Fats and Oils

Fats AND Oils

The Complete Guide to Fats and Oils in Health and Nutrition

UDO ERASMUS

vancouver
canada

Published by
alive books
P O Box 80055
Burnaby BC
Canada V5H 3X5

Printed and bound in Canada.
Illustration: Evelyn Mielke
Cover Art: Anne McDonald
Typesetting: Carter Camera-Ready Limited
Design: Steven Carter and Carolyn Zonailo

Canadian Cataloguing in Publication Data

Erasmus, Udo.
Fats and oils

ISBN 0-920470-10-6 Hardcover
ISBN 0-920470-16-5 Softcover

1. Lipids in nutrition. 2. Oils and fats, Edible. 3. Acids, Fatty - Physiological effect. I. Title.

TX553.L5E73 1986 641.1'4 C86-091191-8

First Printing — August 1987
Second Printing — March 1988
Third Printing — January 1989
Fourth Printing — February 1991

Printed on paper containing over 50% recycled paper including 5% post-consumer fibre.

Foreword

Fats and Oils is filled with interesting and accurate information concerning both the science and physiology of fatty acids in nutrition and health.

The role that dietary fats play in modulating physiology is now becoming better understood and represents one of the frontiers in nutritional medicine. It is for this reason that Udo Erasmus has written a very timely and important book. This book will enable us to better understand the complex science that underlies the metabolism of fatty acids, and the effects that various fats have upon cellular processes such as the production of prostaglandins.

I also appreciate the lucid discussion of lipid peroxides produced from polyunsaturated fatty acids and the health implications of this. *Fats and Oils: The Complete Guide to Fats and Oils in Health and Nutrition* is an excellent contribution to the field of clinical nutrition.

Jeffrey S. Bland, Ph.D.
Publisher, *Complementary Medicine Magazine*

A Note to The Reader

The information contained in this book is given for the purpose of teaching those people who want to learn about edible fats and oils, and their importance in human health. The information is not intended to replace the services of a physician for those conditions which require the services of one.

I dedicate this book to Senta Erasmus, my mother,
and to Sharon, the mother of my children.

Contents

SECTION ONE

Facing the Fats

Molecules and Components of Fats and Oils

SECTION TWO

Life in the Fat Lane

Fats and Oil Business, Processes, and Promotion

SECTION THREE

Fats and Figures

The Human Body

SECTION FOUR

Fat Options

Fats in Food Products

SECTION FIVE

Researching the Fats

Findings, Breakthroughs, and Applications

SECTION SIX

Fats and Fates

Fats and Disease

List of Figures

SECTION ONE

Facing the Fats

Molecules and Components of Fats and Oils

SECTION TWO

Life in the Fat Lane

How Air, Light and Heat Break Down Oils

SECTION THREE

Fats and Figures

How Cells Burn Food for Energy

SECTION FOUR

Fat Options
Food Products

SECTION FIVE

Researching the Fats
Findings, Breakthroughs, and Applications

SECTION SIX

Fats and Fates
Wrong use of fats and use of wrong fats

List of Tables

Preface and Acknowledgements

Since the entire human body is made from food, air and water, food and eating must be an important aspect of physical health. We cannot control the biochemical processes which take place after we swallow. We *do* choose *what* we swallow. Our health depends on those choices. This book provides information about fats and oils, which will enable us to make choices for health.

The information contained in this book comes from many sources, which include the works of Dr. Johanna Budwig, who dedicated her life to research and communication about the usefulness of the essential fatty acids in healing the diseases of fatty degeneration; *Biochemistry*, edited by G. Zubay (Addison-Wesley), which contains a thorough overview of the biochemistry of fats, oils and cholesterol; *Biochemistry: an introduction*, by M. I. Gurr and A. T. James (Chapman and Hall), from which Figure 22 was adapted; *Structure and Function of the Human Body*, by R. L. Memmler and D. L. Wood (Lippincott), which inspired parts of Figure 15; *Dietary Fats and Health*, edited by E. G. Perkins and W. J. Visek (American Oil Chemists' Society), which provided the basis for Figure 7 and contains much useful recent information; *Fats and Oils: an outline of their chemistry and technology*, by H. G. Kirschenbauer (Van Nostrand Reinhold), which describes the industry; *Bailey's Industrial Fats and Oils*, edited by D. Swern (Wiley and Sons), which contains a wealth of information of both chemistry and technology; and *Human Physiology*, by J. J. Previte (McGraw-Hill), from which the diagram that heads Section Three was adapted, and which served as inspiration for Figures 37 and 39. I am grateful for the efforts and contributions that these and other researchers, authors and editors have made to our understanding of fats and oils.

My publisher, Siegfried Gursche, first introduced me to Dr. Budwig's work and sparked my interest in the field. My friend, Christoph Quest invited me to Germany to study and teach. The example of Terry Fox, athlete and Canadian hero, inspired me to keep going whenever I felt like quitting.

Many people in Germany, Canada and the United States reported their experiences with the use of oils containing fatty acids. The positive results of these oils on their health gave me the practical assurance to go ahead with my writing.

Fats and Oils is a family affair as well as a community effort. Senta Erasmus provided the support that made it possible for me to write. Gerd Erasmus introduced me and my material to grade 9 to 12 students and their teachers in Nechako Valley Secondary School, and boosted my confidence in my ability to explain this complex field in an understandable way.

Several people helped to transform the concept of the book into reality. Lorna Smith turned an impossible rough draft into a workable first manuscript. Evelyn Mielke, with patience and good humour, made illustrations out of illegible scribbles. Danae Tilley typed, and typed, and typed. Steven Carter helped with re-writes. Carolyn Zonailo edited for style and clarity, and then, with the help of Anne McDonald and Bir Singh took the manuscript and made of it this book. Diane Tanchak typset, Ruth Wilson proofread, and Margaret Gibbs compiled the index.

Finally, I wish also to acknowledge those people who, by wholesome eating habits, have set a model for us to follow and those who, in changing from mistaken eating habits to healthy ones, have shown us the healing power of nutrition.

Introduction

Diseases of fatty degeneration today kill upward of 75% of the people living in the affluent, industrialized nations of planet Earth before their natural 'three score years and ten' are up. 'Fatty Degeneration.' It doesn't take a genius to realize that if we want to get to the root of the problem of fatty degeneration, we ought to look at the whole field of fats and oils: what they are, what we do to them, how the body deals with them, their food sources, their involvement in disease, and how to use them to enhance our health.

There is enough research information available in scientific journals, enough documented clinical information, and enough information from studies of the food traditions of diverse cultures to show that in order to maintain health, avoid disease, and regain health once we've lost it, we need to increase our understanding, and change our choices and consumption of fats and oils. If we want to avoid premature death from cardiovascular disease, cancer, diabetes, and other diseases of fatty degeneration, and if we want to avoid the suffering of arthritis, obesity, and some types of mental malfunction, we need to become knowledgeable in this least well understood area of human nutrition.

This information is available, 'buried' in different journals, written in the boring style of 'scientific' writing, hidden behind a technical language that most readers have not been taught, and confused by half-truths of advertising.

Bits and pieces of this information have trickled down to us, more in the form of rumours and myths than as clear factual information. There is the controversy between butter and margarine, for instance. There is the talk of the polyunsaturates, and whether they are good for us, or whether they enhance the potency of cancer-causing substances. There is talk of beef fat being bad for us, and fish oils being good for us. There are rumours about hydrogenation and processed oil products. There are stories about fried fats, and of course there's cholesterol. Enough information (or misinformation) has come to us, through the grapevine of friends, hearsay, ads, magazine articles, doctors, and other 'experts' to spark a popular interest in the subject. In my travels, everyone I meet these days has heard something about fats and oils, is interested, is confused about what's what, and wants to know.

Every current book on nutrition has a small section on fats and oils, but alas, the opinions of the various authors diverge so very much, and are so full of contradictions, that they leave us confused. The reason for this is that most of the writers are not knowledgeable on the whole field, and that much of their information on fats and oils come from the industries which market fat and oil products for profit.

Medical doctors, who hold our trust in matters of health and illness (unless we accept more of that responsibility ourselves), study very little nutrition in medical school. While some, especially younger doctors, are changing their approach to healing in response to overwhelming evidence of the importance of foods to health, many doctors steeped in the older medical practises are still skeptical about the nutritional approach. They are therefore of limited help to patients in their endeavours to improve their health through better nutrition, beyond advising them of the woefully inadequate four daily food groups.

In this book, I have addressed all aspects of fat and oil nutrition. The book brings together the findings of the major research work that has been done on fats and oils processes, products, and diseases, in a way that is not mysterious and is easy to understand.

While the book gives you important information, it leaves you free to decide what you will do to maximize your chances of maintaining health and avoiding degenerative disease. I have explained the chemistry of fats in a way that someone with little scientific training can follow. (The explanations were tested on 14 to 17 year old students, and the students were able to understand.) A knowledge of these basics is important so that the buyer of fats and oils products can separate fact from advertising fiction. It also provides consumers of fats and oils with the understanding necessary to assess future developments in the field.

The book is intended to shed light on the processes by which fats and oils are made into marketable products, and it highlights the changes which take place in essential food substances through the techniques of food processing. It outlines how fats and oils are used in the human body. It looks at the various food products available to the modern consumer, and the changes that have taken place in these products by the application of human skills: by breeding, domestication, and processing.

The book describes the connections between fats and oils and human health and disease, in so far as these connections are known. It summarizes the latest findings and breakthroughs in the field. The text is divided into sections which follow a logical sequence, continuity, and progression. However, each section is written to stand on its own as a complete story, cross-referenced with other relevant sections, to avoid unnecessary repetition.

I have intended that the book can be read in several different ways. Those who want to learn the whole story of fats and oils will want to read it from cover to cover. For those who want a handy reference book on fats and oils in health and nutrition, the book provides all of the basic information in the field under separate headings. Those who like to follow their own particular interests in fats and oils nutrition, processes, and topics in health and disease, can skip from section to section.

Ultimately, however, it is hoped that the reader's interest will be sparked to read the entire book, because it provides the information necessary to make wise choices in purchasing fats and oils products for human consumption. Our choices, in large measure, determine the health (or illness) of those affected by these choices: ourselves, our children, and our fellow humans.

SECTION ONE

Facing The Fats

Molecules and Components of Fats and Oils

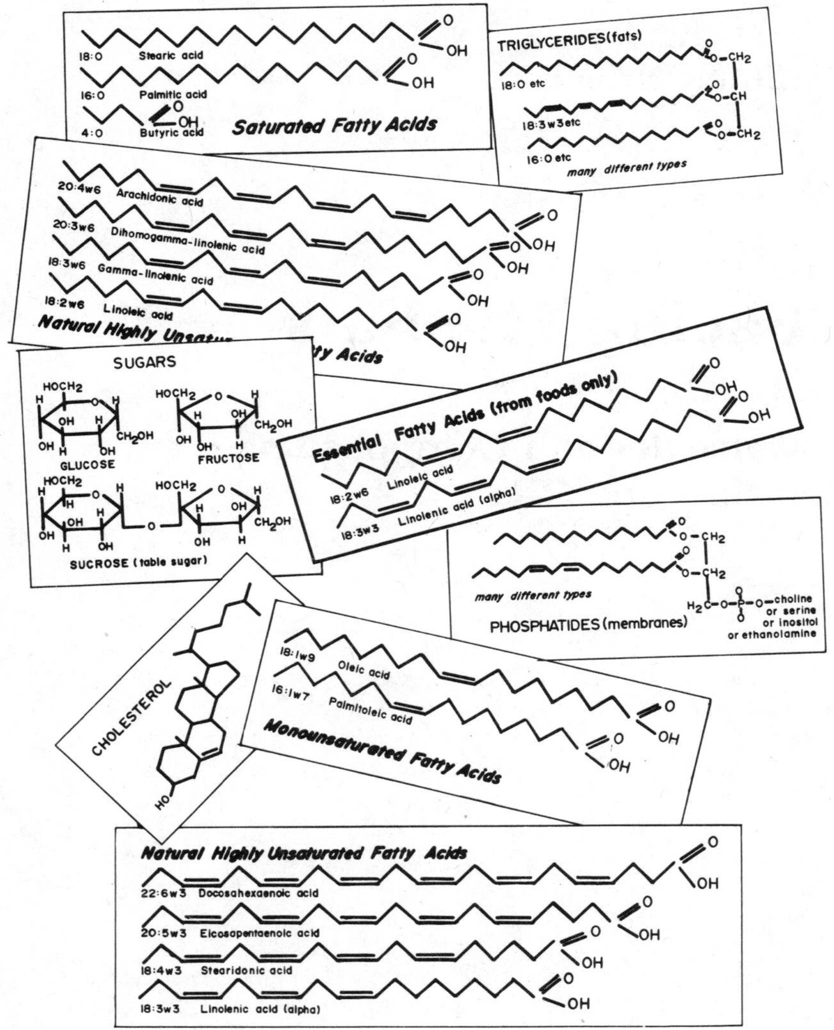

18:0 Stearic acid
16:0 Palmitic acid
4:0 Butyric acid
Saturated Fatty Acids
TRIGLYCERIDES(fats)
18:0 etc
18:3w3etc
16:0 etc
many different types
20:4w6 Arachidonic acid
20:3w6 Dihomogamma-linolenic acid
18:3w6 Gamma-linolenic acid
18:2w6 Linoleic acid
Natural Highly
SUGARS
GLUCOSE
FRUCTOSE
SUCROSE (table sugar)
Essential Fatty Acids (from foods only)
18:2w6 Linoleic acid
18:3w3 Linolenic acid (alpha)
many different types
PHOSPHATIDES (membranes)
choline
or serine
or inositol
or ethanolamine
CHOLESTEROL
18:1w9 Oleic acid
16:1w7 Palmitoleic acid
Monounsaturated Fatty Acids
Natural Highly Unsaturated Fatty Acids
22:6w3 Docosahexaenoic acid
20:5w3 Eicosapentaenoic acid
18:4w3 Stearidonic acid
18:3w3 Linolenic acid (alpha)

1

Fatty Acids — An Overview

Definition

What are fatty acids? Fatty acids are the major building blocks of the fats in human bodies and foods and are important sources of energy for the body. They are also major structural components of the membranes which surround cells, and within each cell, of the membranes which surround subcellular organelles (see: Phosphatides), and thus fatty acids have important functions in the building and maintenance of healthy cells.

Structure of Fatty Acids

What do fatty acids look like?

Basic Structure. A fatty acid molecule is composed of two parts, one fatty and the other acid. Linked together, they are aptly named: fatty acid. A fatty acid molecule contains a non-polar, fatty, and water-insoluble (hates water!) carbon chain of variable length, made entirely of carbon and hydrogen atoms, ending in a methyl (-CH3) group. The other end of the molecule is a weak organic acid called a carboxyl (-COOH) group. Figure 1 shows what a fatty acid looks like.

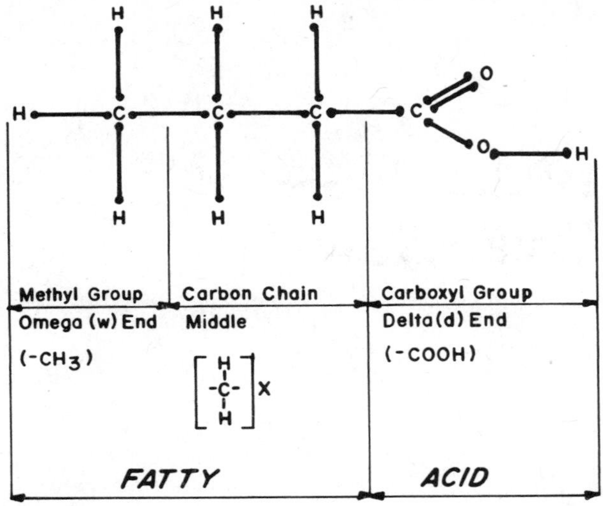

• Electron

•—• Bond formed when 2 electrons from different atoms are shared

H Hydrogen Atom

C Carbon Atom

O Oxygen Atom

Figure 1. Basic structure of a fatty acid.

Chain Length. There can be any number of carbon atoms in the fatty carbon chain, but the most common lengths vary between 4 carbons (butyric acid, found in butter) and 24 carbons (found in fish oils and brain tissue). Formic acid with 1 carbon (bee sting and ant bite) and acetic acid with 2 carbons (vinegar) are also part of this family of compounds, but are not included among the fatty acids because their fatty carbon chains are so short that they behave as water-soluble acids. Figure 2 shows some fatty acids commonly found in nature.

Double Bonds. The fatty acids shown in Figure 2 are saturated, meaning that they contain no double bonds. Each carbon atom in the fatty chain is 'saturated' with as many hydrogen atoms as it can possibly hold. Such saturated fatty acids can be modified by the insertion of one or more double bonds into the carbon chain by removing two hydrogen atoms. This insertion

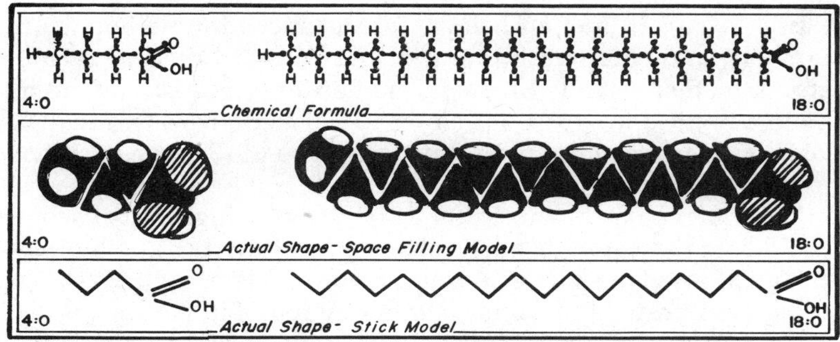

Figure 2. Some (saturated) fatty acids found in nature.

produces unsaturated fatty acids, which differ from the saturated ones in shape, physical properties such as melting point, and chemical properties such as their ability to react with other molecules, including water, oxygen, other chemical groups such as hydroxyl (-OH) or sulphydryl (-SH), or light. Unsaturated fatty acids are more unstable and chemically more active than saturated fatty acids, which are relatively inert.

Chemists assign numbers to the carbon atoms in fatty acid chains to make it easier to talk about the fatty acids. The numbering system we will use in this book is called the omega (*w*) system. This system numbers the carbon atoms in sequence, starting from the methyl end[1]. Figure 3 illustrates the omega numbering system for fatty acids.

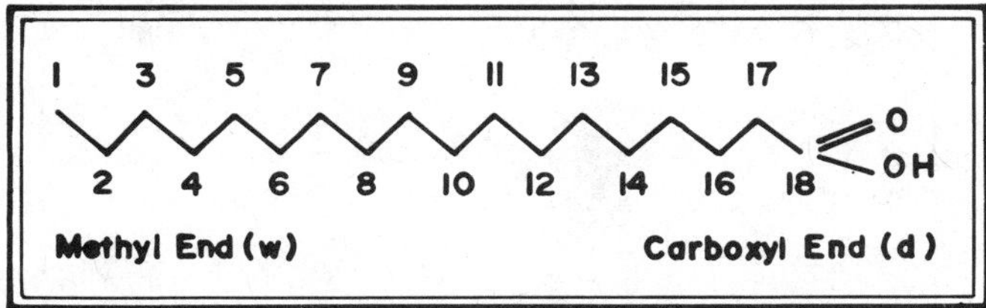

Figure 3. The w (omega) numbering system for fatty acids.

Double bonds can occur in the fatty carbon chain at any point, and various types of plants and animals differ fom each other in their ability to insert double bonds in different places along the chain. This is very important in nutritional terms (see: Essential

Fatty Acids). In human beings, for instance, double bonds are rarely (if ever) inserted into fatty acids with less than 16 carbon atoms in their chain. Likewise, human enzymes cannot insert double bonds into positions closer to the methyl (*w*) end than 7, whereas plants can insert double bonds into the 3 and 6 positions from the methyl end.

There can be from 1 to 6 double bonds in a single fatty carbon chain, and these double bonds change the properties and biological functions of the fatty acid which contains them. Figure 4 shows some unsaturated fatty acids commonly found in nature.

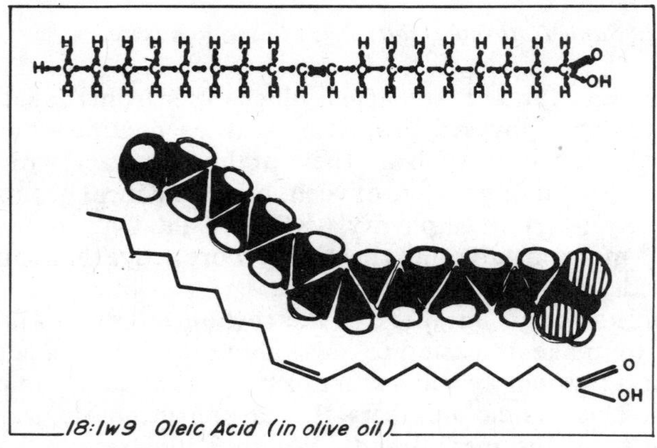

18:1w9 Oleic Acid (in olive oil)

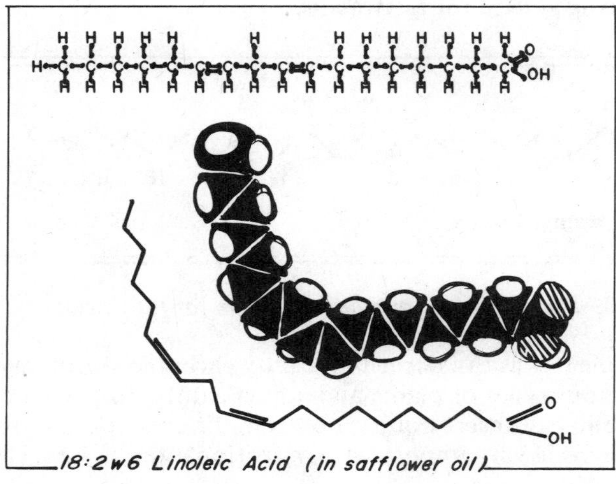

18:2w6 Linoleic Acid (in safflower oil)

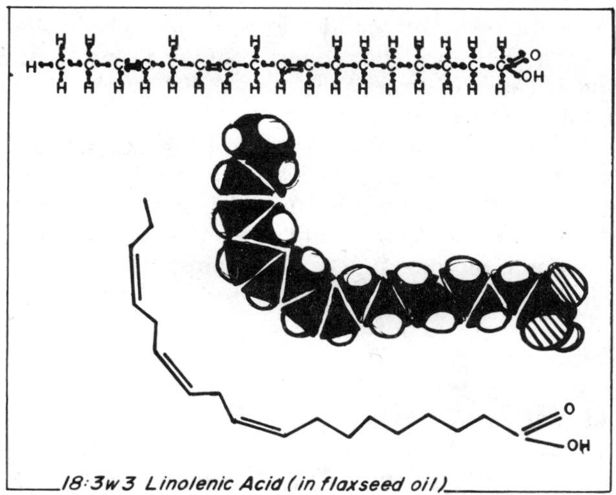

Figure 4. Some (unsaturated) fatty acids commonly found in nature.

If more than 1 double bond is present in the fatty carbon chain, the double bonds almost always start 3 carbon atoms apart. This spacing of double bonds is standard in fatty acids occurring in nature, and is called 'methylene interrupted' double bonds. Figure 5 shows the methylene interrupted arrangement of double bonds in unsaturated fatty acids containing more than one double bond.

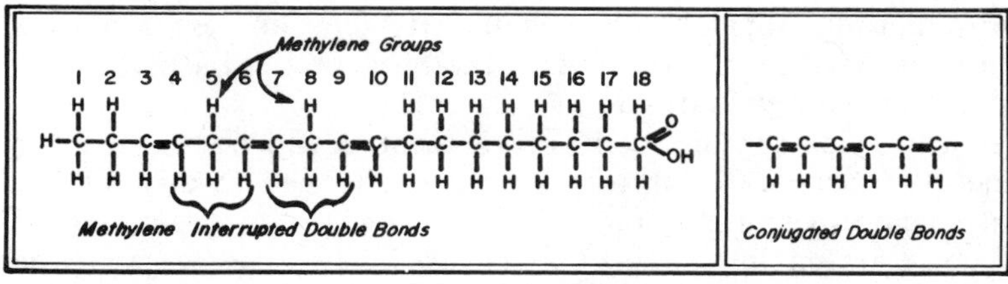

Figure 5. Methylene interrupted double bonds in a fatty acid.

Cis- and Trans- Configuration. The double bonds in all the nutritionally important fatty acids are in an arrangement called the *cis-* configuration. In this configuration the hydrogen atoms on the carbons involved in the double bond are on the same side of the molecule. The hydrogen atoms repel one another and the fatty carbon chain kinks, taking up some of the empty space on the side of the molecule opposite the hydrogen atoms. The kink changes the shape and, therefore, the properties of the molecule, and this is important because it determines the way in which the molecule will function in the body. A double bond in the fatty carbon chain can also be in the *trans*- configuration. In this arrangement, the hydrogen atoms on the carbons involved in the double bond are on opposite sides of the molecule. The *trans*- configuration is more stable, the molecule is not kinked, and the fatty acid's properties and biological functions are altered (see: Trans- Fatty Acids). Figure 6 shows the *cis*- and *trans*- configurations.

Functions of Fatty Acids

What do fatty acids do? Fatty acids have many different functions. Fatty acids, as part of the body fat under the skin and around organs, are useful for insulation and shock absorption. All fatty acids can be used for energy production, though some of them are saved for more important functions, to be considered later.

Fatty acids containing less than 16 carbon atoms, and all saturated fatty acids are 'burned' or oxidized in the body to provide energy, calories, heat. The shorter the saturated fatty acid, the more readily it 'burns', and the easier it is to digest. This is important for people who suffer from weak or diseased liver. Since one of the important functions of the liver is the metabolism of fats, one of the symptoms of liver malfunction is difficulty in digesting fatty foods, and a feeling of tiredness or heaviness after a fat-containing meal. Shorter chain fatty acids are less taxing on the liver than longer ones, and are therefore preferable in the diets of people with liver afflictions.

Fatty acids containing 16 or 18 carbons can be 'burned' for energy, incorporated into membranes, changed to unsaturated fatty acids, or stored in fat tissue.

Unsaturated fatty acids can be used in special ways in the structure of membranes, in the creation of electrical potentials, in the movement of electric currents, as well as being available to be 'burned' for energy.

Unsaturated fatty acids can be lengthened (elongated), more double bonds can be inserted (desaturated), and the highly unsaturated molecules which result are used for special functions in the most active tissues such as brain, sense organs, adrenal glands, and testis. In these tissues, the highly unsaturated fatty acids function in attracting oxygen, the generation of electrical

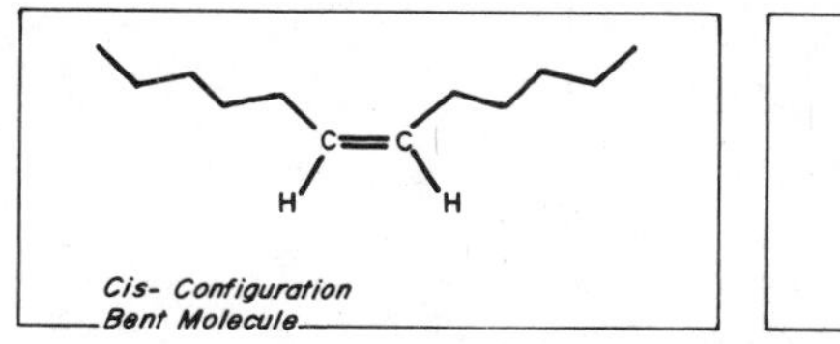

Trans- Configuration
Straight Molecule

Figure 6. Cis- and trans- configurations around a double bond.

currents, and the transformation of light energy into electrical energy into nerve impulses.

Two types of unsaturated fatty acids, the essential fatty acids, can be partially oxidized, and this process, which is enzyme-controlled and very precise, changes essential fatty acids into prostaglandins, which regulate many functions of all tissues in a hormone-like way (see: Prostaglandins).

Figure 7 shows the overall scheme of fatty acid metabolism: the ways in which the human body can lengthen and insert double bonds into the various fatty acids found in nutrition. It also indicates the fatty acids from which, by oxidation, the prostaglandins are made.

Food Sources of Fatty Acids

In which foods do we find the fatty acids? The short chain saturated fatty acids are found especially abundantly in butter, coconut, and palm kernel fats, and in minor quantities in all fats and oils.

Long chain fatty acids are found in all fats and oils, but we will list below only those foods in which they make up a large part of the total fats or oils content.

W3 Family. Alpha-linolenic Acid, commonly referred to as linolenic acid, (LNA, 18:3*w*3), (see: Naming the Fatty Acids) is found in flax, hemp seed, pumpkin seed, soy bean, walnut, and dark green leaves. Flax seed is the best source, containing almost 60% of its oil as LNA. Hemp seed is marijuana and illegal, but its seed oil contains 25% LNA. Pumpkin seed oil contains up to 15% LNA. Soybean oil runs about 7-9% LNA. Other seed oils contain less LNA than these, or none. Dark green leaves contain only a little oil, but this oil is more than 50% LNA.

Stearidonic Acid (SDA, 18:4*w*3) is found in certain wild seeds, which are not yet commercially available. Eicosapentaenoic Acid (EPA, 20:5*w*3) and Docosahexaenoic Acid (DHA, 22:6*w*3) are found in fish and marine animal oils. Salmon, trout, mackerel,

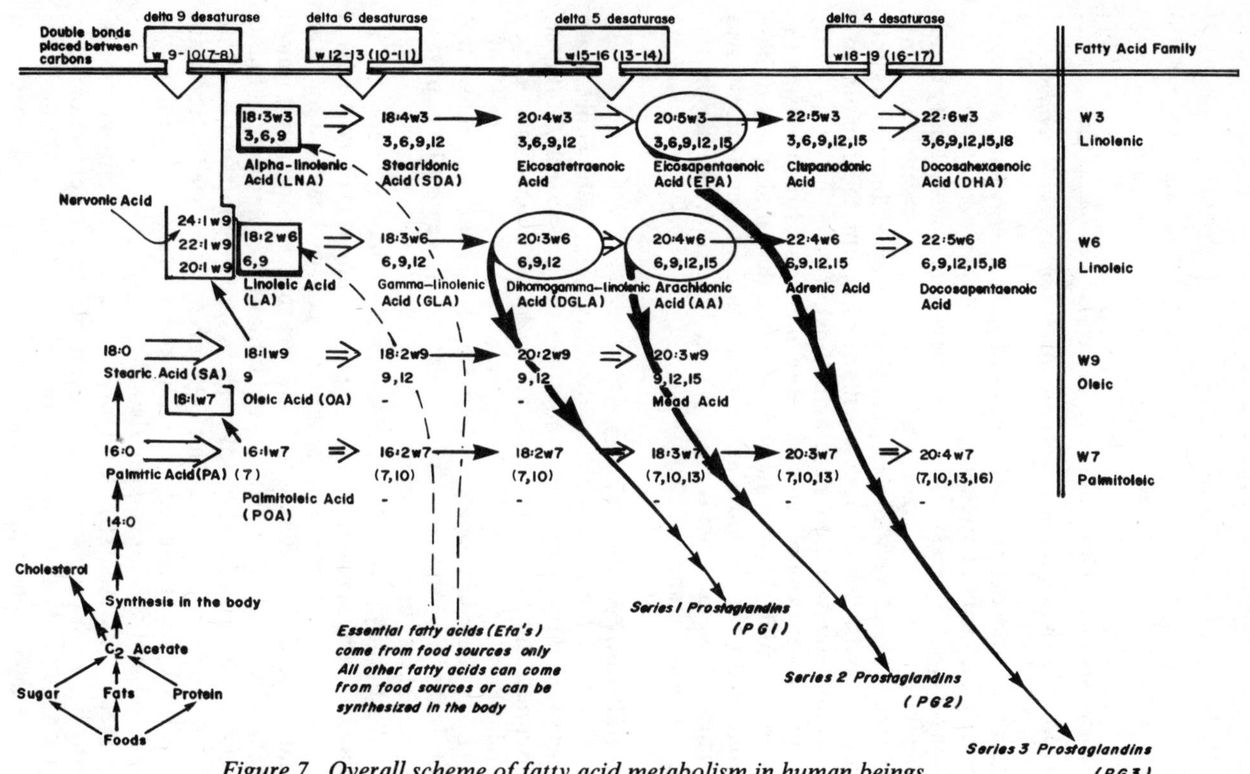

Figure 7. Overall scheme of fatty acid metabolism in human beings.

sardines, and other cold water marine animals are high in these oils. Among land animals, brain, eyeball, adrenal, and testis are high in these oils, which explains why primitive tribes considered these tissues delicacies (or holy). They ate them raw immediately after the kill, because, as science found out centuries or millennia later, these highly nutritious oils deteriorate and spoil very rapidly after the animal dies.

W6 Family. Linoleic Acid (LA, 18:2*w*6) is found in safflower, sunflower, hemp, soybean, walnut, pumpkin seed, sesame seed, and flax. Safflower is the highest source of LA, but new commercial varieties of safflower seeds have been bred, which contain only small quantities of LA. Gamma-linolenic Acid (GLA, 18:3*w*6) is found in mothers' milk and evening primrose oil. Several other seeds also contain GLA, but these are not yet available commercially. Arachidonic Acid (AA, 20:4*w*6) is found in meats and other animals products.

W9 Family. Oleic Acid (OA, 18:1*w*9), is found in high quantities in the oils of olive, almond, pecan, cashew, filbert, and macademia nut.

Saturated Family. Stearic Acid (SA, 18:0), is found in high quantities in beef, mutton, and pork. Palmitic Acid (PA, 16:0), is found in high quantities in coconut and palm kernel oils.

Butyric Acid (BA, 4:0) is most abundant in butter. All oils contain mixtures of the different fatty acids in different proportions (see: Oils in Seeds).

2

Naming the Fatty Acids

Introduction

Every fatty acid has several names. It may have a nickname, and it always has a proper name. Or one can draw its molecular structure in any one of several ways. And it also has a shorthand name. We'll briefly describe the different naming systems, because some of them will be used in the book, and if you are familiar with them, it will make the text easier to follow. It's really quite simple.

Nicknames

A fatty acid gets its nickname from the scientist who discovered it, and the name may be as eccentric as the scientist. If he knows Greek or Latin word roots, then the name may reflect that erudition. Perhaps he will name it by the animal or plant from which he isolated it. Or perhaps some other whim will move him in his eagerness to call his new chemical by name.

For example, butyric acid was so named because it was found in butter. Caproic, caprylic, and capric acids were found in goat's milk. The same Latin root is also found in the sun sign capricorn, the goat, and explains those names. Oleic acid got its name from the olive oil in which it is found, and linoleic and linolenic acids got theirs from the Latin name for flax, which is *Linum.* Stearic acid comes from the Greek root word for fat, which is stea-, lauric acid from the laurel; palmitic acid from the palm tree; vaccenic acid, a fatty acid found in cow's milk, got its name from the Latin word for that animal, which is vacca. And so on, the names go.

But those names do not tell us what the fatty acid is, what its structure or properties are, or what it does. And so, each fatty acid also has a proper chemical name, which tells us exactly what it is.

Proper Names

The proper name for a fatty acid contains within it all the information that a chemist needs in order to draw its structure and know its properties, even if he has never seen this fatty acid before. This kind of naming follows strict rules laid down by the chemists at meetings. These meetings are much like christenings. The parents come, the aunts and uncles attend, the friends of the family are invited. They choose a name for the new baby, and afterwards they have a party. At these meetings, scientists discuss and all agree on a naming system for future additions to the chemical family so that when they talk to one another, they can understand each other. Whenever a new group of chemical compounds is found or synthesized, another christening party is held to decide how and what to name the new chemical children. Here's an example. The proper name for palmitic acid is hexadecanoic acid. Hexadeca means 16; -oic acid, they have decided, is the name for a fatty acid. All together, the name tells me that this is a fatty acid with 16 carbons in its chain. Simple.

The proper name for linoleic acid is a little more complicated, because the molecule has more character. It is called: all *cis*- *w*6,9-octadeca/di/en/oic acid; -oic acid makes it a fatty acid. Octadeca means 18 carbons. The 'di' means 2, and the 'en' means double bonds; *w*6,9- describes where the double bonds are in the chain; they start on carbons 6 and 9, counting from the *w* or left end of the molecule (the methyl end rather than the acid end) and go to the next carbon, i.e. there is a double bond between *w* carbons 6 and 7, and another double bond between *w* carbons and 9 and 10. All *cis*- tells me that both hydrogen atoms on the carbons involved in each double bond are on the same side of the molecule. Well, that's not so bad, but you can see that it gets a little complicated.

The other day I ran into a good one. It was called 1-(1-(2-cyanoaziridinyl)isopropyl)aziridin-2-carboxylic acid amide. They lost me on that one. Since they also showed the structure of the molecule, I looked at that instead, which brings us to the third kind of name, the structural formula.

Structural Formula

When we use a structural formula to make one of our chemical children known to others, we draw a picture of the whole structure, to show which atom joins to which. This is like taking a photograph of the child with you and showing it to people, so they can see for themselves what it looks like. This is often much simpler than bringing the whole child's living presence.

For example, here is the structure of the saturated fatty acid, palmitic acid, also known as hexadecanoic acid:

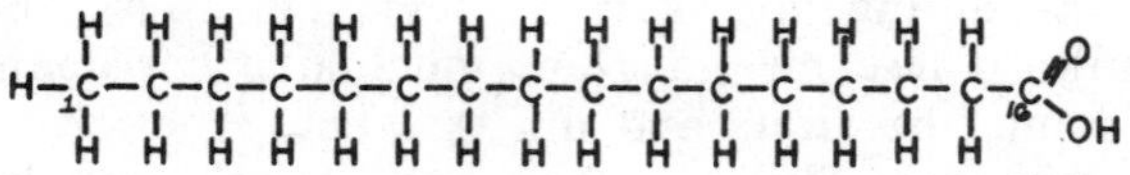

16:0

And here is the structure for linoleic acid, also known as *cis, cis-w*6,9-octadecadienoic acid:

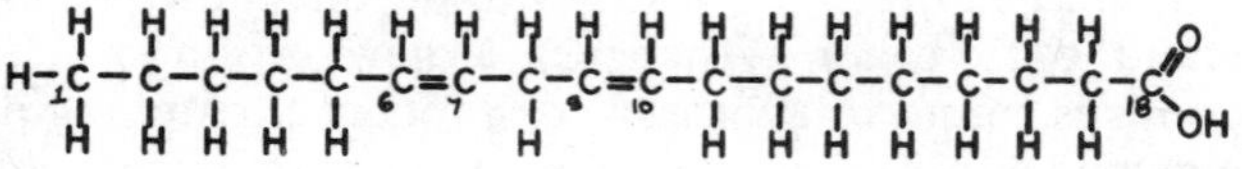

18:2w6

As you can see, this method makes it easy for someone to identify the molecule that you are talking about. Drawing the whole structure, however, is slow and cumbersome, and on the typewriter, often impossible. So finally, a system of shorthand has been developed, by which the fatty acids can be named.

Shorthand Names

The shorthand used to name fatty acids is simple and convenient to use. We'll use some examples to illustrate it.

Butyric acid is the nickname. The structure looks like this:

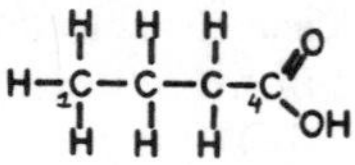

4:0

The shorthand name is 4:0. 4 is the number of carbon atoms in the fatty acid chain. 0 is the number of double bonds. We know that there is a methyl group (-CH3) at one end, and an acid group (-COOH) at the other, because this is true for all fatty acids.

Let's take another example. Linolenic acid (LNA) is the nickname. The proper name is all *cis*- *w*3,6,9-octadecatrienoic acid. The structural formula is:

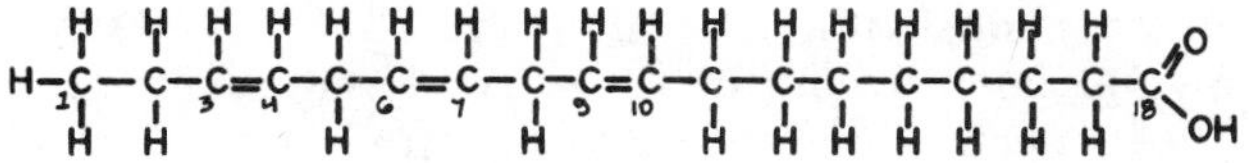

18:3w3

The shorthand name is 18:3*w*3. 18 is the number of carbon atoms, 3 is the number of double bonds, *w*3 gives the position, from the methyl end, of the carbon atom at which the first double bond starts. Scientists know, and we learned in Chapter 1, that in all natural fatty acids, the double bonds are methylene interrupted. From this we can figure out that the second double bond starts at carbon 6 and the third double bond starts at carbon 9. The first double bond unites carbons 3 and 4; the second, carbons 6 and 7; the third, carbons 9 and 10. We also said that natural fatty acids have all their double bond hydrogens in the *cis*- configuration, on the same side of the molecule[1]. It's simple, once you get the hang of it.

Let's do it the other way around. 18:2*w*6 means: an 18-carbon chain, 2 double bonds (methylene interrupted and in *cis*- configuration), and the first double bond starts at the *w*6 carbon, the sixth carbon from the methyl (left) end. The second bond must start at carbon *w*9. So the structure of 18:2*w*6 is:

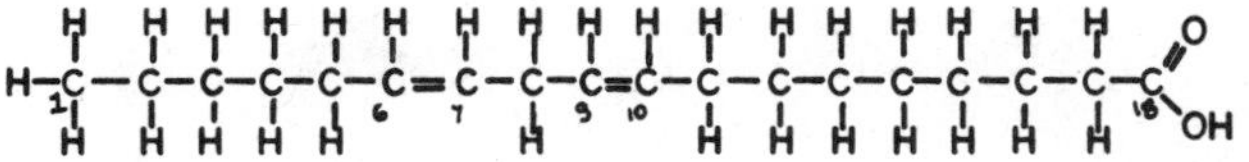

18:2w6

22:6*w*3 means: 22 carbon atoms, 6 double bonds (methylene interrupted and in *cis*- configuration), and the first double bond is on carbon 3, counting from the *w* (methyl), or left end. Always there is the carboxyl (-COOH) acid at the right end. So here we go:

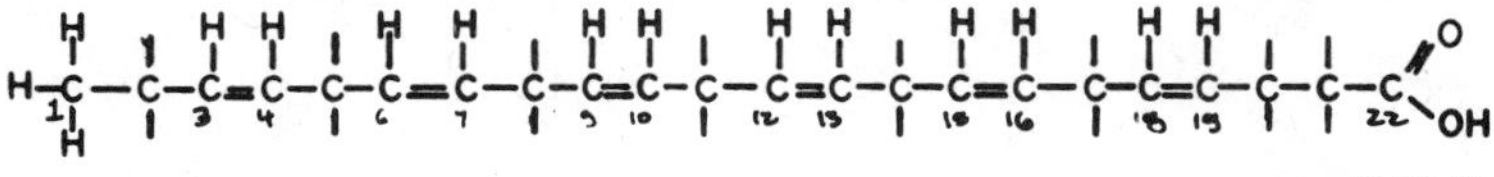

22:6w3

First we made 22 C's. To the carbon at the left end we added three hydrogens to make a methyl. To the carbon at the right end we added =0 and -OH to make the acid group. Then we put in the double bonds. The first double bond goes between carbons 3 and 4, the next ones between C6 and 7, between C9 and 10, between C12 and 13, between C15 and 16, between C18 and 19. Then we put the hydrogens of both carbons involved in each double bond on the same side of the molecule. Then we connected all the remaining carbons with one bond each. That's how far we got in the drawing. Then we put in all the remaining hydrogens (2 per carbon, 1 on each side of the molecule), and presto 22:6*w*3. Now wasn't that easy? And fun?

We will use these shorthand designations (as well as structures and common names) in the book, and you'll be able to figure out what they mean from these shorthand designations.

Just in case you miss, we've prepared a list of the names and structures of the most common and important fatty acids in nutrition. Look at them. There are only a few. And we're going to skip the proper names.

		nickname	abbreviation used in book	shorthand	structural formula
Saturated Fatty Acids	short chain	Butyric Acid	BA	4:0	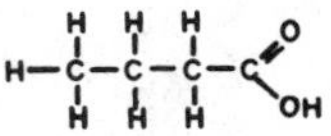
		Caproic Acid		6:0	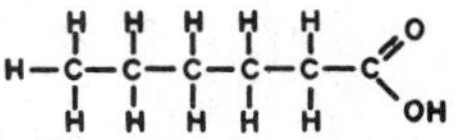
		Caprylic Acid		8:0	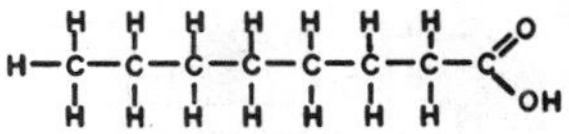
		Capric Acid		10:0	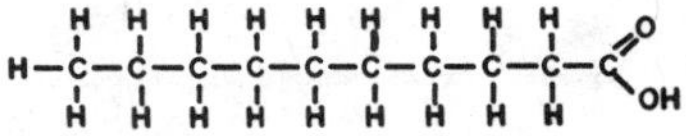
	intermediate chain	Lauric Acid		12:0	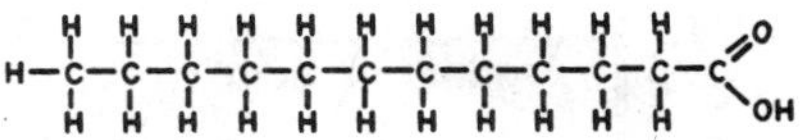
		Myristic Acid		14:0	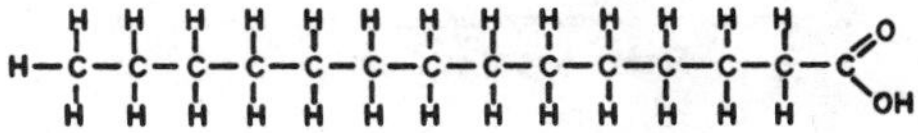
	long chain	Palmitic Acid	PA	16:0	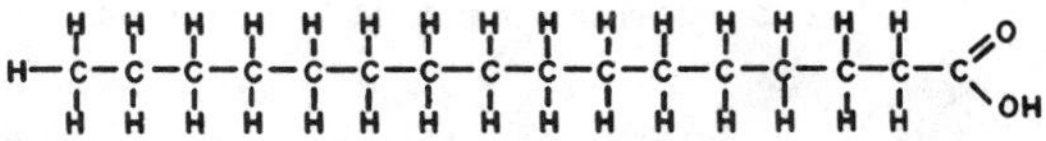
		Stearic Acid	SA	18:0	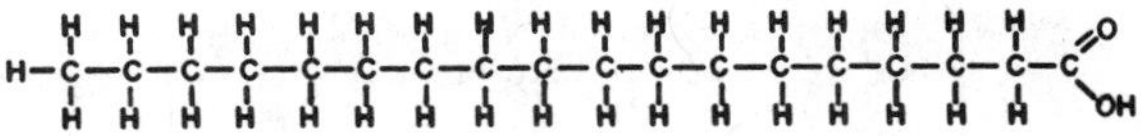

		nickname	abbreviation used in book	shorthand	structural formula
Monounsaturated Fatty Acids		**Palmitoleic Acid**	POA	16:1w7	
		Oleic Acid	OA	18:1w9	
Essential Fatty Acids (Efa's)		Linoleic Acid	LA	18:2w6	
		Linolenic Acid	LNA	18:3w3	
Fatty Acid's made from Efa's	from linoleic acid	Gamma-Linolenic Acid	GLA	18:3w6	
		Arachidonic Acid	AA	20:4w6	
	from linolenic acid	Stearidonic Acid	SDA	18:4w3	
		Eicosapentaenoic Acid	EPA	20:5w3	
		Docosahexaenoic Acid	DHA	22:6w3	

3

Saturated Fatty Acids

Introduction

The saturated fatty acids (SFAs) are the simplest fatty acids. At one end, they carry the carboxyl acid group; the rest of the molecule is fatty material. The fatty material is an arrangement of carbon atoms hooked together in a chain, and each of the remaining positions on the carbon atoms are taken up by hydrogen atoms. This explains why they are called saturated: they carry as many hydrogens as possible; they are 'saturated' with hydrogen atoms. Figures 1 and 2 illustrate saturated fatty acids.

General Properties

The carbon chain can be anywhere from 4 to 24 carbon atoms long. The carbon chain of SFAs is straight, has no kinks, contains no double bonds, is slow to react with other chemicals, and carries no electric charges. Only the acid group reacts readily, either with glycerol in the production of fats and membranes, or with strong bases to make soaps. But essentially, it is a sluggish molecule, a little bit uninteresting in comparison to some other fatty acids which we will consider in the next chapter (see: Unsaturated Fatty Acids).

Melting Points

The longer the carbon chain in a SFA, the higher its melting point, the harder it is. The acid part of the molecule is usually hooked up to a glycerol molecule. The fatty part, on the other hand, wants to aggregate. Fat likes to dissolve in fat, and hates water, so the fatty parts of the molecules tend to stick together. The longer the fatty part of the molecule, the greater is its tendency to aggregate. Hence, the more 'sticky' and harder is the fat, and the higher is its melting point. Table A1. compares the chain lengths and melting points of the common SFAs.

Table A1. Chain lengths and melting points of saturated fatty acids.

Name of Fatty Acid		Number of Carbon Atoms	Melting Point
1.	butyric (4:0)	4	-8°C
2.	caproic (6:0)	6	-3°C
3.	caprylic (8:0)	8	17°C
4.	capric (10:0)	10	32°C
5.	lauric (12:0)	12	44°C
6.	myristic (14:0)	14	54°C
7.	palmitic (16:0)	16	63°C
8.	stearic (18:0)	18	70°C
9.	arachidic (20:0)	20	75°C
10.	behenic (22:0)	22	80°C
11.	lignoceric (24:0)	24	84°C

Short Chain Saturated Fatty Acids

Short chain SFAs (4:0 to 10:0) make up about 10% of the total fatty acids found in butter and milk fat, and also a part of coconut oil. Up to a length of 10 carbons, they are liquid at body temperature, 37°C; above 10 carbons they are solid at body temperature.

The human body uses SFAs up to 14 carbons in length mainly for the production of energy. As they are relatively easy to digest, they are used in some hospitals in the diets of people suffering from liver and other digestive ailments. Other than this, they have no special functions in the body or in nutrition.

The short chain butyric acid (4:0) will dissolve in water. The 6:0 and 8:0 SFAs are partly water-soluble, and the SFAs with longer chains will not dissolve in water, but dissolve readily in oil.

As the chain lengthens, the water-soluble acid group makes up a smaller and smaller part of the molecule, and this explains the decreasing water solubility. It also explains the increasing ability of the SFA molecule to dissolve in oily, organic or non-polar solvents, solvents which carry no electrical charge.

Long Chain Saturated Fatty Acids

Long chain SFAs have melting points higher than body temperatures, are insoluble in water, and form crystal structures, i.e. they tend to aggregate or stick together to form droplets or, if hard, plaques. This tendency to aggregate is involved in one of the major health problems related to human nutrition. When the intake of the long chain SFA-containing fats is high, they tend to stick together and deposit within cells, within organs, and within the arteries (along with proteins and cholesterol, which is also non-polar and very sticky, and has an extremely high melting point of 149°C). This aggregating tendency of long chain SFAs is a part of the problem in cardiovascular and other diseases of fatty degeneration, which plague those populations whose diets are high in beef, mutton, pork, and dairy products, all of which have a high percentage of long chain SFAs in their fats[1]. These diseases also plague those whose diets are high in refined sugars and starches, because these too, are converted into SFAs in the body (see: Sugars and Starches).

Long chain SFAs are used to build cell membranes (see: Phospatides and Membranes). Their tendency to aggregate balances the tendency of unsaturated fatty acids to disperse (see: Unsaturated Fatty Acids). Both kinds of fatty acids are found in membranes.

SFAs also prevent unsaturated fatty acids in membranes from taking part in unwanted chemical reactions with one another, by keeping the unsaturated fatty acid chains physically separated from one another (see: Phosphatides and Membranes).

4

Sugars and Starches

Introduction

A book on fats and oils would not include a chapter on sugars and starches, except for the fact that these carbohydrates are — I was going to say kissing cousins, but their relationship is even closer — these carbohydrates are parents to the fats. Sugars and starches can turn into fats. Figure 8 shows illustrations of several carbohydrates. First of all, let's list the food products which we include in the category of sugars and starches.

Sugars

All refined sugars and syrups, which include the simple sugars glucose (or dextrose), fructose (or levulose), and galactose, the double sugars sucrose (table sugar), maltose (in beer), and lactose (in milk), the dextrins and the syrups made from sugar cane, sugar beets, from sorghum, and from maple, fall into this category. Even honey is included. All of these products are concentrated sources of sugars, are rapidly digested and absorbed, and are quickly turned to fats. More about that a little later.

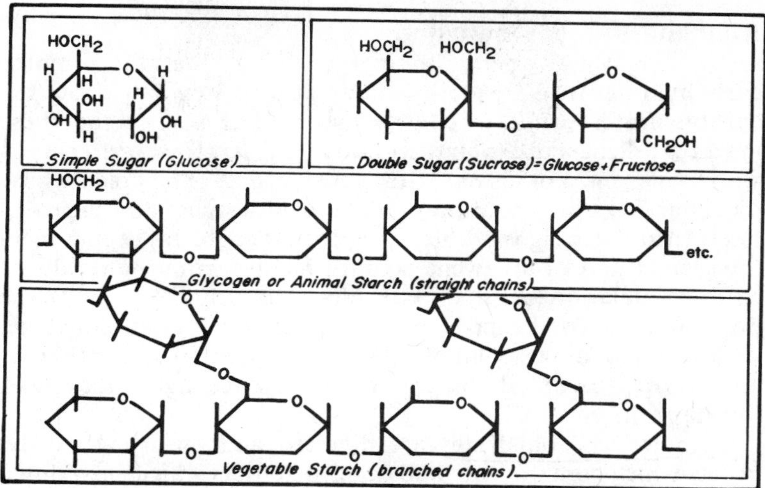

Figure 8. Carbohydrates.

Starches

Starches are sugar molecules chained or bonded together. Enzymes in the body break the bonds between the sugar molecules, and turn starches into sugars. Among the starch-containing foods, the worst for turning into fats are the refined sources. These include white flour, white rice, pasta, enriched flours (both white and dark), corn starch, tapioca, and most of the breakfast cereals found on supermarket shelves, as well as all the products made with these ingredients.

Not usually dangerous, because they are less refined, more complex and therefore more slowly digested and absorbed, and also because they are rich in the vitamin and mineral co-factors necessary to enable our bodies to burn them for energy, are the complex carbohydrates. These can only make us fat if we live a sedentary life style, eat compulsively for psychological reasons, and get no exercise. Complex high carbohydrate foods include starchy vegetables and fruits: potatoes, yams, corn, figs and bananas, and of course, the grains.

Products which contain hidden sugars and starches include soft drinks, cakes, cookies, and pies; candies and confections; many canned fruits and juices; ice creams and shakes; jams and jellies; and desserts. Ketchup contains huge amounts of sugar, and many meat and sausage products are extended with refined starch.

Metabolism of Carbohydrates

A normally active person eating a diet high in natural, complex carbohydrates (usually grains) does not have to worry about the carbohydrates turning into fat. In fact, for an *active* person, these are an excellent source of nutrition and energy. However, a person who spends most of his day sitting in an office, or a person whose diet contains a high amount of the refined starches and sugars, is likely to have a weight problem (really a fat problem) beginning in the second half of his twenties, until he dies from the results of cardiovascular disease in his late thirties to early sixties. With the popular junk food diets that the children of today consume, weight and cardiovascular problems often occur at an even earlier age, and are found to be quite severe even in teenagers. How does this happen?

Complex carbohydrates are digested and absorbed slowly, because they contain fiber and other materials which slow down digestion, and because the starches they contain are only slowly converted into sugars. For this reason, the energy they provide is burned up in body functions at the rate at which it is produced. They also contain the vitamin and mineral factors that allow the carbohydrates to 'burn clean' into carbon dioxide and water.

Refined carbohydrates, on the other hand, are digested and absorbed much more rapidly, and can overload the blood with glucose. Also, because they lack important minerals and vitamins, the body cannot burn them properly, and therefore has to deal with them another way, for instance by turning them into fat.

Sugars are absorbed even faster than starches, and are therefore more dangerous than starches. The body has to do something about the high glucose levels because when the blood glucose level goes too high, a dangerous condition is created which may result in sugar shock, coma, or death. And such a condition must be prevented.

Excess Glucose

There are two ways in which the body deals with excess glucose: It can spill the excess glucose over into the urine, and this is the most common symptom of diabetes. However, spilling glucose is the body's way of handling excess sugar only when the preferred way fails. The body prefers to store the excess glucose it gets in times of feasting for future times of famine. This is a very smart thing to do, unless the body lives in the 20th century, in an industrialized nation, where feasting is followed by more feasting, and famines are largely avoided. The human body hasn't been equipped by nature to deal with such a situation, and we can avoid the health problems caused by consuming excess refined carbohydrates by making wise food choices, by eating only when hungry and by exercising to burn off our caloric indulgences.

But, let's go back to the story of excess refined carbohydrates. We haven't made wise food choices, have stuffed ourselves on refined starches and sugars, and overloaded our body with glucose. The body responds in the following way. High blood glucose triggers the pancreas to secrete insulin, which stimulates the conversion of sugars into fatty acids, three of which are then hooked to glycerol molecules to make fats (triglycerides). The fats are taken to the fat tissues and stored, or deposited in various organs.

There are fatty acids of high quality and there are fatty acids of low quality. The former heal, and the latter kill, and so an important question to ask here is: what kind of fatty acids are produced by excess sugars and starches in our body? You guessed it. The kind that kill, the sticky, saturated kind of fatty acid, the kind that increases the chance of stroke, heart attack and arteriosclerosis.

The body can insert one double bond into these sticky, saturated fatty acids, making them once unsaturated. Saturated and once unsaturated fatty acids are good as a source of energy for the body, but are not essential. They cannot help fill the body's need for essential fatty acids, or help cure deficiency (see: Essential Fatty Acids). On the contrary, the fatty acids made from sugars and starches increase the likelihood of diseases of fatty degeneration. Excess refined starches and sugars also increase the cholesterol level in the blood.

How Sugars Become Fat

How does the conversion of starches and sugars to fats and cholesterol happen? Two-carbon acetate fragments, which are the building blocks for cholesterol (see: Cholesterol), are also the building blocks for saturated fatty acids. When glucose is broken down to produce energy in the body, one of the steps involved is the creation of these acetate fragments. It is easy to see that if these fragments are produced faster than they can be burned by the body into carbon dioxide and water, then the excess fragments put pressure on the body to make saturated fatty acids and cholesterol, in this way cutting down the metabolic problems that excess acetate fragments would cause, were they allowed to accumulate in our system. Excess acetate is more toxic than excess fat and excess cholesterol.

While the human body can turn excess sugars into fats, it cannot turn these fats back into sugars, but must 'burn' off the fats through activity. This is okay for most of our organs, which can perfectly well use fats as their energy source. The brain, however, is very fussy about its fuel supply, and demands glucose to function. If there is no glucose in the diet, the body has to make it. It cannot use fat to make glucose, and so it has to use protein for this purpose. For this reason, people who are intolerant or allergic to carbohydrates[1], need to eat extra protein. For them, proteins have to do the double duties of providing the building materials for enzymes and body structures, and of providing the materials for making glucose.

Refined Carbohydrates and Disease

Refined sugars are digested and absorbed into the bloodstream with unnatural speed. Insulin does its job of removing excess glucose from the bloodstream with amazing efficiency. As a result, the blood glucose level rises very rapidly after the consumption of sugar, and then, by the action of insulin, may fall too rapidly or too low. The result is hypoglycemia, with mental symptoms ranging from depression, to dizziness, to crying spells, to aggression, to lack of sexual interest, to insomnia, to black-out.

When the blood glucose goes too low, the adrenal glands kick in and mobilize the body's stores of glycogen[2]. They also stimulate the synthesis of glucose from proteins and other substances present in the body. On a diet high in refined carbohydrates, the pancreas and adrenal glands are caught in a biochemical yo-yo, and are overworked. If the pancreas weakens, it secretes less insulin, the blood glucose remains high, and diabetes (hyperglycemia) results, with glucose in the urine, and cardiovascular complications. If the adrenal glands give out, adrenal exhaustion — the inability to respond biochemically to stress, and susceptibility to stress diseases — occurs. Hypoglycemia becomes severe because the overworked adrenals fail in their blood sugar-raising function. Low blood sugar caused by the action of insulin gives rise to cravings for sugar, and the rapid absorption of the sugar eaten starts another insulin cycle which repeats the vicious hypoglycemia — sugar-craving circle.

If the body is unable to carry the extra fats and cholesterol produced from sugar, it has to dump the additional load. Fats can be deposited in the liver, heart, arteries, fat tissues, kidneys, muscle, or just about anywhere, and such deposits of fats characterize the diseases of fatty degeneration. Fatty degeneration can be defined as the deposition of visible fat in places where it is not normally found, and included in this definition are atherosclerosis, liver and kidney degeneration, tumours, obesity, rheumatic diseases and diabetes.

Saturated and monounsaturated fatty acids increase tissue anoxia (lack of oxygen), literally choking the body's tissues. By increasing the body's load of these unnecessary fatty acids, the refined carbohydrates lower the body's available oxygen supply. Lowered oxygen supply is involved in all forms of degenerative disease, in all forms of fatty degeneration (see: Fatty Degeneration).

Refined carbohydrates are involved in another way in these diseases. Because they lack the vitamins and minerals required for their own metabolism, they draw on the body's stored supply of these factors, and if the stores are depleted, the body becomes unable to metabolize fats and cholesterol properly. This means that it cannot get rid of excess cholesterol (by changing it into bile acids and discarding some of both cholesterol and bile acids through the stool), and cannot burn off the excess fats as heat or increased activity, because vitamins and minerals are required for the biochemical reactions involved in these processes. As a result, cholesterol level rises; metabolic rate goes down; fats burn more slowly; the person feels like exercising less; obesity results. Obesity increases the risk of diabetes, cardiovascular disease, and cancer. Decreased metabolic rate is also involved in aging, arthritic diseases, cancer, and cardiovascular disorders, and is another general symptom of degenerative diseases.

Sugar causes degeneration in still another way. High blood sugar inhibits the release of the essential linoleic acid (LA, 18:2*w*6) from storage in fat tissue and thereby contributes to essential fatty acid deficiency. Here, although LA is present in the body, it remains stored, unable to fulfill its functions. In spite of the presence of adequate LA within us, we may still be *functionally* deficient in LA.

Finally, the lack of bulk and fiber in the refined carbohydrates slows down the speed at which foods pass through the digestive tract. They sit around in the colon, and bring on constipation, inflamed (diverticulitis) and ballooned (diverticulosis) colon, toxin retention which weakens the liver, bowel cancer, hemorrhoids, and varicose veins. Some types of fiber aid in the removal of excess cholesterol, and the refined carbohydrates are of no help in this matter.

Sugars and starches thus play a considerable role in the cause of fatty degeneration, by their contribution to the fat and cholesterol the body must carry, by their depletion of the body's stores of vitamins and minerals, by interference with the functions of the essential fatty acids, and by their lack of bulk and fiber.

Identifying the real culprit. Sugars are considered by many researchers to be the major dietary cause of degenerative diseases. While they do play a major role in degeneration, much of their effect is due to the fats into which the body converts excess sugars, and the fats produced from them then create major health problems for the body.

If one compares changes in total sugar consumption, total fat consumption, and consumption of altered (vegetable) fat substances with the vast increase in degenerative disease over the last 100 years, one finds the *best* correlation between altered (vegetable) fat substances and disease, a less strongly positive correlation between sugar consumption and disease, and an even less strongly positive correlation between total fat consumption and disease. All three, however, show positive correlations with degenerative disease.

5

Unsaturated Fatty Acids

Introduction

Unsaturated fatty acids (UFAs) differ from the simpler saturated fatty acids in only one respect. They contain one or more double bonds between carbon atoms in their fatty carbon chain, and for each double bond, they give up 2 hydrogen atoms. Aside from this, they are identical in structure: they have the acid end and have carbon chains of varying lengths, just like the saturated fatty acids. Figure 9 shows the formation and structure of an unsaturated fatty acid.

Properties of the Double Bond

However, this small difference in structure, the double bond, drastically changes their properties. Because of the way the hydrogen atoms are placed on the carbons involved in the double bonds[1], the chain is kinked at the double bond position. This so-called *cis-* configuration and the resulting kink in the molecule was illustrated in Figure 6, in the first chapter. The kinks created by *cis-* double bonds in fatty acids make it difficult for the fatty acid chains to fit together well, and therefore they aggregate

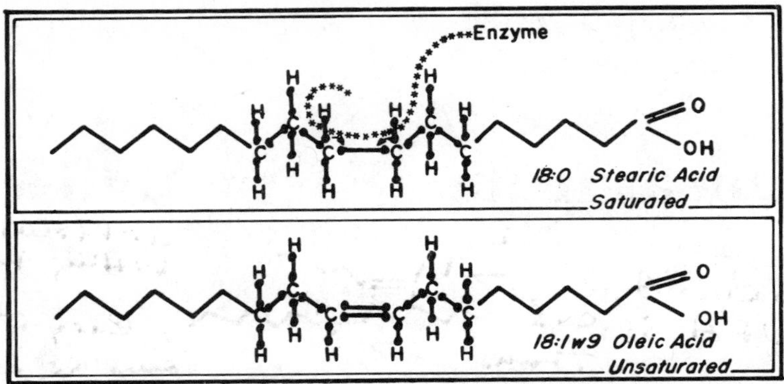

Figure 9. Formation and structure of an unsaturated fatty acid.

poorly. For this reason, they melt at a lower temperature (are more liquid) than saturated fatty acids identical in every respect except for the double bond.

The double bond, because it has a pair of extra electrons, carries a slight negative charge. Since like charges repel one another, this results in UFA chains repelling one another, and this repulsion gives them the tendency to spread out over surfaces in a very thin, 1-molecule thick layer. Thus, while saturated fatty acids tend to aggregate, UFAs tend to disperse, to move apart, to be anti-sticky. Figure 10 compares some properties of different fatty acids.

This property of UFAs provides the fluidity needed in membranes. It allows molecules within the membrane the freedom to swim and dive, to make and break contacts with one another, to fulfill their important chemical and transport functions.

Monounsaturated Fatty Acids (MUFAs)

MUFAs are unsaturated fatty acids with one double bond. The length of their carbon chains can vary.

The shortest MUFAs are 10 carbon (C10) chains. C12 and C14 MUFAs also occur. All of these are found in small quantities in milk. Their double bonds are found in various locations along the chain. They are of minor importance in nutrition.

More important is a MUFA with a 16-carbon chain and a double bond between carbons 7 and 8. It is called palmitoleic acid (POA, 16:1*w*7) and occurs in larger quantities in milk, and also in coconut and palm kernel oils. An excess of this MUFA can lead to health problems by interfering with the functions of the essential

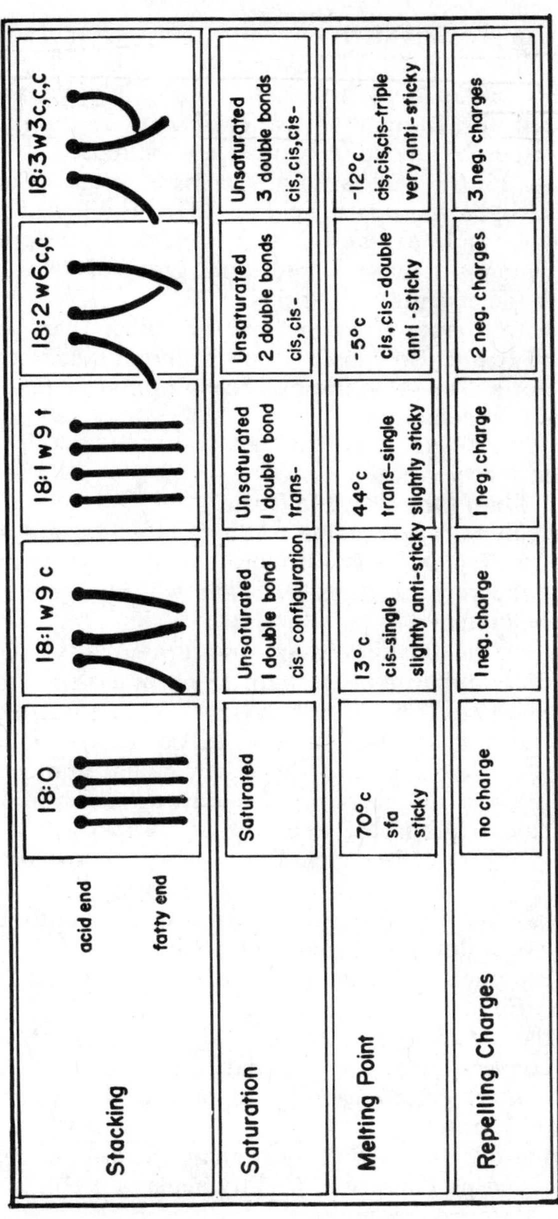

	18:0	18:1 w 9 c	18:1 w 9 t	18:2 w6c,c	18:3 w3c,c,c
Stacking (acid end / fatty end)					
Saturation	Saturated	Unsaturated 1 double bond cis-configuration	Unsaturated 1 double bond trans-	Unsaturated 2 double bonds cis, cis-	Unsaturated 3 double bonds cis, cis, cis-
Melting Point	70°c sfa sticky	13°c cis-single slightly anti-sticky	44°c trans-single slightly sticky	-5°c cis, cis-double anti-sticky	-12°c cis,cis,cis-triple very anti-sticky
Repelling Charges	no charge	1 neg. charge	1 neg. charge	2 neg. charges	3 neg. charges

Figure 10. Some properties of different types of fatty acids.

fatty acids (see: Essential Fatty Acids).

The most important MUFA in nutrition has an 18-carbon chain, and its double bond is always between carbons 9 and 10. It is called oleic acid (OA, 18:1*w*9). OA is found in olive, almond, and other seed oils, in the membranes of plant and animal cell structures, and in the fat depots of most land animals. OA is quite fluid (melts at 13°C), and its fluidity helps to keep the arteries supple. It is also the major fatty acid found in the oil produced by human skin glands. In excess, however, oleic acid interferes with important functions of the most interesting group of UFAs, which are known as the essential fatty acids.

MUFAs with double bonds in positions other than between carbons 9 and 10 are also known. Many different kinds exist, but as they are not of any great importance in human nutrition, we will not consider them here.

Unsaturated Fatty Acids With More Than One Double Bond

These are the most interesting of the fatty acids, and we will devote several chapters to a consideration of the structure and functions of the various kinds. Here we will just give a short preview of the kinds.

Nutritionally, the most important unsaturated fatty acids with more than one double bond contain 18 carbon atoms in their chains. There are 2 of these 18 carbon UFAs. They are also known as essential fatty acids (EFAs). One, called linoleic acid (LA, 18:2*w*6), has 2 double bonds; the other, called linolenic acid (LNA, 18:3*w*3), has 3 double bonds. These are extremely important in nutrition and health (see: Essential Fatty Acids).

Another group of UFAs includes a member with 20 carbon atoms and 5 double bonds, known as eicosapentaenoic acid (EPA, 20:5*w*3), and a member with 22 carbon atoms and 6 double bonds, known as docosahexaenoic acid (DHA, 22:6*w*3). These too, have very important functions in the body (see: Oils from Fish and Sea Foods).

Between these 2 groups of UFAs we find the intermediates in the body's conversion of the essential fatty acids to EPA and DHA. These intermediates have 18, 20, or 22 carbon chains, and 3, 4, or 5 double bonds.

Unsaturated fatty acids with more than one double bond are sometimes called polyunsaturated fatty acids or PUFAs. There are the natural PUFAs mentioned in the preceding 2 paragraphs, which are very important in the body's functions, but there are also PUFAs which are non-natural and man-made, which interfere with biological functions (see: Polyunsaturates).

Essential fatty acids can be slowly converted within the body into larger and more highly unsaturated fatty acids (20:5*w*3 and 22:6*w*3) which have important functions in the brain cells, the nerve endings called synapses, the sense organs, the adrenal glands, and the sex glands. 20:5*w*3, called EPA for short, is also used to make one family of prostaglandins. Alternately, EPA and DHA can be supplied to the body through the diet, from the oils of certain fish and marine animals (see: Oils from Fish . . .).

If this all sounds a little complicated, don't worry. We will take up each of these topics in turn and explain them simply, to unravel a mystery on which life and health depends.

6

Essential Fatty Acids

Introduction

The most important fatty acids in human nutrition and health are two fatty acids with 18 carbon links in their chains. Their names are linoleic acid (LA) and linolenic acid (LNA).

Linoleic Acid

The proper scientific name for LA is: all *cis*- *w*6, 9-octadecadienoic acid, abbreviated to 18:2*w*6. The abbreviation 18:2*w*6 means that there are 18 carbon atoms in the chain, there are 2 double bonds, the double bonds are methylene interrupted, the first double bond starts at carbon atom number 6, counting from the methyl end, and the double bonds are in the *cis*- configuration (see: Naming the Fatty Acids).

Linolenic Acid

The proper scientific name for LNA is all *cis*- *w*3,6,9-octadecatrienoic acid, abbreviated to 18:3*w*3. It is very similar to LA, but has three double bonds, the first one of which is on carbon atom number 3, counting from the methyl end. Figure 11 shows the molecular structure of the two essential fatty acids.

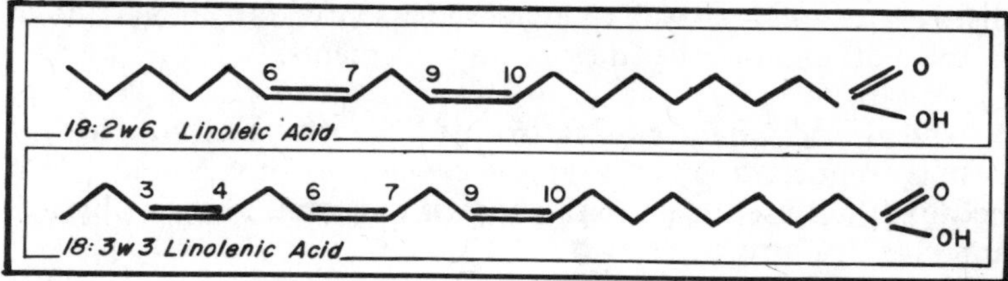

Figure 11. Stick models of the essential fatty acids.

Both LA and LNA are essential fatty acids. This means that the human body has to have them, cannot make them, and must therefore get them from food sources. A third fatty acid, called arachidonic acid (AA, 20:4*w*6), was thought to be essential for a time, but the human body can make it from LA, and therefore AA is not essential. If either LA or LNA is missing or deficient in the diet, deficiency diseases develop.

LA Deficiency Symptoms

The symptoms of LA deficiency include: eczema-like skin eruptions, loss of hair, liver degeneration, behavioural disturbances, kidney degeneration, excessive water loss through the skin accompanied by thirst, drying up of glands, susceptibility to infections, failure of wound healing, sterility in males, miscarriage in females, arthritis, heart and circulatory problems, and retardation of growth. Prolonged absence of LA from the diet is fatal. All of the deficiency symptoms (except death) can be alleviated by adding LA back to the diet from which it was missing.

LNA Deficiency Symptoms

The symptoms of LNA deficiency include: retardation of growth, weakness, impairment of vision and learning ability, motor incoordination, tingling in arms and legs, and behavioural changes. These symptoms can be removed by adding LNA back to the diet from which it was missing.

Experts have recently begun to suggest that essential fatty acid deficiency is far more widespread than was formerly believed. The symptoms closely resemble some of the symptoms of the diseases of fatty degeneration. It comes as no surprise, therefore, that the tissue and/or blood levels of people with these diseases are low in essential fatty acids, or that they are functionally deficient, even if essential fatty acids are present. Nor is it surprising that this set of diseases responds so well to increased essential fatty acid content in the diet, and to other dietary improvements.

Physical and Chemical Nature of Essential Fatty Acids

It is important to look at the properties of LA and LNA, because their usefulness to the body is the result of their physical and chemical properties.

Essential fatty acids attract oxygen. This property has made them useful in the paint industry in 'drying' oils, which when exposed to air, dry and harden. Safflower oil, which is 80% LA, and linseed oil, which is almost 60% LNA and about 20% LA, are oils commonly used for this purpose. These two oils are also the best oils in nutrition, and for the same reason. Flax oil (the undenatured version of linseed oil) is better than safflower oil, because it contains both of the essential fatty acids (safflower contains only LA) and because it is more active (it contains more double bonds in an equal volume of oil).

Essential fatty acids absorb sunlight. The absorption of light energy increases their ability to react with oxygen by about 1000-fold, and makes them chemically very active indeed[1].

The essential fatty acids carry a slight negative charge, which makes them capable of a number of activities important in the body. Their molecules repel one another because of this charge. This means that they spread out in a very thin layer over surfaces, and do not form aggregations. This property is called surface activity. In biological systems, surface activity provides the power to carry substances such as toxins to the surface of the skin, intestinal tract, kidneys, or lungs where these substances are discarded. The surface activity of the essential fatty acids also helps to disperse concentrations of any substances which either react with or dissolve in these fatty acids.

The negative charge also makes the essential fatty acids weakly basic (as opposed to acidic), and able to form weak hydrogen bonds with weak acid groups such as the sulphydryl groups found in proteins. Sulphydryl groups are especially important in oscillating reactions which take place between them and the double bonds of the essential fatty acids. They allow the one-way movement of electrons and energy in molecules to take place. According to one of the world's best chemists, the Nobel Laureate Linus Pauling, such movement is required to make possible the chemical reactions on which life depends.

Because of their special arrangement, the electrons involved in the double bonds of the essential fatty acids can be induced to become loose and move, as so-called de-localized pi-electrons, which resemble clouds floating along the fatty acid chain. This concept is illustrated in Figure 12.

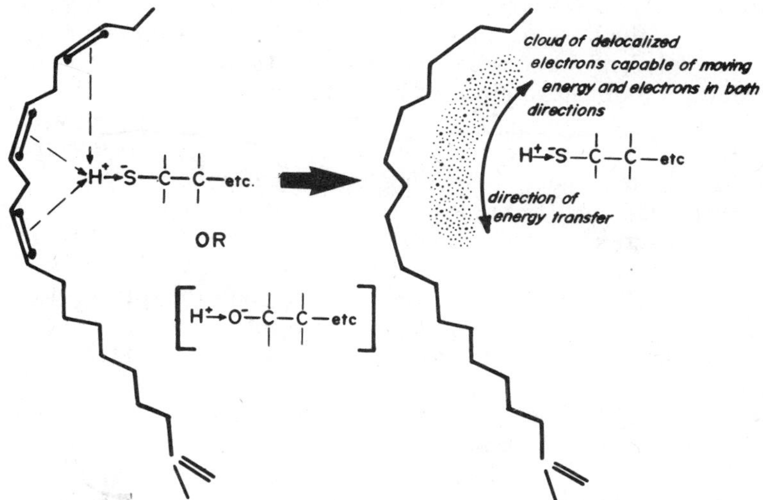

Figure 12. Electron and energy transfer in a pi-electron cloud.

They are able to form phase boundary potentials (like charges of static electricity in a capacitor), which are caught between the water within and outside cells, and the oils within the membranes. These charges can produce measurable bio-electric currents (like the zap when static electricity discharges), which are important in nerve, muscle, heart, and membrane functions.

The Functions of LA and LNA in the Body

Much is still unknown about the functions in the body of the essential fatty acids. Of the two, LA has been studied far more extensively than LNA. Both of the essential fatty acids are difficult to work with, because they are easily destroyed. LNA is even more sensitive to destruction than LA.

Still, although much work still needs to be done before we completely understand the nature of their activity (and this is true for all the other essential nutrients as well — the vitamins, minerals, trace elements, and amino acids), a long list of functions in which they are involved can be given, based on scientific studies and an understanding of their chemical and physical nature. Overall, they are involved with the production of life energy in the body from food substances, and the movement of that energy in our systems. They govern growth, vitality and mental state. They hook up oxygen, electron transport, and energy in the process of oxidation, the burning of food for the production of the energy required for life processes. Oxidation is the central and most important moment to moment living process in the body.

LA and LNA are involved, in a way not well understood, with the transfer of oxygen from the air in the lungs, through the alveolar membrane (the thin lung tissue membrane), through the capillary wall, into the blood plasma (the watery fluid in which the blood cells are suspended), across the membranes of the red blood cells, to the hemoglobin, which then carries the oxygen to all cells of the body. At the cell end, they are needed in the transport of oxygen from the red blood cells, through the plasma, across the walls of the capillaries, across the cell membranes, and, in the cell, to transport the oxygen to the exact location(s) where it is needed.

They can be likened to an oxygen 'magnet' in the body, which pulls oxygen into the body in the same way that a magnet pulls iron filings. Figure 13 shows the attraction between oxygen and essential fatty acids.

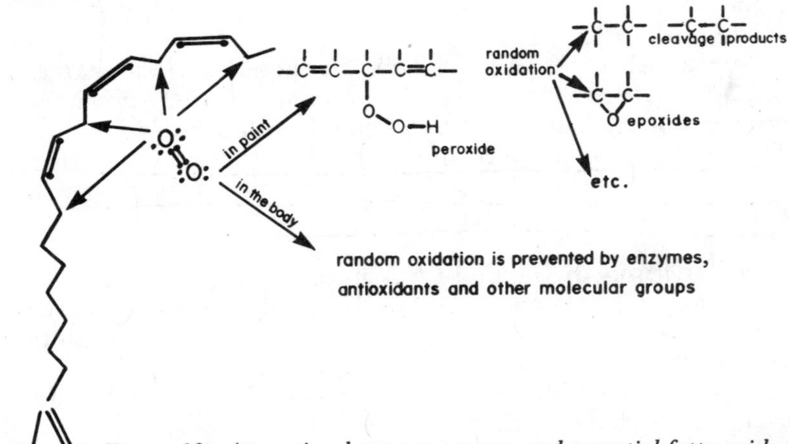

Figure 13. Attraction between oxygen and essential fatty acids.

LA and LNA have a function in holding oxygen in the cell membranes, where it acts as a barrier to viruses and bacteria, because these foreign organisms will not thrive in the presence of oxygen. LA is involved in the production of the red blood pigment hemoglobin from simpler substances. They are both involved in a process which makes oxygen available to the tissues, by 'activating', or opening the oxygen molecule. This appears to occur by way of free radicals or electrostatic forces, regulated by sulphur-containing proteins.

The essential fatty acids form a structural part of all cell membranes, where they hold proteins in the membrane by the electrostatic attractive force of their double bonds, and thus they are involved in the traffic of substances in and out of the cells via protein channels, pumps, and other special mechanisms. Figure 14 shows the relationship of essential fatty acids to sulphur-containing proteins in membranes. They have a part in maintaining the fluidity of membranes, and in creating the electrical potentials across the membranes, which when stimulated, can generate bioelectric currents which travel along the cells to other cells, transmitting messages.

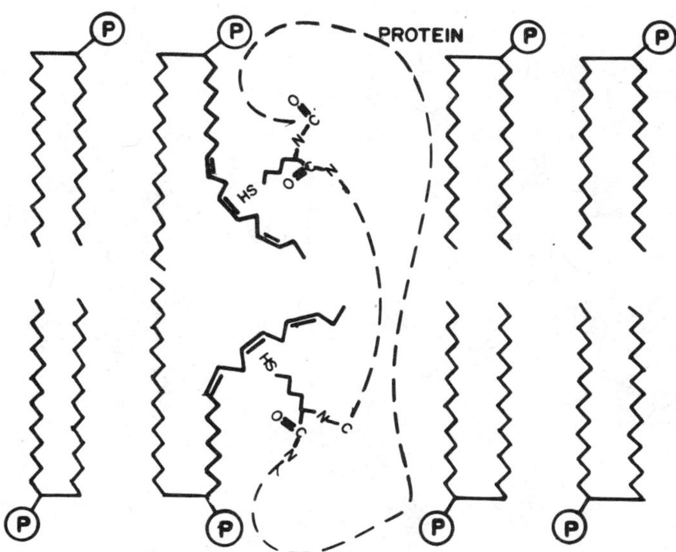

Figure 14. Relationship of essential fatty acids and sulphur-containing membrane proteins.

The essential fatty acids are also structural parts of the membranes of the subcellular organelles or 'small organs' within the cell. Let's list them and briefly describe their functions. There's the 'endoplasmic reticulum', where protein synthesis takes place. There's the 'Golgi apparatus', which is involved in the secretion of substances within the cell. There are the 'vesicles', which transport substances into and out of the cells. Then there are the 'mitochondria', those factories within each cell which burn (or oxidize) food to release the stored sunlight energy in them for use in our life functions, both on the biochemical and the human level. Finally, there's the 'nucleus', which contains the chromosomes. These carry the master plan according to which the whole body is constructed, and control the sequences of biochemical events that we know as development and cell function, which begin at conception and continue constantly until death. Information carried on the chromosomes determines eye colour, hair colour, body type, gender, and so on. Figure 15 shows a cell with its organelles. Figure 16 shows all of the fatty acids commonly found in membranes, including the essential fatty acids and their derivatives.

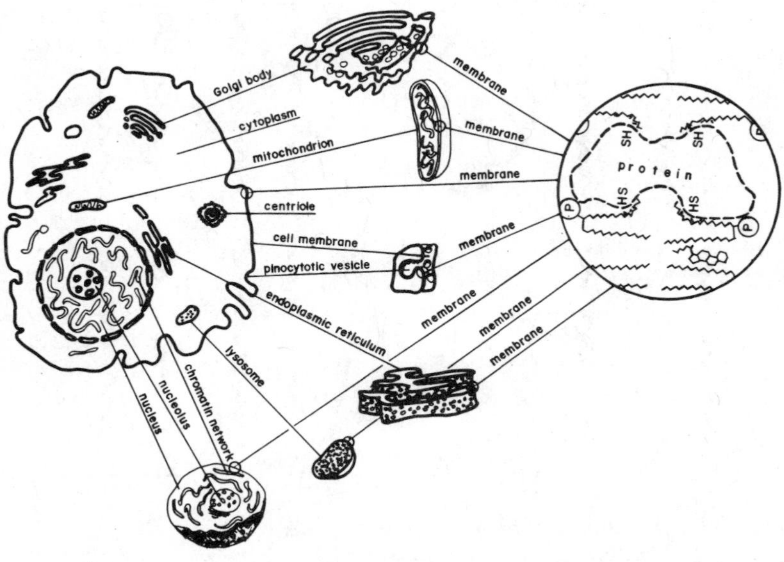

Figure 15. A cell, its organelles, and membranes.

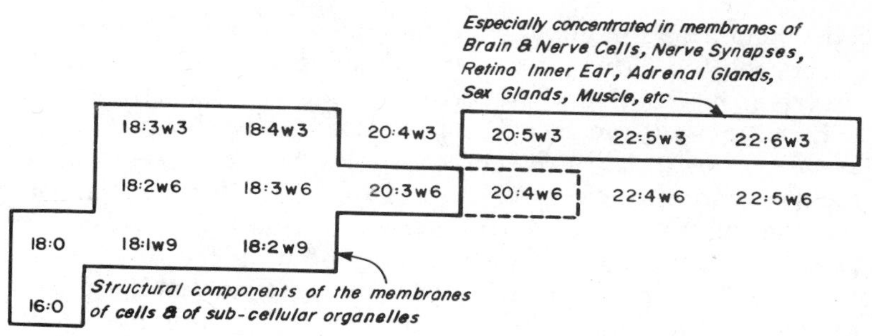

Figure 16. Fatty acids commonly found in membranes.

LA and LNA shorten substantially the time required for the recovery of fatigued muscles after exercise, by facilitating the conversion of lactic acid to water and carbon dioxide. Both LA and LNA are involved in the secretion of all glands, both juice-producing (exocrine) and hormone-producing (endocrine).

Essential fatty acids are the precursors of a family of substances, the hormone-like, short-lived prostaglandins, which regulate many functions of all tissues on a moment to moment basis. Some prostaglandins affect the tone of smooth (involuntary) muscles in the blood vessels. Some prostaglandins lower blood pressure, some relax coronary arteries, some inhibit platelet stickiness. Others have opposite effects, and a delicate balance exists in our bodies between opposing effects, which determines the state of physical health of our cardiovascular systems (see: Prostaglandins). The essential fatty acids are also the precursors for even longer and more (5 and 6 times) unsaturated fatty acids which are needed in the most active energy-exchanging and electron-exchanging, as well as oxygen-requiring tissues, especially the brain, retina, inner ear, adrenal, and testicular tissues. They carry the high energy required by these most active tissues, and ensure very high oxygen availability.

The essential fatty acids are growth-enhancing. At levels above 12-15% of total calories, they increase the rate of metabolic reactions in the body, and the increased rate 'burns' more fat into carbon dioxide, water and energy (heat), resulting in fat burnoff and loss of excess weight. Essential fatty acids seem to be involved in electron and energy transport in ways which are not well understood and require much further study. Essential fatty acids are involved in the transport (esterification) of excess cholesterol.

They help keep the body depot fats fluid. They are involved in generating the electrical currents that make the heart beat in orderly sequence. Heart tissue requires LA for proper functioning.

Essential fatty acids are found around the chromatin, the hereditary material in the chromosomes, where they appear to regulate chromosome stability, and may have functions in the starting and stopping of gene expression. Essential fatty acids help govern the movement of chromosomes during cell division by their functions in spindle fiber development. Essential fatty acids are required in the formation of the new cell membranes which separate the two daughter cells after a cell has divided. Essential fatty acids are involved in the function of the immune system, which acts to fight infections and confers resistance to disease and allergies.

In the young, LNA is required for brain development. Deficiency of LNA during fetal development and early infancy results in permanent learning disability. Essential fatty acids can buffer excess acid in the system, as well as excess base. Essential fatty acids are involved in the absorption of visible sunlight and ultraviolet light through the skin for storage in the body in the form of chemical bonds. Essential fatty acids are the highest source of energy in nutrition.

In short, essential fatty acids govern every life process in the body. Life without essential fatty acids is impossible. When essential fatty acids are deficient, we can expect a diversity of health problems.

Daily Requirement for Essential Fatty Acids

How much is enough? Of the 45 essential nutrients discovered so far (there may be as many as 75-100 in all), linoleic acid (LA, 18:2*w*6) is the one the body contains and needs the most of, but estimated amounts differ among different researchers on the subject. The amount needed varies, depending on physical activity, stress, nutritional state, and individual differences. Because of hormonal differences, males may require up to 3 times as much as females. Requirement also varies from time to time for the same person. Although 1-2% of calories or 3-6 grams per day is enough to prevent symptoms of deficiency in most healthy subjects, an optimum amount might be in the range of 3-10% of calories, or 9-30 grams per day. The obese and people on diets high in saturated fatty acids and olive oil require even more. In animal studies, as much as 28.5% of calories as LA has been given without problems in long term feedings, provided enough vitamin E was also included (about 1 part vitamin E for 1500 parts LA). 30 grams of LA/day would require less than 50 I.U. of vitamin E. Other nutrients required for LA to properly unfold its functions in the body are vitamins C, B3, B6, and zinc. Vitamin A or its precursor carotene, is also important.

Body Content of Essential Fatty Acids

In the average human being, about 10% of the total of 10 kilograms of body fat tissue, or 1 kilogram, is LA. Vegetarians contain up to 25% of their total body fat as LA. In view of the fact that vegetarians on the average are less prone to fatty degeneration than the average person and that people with degenerative diseases are generally lower than average in LA (about 8% of their fat tissue), it appears that a healthy person would contain more than 1 kg of LA in his body. The amount of linolenic acid (LNA, 18:3*w*3) needed for health is less than that of LA, perhaps between 1/5 and 1/2 of that of LA, or between 2 and 10 grams per day. Newest estimates recommend 2% of daily calories as LNA. The body's content of LNA is correspondingly less than that of LA.

Sources of Essential Fatty Acids

Where can we get the essential fatty acids we need? Plants have enzymes which can insert a double bond into fatty acids in positions 3 and 6, but humans do not have such enzymes. That is why LA and LNA are 'essential' in our food supply, and why they come primarily from plant sources.

The best source of essential fatty acids are the oils of certain seeds and nuts. The richest source of these vital substances is flax oil. Safflower oil is also good, but contains only one of the essential fatty acids, LA. For therapeutic purposes, evening primrose oil is excellent, but it, like safflower, does not contain any of the second essential fatty acid, LNA. The best sources of the essential fatty acids can be found in the table in chapter 43 (see: Oils in Seeds).

Caring for the Essential Fatty Acids

As essential as LA and LNA are to our health, they are also very tempermental, and easily destroyed by light, air, and heat. For this reason, care needs to be taken in the processing, packaging, and storing of the oils containing them. Nature packages these oils in seeds, in a way that keeps light, air and heat out. In this package, the oils can sometimes be kept for up to several years without spoiling.

When man extracts the oil from such seeds, he needs to make sure that light, air, and heat are kept out of the oil from before pressing until the oil is consumed, but to set such conditions is expensive, and the necessary care is not usually taken (see: Oil Making).

Light. Light is the greatest enemy of the essential fatty acids, because it speeds up to 1000 times the reaction of oils with oxygen from the air, resulting in rancid oil. Polymerization reactions, which produce rubber-like substances that are often found around tumours, can be induced by light. Light fosters free radical chain reactions (see: Free Radicals) which break down the essential fatty acids into many different kinds of products, including aldehydes, ketones, and other toxic and non-toxic components. Worst of all, light destroys the vital biological properties of the essential fatty acids through its reactions with them.

Oxygen. Oxygen from the air, even in the absence of light, breaks down the essential fatty acids because of their very active nature. The result is what we know as rancid oil, which has a particular acrid, scratchy taste, and a characteristic unpleasant smell. Dozens of breakdown products form, with toxic or unknown effects on the body's functions.

Heat. High temperatures, which are reached in some of the processes to which the oils are subjected in refining, hydrogenation (to make margarines and shortenings), deodorizing, and other commercial methods used for making consumer items, destroy the essential fatty acids by twisting the molecules from their natural *cis-* shape to the unnatural *trans-* shape (see: Trans- Fatty Acids). Frying also twists these oils (see: Frying).

In order to make oils that will not spoil, they must be pressed and packaged in the dark, in the absence of oxygen, and without heat. They must be stored in opaque containers to prevent light from spoiling them on the shelf. They must be in containers which exclude air or oxygen. With this kind of packaging, good oils will remain fresh for years.

7

Triglycerides

Introduction

Triglycerides are the main class of food fats. They make up about 95% of all the fats we eat, as well as most of the stored fat we carry around in our bodies. They are the major way of storing energy for future use, in the seeds of the plants from which we press edible oils, in egg yolks, and in the depot fats of animals. In a wholesome diet, the triglycerides also serve as the body's reserve of the valuable essential fatty acids, LA and LNA.

Structure of the Triglycerides

Figure 17 shows the way a triglyceride is built. A glycerol molecule is the backbone, and on to each of its 3 carbon atoms, one fatty acid is hooked, to make a 3 pronged fork.

The 2 outside carbon positions of the glycerol prefer to hold a saturated fatty acid, whereas the middle position prefers an essential fatty acid. The preference is not 100% however, and so one finds the positions switched to a small extent. The type of oil or fat in question also determines to some extent which fatty acids will be found on which position. Beef fat, for instance, is made of

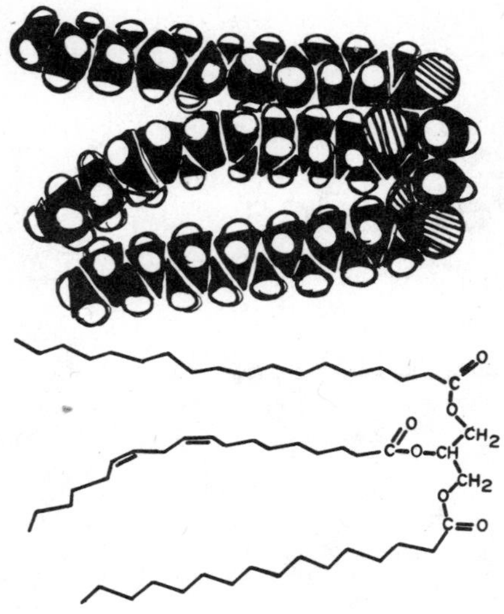

Figure 17. Structure of a triglyceride (fat).

triglycerides which carry mostly saturated and monounsaturated fatty acids in all positions (it contains hardly any essential fatty acids).

Completely hydrogenated fats carry almost 100% saturated fatty acids on all positions. Flax oil and high LA strains of safflower oil, on the other hand, carry essential fatty acids in all 3 positions much of the time, because both of these oils contain more than 70% essential fatty acids, which obviously can't all fit on the middle position.

The fatty acids attached to the glycerol molecule can be short or long. Butter for instance, has many short chain fatty acids (between 4 and 14 carbon atoms in length) hooked to glycerol, whereas most plant seed oils and animal depot fats have mainly 18-carbon fatty acids in their triglycerides. Fatty acids in the triglycerides of fish oils are even longer. As you can imagine, the number of possible combinations or arrangements of the fatty acids is very large, since there are 3 positions, at least 4 different degrees of saturation (saturated, monounsaturated, twice unsaturated, and three times unsaturated), and at least 8 different possible carbon chain lengths (4 to 18 carbon atoms, even numbers only), as well as smaller amounts of odd numbered and unusual types of fatty acids on triglycerides.

Figure 18 shows examples of some possible combinations of fatty acids on triglycerides.

4:0	6:0	12:0	18:0	18:1w9	12:0	18:2w6	18:3w3	
18:1w9	16:1w7	8:0	18:0	18:3w3	18:2w6	18:2w6	18:3w3	
10:0	4:0	14:0	18:0	18:0	18:1w9	18:0	18:2w6	
18:2w6	18:0	16:1w7	12:0					*outside position*
18:2w6	18:2w6	18:3w3	18:2w6	etc.				*middle position*
18:2w6	18:0	18:1w9	16:0					*outside position*

Figure 18. Some possible combinations of fatty acids in fats.

All fats and oils are mixtures of triglycerides with such varying compositions (see: Oils in Seeds). In nutrition however, this is not as important as the total amount of each kind of fatty acid present because the body separates the triglycerides into glycerol and fatty acids, and reconstitutes the parts back into triglycerides according to its needs. It burns for energy the short chain fatty acids and the saturated and monounsaturated 16- and 18-carbon fatty acids, while preserving the essential fatty acids for their extremely important structural and metabolic functions in the body.

Functions of the Triglycerides

Triglycerides have several functions. They form a layer of insulation around the body, which conserves heat. Without this layer, more food consumption, more digestion, more absorption, and more metabolism of substances would be required to keep body temperature constant. It is more efficient and less wasteful to conserve the heat rather than to keep producing it, just as it is more efficient to put on a jacket than to heat the whole house.

The adipose (fat) layer around the body and internal organs also protects us from shock and injury when we bump into things and every time we take a step, walking or running. Adipose is singularly effective at dampening the shock waves, which would otherwise destroy delicate tissues. The fat pad under the heel, for instance, takes up a tremendous amount of shock each time the heel hits the pavement. One can still feel the shock wave travel up one's body at every step, but in much reduced intensity.

However, the main purpose of adipose tissue is as a reserve of energy on which the body can draw between meals, during times of increased exertion, while asleep, during famine, or while pregnant. Since man evolved as a natural being subject to times of feast and times of famine, the adipose tissue system evolved to mellow out the fluctuations between these two extremes. Plants did not evolve such a system. For this reason they stop growing when the sunshine fades or when it gets cold.

Another purpose for the triglycerides is that substances such as sugars, which are necessary for brain function, but are toxic in excess, can be converted to triglycerides which are less harmful in large quantities. So the triglycerides provide a kind of safety mechanism for the body, a way of changing potentially toxic substances into neutral ones.

The fatty acids from triglycerides are the fuel on which all the organs work, except for the brain. The brain requires glucose, and this can be made from glycerol, so the triglycerides store brain fuel too (glucose can also be made from protein).

The triglycerides store the body's reserve of the essential fatty acids, which are required for the structure and functions of the membranes, are the precursors of the prostaglandins (see: Prostaglandins), and are also the precursors of the highly active, very highly unsaturated fatty acids required for brain cells, synapses, retina, adrenal glands, and testes to function properly.

Triglycerides and Disease

Excess triglycerides cause problems, and are associated with disease. High triglyceride levels in the blood are associated with heart disease, and are produced by overeating, and especially by a high intake of refined sugars in the diet.

Excess body fat, or obesity correlates with high cholesterol level and high triglyceride level, both of which are associated with cardiovascular disease, high blood pressure, and heart and kidney failure.

High blood triglyceride levels increase the tendency of blood cells to clump together, decreasing the amount of oxygen the blood can carry, and increasing the risk of all degenerative disease, including cancer.

Protection

Diets which are high in fats but which are also high in quality protein, vitamins and minerals lessen the danger of the problems of degeneration. Vitamin B6 is particularly necessary in a high fat diet. The same vitamin is important in high protein diets.

A diet high in the highly unsaturated *w*3 fatty acids EPA (20:5*w*3 and DHA (22:6*w*3) found in fish and marine animal oils (see: Oils from Fish and Other Sea Foods), lowers the blood triglyceride level. People regularly eating such a diet don't suffer from cardiovascular and other degenerative diseases. People who begin to take these oils show remarkable reductions in their blood triglyceride levels, although their cholesterol levels are lowered only a little. Cholesterol levels are lowered by increasing the intake of the *w*6 fatty acids, especially linoleic acid (18:2*w*6). Exercise lowers blood triglyceride levels by burning up the excess for energy. Safe blood triglyceride levels should be 100 mg/dl or lower. The level in the North American population is often above that.

8

Phosphatides (phospholipids) and Membranes

Introduction

Phosphatides are the second major class of lipids (besides the triglycerides) found in foods and in the body. They are the major structural lipids of all organisms.

Structure of Phosphatides

Phosphatides are similar to triglycerides, in that two fatty acids (usually 16- or 18- carbon chains) are attached to a glycerol molecule, but phosphatides differ from triglycerides in that, whereas the third position on the glycerol of triglycerides holds a third fatty acid, this position in the phosphatides holds a phosphate group. The phosphate group changes the properties of the molecule drastically. Whereas a triglyceride is a non-polar, fat-soluble molecule which dislikes water and likes to aggregate into an oil droplet with other triglyceride molecules, the phosphatide is polar and water-soluble, tends to disperse over surfaces, (because the negatively charged phosphate groups repel one another) and is dual in nature. The fatty acid part of the molecule is fat soluble, and the phosphate group is water soluble. Figure 19 shows the structure of a phosphatide molecule.

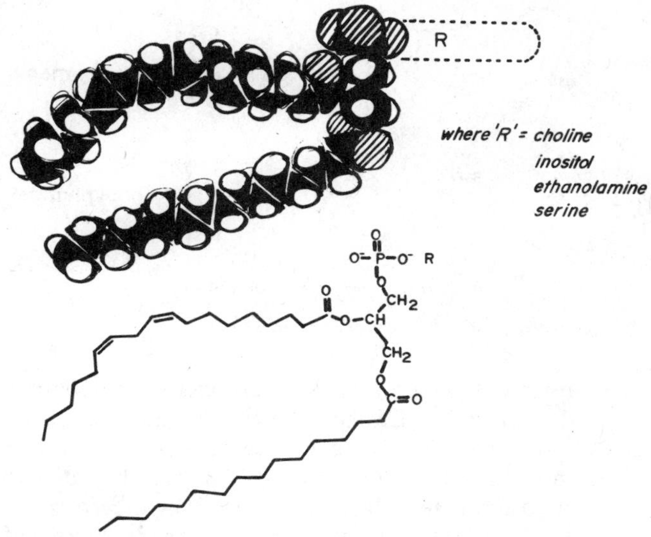

Figure 19. Structure of a phosphatide.

Biological Membranes and Phosphatide Function

The dual nature of the phosphatides, and their tendency to spread out in a thin layer wherever water and oil meet, suits them in a unique way to form biological membranes, and sure enough, that's where we find phosphatides — in membranes. They form the double-layered membrane, the 'skin' of every living cell of every living organism: bacteria, plants, animals, and humans. Figure 20 shows the structure of a biological membrane.

Phosphatides also form the 'skins' of the little organs, the organelles, within the cells. They surround the mitochondria, the Golgi, the endoplasmic reticulum, the nuclear membrane, the lysosomes, and the other less well-known, though not less important, intracellular factories.

Within the membrane, the phosphatides have many functions. They form the basic barrier which keeps the outside outside, and the inside inside the cell or organelle. Along with proteins, they determine the selectivity of the membrane, regulating which substances are allowed or transported into the cell or organelle from the outside, and which substances from within the cell are allowed or encouraged to leave. Their selectivity is not perfect, however, and fat-soluble substances such as alcohol, barbituates,

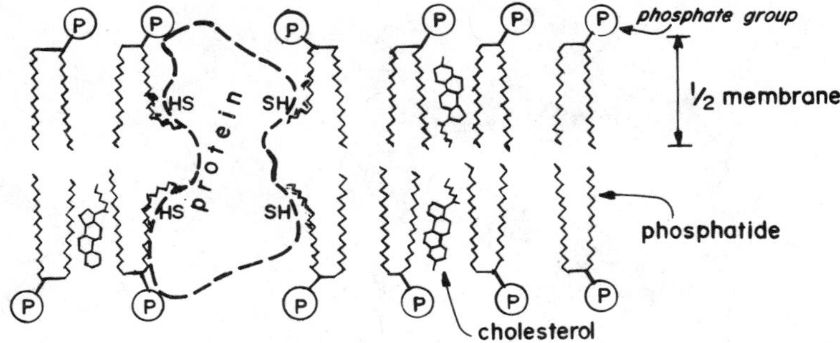

Figure 20. Structure of a biological membrane.

many prescription drugs, and many carcinogens can penetrate the phospholipid membrane. Cancer-causing substances are potent only to the degree that they are able to dissolve in the cell membrane and able to get into the cell, where they disrupt its functions and convert the cell from normal to cancerous.

The phosphatides help to prevent the membrane proteins from falling out of the membrane; they help to hold them in place in the membrane, where these proteins fulfill many special enzyme and transport functions.

As in triglycerides, the fatty acid on the middle carbon of the glycerol molecule prefers, and therefore usually holds, an essential fatty acid. The highly unsaturated fatty acid molecules are bent and cannot be tightly packed. They take up more space than the straight saturated fatty acid molecules, and therefore make the membrane more fluid. Figure 21 illustrates this point. Thus the phosphatides ensure that the membrane is fluid, so that the molecules in it can move and the proteins within the membrane can float around the surface of the cell, performing their vital functions.

The highly unsaturated fatty acid molecules attract oxygen, in the presence of which infectious organisms such as bacteria and viruses can't thrive. In this way, the phosphatides protect the cell from invasion by foreign organisms.

A saturated fatty acid is usually found on the outside position of the glycerol molecule, and gives some rigidity to the membrane. It also separates the highly unsaturated fatty acids, thereby preventing them from chemically reacting with one another in ways not conducive to life.

The phosphate group ensures that each molecule of the

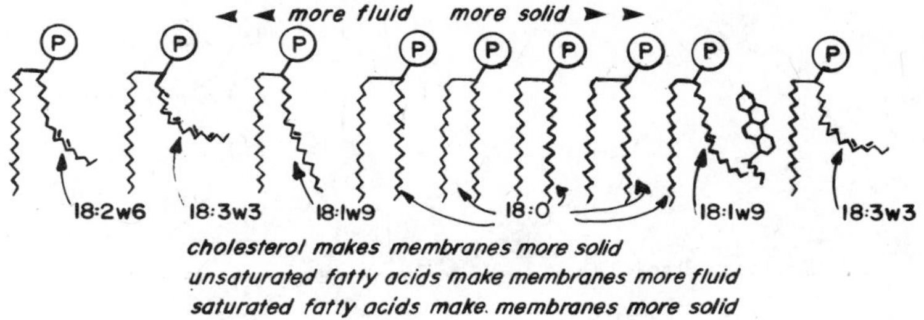

Figure 21. How a membrane becomes more fluid or more solid.

membrane phosphatides lines up in the same direction and in precise regularity.

Phosphate groups can have attached to them one of several other chemical structures, whose exact function in membranes is still a mystery. The names of the main ones are choline, inositol (both are sold as supplements in health food stores), serine, and ethanolamine. Phosphatidyl choline is a phosphatide with a choline group attached to its phosphate.

Besides the phosphatides and proteins, the membranes contain cholesterol, which fine tunes the fluidity of the membranes under constantly fluctuating conditions of food fat intake (see: Cholesterol). Membranes also contain vitamins E and A, both of which help to protect the membranes from destruction by free radicals (see: Free Radicals). Vitamin A also appears to help with energy and electron transfers across membranes.

Single Membranes

Phosphatides are also important in the single-layered membranes which surround the fats and cholesterol being transported from the intestines to and from the liver, and to and from the cells. The main types of these fat and cholesterol carrying vehicles are shown in Figure 22.

The chylomicrons are made in the intestinal cells and carry the food fats. The very low density lipoproteins (VLDL) are made in the liver. The high density lipoproteins (HDL) and low density lipoproteins (LDL), which are related to cardiovascular health and disease are described in more detail elsewhere (see: Blood Cholesterol). The relationships of these carriers to one another are complex, and not yet fully understood (see: Digestion).

Phosphatides keep the fats and cholesterol soluble in the blood.

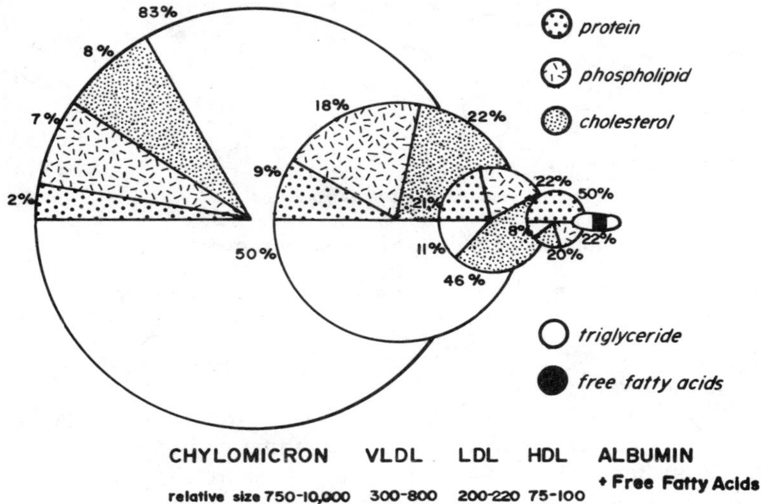

Figure 22. Transport vehicles for fats and cholesterol.

If phosphatides (and proteins) did not surround these lipids, the lipids would coalesce, form 'greasy' bubbles in the blood, and rise within us in the same way that cream rises to the top of a bottle of milk. Our head and shoulders would be all oil and the rest of us protein and water. The phosphatides prevent this from happening.

Phosphatides and Disease

The phosphatides are so important to life that no diseases are associated with them. This means two things. One is that they are extremely well regulated by body mechanisms because of their importance. The other is that any genetic defect or fault in the body's ability to make or use them immediately kills the organism. That is why no diseases are associated with the phosphatides.

9

Lecithin

Introduction

Lecithin, its name derived from the Greek word for egg yolk from which it was first isolated, is the best known member of the phosphatides (see: Phosphatides), and is valuable in nutrition for three reasons. Figure 23 shows a molecule of lecithin.

Biological Value of Lecithin

Lecithin supplies choline, which is necessary for liver and brain function. Choline also helps the body to utilize fats and cholesterol properly, and is known as a lipotropic factor because of this ability. Phosphatidyl choline, sometimes known as triple strength lecithin, contains 3 times the amount of choline than does ordinary lecithin. The second reason for the biological value of lecithin is that about half of its fatty acids are usually essential fatty acids. The third value of lecithin is its activity as an 'edible detergent'. A detergent breaks up fats into smaller droplets held in suspension, or 'emulsifies' fats. The emulsifying action of lecithin, as we will see a little later, is extremely important.

Most seed oils contain some lecithin. The commonest and best commercial source of lecithin is soybean oil, which contains up to

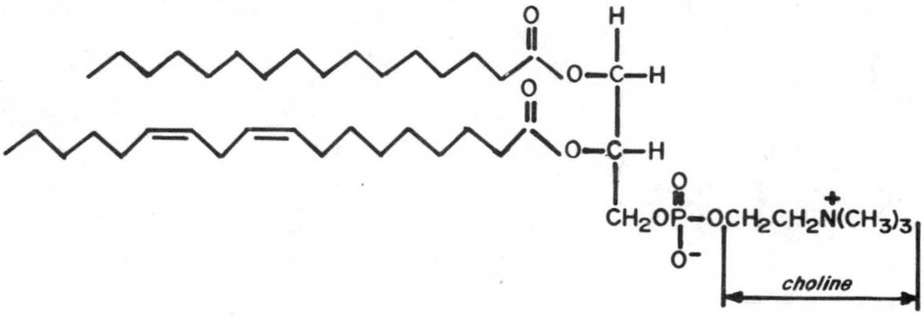

Figure 23. Stick model of lecithin (phosphatidyl choline).

2% lecithin. Soybean lecithin contains both essential fatty acids [the oil contains 57% linoleic acid (LA, 18:2*w*6), and 9% linolenic acid (LNA, 18:3*w*3)], whereas the lecithin from most other oils contains only LA. That's the 'good news' about lecithin.

Commercial Changes

Now the 'bad news'. Because the essential fatty acids, and especially LNA, spoil very easily, breeding experiments are being carried out to develop genetic strains of soybeans which contain only 3% LNA instead of the 9% that the oil of natural strains contains. When oils and lecithins from these new strains become commercially available, the nutritional quality of both will be less than that of the natural oil and lecithin. But, and this is the reason for making the changes, the shelf life of the oils will be better. For this convenience of storage, we sacrifice the nutritional quality of the products and compromise our health.

A similar problem occurs when animals are fed man-made feeds, from which, in order to increase their shelf life, the essential fatty acids have been largely removed. The more stable but less nutritionally valuable oleic acid (OA, 18:1*w*9) replaces them. The types of fatty acids that eggs, chickens, and meats contain depend on the kinds of fatty acids present in the foods consumed, and so eggs and meats from animals raised on commercial feeds contain 'lecithin' which is low in essential fatty acids, and such lecithin cannot perform one of the important functions of natural lecithin in the human body (see: Eggs).

The Functions of Lecithin

Lecithin helps to keep cholesterol soluble. In a food like eggs, which contain a large amount of cholesterol, it is especially important that the lecithin be of high quality.

Lecithin keeps cholesterol from depositing in arterial linings, and prevents and dissolves gall and kidney stones by its emulsifying action on fatty substances.

Lecithin is necessary in the liver for that organ's detoxification functions, which keep us from slowly being poisoned by breakdown products from the metabolic processes that take place in our bodies. Poor liver function is often a forerunner of cancer. Deficiency of either choline or essential fatty acids can be used to induce cancer in experimental animals, and is likely involved in causing some human cancers.

Lecithin is important in increasing resistance to disease by its role in the thymus gland. Here, it is the essential fatty acids, especially LA, which is the precursor of several prostaglandins (see: Prostaglandins), which are vital to the body's immune function.

Lecithin is a member of the phosphatides, which make up a large portion (22%) of the high density lipoprotein (HDL) and low density lipoprotein (LDL) cholesterol-carrying vehicles in the blood. These vehicles keep cholesterol and triglyceride fats in solution in the blood stream and prevent them from being deposited in arterial walls; in this way, lecithin is involved in the prevention of atherosclerosis and cardiovascular problems such as high blood pressure, heart attack, stroke, and kidney and heart failure which result from atherosclerosis.

Lecithin is an important part of the membrane phosphatides, where it is involved in electric phenomena, membrane fluidity, and the other functions for which the essential fatty acids are responsible (see: Essential Fatty Acids).

Finally, lecithin is an important component of bile, where its function is to emulsify — break into small droplets — food fats, to increase their surface area, making digestion of fats by enzymes easier (see: Digestion).

10

Cholesterol

Introduction

There is probably no nutritional substance as controversial as cholesterol, no substance about which there is more confusion, no substance as able to strike instant terror into the hearts of people.

A hard, waxy lipid substance which melts at 149° C, cholesterol is essential for physical health, even though it is not required in our food supply, since our bodies can manufacture it from simpler fragments (2-carbon acetate groups) which it derives from the breakdown of sugars, fats, and even proteins. Figure 24 shows the structure of cholesterol.

The more sugars and fats (especially saturated and other non-essential fatty acids) are present in our diets, the more pressure there will be to make cholesterol, and for this reason, diets high in sugars and non-essential fatty acids tend to result in high cholesterol levels. But before we get into the evils of cholesterol, let's look at the natural and vital functions of cholesterol in the body.

Functions of Cholesterol

What are the vital functions of cholesterol? Cholesterol keeps

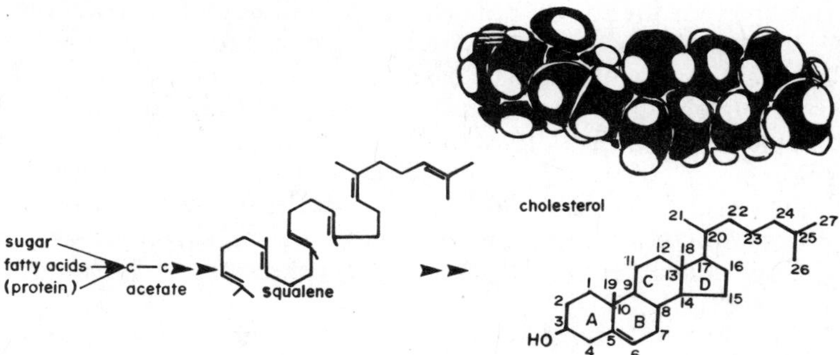

Figure 24 Synthesis and structure of cholesterol.

the membranes of our cells functioning properly. If the membrane has too little cholesterol in it, it becomes too fluid and falls apart. If there is too much cholesterol in it, the membrane becomes stiff and breaks. The content of fatty acids in the human diet varies from day to day, and these fatty acids are used to build the basic structure of the membranes. The more highly unsaturated fatty acids make membranes more fluid, and the more saturated ones make it more hard.

Cholesterol has the function of compensating for the changes in membrane fluidity, keeping it within the narrow limits that assure optimal membrane function. This function is so important that nature has equipped each cell with the means to synthesize its own membrane cholesterol.

The steroid hormones are made from cholesterol. The male and female steroid hormones, better known as the sex hormones, develop and maintain the delightful differences between the genders. The female hormones estrogen and progesterone, and the male hormone testosterone are the three best known of these hormones.

The adrenal corticosteroid hormones are also made from cholesterol. They include aldosterone, which regulates the body's water balance through the kidneys, increasing sodium retention by the renal tubules. Cortisone, which promotes the synthesis of glucose to prepare the body for fight or flight in response to stress, and which suppresses inflammation reactions, is another corticosteroid hormone made from cholesterol. Cortisone finds application in medicine for the suppression of inflammatory reactions[1].

Vitamin D, the sunshine vitamin, required for the metabolism of calcium and phosphorus, also comes from cholesterol.

The bile acids, which break up (emulsify) food fats into small droplets in our intestines to make them easier to digest and absorb, are derived from cholesterol. Through the bile acids, cholesterol performs vital functions in the entire digestion and absorption of fats, oils, and fat-soluble vitamins from foods. Via the bile acids, the body discards excess cholesterol which it does not need.

Finally, cholesterol is one of the substances secreted by the glands in the skin, which cover and protect the skin against dehydration, cracking, and the wear and tear of sun, wind, and water. In its capacity as skin covering, cholesterol also aids in the healing of skin tissue and prevents foreign organisms from infecting the skin.

Recently, it has been suggested that cholesterol also functions as an antioxidant, especially when the body is low in the other antioxidant factors. This is indicated by the finding that high cholesterol levels are found in the blood when the body is deficient in the antioxidant substances which are normally present. Conversely, the antioxidants, which include the vitamins C and B3 and the mineral zinc, have powerful cholesterol-lowering effects, supporting the theory. Several other antioxidants also lower cholesterol levels, but more work needs to be done with these others before the extent of their cholesterol-lowering ability is known with certainty.

The Dark Side of Cholesterol

The dark side of cholesterol, which has gotten so much attention over the last 40 years that the word cholesterol is equated with cardiovascular disease, is the fact that it is often found deposited, along with other fatty substances, the protein fibrin, and calcium ions, in the inner lining (the intima) of human arteries, where it narrows them.

There are a number of theories of why it is deposited, and these theories change every few years. One current theory suggests that the arterial walls are first damaged by free radicals in the blood stream, and that cholesterol deposition is a part of the mechanism that attempts to repair the arterial damage caused by the free radicals (see: Free Radicals).

Another theory suggests that cholesterol deposition is secondary to proliferation (unnaturally rapid division) of some of the cells in the arterial walls in a manner which resembles the proliferation one sees in cancer cells during tumour formation. The proliferation is now suspected to be free radical-induced.

A third theory proposes that cholesterol is deposited in the arteries because the levels of the micronutrients which are required to destroy free radicals in the body are deficient in those individuals in whom these deposits occur.

That free radicals are involved in the biochemical processes which lead to the intraarterial cholesterol deposits is beginning to be more widely accepted, and is in the process of becoming the new, accepted, popular theory to explain the cause of the degenerative changes that occur in human arteries, but the exact details of the steps involved have not yet been nailed down. But whatever these steps may be, it is agreed that cholesterol-containing deposits in the walls of the arteries are dangerous. About 2/3 of the North American population suffers from such atherosclerotic deposits to some degree. They narrow the arteries and slow down the flow of blood.

In addition, a high level of cholesterol and saturated or denatured fatty acids in the blood makes the platelets more sticky, and increases the risk of a clot forming. The combination of atherosclerosis and sticky platelets may completely block an artery, cutting off the oxygen and nutrients to the cells of the part of the body supplied by that artery. The deprived cells then die. If an artery to the brain is blocked, a stroke occurs, and depending on the size and location of the artery, the stroke may be minimal or fatal. Blockage of an artery supplying the heart results in a heart attack, or coronary[2]. If a clot blocks an artery in the lungs, pulmonary embolism occurs. A blocked artery to the legs results in impairment of peripheral circulation, and can lead to gangrene. Blindness and deafness can occur when arteries supplying these sense organs are blocked. Narrowed arteries to the heart result in chest pains (angina pectoris) after exertion or after consuming a meal high in fats, because fats make the blood more sludgy and less capable of carrying oxygen.

Atherosclerotic deposits also 'harden' the arteries. Hardened arteries raise the blood pressure because the arteries' resilience, which normally takes up the pressure generated by heart contraction, is lost. This results in a heavier load on the heart and kidneys, which, if prolonged, results in heart and kidney failure, as well as water retention, or edema.

These are the major charges against cholesterol. Whether cholesterol is the main culprit or whether cholesterol deposits result from some other primary metabolic problem is still being hotly debated. When the dust of this debate settles, it looks like cholesterol will be found not guilty as the primary cause of cardiovascular disease, though it is clearly involved in the later stages of this disease. A large body of accumulating evidence points in that direction, and we will look at this evidence a little later in this chapter. Right now, let's find out where the cholesterol present in the body comes from.

Sources of Cholesterol

Home made cholesterol. The body makes cholesterol. The cells in the human body can make all the cholesterol they need for their membrane requirements. Cells manufacture cholesterol in response to demand. For instance, when someone drinks alcohol, the alcohol dissolves in the membranes, making them more fluid. In response, the cells will manufacture cholesterol, build it into the membrane, and thereby bring the membrane back to its proper (less fluid) state. As the alcohol wears off, hardening the membrane, no more cholesterol is made, and some of the cholesterol in the membrane is taken out, again establishing the normal membrane fluidity. The extra cholesterol is then hooked up (esterified)[3] with linoleic acid (18:2*w*6) and shipped off to the liver to be changed into bile acids, provided that the vitamins and minerals necessary for this change are present. The bile acids are dumped into the intestine, help there with fat digestion, and are then removed from the body with the wastes, provided that the food contains sufficient fiber and that bowel action is regular enough to prevent the bile acids from being reabsorbed and recycled.

Besides the cells' production of cholesterol, the liver, intestine, adrenal glands, and sex glands all make cholesterol for the other functions in which cholesterol is involved. During pregnancy, the placenta also makes cholesterol, and from it manufactures progesterone, which keeps the pregnancy from being terminated.

Making home made cholesterol. How is cholesterol made? Since the body makes cholesterol, it might be interesting to find the building blocks for its production.

The building blocks for the manufacture of cholesterol are 2-carbon fragments called acetate, which are hooked end-to-end until 30 of them are chained together. Through many steps, involving many different enzyme catalysts, this chain is cyclized, and finally 3 carbons are clipped from different parts, to arrive at the 27 carbon cholesterol molecule. The process is complex and interesting for biochemists, but the important question which bears on nutrition is: where do the 2-carbon acetate fragments come from?

When fatty acids are broken down for energy, they are broken into 2-carbon fragments. Since the essential fatty acids are conserved by the body for other vital functions, the saturated and monounsaturated fatty acids are the main source of acetate fragments from the fats. When carbohydrates (sugars and starches) are broken down for energy, they too produce the 2-carbon fragments. Proteins (amino acids) also, can be broken down to produce acetate fragments, but the body conserves amino acids for building important structures, so proteins are burned for energy only in extreme circumstances such as fasting, some disease states, and when inordinately large amounts of protein are consumed.

A diet high in non-essential fatty acids and refined carbohydrates produces an excess of acetate fragments in the body, and thus 'pressures' the body into increased cholesterol production. And there you have the reason for the high cholesterol levels of most of the people in the 'processed foods' nations. Some of the excess cholesterol may finally find its way into the arterial walls and create the problems of atherosclerosis. Additional cholesterol which enters our bodies in foods may aggravate the problem.

Cholesterol from food sources. What foods contain cholesterol? Only foods from animal sources contain cholesterol. Plant foods contain none. Eggs, meat, dairy products, fish, and shell fish all contain it. One egg, 1/4 pound of liver, and 1/4 pound of butter each contain about 250 milligrams of cholesterol. Fish and shell fish contain somewhat less.

The average North American diet contains about 800 mg of cholesterol daily. Of the cholesterol consumed, about 45% comes from eggs, 35% from meat, and 20% from dairy. About half of the dietary cholesterol is actually absorbed into the body. The rest passes on through, unused.

Cholesterol Content of the Human Body

How much cholesterol is there in a human body? The average human body contains about 150 grams (150,000 mg) of cholesterol in all. Most of this is found in the membranes, and about 7 grams is carried in the blood. The daily turnover of cholesterol is about 1100 mg, or just over 1 gram. These figures can vary of course, depending on the diet, state of health, and size of the person. The daily cholesterol turnover of a strict vegetarian (no meat, no eggs, no dairy) is quite a bit less than 1 gram; and meat eaters will turn over more cholesterol as their consumption of cholesterol increases.

Controversy About Cholesterol

The more cholesterol we eat, the less our body needs to make. The less we eat, the more our cells need to make. Since making cholesterol requires energy, some researchers suggest that having cholesterol in our diet is an evolutionary advantage, and claim that meat, egg, and dairy eaters are better adapted for survival than vegetarians. However, the fact that so many people have cholesterol deposited in their arteries has led other researchers to suggest that the human being cannot metabolize large amounts of dietary cholesterol effectively, or that the mechanism which regulates the human body's cholesterol levels does not compensate very well for dietary cholesterol.

Some researchers, including the proponents of orthomolecular nutrition (see: Orthomolecular Nutrition) feel that the 'cholesterol' problem is really caused by dietary deficiencies in the micronutrient vitamins and minerals required to properly metabolize cholesterol in the body. The researchers have shown that a diet moderately high in cholesterol, which also includes sufficient quantities of all the micronutrients (usually given as multi vitamin and mineral supplements), keeps the blood cholesterol level low and prevents the occurrence of atherosclerosis. Orthomolecular therapists lower high blood cholesterol levels simply by giving high doses of certain vitamins and minerals, and have clinical evidence which shows that atherosclerosis, considered irreversible by the medical profession, can be reversed by micronutrient supplements. High doses of vitamins C and B3 lower a blood cholesterol level of 260mg/dl by about 50 mg each, and the minerals calcium, zinc, chromium, and selenium are also effective. The essential and other highly unsaturated fatty acids (fresh flax or fish oils are best) in their natural all *cis-* state also lower high cholesterol levels by up to 15 or 20%. Some types of dietary fiber also help to lower cholesterol levels[4].

Other researchers, like those at the Loma Linda School of Nutrition, explain the high incidence of atherosclerosis among meat eaters in a different way. They believe that man is by nature a vegetarian, like the other primates to whom, according to evolution (in which they don't believe), he is related. Strict vegetarians have less than 1/4 the meat eaters' rate of death from cardiovascular disease (CVD), and people who include eggs and dairy products but exclude meat from their diet, have only a slightly lower risk of death from CVD than meat eaters. These figures represent people who don't take nutritional supplements.

Resolution

Who is right? Perhaps both sides are right. A vegetarian diet is usually a better source of vitamins and minerals than a non-vegetarian diet, because muscle meats (see: Fats in Meats) and dairy products (see: Fats in Milk and Dairy Products) are not good sources of most of these factors. Eggs are better, but those that come from chickens fed artifical commercial mash are lower in protective factors than the eggs of chickens that forage for their own food (see: Eggs). But when a diet based on these foods is augmented with the missing vitamin and mineral factors, it too, presents fewer cholesterol problems (see: Cholesterol and Disease).

It appears likely that neither the animal eater nor the plant consumer need to fear high cholesterol or CVD if they take their foods from natural sources, unrefined, and that the accusing finger will point at refined sugars and starches from which vitamins, minerals, fiber, and protein have been removed, and also at refined, denatured and altered fat and oil products which too, have had their vitamins, minerals, fiber and proteins removed.

11

Essential Nutrients

Introduction

No book on nutrition would be complete without some mention of all of the essential nutrients required by the human body for health and growth. Why? Because none of the nutrients work in isolation. All essential nutrients work together as a team to maintain health and to repair damage. The absence of any one of these essential nutrients is enough to destroy our physical health.

If we attempt to keep ourselves healthy by making sure that our fat intake is optimal without also making sure that the other essential nutrients are present in our diets, our attempts to maintain health will fail. When we design a nutritional program for the maintenance of health, we must design it to contain all known essential nutrients. I have yet to meet a person whose health did not improve in some way from this approach. In a healthy person, there is no room for disease. Disease results from the absence of health. Physical health is based on the presence of the molecules of health in adequate to optimum quantities. These molecules of health are the essential nutrients, out of which a healthy body is built.

One would think that in the affluent nations of the world, the industrial nations, the diet would be adequate in essential nutrients. Money is no problem, and time is no problem either, right? Wrong! Over 60% (and rising) of the North American population is deficient in 1 or more of the essential nutrients. Judging from the incidence of degenerative disease in Europe, their nutritional state seems to be about the same as ours. The poorer nations of the earth are better nourished than the majority of the affluent, though the former consume less food.

Impressive work is being done with vitamins, minerals and essential fatty acids in the treatment of degenerative diseases. Much is being learned, and people are being relieved of different afflictions which resist orthodox medical treatment with drugs, surgery, and radiation.

However, the information is incomplete, because our knowledge of nutrition is incomplete. The systematic study of biochemical nutrition is just in its infancy, and much work needs to be done before we have all the information.

Essential Fatty Acids

The body content of essential fatty acids fluctuates with its content in the diet. The optimum dose of LA appears to be between 10 and 30g/d, although this varies with state of health, stress, season, and climate. Therapeutically, very high doses of both essential fatty acids are used in the treatment of degenerative diseases. Their success depends on the presence of the other essential nutrient factors also being present in the amounts

Table A2. Essential fatty acids.

Name	Body Content	Minimum Daily Requirement	Estimated Optimum	Therapeutic Dose	Toxic Dose
Linoleic Acid (LA) 18:2*w*6	2000 grams or more	3 g/d	9-30 g/d	up to 60 g/d	none known*
Linolenic Acid (LNA) 18:3*w*3	variable	1.5 g/d	6 g/d	up to 60 g/d	none known*

* provided that the natural antioxidants found in the seed are present, or vitamin E at the rate of 1:1500 is added to the oil.

required for optimal cell functions. For successful therapy, junk foods must be discontinued. Vitamin E is especially important to ensure the proper use of the essential fatty acids in the body. Table A2 gives an overview of the essential fatty acids. Sulphur-rich proteins are also required for the functions that the essential fatty acids fulfill in the body.

The requirement for essential fatty acids varies with the total fat content of the diet, but should be at least 1/4 of total fats consumed. Thus a low fat diet requires less essential fatty acids, and a high fat diet requires more.

Vitamins

Vitamins have been used therapeutically with a good success rate for many years now. The results that have accumulated are very impressive. The total body content for most vitamins is not yet known. Such measurements are difficult to carry out, because the vitamins (unlike minerals) degrade rapidly; furthermore, such measurements would not be particularly useful. Serum levels, and the levels of vitamins in particular tissues, organs and glands where they serve particular functions are more useful, and some of these measurements are used in therapy. Table A3 gives an overview of the vitamins essential in human nutrition.

Table A3. Vitamins.

Name	Body Contains	Minimum Daily Requirement (RDA)	Therapeutic Dose	Toxic Dose
Vitamin A or Carotene	500,000 IU (172 mg)	5000 IU/d	50,000 IU/d up to 500,000 short term only	100,000 IU for several months 18,500 daily for kids carotene is non-toxic
Thiamine (B1)	25 mg	1.2 mg/d	up to 100 mg/d	—
Riboflavin (B2)	?	1.7 mg/d	up to 100 mg/d	—

Table A3. Vitamins cont'd

Name	Body Contains	Minimum Daily Requirement (RDA)	Therapeutic Dose	Toxic Dose
Niacin (B3)	?	20 mg/d	up to 3,000 mg or more/d	niacin flush
Pantothenic Acid (B5)	?	10 mg/d	up to 300 mg/d	—
Pyridoxine (B6)	?	2 mg/d	up to 500 mg/d	over 500 mg/d
Biotin (B7)	?	.3 mg/d	up to .3 mg/d	—
Folic Acid (B9)	?	.4 mg/d	up to 5 mg/d (Canada)	—
Cobalamin (B12)	5 mg	.006 mg/d	up to .1 mg/d	—
Orotic Acid (B13)	?	—	—	—
Pangamic Acid (B15)	?	?	up to 150 mg/d	—
Choline (not essential)	?	—	up to 5,000 mg/d	—
Inositol (not essential)	?	—	up to 3,000 mg/d	—
Para Amino Benzoic Acid	?	?	up to 1,000 mg/d	—
Vitamin C	1400 mg	60 mg/d	up to 10,000 mg/d or more	above bowel tolerance
Vitamin D	?	400 IU/d	up to 1,000 IU/d	25,000 IU over extended time
Vitamin E	?	30 IU/d	up to 1200 IU/d or more	—
Vitamin K	?	?	up to .3 mg/d	over .5 mg
Bioflavonoids	?	?	up to 500 mg/d	—

Table A4. Minerals.

Name	Body Content	Minimum Daily Requirement (RDA)	Therapeutic Dose	Toxic Dose
Calcium (CA)	1050 grams	800-1200 mg/d	800-2000 mg/d	?
Phosphorus (P)	1000	800-1200 mg/d	?	?
Potassium (K)	300	(900 mg)	?	25g KCl
Sulphur (S)	175	(adequate protein)	?	?
Sodium (Na)	150	(1g NaCl)	?	?
Chlorine (Cl)	140	(1g NaCl)	?	15 g
Magnesium (Mg)	35	300-400 mg/d	?	?
Silicon (Si)	30	?	?	?
Iron (Fe)	4.2	18 mg/d	?	5g
Fluorine (F)	2.6	(1 mg)	?	?
Zinc (Zn)	2.3	15 mg/d	up to 100 mg/d	over 300 mg
Strontium (Sr)	.32	(1-3.2 mg)	?	?
Copper (Cu)	.125	(2 mg)	?	?
Vanadium (V)	.018	(1-3.2 mg)	?	?
Selenium (Se)	.013	(.05 - .1 mg)	?	.2 mg
Manganese (Mn)	.012	(2.5 - 7 mg)	?	?
Iodine (I)	.011	.080 - .150 mg/d	?	?
Nickel (Ni)	.010	(less than .5 mg)	?	?
Molybdenum (Mo)	.009	(.045 - .5 mg)	?	?
Cobalt (Co)	.0015	(.008 mg)	?	?
Chromium (Cr)	.0015	(.090 mg)	?	?

Minerals

The brackets indicate that no government RDA has been set for that mineral; the figure indicated has been suggested by researchers in the field. Strontium may not be essential, as no function for it has been found so far. Since strontium is found in the body, however, we'll have to wait to find out what it is doing there. Table A4 gives an overview of the minerals essential in human nutrition.

Essential Amino Acids

Traditionally, nutritionists were only concerned with whether a protein was complete (containing all of the essential amino acids in adequate quantities) or not.

Individual amino acids are just beginning to be used for their

Table A5. Essential amino acids.

Name	Body Content	Daily Requirement (RDA)	Therapeutic Dose	Toxic Dose
Protein	12% of total wt.	45-120 g/d	?	?
Isoleucine		between 1-3 g/d	?	?
Leucine		between 1-3 g/d	?	?
Lysine		between 1-3 g/d	food + 1 g/d	?
Methionine		between 1-3 g/d	?	?
Phenylalanine		between 1-3 g/d	food + 500 mg/d	?
Threonine		between 1-3 g/d	?	?
Tryptophan		between 1-3 g/d	food + 1-2 g/d	?
Valine		between 1-3 g/d	?	?
(Histidine)		between 1-3 g/d	?	?
(Arginine)		between 1-3 g/d	?	?

various therapeutic effects. Phenylalanine is used as an anti-depressant and to increase assertiveness. Tryptophan is used as a sedative. Arginine appears to decrease atherosclerosis and gall stones. Lysine is used to inhibit the growth of viruses. Methionine and cysteine are useful in their relationship to essential fatty acids. Several other amino acids which are not essential are also used for various special purposes. Amino acid therapy is a recent development in nutritional medicine, and as you can see, a lot remains to be discovered. Table A5 gives an overview of the essential amino acids.

SECTION TWO

Life In The Fat Lane

Fats and Oils Business, Processes, and Promotion

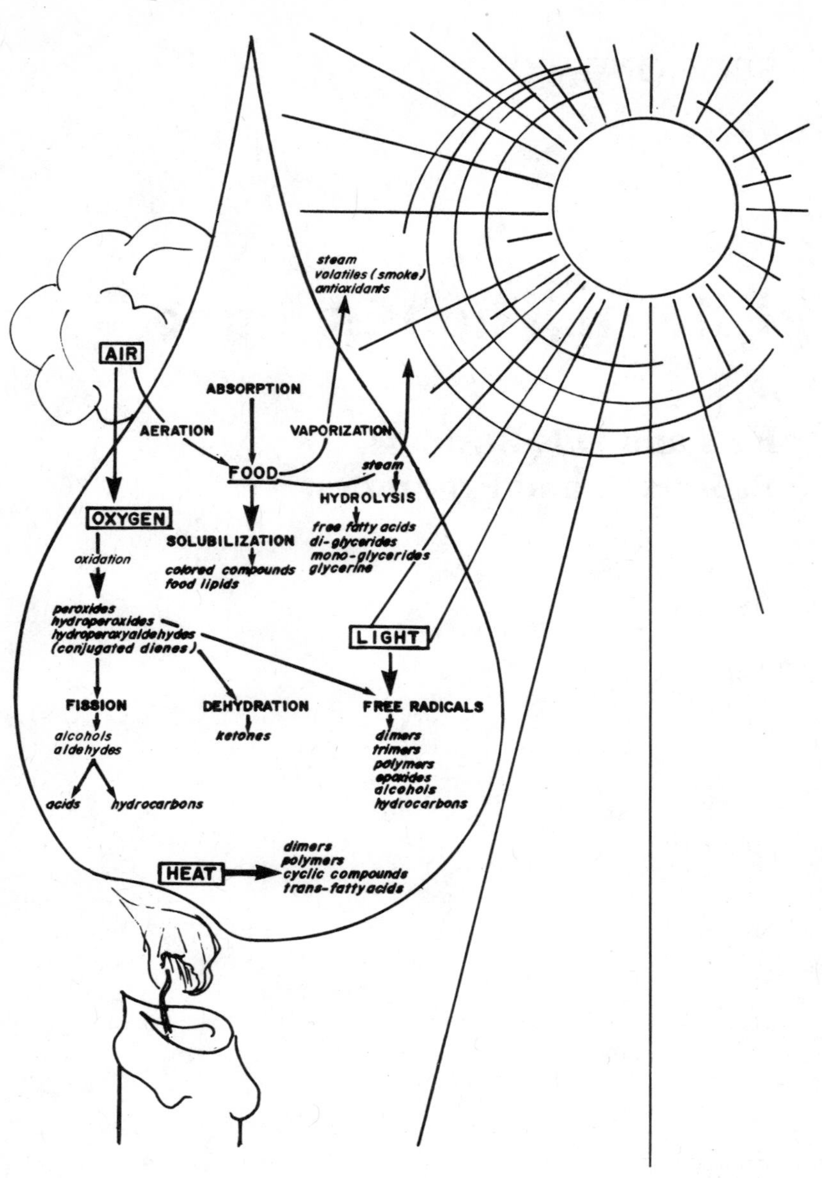

steam
volatiles (smoke)
antioxidants
AIR
ABSORPTION
AERATION
VAPORIZATION
FOOD
steam
HYDROLYSIS
OXYGEN
SOLUBILIZATION
free fatty acids
di-glycerides
mono-glycerides
glycerine
oxidation
colored compounds
food lipids
peroxides
hydroperoxides
hydroperoxyaldehydes
(conjugated dienes)
LIGHT
FISSION
DEHYDRATION
FREE RADICALS
alcohols
aldehydes
ketones
dimers
trimers
polymers
epoxides
alcohols
hydrocarbons
acids
hydrocarbons
HEAT
dimers
polymers
cyclic compounds
trans-fatty acids

12

History of Oil Making

In The Beginning

Traditionally in Europe, oil pressing was a home and cottage industry. Every large estate and little town had its own oil mill. Many older people who lived in Europe before the Second World War remember how every week, fresh flax oil was sold door to door, just like milk and eggs. Fresh flax oil was delivered in small (100 ml) bottles.

People knew that good oil has to be bought in small quantities and used fresh, because it is alive and spoils, just like fresh vegetables, milk, and eggs. And just like these, fresh oil was a staple in most homes. Fresh flax oil was known for its delicate nutty taste, its lightness and easy digestion, its health-sustaining properties, and its therapeutic value in the treatment of many diseases, among them mood disorders, low vitality, liver disorders, and cancer.

Bigger Is Better

In the 1920's, the 'bigger is better' philosophy gradually took over the oil trade. Huge oil firms developed. Huge fields of oil seeds were planted. Huge continuous feed, screw type, heat producing oil presses were built to replace the small, slow, cool-running batch presses in use prior to that time. The new presses were built to run around the clock, some pressing over 100 tons of seed per day. Automation made the operation very efficient, and cut down on labour costs. Figure 25 illustrates the batch and the screw presses.

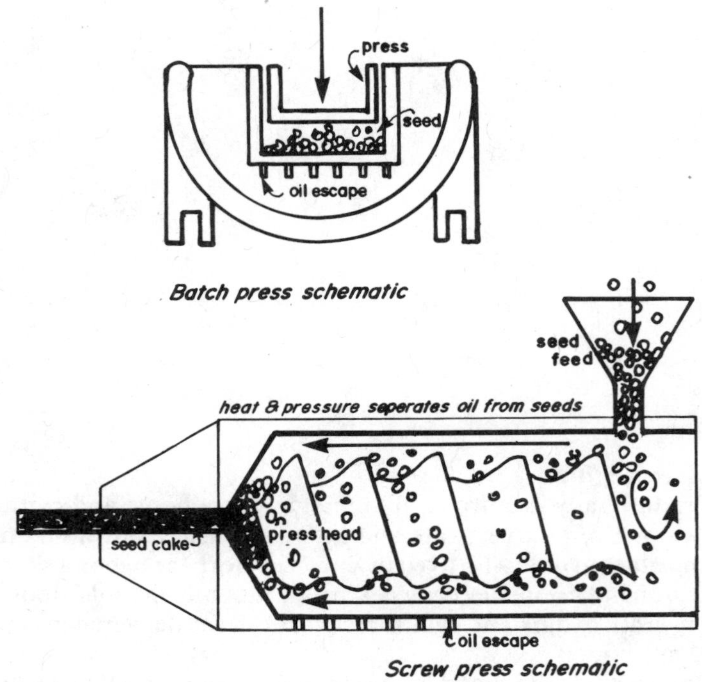

Figure 25. Batch and screw presses.

Pesticides came into widespread use, and bigger crops resulted from not having to share the land and yield with weeds and insects.

Processes of seed preparation, extraction, refinement, bleaching, deodorization, and other processes were developed to make oil pressing easier, and to remove 'impurities' of natural substances from the oil to keep it from spoiling. Synthetic antioxidants began to be added back to the now refined oil to stabilize it and lengthen its shelf life.

The cottage industry folded. They couldn't compete with the lower costs of mass production, or with the new methods of advertising, which were clever and consistent in the mass media, though not entirely correct in their praise of the 'new and improved' oil products.

Nutritional Effects of the Mega Oil Industry

By the end of the Second World War, flax oil, the most nutritious of all the oils, had disappeared from the market, because the 'impurities' it contains make it unstable and make it spoil. The spoilable 'impurities' in flax oil are the two nutritionally essential fatty acids LA (18:2*w*6) and LNA (18:3*w*3) and flax oil contains them in such high quantities (over 70%) that if they were removed, very little oil would be left to sell. Flax oil was replaced by more stable oils, oils with less of the essential fatty acids in them, and therefore less chance of spoilage during transport and storage, but also, therefore, oils of inferior nutritional value. The only use which remained for flax seed oil was in the paint industry. The oil was boiled and lead was added to make linseed oil, which was and still is used as a 'drying oil', because it attracts oxygen from the air, reacts with it chemically, and 'dries' in a thin film rapidly. In paints, this 'drying' property is very important.

What else happened? We got bland refined oils without taste. We've come to think that oil *should* be tasteless, which is not true at all. Each fresh, natural seed oil has its own particular, delicate flavour and aroma.

We got pesticide residues in our edible oils that interfere with nerve functions and oxidation processes, and therefore lower our vitality. We got chemically extracted oils with chemical solvent residues in them. These are lung irritants and nerve depressants. We got non-natural antioxidants in our oils, which improve the oil's shelf life, but which may interfere with energy production, cell metabolism, and respiration because they do not fit into the incredibly precise architecture of our enzyme systems and membranes, and, over time, may contribute to many diseases, and to our lack of vitality.

We got low quality oils, oils with much of their health value removed, altered, or destroyed in place of the fresh, natural, high quality oils with their complex composition of oil-related, mineral, and vitamin substances. These substances help in the digestion and metabolism of oils and have nutritional value of their own. Among the substances removed are the phosphatides including lecithin, which have important membrane functions (see: Phosphatides); the phytosterins; the fat-soluble vitamin complexes A and E and their precursors, which protect the oils against damage in storage and in the body; chlorophyll; aromatic and volatile compounds; and minerals. Some of these substances are removed from the oils and sold separately as supplements in health food stores to 'health nuts', while the refined (but impoverished) oil is sold in the supermarket to the general public.

The fatty acid composition of our diet was altered. Oils low in the essential fatty acids became the standard item on the shelf of every grocery store. With this reduction in essential fatty acids in our diets, the incidence of the diseases of fatty degeneration rose to epidemic proportions.

We obtained oils that have been altered by heat and alkali from their natural nutritious form into oils which contain substances detrimental to health: *trans-* fatty acids, polymers, cyclic compounds, aldehydes, ketones, epoxides, hydroperoxides, and many other compounds not yet identified, many of which are toxic to our bodies (see: Toxic Products). The processes used to refine oils produce many dozens of different substances. The process is random, and cannot be controlled, and different batches of oil contain widely varying amounts and kinds of chemically altered fat breakdown products.

Hydrogenation, a process also introduced on a large scale in the 1930's[1] for making margarines and shortenings as cheaper substitutes for butter and lard, respectively, has resulted in so many altered fat substances in our diet that just one of them, the *trans-* fatty acids, makes up twice as much food additives in our diet as all other food additives combined (see: Trans- Fatty Acids).

We ended up with fats and oils which are the nutritional equivalent of the refined sugars in carbohydrate nutrition: demineralized, de-vitaminized, fiber-less, empty calories, which cannot be properly digested and metabolized, which rob the body of its stores of minerals and vitamins, which lead to deficiency states in these essential substances, and which lead to fatty degeneration in all of its many forms.

In 1900, death from cardiovascular disease accounted for only 15% of all deaths from all causes. Today, it kills 50% of the population, an increase of 350% in just 80 years, in spite of all of our amazing technological medical advances. Cancer in 1900 killed 3% of the population. Today, it kills 23% of us, and soon will kill 25%, because its incidence is still rising. This is an increase of 600% in just 80 years.

These are the greatest killers in affluent nations, but the other degenerative conditions: diabetes, multiple sclerosis, kidney degeneration, liver degeneration, and other forms of fatty degeneration have risen just as dramatically in the past 80 years.

Bigger Is Not Better?

Slowly, we are beginning to get wise. Bigger is not always better. In Europe, fresh flax oil and the cottage industry that supplies it has made a comeback. Slowly people are returning to the eating habits of pre-processing days, regaining the state of health of pre-processing days, and if the trend catches on, the lowered incidence of degenerative disease of pre-processing days will return.

In North America too, people are returning to the crude, mechanically pressed, unrefined, natural oils, although the North Americans are a little slower than the Europeans to give up their faith in progress. Slowly, the assumptions of the mega oil business are being examined, found to be false, and discarded.

13

The Fats and Oils Business

A Lot of Fat

Four and a half billion people live on planet Earth. The average weight of a human being is about 150 pounds or 70 kilograms. The average human carries about 15% of his body weight or 10 kg as fat. According to these figures, human beings carry a total 45 billion kilograms of fat around with them in their bodies.

Fat Consumption

Human body fat is not static, but constantly turning over. In North America and Europe, and in all other industrialized nations and among wealthy people living in the poorer nations as well, fats and oils make up over 40% of the 2,500 calories that a human being consumes daily. This is about 1,000 calories per day as fats. A gram of fat produces 9 calories, so 1,000 calories is contained in just over 110 grams, and this is one estimate of the daily fat consumption for the average well-to-do person. At this rate, the annual consumption of fats is just over 40 kg per year. Actual fat consumption may be closer to 160 g/d, 1500 calories, or 60 kg per year (see: Fat Consumption).

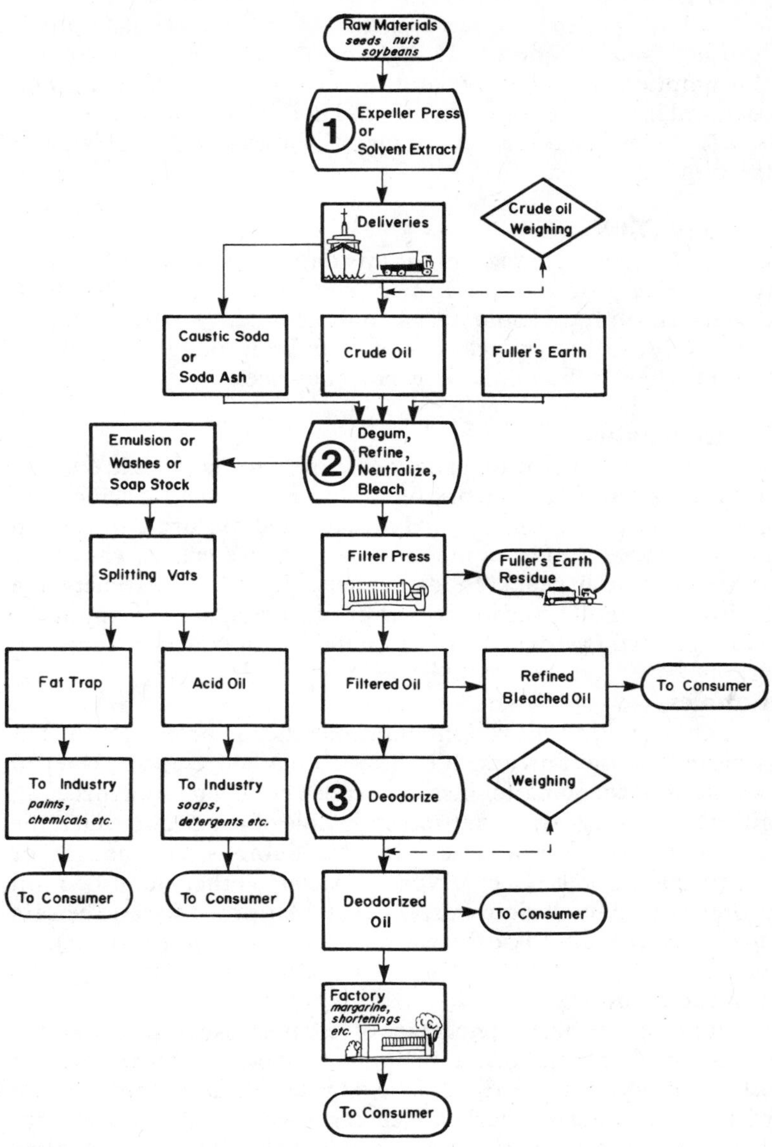

Figure 26. Schematic of the mega oil industry.

For North America alone, this adds up to 10 million tonnes of fat and oil products annually, just for human consumption. Another source quotes 25 kg per person per year as the consumption of edible fats and oils world-wide. The paint and chemical industries, and the soap and detergent industries gobble up a lot of fat and oil as well. Figure 26 shows a schematic view of the mega oil industry.

Fat and Oil Sales

In 1975, the world market for fats and oils was over 41 million tonnes. The producers sold their products for almost 29 billion dollars. In 1981, they sold over 40 billion dollars worth of fats and oils. By 1992, they expect sales of 80 million tonnes, bringing in more than 60 billion dollars by current prices.

Hydrogenation

About 1/3 of all the oil produced is hydrogenated, and ends up in various hardened fat products, the main ones of which are margarines and shortenings. Hydrogenated oils are also used in making baked goods, confections such as ice cream, chocolate and candy, and snack foods such as potato chips where the hydrogenated oil helps to give the product crispness. Without the hydrogenated (hardened) oil, the potato chip would be limp.

Lobbies

With these kinds of volumes of products and profits at stake, it is clear that the fats and oils business has developed powerful political and economic lobbies (now called government advocacies), aimed at making laws that protect the sale of products, even if the health value of some of these products is dubious, as is the case for hydrogenated oils (see: Hydrogenation), other modified oil products used for various purposes in edible products, and certain oils which contain toxic fatty acids (see: Toxic Oil Products).

Competition

From the size of the market involved, it is easy to see why each sector of the fats and oils industry — the beef and meat, the seed oil, the dairy, and the egg — are engaged in fierce competition with one another to market their respective products, and why each uses aggressive advertising campaigns, often short on facts and long on manipulative techniques, to capture the largest possible share of the attention, the interest, and the money of consumers. In the course of these campaigns, health is not a major consideration, although in some advertising, it appears as though health is the issue.

In this frenzy for sales, consumers are 'educated', choices are affected, habits are changed, overconsumption of fat and oil products is encouraged, and . . . degenerative disease increases.

14

Oil Making (commercial style)

Introduction

In a modern oil pressing facility, many things happen to the oil seed and the natural oil that it contains. Figure 27 summarizes the steps by which oils are processed.

Cooking

First, the seeds are mechanically cleaned. Then the seeds are crushed, then cooked for up to 2 hours at varying temperatures, depending on the seed type used. A good average temperature is 120°C. This process makes the next step easier, by destroying the cells which contain the oil.

Expeller Pressing

The crushed, cooked seeds are pressed in an expeller (or screw) press, a continually rotating spiral-shaped augur which moves the seed forward (like a kitchen meat grinder does) and pushes the seed against a metal press head. The pressure generated in the head of an expeller press reaches several tons per square inch. The turning augur further crushes the seeds and creates friction in the seed mass, which produces heat in the head (the press head). Both

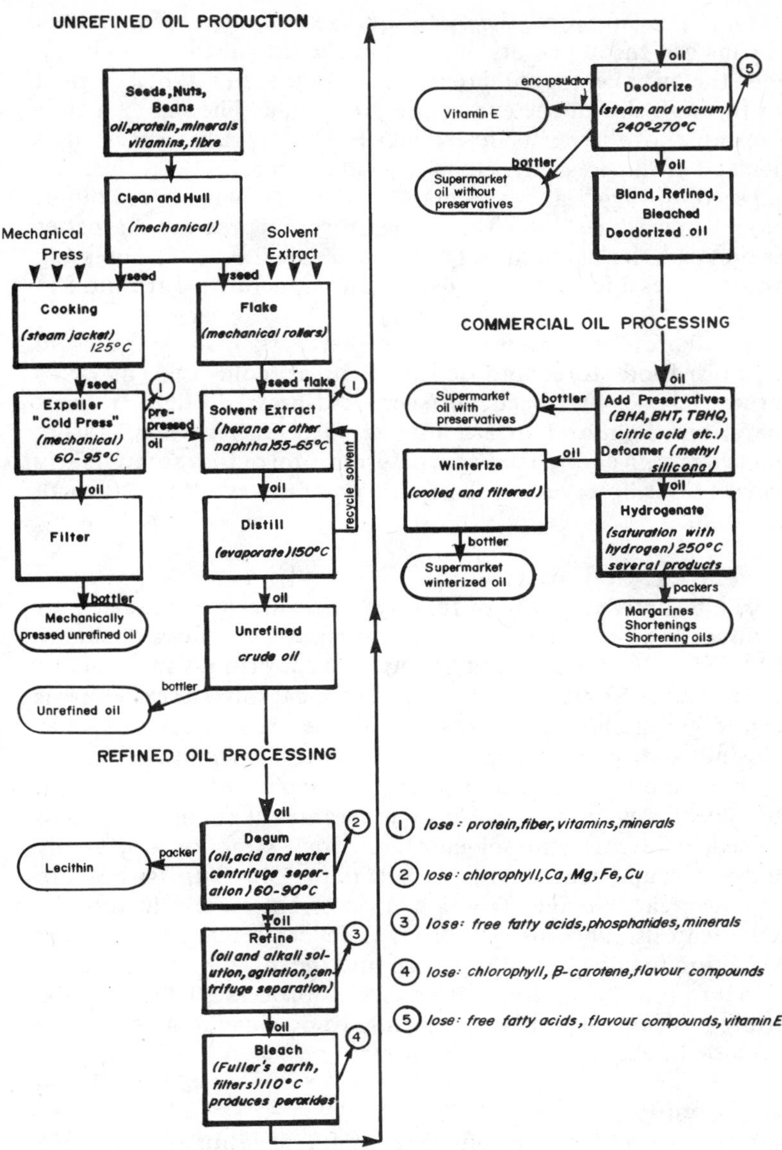

Figure 27. Summary of the steps involved in the processing of oils.

heat and pressure force the oil to squeeze out of the seed, and the oil runs out through slots or holes in the side of the press head, while the oil cake, the solid remainder of the seed mash, is pushed out through slits at the end of the press head. The size (which is adjustable) of these slits determines the back pressure created in the head of the press, which in turn determines how hot the head and seed mash get, and how much of the oil will be forced out of the seed mash. The higher the temperature and pressure, the better the oil yield, the less of the oil remains in the oil cake. The pressing process takes a few minutes, usually at temperatures around 85° to 95°C.

The oil pressed in this way may be filtered, then bottled and sold in health food stores and delicatessens as 'cold-pressed', or as natural, crude, unrefined oil (see: Cold-pressed Oils). In most operations, light and air are not excluded, and the temperature reached is high enough to begin deterioration of the essential fatty acids. This is however, the best oil commonly available in North America.

Solvent Extraction

An alternative method of removing the oil from the seed is to dissolve the oil out of the seed meal with a solvent such as hexane, at 55°-65°C, under constant agitation of the ground and crushed seed material. Sometimes this same chemical solvent procedure is used to get the bit of oil remaining in the oil cake after expeller pressing, and thus increase the yield of the oil from the seed.

Once the oil-solvent mixture has been separated from the seed, the solvent is evaporated off at a temperature of about 150°C, and re-used. The chemical solvents used for extraction are highly flammable, and occasionally, an oil factory blows up, with loss of life and great damage. Traces of the solvent remain in solvent-extracted oils. The oils won from expeller pressing and solvent extraction may be mixed together, and the oil sold as 'unrefined' oil. Unrefined oil is treated by several processes: degumming, refining, bleaching, and deodorizing, to produce refined oil. We will look at each of these steps in turn.

Degumming

In this process, phospholipids including lecithin are removed. True gums, protein-like compounds, and complex carbohydrates called polysaccharides are also taken out of the oil. Lecithin, famous for its health benefits, is isolated and sold separately in health food stores (*you* pay twice). Degumming is carried out at about 60°C, with water and phosphoric acid. Degumming also removes chlorophyll, calcium, magnesium, iron, and copper from the oil.

Refining

In this process, the oil is mixed with caustic soda (Draino), which is sodium hydroxide (NaOH), a very corrosive base, or with a mixture of NaOH and sodium carbonate (Na_2CO_3) agitated, and then separated. Refining removes free fatty acids from the oil, since free fatty acids indicate poor oil quality. Free fatty acids form soaps with NaOH, which then dissolve in the watery part of the mixture. Phospholipids, protein-like substances, and minerals are also further removed in this process. Refining temperature is around 75°C. The oil still contains pigments, and is usually red or yellow at this stage.

Bleaching

Here, filters, Fuller's earth, and/or acid-treated activated clays are used to remove the pigments chlorophyll and beta-carotene, and remaining traces of soap. Also, certain natural polycyclic and aromatic substances are removed. Bleaching takes place at 110°C, for 15 to 30 minutes.

During bleaching, toxic peroxides and conjugated fatty acids are formed from the essential fatty acids present in the oil. If air is excluded during this step, peroxidation is prevented, but a higher temperature must be used, which increases the amount of positional isomers (double bond shifts) of the unsaturated fatty acids present in the oil.

Deodorization

This treatment, which is steam distillation under pressure and exclusion of air, removes aromatic oils and more free fatty acids, as well as pungent odours and unpleasant tastes, which were not present in the natural oil in the seed before the processing began.

Deodoriziation takes place at the incredibly high temperature of 240° to 270°C (464° to 518°F) for 30 to 60 minutes. Above 160°C, *trans-* fatty acids begin to form in substantial quantities (see: Trans- Fatty Acids).

The peroxides produced in the refining step are removed. Tocopherols (vitamin E), phytosterols, and some pesticide residues and toxins are also removed by deodorization. The oil is now (finally!) tasteless, and cannot be distinguished from oils derived from other sources which have been similarly treated. The high temperature necessary for deodorization results in the formation of many unnatural isomers of the unsaturated fatty acids. These isomers include molecules in which the position of the double bond has been moved to another part of the carbon chain; *trans*-fatty acids, formed by twisting the molecule; cyclic compounds, which occur when the fatty acid chain reacts with itself to form a ring; dimers and polymers, which result when fatty acid molecules cross-link with one another to produce something similar to vulcanized rubber and plastics; and other altered fatty acid breakdown products. These changed molecules are different in shape and function from the fatty acids found normally in nature and food, and are a cause for concern to biologists, nutritionists, and health professionals.

The oils which result from these processes are the vitamin and mineral deficient oil equivalents of white (refined) sugars, white (refined) flour, and pure (refined) starch. It is now bottled and sold as refined oil. Believe it or not, this oil can still be sold as 'cold-pressed', because no *external* heat was applied during the pressing of the oil. This kind of oil is sold in supermarkets, and also sold in health food stores, alongside the natural, unrefined oils. It is important to know the difference.

Supermarket Step

For supermarkets only, refined oils have several synthetic antioxidants added to them from a list which includes butylated hydroxytoluene (BHT), butylated hydroxyanisole (BHA), propyl gallate, tertiary butyhydroquinone (TBHQ), citric acid, and methylsilicone, to replace the natural antioxidants beta-carotene and vitamin E which were taken out of the oil in the refining processes. Defoamer is also added, and the oil is bottled and sold.

It may go through another step called winterization, where it is cooled and filtered one more time to prevent its going cloudy in the fridge.

Touring the Refinery

It is not easy to get permission to tour through an oil-pressing facility. It is easy to see why most oil companies do not like the processes to be well known. If more people knew about how the oils are made, what they contain, and what has been taken out, more people would complain, and fewer would buy these oils.

To be fair to the oil makers, what is now known about oils was not known when the huge oil pressing facilities were first developed. But this information has been around for 30 years now, and much of it was discovered under the stewardship of the oil companies themselves, through work they paid university laboratories to do, and through work done in their own labs.

There is great resistance in the industry to make the changes necessary to produce natural, unrefined oils. In essence, these changes would make large presses and the mega oil industry obsolete. Fresh edible oils are really a cottage industry.

Neither the care required to make fresh oils containing the nutritionally essential fatty acids in their natural state, along with the vitamins and minerals required for the human body to metabolize them properly, nor the system necessary to get these oils to the consumer before they deteriorate from light and air exposure are the present mandates of the mega oil industry. The Japanese have a saying for this kind of situation. They claim that 'the bigger the front, the bigger the back'. In the case of the commercial oil makers, certainly, this saying holds true.

15

Hydrogenation

The Process

An excellent way to ruin the nutritional value (the essential fatty acids) in a sample of natural oil is to hydrogenate the oil. In this process, an oil which contains unsaturated fatty acids in their natural, all *cis-* state are reacted at high temperature (120°-210°C or 248°-410°F) and under pressure with hydrogen gas in the presence of a metal catalyst, usually nickel, but sometimes platinum or even copper, for 6 to 8 hours. Figure 28 summarizes what happens to fatty acids during hydrogenation.

Complete Hydrogenation

If the process is brought to completion, all of the double bonds in the oil are saturated with hydrogen. The fatty acids in the fat that results contain no double bonds, contain neither *cis-* nor *trans-* configuration (since *cis-* and *trans-* apply only to double bonds, and therefore only to unsaturated fatty acids), and has no essential fatty acid activity. Such a fat is 'safe' because it contains no *trans-* fatty acids to interfere with essential fatty acid activity in the body. It is also 'safe' because it is dead, does not spoil, and therefore has a long shelf life (if that term can be applied to a dead

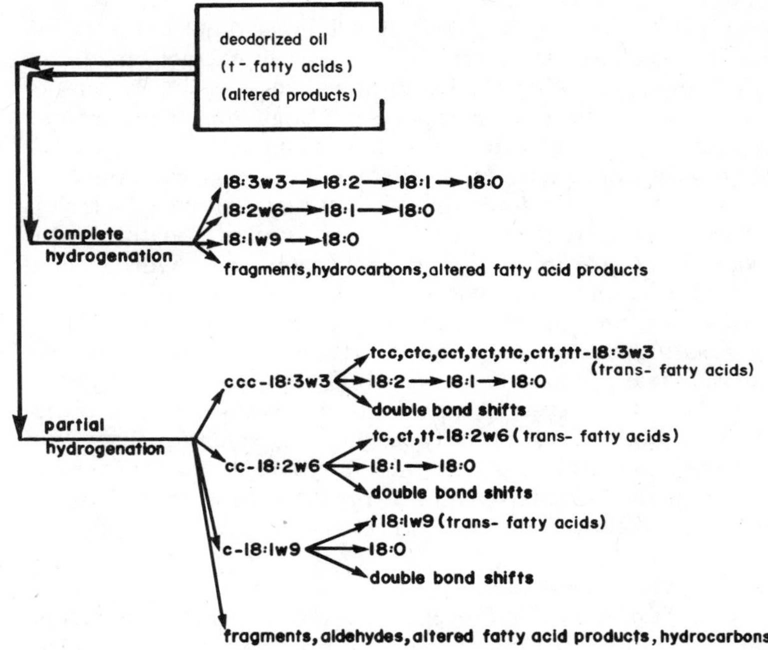

Figure 28. Products of hydrogenation.

substance). Completely hydrogenated oil can be heated: fried, baked, roasted and cooked; the body can use it for energy. But it also contains fragments of fatty acids created during the hydrogenation process, and altered molecules derived from fatty acids. Some of these may be toxic. It may also be contaminated by the metal catalyst used in the process of hydrogenation.

Except for the nutritionist's observation that the body does not need it, hydrogenated fat is both the manufacturer's and the consumer's dream, an ideal substance.

Uses For Completely Hydrogenated Products

Completely hydrogenated oil has some uses. Generally, coconut or palm kernel oils, which are over 90% saturated to begin with, are used as the starting material. The completely hydrogenated fat is relatively inert chemically, and can be used for frying without the danger that it is thereby made more toxic. It is used to make products such as chocolate, hard enough that they do not melt, except in very hot weather, and yet melt in the mouth. It is used in procedures in which oil has to be heated to extract oil-soluble principles out of other food substances, such as the flavours of onions and garlic (see: Recipes), although non-hydrogenated coconut oil is preferable for this purpose. Completely hydrogenated coconut oil can be used in mixtures with natural, essential fatty acid-containing liquid oils to make a 'vegetable butter' which is free of *trans-* fatty acids (see Recipes). While the natural oil is always preferable in a food product, completely hydrogenated coconut or palm kernel oil is not a *major* health risk. However, a word of caution is in order. Most affluent people consume far too much saturated fat, and far too little essential fatty acids. In excess, the saturated fatty acids crowd out the essential fatty acids from the enzyme systems which insert double bonds into (desaturate) both types of fatty acids, and essential fatty acid deficiency can result (see: Essential Fatty Acids). Its presence can also upset the delicate balance of prostaglandins (see: Prostaglandins). For these reasons, it is best avoided.

Partial Hydrogenation

When the process of hydrogenation is not brought to completion, a product containing many (dozens) of intermediate substances results. Double bonds may turn from *cis-* to *trans-* configuration; double bonds may shift, producing conjugated fatty acids; they may move along the molecule to produce positional double bond isomers; fragments may be produced. Figure 29 illustrates some of these chemical changes.

There are so many possibilities of different compounds that can be made during partial hydrogenation that they stagger the imagination. Scientists have barely scratched the surface in studying all the changes induced in fats and oils by hydrogenation. Needless to say, the industry is hesitant to fund thorough and systematic studies on the kinds of chemicals produced and their effects on health. The industry is equally hesitant to publicize the information which already exists on this topic.

Since the hydrogenation reaction occurs at random within the oil being hydrogenated, it is impossible to control the outcome of the process. Nor is it possible to predict the quantities of the different kinds of altered substances that will be present in any given batch of partially hydrogenated oil product.

It is possible, however, to stop the reaction when the desired degree of 'hardening' has been achieved, and this is one of the

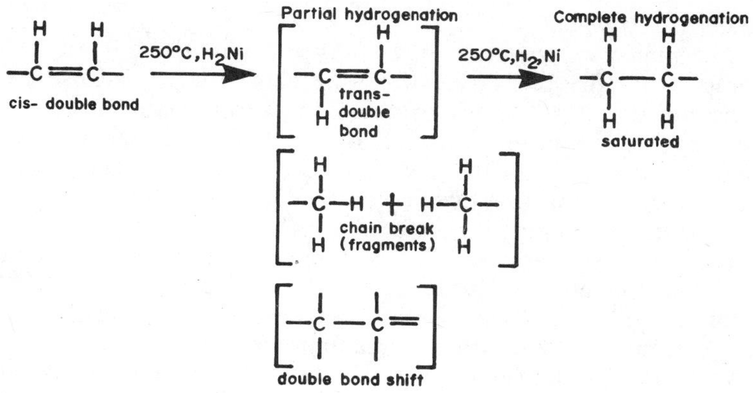

Figure 29. Chemical changes which can occur during hydrogenation.

industry's major reasons for using the process in the first place. It allows a cheap oil to be taken and turned into a semi-liquid, plastic, or solid fat with particular properties of spreadability, shelf life, and texture or 'mouth feel', and this is what the industry wants.

Partial hydrogenation is the process by which margarines, shortenings, and shortening oils are made. Consequently, it is to be expected that these products are high in *trans-* fatty acids and other altered fat substances. Some of these altered substances are known to be detrimental to health because they interfere with normal biochemical processes, and many of them have not been adequately studied to know what their effects on health might be.

Trans- fatty acids in partially hydrogenated products. Several researchers have measured the content of *trans-* fatty acids[1] in various hydrogenated products, and have published their findings. Stick margarines in one such study averaged 31% t- fatty acids, with a range from 9.9 to 47.8%. Tub margarines averaged 17% t- fatty acids, with a range from 4.4 to 43.4%. In some margarine samples from another study, t- fatty acids content of more than 60% was found, and virtually no essential fatty acids at all (less than 5%). Another study found that even diet margarines contain up to 17.9% t- fatty acids.

Vegetable oil shortenings were found to contain up to 37.3% t- fatty acids, with an average of 20%. Vegetable salad oils contained up to 13.7% t- fatty acids. Oils on french fries were up to 37.4%; in candies, up to 38.6%; and oils in bakery products up to

33.5% t- fatty acids.

The major contribution of t- fatty acids to the human diet comes from the margarines and the shortenings, because we consume about 40 grams of these substances daily and they average 20% or more t- fatty acids. The known effects of these altered fatty acids on the body (see: Trans- Fatty Acids) were cause enough for the Dutch government to ban the sale of margarines containing *trans-* fatty acids[2].

Government concerns. A government committee in Canada has expressed concern, and recommends that a minimum of 5% linoleic acid (LA, 18:2*w*6) should be required in all margarines and margarine-like products. This figure is too low, because 5% LA is neutralized and made ineffective by 95% of monounsaturated oleic acid and saturated fatty acids (see: Fats in Meats), and therefore results in functional absence of LA (see: Essential Fatty Acids). Since, according to the World Health Organization's recommendations, the *minimum* functional requirement of LA is 3% for an adult person, 4.5% during pregnancy, and 5-7% during lactation, a product should have 8% (5+3), 9.5% (5+4.5), and 10% (5+5), to 12% (5+7) LA respectively to accommodate these conditions[3]. The presence of t- fatty acids in the product would require the content of LA to be even higher to make up for the LA-lowering effect that the t- fatty acids are known to have.

Why Hydrogenate?

Hydrogenation allows the manufacturer to start with a cheap and low quality source of oil, and turn it into a product that competes with butter in spreadability. Perhaps it can even compete in taste, although margarines often taste slightly rancid, especially in summer, and whereas the summer rancidity of butter can be removed by heating it [the short chain, free fatty acids responsible for this taste which separated (hydrolysed) from the glycerol molecule (see: Triglycerides), evaporate off], heating will not remove the rancid taste from margarine, because margarine's rancidity is based on oxidation of long chain unsaturated fatty acids which won't evaporate.

The low cost of the raw material allows margarine to be sold at a much lower price than butter, while still maintaining good profits, with money left over to mount massive advertising campaigns to capture a large share of the market of bargain-hunting supermarket shoppers. These advertising campaigns appeal to the uninformed person's interest in health, and make claims which have never been proved either experimentally, or even statistically or anecdotally (see: Advertising and Jargon).

Two statements sum up the story of hydrogenation and health. The first statement, made by G.J. Brisson, Professor of Nutrition at Laval University in Quebec, says that "it would be practically impossible to predict with accuracy either the nature or the content of these new molecules [produced in the process of hydrogenation]. Between the parent vegetable oil, sometimes labeled 'pure', and the partially hydrogenated product . . . there is a world of chemistry that alters profoundly the composition and physicochemical properties of natural oils."[4]

The other statement was made by Herbert Dutton, one of the oldest and most knowledgeable oil chemists in North America. It goes like this: "If the hydrogenation process were discovered today, it probably could not be adopted by the oil industry". He adds, "... the basis for such comment lies in the recent awareness of our prior ignorance concerning the complexity of isomers formed during hydrogenation and their metabolic and physiological fate."[5] Translated into more simple English, it means that we now know some of the many ways in which fats are changed by hydrogenation, and also, that the body does not use these changed substances the way it uses normal fats and oils. Because of all the known and unknown effects on health that the 'complexity of isomers formed during hydrogenation' produces, government regulations, passed to protect the health of the people of the nations, would forbid the use of this process in the manufacture of edible products.

But because the process of partial hydrogenation has been used commercially on a large scale since the 1930's and now has a long tradition behind it, and because the oil industry has powerful lobbies in government, hydrogenation is allowed to continue to supply unnatural fat products to our foods.

16

Trans- Fatty Acids

Eyeing the Beast

In the previous chapter, we touched on the fact that *trans-* fatty acids are produced by high temperatures. In this chapter, we will look at *trans-* fatty acids in more detail. A very slight change —just the rotation of the molecule around a double bond — turns a fatty acid from its natural all *cis-* configuration into an unnatural fatty acid with one (or more) double bonds in the *trans-* configuration, a *trans-* fatty acid. None of the atoms in the molecule has been changed. There are still the same number of carbon atoms and the same number of hydrogen atoms; the bonds are still in the same place; only the molecule "has its head on backwards"[1].

Comparing Cis- and Trans-

Cis- double bonds have both hydrogen atoms on the carbons involved in the double bonds on the same side of the molecule. A twist of the molecule which occurs at high temperature (160° C. or higher) places the hydrogens on the carbons involved in the double bonds on opposite sides of the molecule. That's the only

change. Figure 30 shows both *cis-* and *trans-* configurations of a fatty acid.

The results of this miniscule change are quite drastic. In the *cis-* double bond, the hydrogens on the same side of the molecule repel each other in seeking space for themselves, and since there is nothing on the other side of the molecule, it bends to make room. The *trans-* molecule however, remains almost straight because the hydrogen atoms are on opposite sides of the molecule.

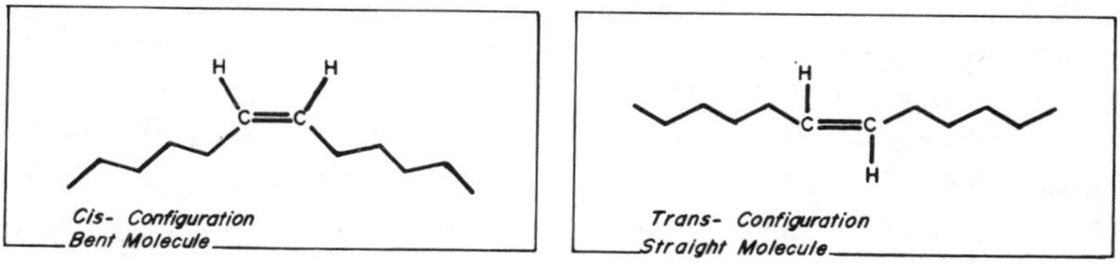

Figure 30. Cis- and trans- configurations of fatty acids.

Any double bond in a fatty acid molecule may be twisted into the *trans-* form. Thus a fatty acid with 2 double bonds may be changed to any one of 3 *trans-* forms of the molecule (one bond twisted, the other bond twisted, or both bonds twisted), and a fatty acid with 3 double bonds can form any one of 7 different *trans-* forms. None of the *trans-* forms are biologically equivalent to the parent molecule. Much of an oil's content of the essential fatty acids, linoleic acid (18:2*w*6) and linolenic acid (18:3*w*3), which are 2- and 3-times unsaturated, respectively, (see: Essential Fatty Acids), is either saturated with hydrogens during the process of hydrogenation or twisted into various *trans-* forms by the high temperatures (up to 250°C) at which this processing takes place. The essential fatty acids are more active chemically than the monounsaturated oleic acid (18:1*w*9), and for this reason, hydrogenation selectively and more rapidly destroys these biologically most valuable molecules, by both *trans-* fatty acid production and saturation with hydrogen (see: Hydrogenation).

Properties and Functions of T- Fatty Acids

The simple change in shape from *cis-* to *trans-* has some important effects on the physical properties and therefore, the functions of the molecules. The *trans-* configuration is more stable than the *cis-* configuration. This means that once a *cis-* fatty acid has been changed to a *trans-* fatty acid, chances of its being changed back to a *cis-* fatty acid are very slim.

The change in shape from the bent *cis-* form to the straight *trans-* form is important, because the molecules fit into body structures differently. In biological systems, the *trans-* form half-fits into enzyme and membrane structures. It can't complete the functions that the *cis-* form performs, and at the same time, blocks out the *cis-* form. Thus the *trans-* forms take up the space, but won't do the work of the *cis-* essential fatty acids.

Cis- and *trans-* molecules pack differently, and therefore their melting points are different. For instance, each molecule of either *cis-* or *trans-* oleic acid (OA, 18:1*w*9) has one double bond. If this double bond is in the natural *cis-* configuration, a pot full of these molecules melts at 13°C and is thus liquid at both room and body temperature. In the *trans-* configuration, a pot full of these molecules melts at 44°C and is thus solid at both room and body temperatures. The natural *cis-* molecules are more dispersed. The *trans-* molecules are more sticky. For this reason, *trans-* fatty acids encourage fatty deposits in the arteries, liver, and other organs, and *trans-* fatty acids also make platelets more sticky, increasing the likelihood of a clot in a small blood vessel, leading to strokes, heart attacks, or circulatory occlusions in other organs, such as lungs, extremities, and sense organs. *Trans-* fatty acids behave more like the saturated (no double bonds) fatty acids than like their *cis-* fatty acid siblings [the saturated equivalent of OA (18:1*w*9) is stearic acid (18:0), and the latter melts at 70°C]. Saturated fatty acids are even stickier than *trans-* fatty acids, but on the other hand, they don't interfere with the functions of the essential fatty acids.

Another difference between *cis-* and *trans-* fatty acids is that the body metabolizes them differently. *Trans-* fatty acids are useful to the body only as energy-creating fuel, unlike the *cis-* essential fatty acids (see: Essential Fatty Acids), which the body conserves for use in important structures in cell membranes. The rate at which our enzymes break down the *trans-* fatty acids is slower than the rate at which they break down *cis-* fatty acids. This is important for organs such as the heart, whose normal fuel is fatty acids, and whose ability to perform may be lowered when the consumption of *trans-* fatty acids is high. In a situation of stress, increased activity, or crisis, lowered heart performance might have fatal consequences.

Another important finding is that *trans-* fatty acids change the permeability of membranes. This means that some molecules, which ordinarily would be kept out of the cell, can now get in, and that some molecules which would ordinarily remain in the cell can now get out. The protective barrier around the cell, which is vital to keeping the cell alive and healthy, is impaired by *trans*- fatty acids.

The effect of the change from *cis*- to *trans*- configuration which is most likely to have negative effects on the well-being of humans has received little research attention so far. It involves the changes which occur in the electrical properties of the twisted *trans*- molecule as a result of the twist and change in shape. The essential fatty acids and their highly unsaturated derivatives are involved in energy and electron exchange reactions which also involve sulphur-rich proteins, oxygen, and light. The *trans*- fatty acids are not able to take part in these most vital reactions, and in fact, they interfere with them, because they almost fit, but not quite. The situation is similar to that which occurs when we use a spark plug with too wide a gap in a car. The spark is unable to jump this gap, and because of this tiny (in comparison to the size of the car) fault, the car goes nowhere. Life is energy, and it flows in the body over molecules set up for just that purpose by the very precise structure and spatial arrangement of atoms and their electrons in relation to one another. When we change the molecular architecture of the body by introducing molecules (building blocks) which are the wrong shape, size, or properties, they do not fit, and throw the flow pattern of the life currents off course. The life currents are responsible for all life functions, including healthy heartbeat, nerve function, cell division, co-ordination, sensory function, mental balance, and vitality. We have to look no further than altered molecules and their capacity to impair, derail, or interrupt the natural flow of energy from molecule to molecule within the body, to explain the degenerative diseases on the molecular level. *Trans*- fatty acids constitute the major class of these altered molecules, because the fatty acids are centrally important in the electrical reactions in the body, and because we consume them in comparatively large quantities in processed food products. Since the disruption they create is primarily electrical and not molecular, it is very difficult to put the finger on them. By the time degeneration becomes visible, the *trans*- fatty acids have been metabolized, although they started the process which led to degeneration.

Finally, the *trans*- fatty acids disrupt the vital functions of the essential fatty acids, and worsen essential fatty acid deficiency, by interfering with the enzyme systems which transform the fatty acids into other important molecules: the highly unsaturated fatty acids found especially concentrated in the brain, sense organs, adrenals, and testes; and the prostaglandins, which regulate the tone of the muscles in the walls of the arteries and thereby increase or decrease blood pressure, and which also regulate the stickiness of the platelets, important in blood clotting. It is easy to see that anything which interferes with the production of the prostaglandins will have important effects on cardiovascular health.

Food Sources of T- Fatty Acids

How much *trans-* fatty acids do we get, and from where? It has been estimated that average intake of *trans-* fatty acids is about 12 grams per day in the U.S. (9.1 grams per day in Canada), of which 95% comes from hydrogenated vegetable oil products, and the rest from animal products, mainly beef and butter fat. This 12 grams is almost 10% of our total fat intake. Our annual consumption of *trans-* fatty acids is almost twice as much as our intake of all other unnatural food additives (and that's what t-fatty acids are) put together.

The main source of *trans-* fatty acids in our diet is partial hydrogenation (see: Hydrogenation). The two main products from which we get t- fatty acids are margarines and shortenings or shortening oils, both of which are made from partially hydrogenated vegetable oils. Margarine accounts for about 3.5 grams of t- fatty acids per day, and shortening for about 4.6 grams per day. Salad oil accounts for around .5 grams. Butter and milk add about .25 grams each, and meat adds another .12 grams.

How the Body Deals With T- Fatty Acids

In the same way as a bricklayer can refuse to use a chipped brick in his building, the human body has ways of dealing with the presence of t- fatty acids in the diet. Some enzymes, lucky for us, recognize the difference in the shape of the t- fatty acids from the natural *cis-* fatty acids, and refuse to use t- fatty acids in functions for which these changed molecules are not suited anyway. Some tissues in the human body also recognize and reject t- fatty acids. The brain is partially protected from them, and the placenta does not pass them easily, protecting the unborn child to some extent; but neither brain nor fetus is completely protected from the t- fatty acids in the diet.

The bricklayer may destroy the broken bricks to prevent their being used in the building. The body deals with some of the t- fatty acids in a similar way. It breaks down some of them as quickly as it can. For instance, *trans-* polyunsaturated fatty acids, which are twisted essential fatty acid molecules, are rapidly metabolized for energy, whereas the body will conserve the natural *cis-* essential fatty acids for more important functions. In this way, the interfering t- fatty acids are selectively destroyed and the interference they cause in essential fatty acid functions is kept to a minimum.

Still, if too many bricks are faulty, the bricklayer will have to use some of them in the structure. There is a limit to the amount of altered material the body can destroy, and when that limit is exceeded, disease begins to manifest, because the body attempts to use the altered molecules for vital functions.

Trans- Fatty Acids and Disease

Atherosclerosis. *Trans-* fatty acids can increase blood cholesterol level by 15% and triglyceride levels by 47% very rapidly when partially hydrogenated vegetable oil, containing 37% t- fatty acids is fed. High triglyceride levels play a part in the development of cardiovascular disease. If the diet contains cholesterol, the effect of the t- fatty acids is enhanced. T- fatty acids increase the size of atherosclerotic plaques in the aortas of pigs in experimental situations. High levels of the natural highly unsaturated *cis-* fatty acids, found in flax and certain fish oils, reverse these effects of the t- fatty acids.

Cancer. It has been shown that many kinds of cancers are associated with diets high in fats. When the information is analyzed and compared to the increase in the incidence of deaths from cancer over the last 80 years (from 1 in 30 in 1900 to 1 in 5 in 1980), it can be shown that the increase in the occurrence of cancer parallels the increase in the consumption of fats of vegetable origin, and even more closely with the increase in consumption of hydrogenated vegetable oils. The increase in the consumption of t-fatty acids can explain much of the increased incidence of cancer. While this statistical analysis is not proof that *trans-* fatty acids *cause* cancer, it serves to alert us to that possibility. Consideration of the vital functions of the essential and other highly unsaturated fatty acids makes it seem likely that the t- fatty acids, which interfere with these vital functions, are involved.

Accumulating evidence indicates that the essential fatty acids and the longer, more highly unsaturated fatty acids made from them play a vital role in the remission of cancer. The fact that at least some cancers involve a functional deficiency in the essential fatty acids (see: Fatty Degeneration) lends further support to this theory.

17

Toxic Products

Introduction

Besides the *trans-* fatty acids which are treated separately in Chapter 16, there are several other toxic oil products that you should know about.

Toxic Fatty Acids Found in Nature

Several natural oils contain toxic fatty acids, and are therefore not good oils for human consumption. *Cotton seed oil* contains from .6 to 1.2% of a *cyclopropene fatty acid* with 19 carbon atoms, which has toxic effects on the liver and gall bladder, and also slows down sexual maturity (at higher levels it causes female reproductive functions to stop, and at much higher levels, it kills rats within a few weeks). On the biochemical level, this fatty acid destroys the desaturase enzymes which make the highly unsaturated fatty acids, and therefore interferes with the functions of the essential fatty acids. It also enhances by many times the power of (fungus-produced) aflatoxins to cause cancer.

Cotton seed oil has the highest content of pesticide residues. The cotton farmers severely over-spray their crops in order to keep boll weevils and other cotton pests under control. Since the natural predators which once kept these pests in check have been killed off by pesticides, the pests are now out of control, requiring intensive pesticide application every year. Even though refining removes part of the toxic fatty acids and pesticides, cotton oil is not a good oil for human (or animal) consumption.

Cotton seed oil also contains *gossypol,* a complex substance containing benzene rings, which irritates the digestive tract, causes water retention in the lungs, shortness of breath, and paralysis.

Rape (canola) and *mustard seed oils* contain *erucic acid,* a 22-carbon, once unsaturated fatty acid (22:1*w*9). Erucic acid causes fatty degeneration of heart, kidney, adrenals, and thyroid. From 1956 to 1974, 'edible' oils made from rape seed were marketed, with erucic acid contents up to 40%. In the meantime, geneticists bred new varieties of rape seed, whose content of erucic acid is lower. Less than 5% of erucic acid is permissible by government standards, but the heart and inner organs don't want any. If the diet persistently contains erucic acid, the body compensates for its presence by making enzymes that shorten the fatty acid chain from 22 carbons to 18 or less, but during the time that elapses before these enzymes become active, fatty deposits and scarring occur in the hearts of the experimental animals studied. Although the fatty deposits are removed after a while, permanent scar tissue remains.

A third toxic fatty acid is *cetoleic acid,* another 22-carbon chain with a double bond on the 11th carbon atom (22:1*w*11). Herring and capelin oils contain between 10 and 20% cetoleic acid, which is similar in its effects to erucic acid. Most other fish oils do not contain it; menhaden and anchovetta oils contain small amounts of this fatty acid.

Another toxic fatty acid is the hydroxy fatty acid *ricinoleic acid* which makes up 80% of the fatty acid content of castor oil. This fatty acid stimulates the secretion of fluids in the intestine, and for this reason is used as a purge before medical intervention in gastro-intestinal problems. Aside from causing very powerful intestinal contractions (the body gets rid of the castor oil and everything else in the intestine as quickly as possible), castor oil has no harmful effects. Prolonged use leaches minerals and vitamins out of the intestinal tissue, and is therefore inadvisable.

Modified Oils

Heating oils to high temperatures (160°C or higher) produces many toxic substances besides the *trans-* fatty acids. Many of these substances have not even been identified, while the structure of others which are toxic are known. So many aspects of our food preparation involve *fried* and *deep-fried oils* that these are a major source of toxic fat substances in our diets. Oils heated in the absence of air form cyclic monomers which are toxic and found in deep frying oils. In experimental animals these cyclic monomers produce fatty liver, and fed to the young, they result in a high death rate. Oils heated in air form less of the cyclic monomers, but produce other substances that are equally toxic to animals. Heated either with or without air, deep fried oils create a great health hazard for human beings.

Another class of modified oil substances, one which rarely gets attention is *brominated oils.* These are made from olive, corn, sesame, cottonseed, and soy bean oils, and are used to enhance cloud stability in bottled fruit drinks and to prevent ring formation on the neck of the bottle; in other words, they serve purely cosmetic purposes.

The solids in bottled natural fruit juices settle out with time, and dry on the bottle necks, forming rings. Fresh juices, on the other hand, are cloudy. Brominated oils give a fresh look to old juices, and have been added to commercial fruit drinks for more than 50 years. Brominated oils cause changes in the heart tissue, enlargement of the thyroid, fatty liver, kidney damage, and withered testicles. They decrease the heart's ability to use saturated fats as fuel, and lower the liver's ability to metabolize pyruvic acid, a very common fuel for cells. They increase the level of several important enzymes in the body, indicating imbalance or difficulty in important metabolic functions. They accumulate toxic bromine in the tissues of children. In Holland and Germany, brominated oils are not allowed in drinks.

Other toxic products are formed by oxidation of unsaturated fatty acids (rancidity). These include: *ozonides* and *peroxides,* which are toxic to lung tissues and can be fatal; *hydroperoxides, polymers,* and worst of all, *hydroperoxyaldehydes,* which are the most toxic of all the toxic substances produced from oxidation.

Last, a substance called *phytanic acid* found perhaps in milk and meat, is toxic for people suffering from a genetic defect called Refsum's disease. When phytanic acid-containing foods are omitted from the diets of people with Refsum's disease, their symptoms are alleviated.

The simple conclusion for health and well-being, supported by scientific evidence as well as clinical experience is to avoid the oils and products which contain these toxic substances. It is true that we are exposed to and have available to us many toxic fat and oil products. But we are not compelled to either buy or eat them.

18

Free Radicals

Terrorists in Your Body?

Free radicals are almost perfect candidates for the honour of the villain in the biochemical drama of diseases and their cause. Even the name 'free radical' has sinister overtones, great for a villain myth-in-the-making in the 1980's — hordes of evil-faced, mean-minded, scruffy (perhaps bearded and long-haired) terrorists loose inside our bodies!

Free radicals contain unpaired electrons, and electrons are very small and difficult to locate. A thousand of them can hide behind the smallest atom, hydrogen, and there are so many atoms in a human body that the number is incomprehensible. Electrons are even smaller, and their numbers even more staggering, more than 4 times 10 to the 28th, or 4 followed by 28 zeroes!! They are impossible to catch or to pin down, because they are constantly flitting from place to place at the speed of light (3 followed by 10 zeroes centimeters per second), and can change from a particle to a wave and back again in a split of a split of a second. When you stop, out of breath from chasing them, you can almost hear them laughing at you.

The free radical theory seems a reasonable theory to explain degenerative conditions such as cardiovascular disease and cancer, (as well as aging), which are widespread and which so far, have eluded man's attempts to cure or control. As a result, the free radical theory can be used as a tool to advertise any number of substances which promise to destroy, remove, capture, scavenge, neutralize, trap, or otherwise immobilize these terrorists in our systems. If we can be convinced that any one of the 4 times 10 to the 28th electrons in our system might just start terrorizing us, a market is created for many 'anti-terrorist' health products, and a great profit. Still, free radicals do exist, and an understanding of their nature will enable us to separate fact from fiction in the market place.

What is a free radical? A free radical is a molecule or element with an unpaired electron. Figure 31 illustrates a molecule with a free radical electron.

```
    H     H     H     H     H
    |     |     |     |     |
  — C  —  C  =  C  —  C  —  C —
    |                 •     |
    H                       H
```

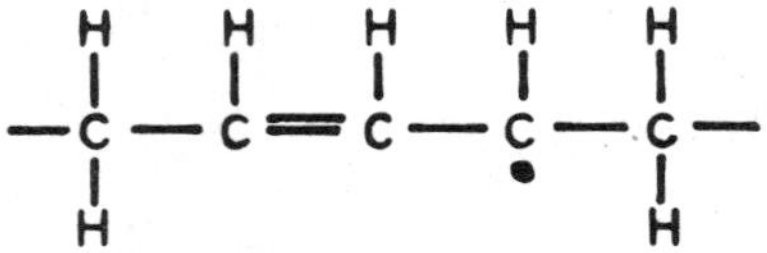

Figure 31. Molecule with an unpaired free radical electron.

Because it is not tied up in a bond or an electron shell with another electron, a free radical electron is loose and very active[1]. It is looking for a partner, because electrons, like humans, hate to be alone, and like to be paired, and will therefore draw an electron from wherever they can, including another electron pair. So a free radical is a sub-atomic, free-wheeling, loose-living electron playing the field for a mate to settle down with, and willing to break up other pairs to find that mate.

Free radicals are intermediates in thousands of normal chemical reactions taking place in the body, so there are lots of them normally present, and the body has ways of keeping them from getting out of hand. This is important, because if natural ways of keeping free radical reactions confined and localized fail, free radical chain reactions can occur, leading to faulty biochemical functions, abnormal and toxic substances, and disease.

Free Radical Chain Reactions

Let's take a closer look at free radical chain reactions that can occur in oils. If we have a bucket of oil exposed to light, a ray

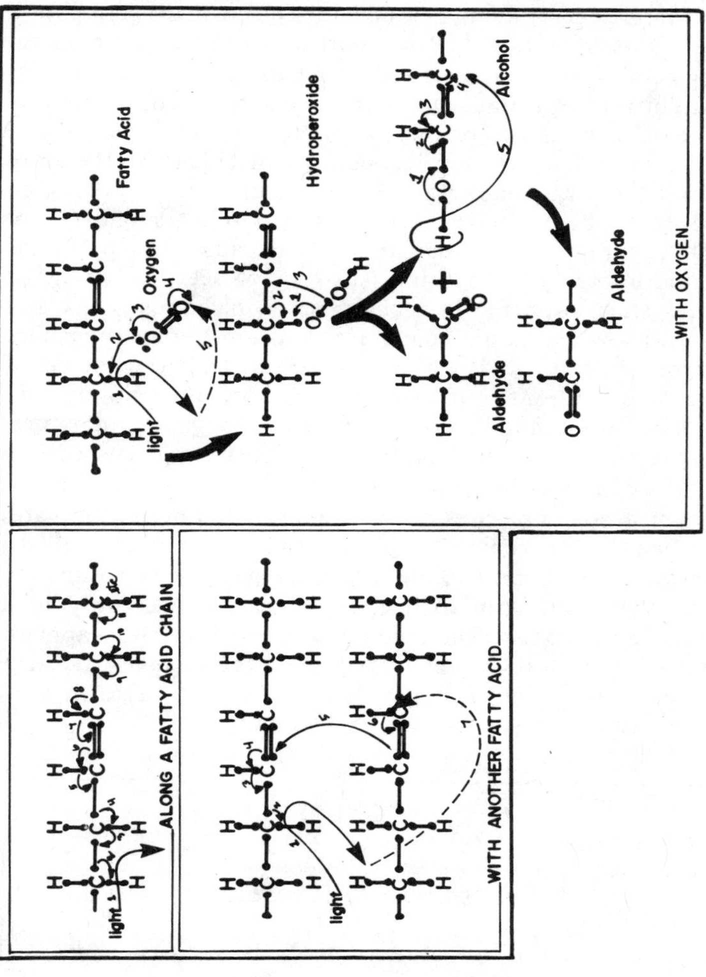

Figure 32. *Some possible light-induced free radical chain reactions.*

(photon) of light may be caught by an electron on a carbon next to the double bond carbon in a molecule of unsaturated fatty acid[2] (see: Fatty Acids). The electron now carries more energy than it did before, is in an excited state, and takes off (perhaps with a hydrogen nucleus), leaving behind a lone electron desperate for a partner. This in turn will grab a partner from wherever *it* can, leaving another electron unpaired, which then repeats the process in a chain reaction, until the original excited electron returns home to pair with the other lone partner (whoever and wherever it may be by this time), or until a special molecule traps the loose electron. A typical chain reaction of this kind may go through 30,000 cycles before it is stopped, and another single ray of sunlight can start another chain reaction. Because chemical bonds are made up of electron pairs, it is easy to see that when the electrons start bouncing in a chain reaction, bonds break and change, and when bonds change, new and different molecules form from the fatty acids with which we started in our bucket of oil. There are billions of photons present even on a cloudy day, and it is by the method described above that they alter, denature, or destroy oils exposed to light. Figure 32 illustrates a few possible light-induced free radical reactions.

Oxygen destroys oils in a similar way. Here, light first activates the oxygen to a form containing an unpaired electron and called a singlet oxygen radical, and the singlet oxygen radical's unpaired electron then pairs with an electron stolen from the fatty acid, starting the chain reaction. Figure 33 shows how this happens. Light however, spoils oil 1000 times faster than oxygen, because light reacts 1000 times faster with the oil directly than it does through oxygen.

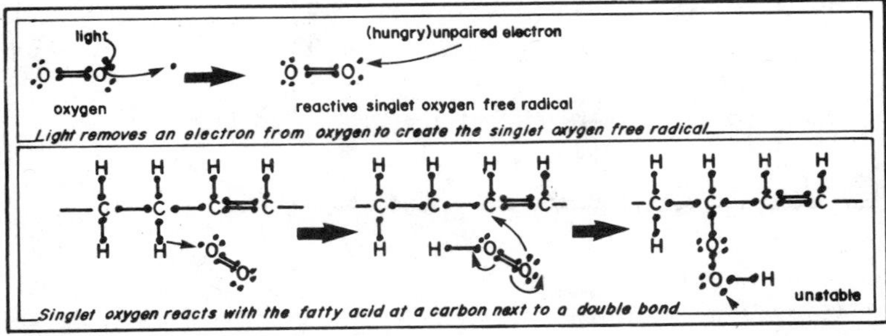

Figure 33. Oxygen-induced free radical reactions.

In a natural oil, there are molecules such as vitamin E (Figure 34) and others which are able to trap loose electrons, and singlet oxygen 'quenchers' such as carotene (Figure 35) and others.

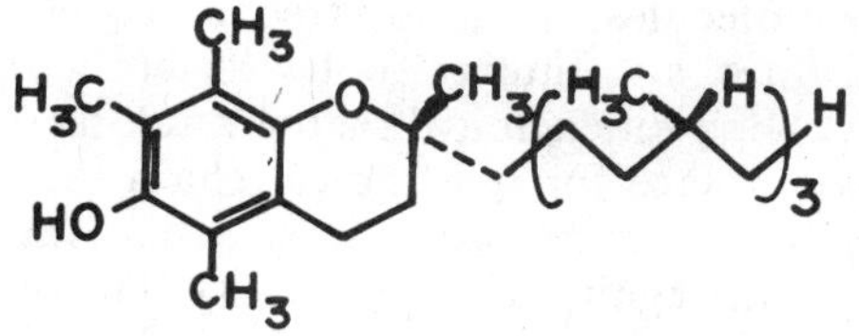

Figure 34. Vitamin E.

Figure 35. Carotene.

On the other hand, chlorophyll and finely divided metals such as iron and copper enhance the free radical reactions, and help light to destroy oils even more rapidly. In refined oils, the vitamins E and carotene, as well as the chlorophyll and most of the metal are taken out of the oil. Artificial substances such as BHT and BHA, which are free radical traps and slow down the light-induced destruction of the oil may then be added to replace the natural substances which were removed.

Protection From Free Radicals

In the human body too, vitamin E, carotene, and a number of other substances protect the essential fatty acids and other important highly unsaturated fatty acids from free radical chain reactions.

Since free radicals are necessary intermediates in vital biochemical reactions, there must be present in the body a way to protect the free radicals from being destroyed at the wrong time, and at the same time to protect the body from free radical chain reactions. There is indeed a way. The structures and shapes, the architecture of the enzymes responsible for facilitating the body's vital reactions, keep the free radicals confined so that they can't just go anywhere they please, but are directed to go only where they are needed. The reaction is completed, and the free electron reunites with the other lone partner as soon as the natural chemical reaction is complete. In this way, a chain reaction is prevented. The molecules which trap free radical electrons do not fit into the enzymes, and thus cannot interfere with the natural free radical-involving biochemical reaction taking place.

The most likely place for free radical chain reactions to take place is in the cell membranes, and it is here that vitamins E and A are found, protecting against that possibility. The rest of the body is protected against damage from free radicals by other substances as well, including some of the B complex vitamins (B1, B5, and B6), vitamin C, the sulphur-containing amino acid cysteine and sulphur-rich proteins, the metals zinc and selenium, vitamin C's bioflavinoid co-factors, and various naturally made cyclic (phenolic) compounds which are found in foods and proteins. Perhaps many other substances exist in the body to protect against free radical damage, but they are not yet known to us. What is known, however, is that the human body is able to prevent and even to reverse and repair free radical damage very efficiently, provided the food substances listed above are present in optimum quantities.

Free Radicals and Nutrition

Some writers on nutrition, knowing that the highly unsaturated fatty acids form free radicals easily, suggest that people should minimize their intake of all unsaturated fatty acids. This suggestion is ill advised for several reasons. First, the essential fatty acids, which are unsaturated, are absolutely necessary for life and health, and most modern diets are already deficient in them. Second, a healthy body contains more of the essential linoleic acid (LA, 18:2*w*6) than of any of the other 45 essential nutrient substances. The people least prone to degenerative disease: strict vegetarians, Japanese fishermen, and traditional Eskimoes have the highest tissue content of the highly unsaturated fatty acids. People suffering from degenerative diseases: obesity, cancer, cardiovascular disease, diabetes, and liver degeneration are usually also low in their tissue content of the essential fatty acids[3]. Third, the essential fatty acids, combined with sulphur-rich proteins (see: The Oil-Protein Combination) are used successfully in the treatment of degenerative diseases. Finally, the essential fatty acids and oxygen, both of which form free radicals very readily, are both extremely important to health and life. It appears, therefore, that the ability to form free radicals is important to normal biochemical functions in health and only becomes dangerous when the free radicals get out of control.

In a diet deficient in the factors which are required to keep free radicals in check, it might seem to make sense to also decrease the intake of essential fatty acids, but it makes a lot more sense to bring the intake of the protective factors (which, in any case, are also essential, and thus necessary in the diet), up to optimum levels. We need to assure ourselves of adequate intake of both. Since the essential fatty acids help to bring oxygen into the system, and lack of oxygen in the system is a main factor in the cause of degenerative diseases including cancer, aging, cardiovascular disease, obesity, and arthritis, and since these diseases are often associated with deficiency or functional deficiency of essential fatty acids, the supply of these should never be compromised. But they *must* be accompanied by optimum intake of the necessary vitamins and minerals.

History of Free Radicals

Why are free radicals a problem now? Free radicals are not a new creation of nature. They have been around for millions of years. So have the essential fatty acids, the vitamins, minerals, and the protective natural substances found in foods. Oils high in essential fatty acids from seed such as flax, sunflower, and sesame have been pressed, enjoyed, and known for their health-giving properties for at least a few thousand years. But degenerative diseases on a large scale are recent in origin. What could be the reason for the epidemic increase in their occurrence during the last 100 years?

There are at least two good reasons for this increase. The first is the rising deficiency in modern refined food diets of the vitamin and mineral factors which are required to metabolize the fatty acids properly, and which protect us from free radical chain reactions. Better eating habits and a good multi-vitamin, multi-mineral supplement take care of this deficiency.

The second is the presence of synthetic substances in larger and larger (pharmacological) doses in our diets and medicines. When a synthetic substance is made in the laboratory which in some ways mimics the activity of one of the natural substances in our bodies and is in other ways quite different from the natural substance, this synthetic substance is likely to 'misfit' into the body's enzyme architecture. One would expect that the free radicals (unpaired electrons) from such a 'misfit' molecule, involved in a biological reaction, cannot be as easily kept confined as those of the natural substance. Might it be that the 'side effects' which so often accompany the action of prescription drugs are based on consistent free radical chain reactions initiated by these drugs?

Drugs that 'misfit' the body's natural architecture are monkey wrenches into the body's natural works, and misroute metabolic processes, leading to toxic products and degenerative disease. A study on this subject would be extremely worthwhile, but would not likely be funded by a pharmaceutical company. Common sense suggests that there are better ways to heal our aches and pains than with unnatural substances. An improvement in our diets, and more care in the way we live seem far more likely to bring lasting relief. When our diets are natural, and our levels of the essential nutrients are optimal — and we do have the option to choose — free radicals cease to be a health problem.

19

Frying

Introduction

Now that we have looked at the chemical changes which occur in oils not protected from light, air, and heat, it might be useful to look at what happens when we fry oils in the household.

It seems that nothing in our use of fats and oil products is safe from scrutiny, and so frying has come in for its share of bad publicity lately. Deep frying operations in restaurants and homes have been insulted. Pan frying has been accused of evil effects on health. Some people have gone so far as to condemn frying altogether — a drastic change in our way of life. What's the truth?

The dangers of frying result from the oxidation that takes place when oils are subjected to high temperatures in the presence of light and oxygen or air. Free radicals are produced, which start chain reactions in the oil molecules (see: Free Radicals). Under frying conditions, many chemical changes take place in oils, including the production of *trans-* fatty acids (see: Trans- Fatty Acids), oxidation products of many different kinds, some of which are highly toxic and appear around tumours, and scores of other unnatural breakdown and polymer products whose effects on health are not known.

Frying with oils once won't kill you, and so seems harmless. The body has ways of coping with toxic substances. But over 10, or 20 or 30 years, it is possible to accumulate enough altered and toxic products that the chemistry of the body, the bio-chemistry, is seriously impaired, and degenerative disease occurs.

Safe Frying

Not all substances used for frying, and not all frying conditions lead to health problems. The changes due to heat, air and light take place very rapidly in unsaturated fatty acids, but only slowly in saturated fatty acids, because the saturated fatty acids are chemically less active. They are therefore not as valuable to human health as are the unsaturated ones, but at the same time they are more stable in the presence of light, heat, and air. So whenever a fat is needed for frying, one which is mostly saturated is preferable. None of the oils that come in bottles qualifies for frying, because what makes oils liquid is their content of unsaturated fatty acids.

There are two good substances useful for frying purposes. One is coconut or palm kernel 'oil'. The other is butter. A third fat used traditionally for frying was lard, but this has largely been replaced by shortening. Shortening and margarine are not good substances to fry with, because they are not good substances to consume (see: Trans- Fatty Acids).

Coconut oil contains mostly saturated fatty acid chains between 10 and 16 carbons in length, and only about 8% unsaturated fatty acids. Usually, the 'oil' is hydrogenated, which means that even the small amount of unsaturated fatty acids in them has been saturated. Thus coconut butter is almost completely saturated, and so therefore light, air, and heat destroy it only slowly.

Butter contains mostly saturated fatty acid chains between 4 and 12 carbons in length, and only about 5% unsaturated fatty acids, about 3% of which is an easily digested *trans-* form. It is not hydrogenated commercially, because it is too expensive a starting material. The shorter fatty acids are easier to digest than the longer chain fatty acids, and especially the longer 16- and 18-carbon saturated fatty acid chains can cause some problems in the metabolism of the essential fatty acids. Used in moderation, neither butter nor coconut fat creates any health problems. On the other hand, they also supply almost no essential fatty acids, and in this sense, they are not very useful nutritionally. They provide fats which can be burned by the body for energy only.

Frying With Oils

There is a way of frying with oils which contain essential fatty acids, but this way of frying requires more care on our part than we ordinarily take in our frying operations.

No-No's

The highly refined oils which we find in transparent bottles on supermarket shelves should not be used for anything. Why? Because they have been degraded by light, have lost much of their nutrient value during the refining processes, and are usually made from the cheapest, most inferior, most intensely pesticide-sprayed oil plants (cotton seed oil is especially bad). Oil should be fresh, unrefined, mechanically pressed, organically grown, and stored in dark containers. Only the health food stores carry acceptable oils, and not all oils in health food stores are acceptable. Fresh flax, safflower, sunflower, sesame, and pumpkin seed oils are all acceptable.

More No-No's

In frying, here is what we usually do. It is our custom to pour oil into the empty frying pan, and let it sizzle for a while before adding the foods we want to fry, and during this sizzling time (sometimes the oil begins to smoke!) the oil is destroyed. The temperature it reaches is too high, and at this temperature, light-catalyzed oxidation reactions occur very rapidly. And this is the essence of the frying dilemma. Oil kept at 215°C for 15 minutes or more consistently produces atherosclerosis in experimental animals. In commercial deep-frying operations, the same batch of oil is often kept at a high temperature constantly for days. Many altered substances have been isolated from such oils. Some are known to be toxic; the effects of many are not known; and you can be fairly confident that none of them will improve your health. What keeps the level of these altered and toxic substances from getting too high is the fresh oil added to replace the oil that stuck to the fish and chips, or onion rings, or whatever was deep-fried, which you ate.

Safe Frying With Oils

Now here is an alternative, a safe way of frying with oils. In traditional Chinese cooking, the first thing the cook puts in the wok is not oil, but water (North American Chinese cooks have largely abandoned this wise practice). The water keeps the temperature down to 100°C, and the water vapour (steam) protects the oil from air. In European gourmet cooking, the vegetables are placed in the frying pan *before* the oil is added, and protect the oil from overheating and oxidation. The food tastes less burnt, retains more of its natural flavours, and most important, we retain our precious health.

It requires more care to fry foods in this way, because we can't be off doing something else at the same time, and perhaps the best thing to do would be not to fry at all, but to eat our fresh oils on salads, or in seeds. We are creatures of habit, but only a very small change in the way we fry with oils pays large dividends in health and well-being.

Baking and Cooking

Baking is similar to frying. The temperature gets very high, and so butter or coconut fat should be used to line the baking pans. The temperature inside the bread or whatever is being baked only goes up to 100°C, actually cooking the bread inside. Only the crust is actually baked. Cooking is less destructive of oils than frying because the temperature goes only to 100°C, but the less oils are heated, the less they are destroyed, and the better they are for us.

20

Advertising and Jargon

Winners and Losers

Winners don't need much advertising. They radiate success on their own merit, by what they are and what they do. Their reputation spreads by word of mouth, based on high performance. When a winner is in town, you just need to be told, and you want to go. Quality speaks for itself.

Losers require cosmetic jobs and a lot of advertising to make it. They have no track record and never will have, because they don't perform. When a loser is in town, you have to be informed, then you have to be sold with a lot of fancy talk and pleasant imagery.

Advertising Foods

The same is true for foods. Really natural and nutritious foods don't need a lot of advertising. A fresh, crisp apple looks good, smells good, and tastes good. It doesn't cause upset stomach, varicose veins, or other illness. Fresh fruit, fresh vegetables, whole grains, nuts and seeds, and spices need, and therefore get, little advertising. Occasionally, someone will advertise his particular brand of one of these, but that's about all.

But all of the refined, denatured, nutrient-impoverished food items require much hype, much flash, much dress-up. The worse the product, the better the ad, because the more pleasant results have to be implied from the use of the product to get humans motivated: to buy the unnourishing products, consume them, and develop the habit of their consumption. Cigarettes, alcohol, ice creams, most boxed breakfast foods, soft drinks, chocolates, snacks, powdered soups, candy, many canned things, and children's junk foods belong to this category. If these products were not constantly advertised, people would not buy them because while they may have been doctored to taste good, they cannot keep us healthy.

Body Language

Advertising for inferior products, therefore, has to be vigorous enough to overide our bodies' signals, which flash: 'Deficient'!

The feeling of health is subtle. When we are free of pain and illness, we usually don't notice, and are free to focus on and get involved with something else. Only when the feeling of health and well-being is replaced by pain and discomfort are we drawn to focus on that, and become motivated to find ways to make ourselves feel good again. It's similar to our response to the room temperature. When the temperature is just right, we usually don't notice. But when it gets either too hot or too cold, we perk up from what we are doing and take notice. Then we make the necessary changes and adjustments to the windows and thermostat to make it just right, so that we can forget about room temperature again, and carry on with whatever else we were doing.

Food products, when they are new to a particular market, may need a little advertising exposure to let people know they exist, and are advertised only in terms of their own qualities. Beyond that, the most effective advertising is word of mouth. Repeat customers are made by product satisfaction (there are stores which are known for their good products and service, and don't need to advertise at all).

Myth-Bashing; Exposing Advertising Claims

Of course, there are laws against false advertising practices. But words are flexible, and can be used creatively to get around legal restrictions. One simply says something which is true about the product, but implies to the customer something desirable which is not actually true of the product. Here are some examples from the world of oils.

'From 100% Corn Oil!' There is a margarine on the market which is made 'from 100% corn oil'. This statement is true. The consumer's association with this statement is that this must be good margarine. Why? Because corn oil is high in polyunsaturates, and polyunsaturates are associated with good health. Corn oil in its natural state contains over 50% of the essential linoleic acid (LA, 18:2*w*6)[1]. But the oil used to make margarine is refined, which means it is missing some of the substances which protect it from chemical deterioration during storage or in our bodies, and it also contains chemically altered breakdown products made from essential fatty acids, as well as other unnatural or toxic products (see: Oil Making). The oil, to harden it, is partially hydrogenated (see: Hydrogenation), which usually causes the majority of the essential fatty acid molecules to be saturated, and some of the remaining essential fatty acid molecules to be broken or twisted. The margarine contains (and the advertising leaves out this important information) an average of 25% *trans-* fatty acids, both mono- and poly-unsaturated (See Trans- Fatty Acids), neither of which function in the body like essential fatty acids, and even worse, some of which interfere with the functions of the essential fatty acids which are still present. If we are lucky we end up with 25% LA (it is likely to be much less, more like 10%) remaining in the margarine out of the more than 50% we started with. One writer puts it this way: "Hydrogenated corn oil is similar to hydrogenated soy bean oil, and offers no advantages over it, [except] the promotional claim: 'contains 100% corn oil'!"[2]

'Polyunsaturated'. Another example is the use of the term 'polyunsaturated'. We think that polyunsaturated means 'healthful' or 'essential fatty acids'. It doesn't but the advertiser uses our ignorance. There are only two essential fatty acids, LA (18:2w6) and LNA (18:3*w*3). Both are polyunsaturates. There are about 8 other natural and very valuable polyunsaturates which the human body can make from LA and LNA, or can get from foods. Total 10. That's all. But there are literally hundreds of polyunsaturates possible, many of them unnatural, some harmful, and many of them present in refined and hydrogenated oils. All of these are included in the term 'polyunsaturates' (see: Polyunsaturates).

'High in Polyunsaturates'. How high is high? 2% of polyunsaturates in an oil is high, compared to zero. But 2% is low in terms of body needs and health.

'Contains lecithin'. How much? Even if only a very small amount of lecithin is present in the product, the term can be put on the label. We know that lecithin is nutritious so we like to see that on the label, but there may be less lecithin than the cat (the mouse even) could carry away on its tail. Another problem is that while the label 'lecithin' might make bells ring in our heads, the lecithin itself might make no bells ring in our bodies, if it is the kind that contains no LA (see: Lecithin).

'For cooking, frying, and baking'. Any oil with this term on the label is a low quality oil (cotton, peanut, canola, for instance) which is made even worse by cooking, frying, and baking. No oil is good for cooking, frying, and baking, because heat destroys the essential fatty acids, and oxidation and light reactions occur far more rapidly at high temperatures, deteriorating the oil and making it harmful to eat.

'No preservatives'. This doesn't mean the oil is clean, because it can still contain pesticide residues, toxic fatty acids, residues of extractant and soap, and *trans*- fatty acids. The worst oils on the market are cotton, peanut, rape, and mustard oils. They are usually refined, which means the natural protectant vitamins and minerals have been taken out and not replaced. In this case, they deteriorate very rapidly if light (especially when sold in clear glass bottles) or oxygen come in contact with the oil.

'No cholesterol'. True for all products of plant origin. What a wonderful way to cash in on our fear of cardiovascular disease, for which cholesterol is not even primarily responsible (see: Cholesterol).

'For the good of your heart' or 'For health'. There is not a single shred of scientific evidence to back up the claim that any margarine is good for your heart, or that it has any health benefits. Heart disease and cancer deaths have increased at a rate parallel to the increase in margarine sales (and the sale of other hydrogenated and partially hydrogenated products). The claim is based on the fact that essential fatty acids are necessary for health, and that products made from vegetable oils, or at least the vegetable oils from which they were made, contain some essential fatty acids. The claim selectively avoids mentioning that hydrogenated and partially hydrogenated products contain many substances detrimental to health as well. Not a shred of evidence for health benefits!

These are just a few examples of advertising for inferior products in which the advertisement tells only a part of the story.

We get taken in only as long as we don't know what's what in fats and oils nutrition.

Advertising and Media

Advertising is based on a whole field of research which studies how people's buying responses are affected by such factors as colour, shape, imagery, music, movement, setting, and other such considerations. Advertising is brought to us by the media (TV, radio, newspaper), and then we program ourselves with the information we are given. Advertising works — we keep going out and buying products we don't really need!

Businesses are created to make profits and they do whatever is necessary to convince the consumer to buy. If you insist on quality, then you'll be sold quality. If you demand service, you'll be given service. Advertising is business putting its best foot forward — the standard method used by anyone who wants to sell anything. But, if the truth were known .... .

21

Polyunsaturates

Introduction

We generally equate the term 'polyunsaturates' with the health-giving value of oils and fats products, because the essential fatty acids, which are polyunsaturates, are necessary for health. Therefore, we conclude, the polyunsaturates must be necessary for health. Unfortunately, this is not true. Only some polyunsaturates are necessary for health; some others are not necessary and some are detrimental to our health.

The value of oils, margarines, and other oil-based products can be estimated by knowing their content of the essential fatty acids, which are polyunsaturated. Polyunsaturates, or more properly, polyunsaturated fatty acids, are all fatty acids with two or more double bonds in their carbon chains (see: Fatty Acids), but there are two kinds: natural and unnatural.

Natural Polyunsaturates

There are only 2 essential fatty acids which are required in our diet, and both of these are polyunsaturates. We call these 2 fatty acids linoleic acid (LA, 18:2*w*6) and linolenic acid (LNA, 18:3*w*3) and from these 2, a healthy human being can make all of the other natural polyunsaturates it needs. It can also get these other natural polyunsaturates from food sources.

From LA, the body can make: gamma linolenic acid (GLA, 18:3*w*6) which is also found in mother's milk, evening primrose seed oil, and several other seed oils not yet available commercially; arachidonic acid (AA, 20:4*w*6) also present in meats; and docosapentaenoic acid (DPA, 22:5*w*6) which is found in the oils of certain fish and marine animals.

From LNA, the body can make: stearidonic acid (SDA, 18:4*w*3) found in the seed oils of a number of wild plants; and eicosapentaenoic acid (EPA, 20:5*w*3) and docosahexaenoic acid (DHA, 22:6*w*3), both of which are found in the oils of some fish and marine animals, among them trout, salmon, sardines, and shell fish.

All of the above polyunsaturates are natural, valuable, all *cis*- , methylene interrupted, polyunsaturates. We want one or both of the essential fatty acids in their natural state in the products we buy, since these provide the basis for making all the others. For special health needs, special oil preparations are available (see: Oil of Evening Primrose; and: Oils from Fish and other Sea Foods: EPA and DHA).

Unnatural Polyunsaturates

There are many fatty acids which are neither natural nor beneficial, although they are polyunsaturated. In this group we find: conjugated fatty acids, in which one or more of the double bonds has moved closer (2 carbons apart) to another double bond than methylene interrupted (3 carbons apart); fatty acids where one or more double bond has moved to a position further away (4 or more carbons apart) from the other double bond(s); *trans*-fatty acids, in which the molecule has been twisted at the location of one of the double bonds (see: Trans- Fatty Acids), or any combination of the above.

The *trans*- fatty acids pose the major problem in nutrition and advertising of polyunsaturates. In one study of margarines on the Canadian market, different samples were found to contain up to 20% *trans*- polyunsaturates.

The manufacturer is allowed to advertise this product as 'high in polyunsaturates', which is technically true and therefore legally permissible, but entirely misleading, because the *trans*- polyunsaturates not only are not health-giving, but are antagonistic to the health-giving essential fatty acids. *Trans*- polyunsaturates compete for enzymes, produce biologically non-functional derivatives, and interfere with the work of the essential fatty acids in the body.

Because of our association of the word polyunsaturates with health, we are fooled into thinking that we are buying a health-giving product, when in reality we may be getting a product of poor quality, a product that is actually health-destroying.

Not all margarines have 20% of their polyunsaturates in the detrimental *trans-* form, but it is not possible for the average housewife (or biochemist, for that matter) to determine whether a sample of margarine in the supermarket is high, medium, or low in these unnatural 'polyunsaturates', or even free of them. For this reason, they are perhaps best left in the supermarket cooler.

The manufacturer himself will not give out this information either, because it is not required of him. Furthermore, he probably does not even know it himself, because the hydrogenation process (see: Hydrogenation), which is used to make the margarine, is not controllable. Different batches of the same brand of margarine or shortening often contain widely different amounts of *trans-*polyunsaturates, and the procedure required to measure the content of the many types of unnatural substances found in partially or totally hydrogenated products is both expensive and time-consuming and would have to be done for each new batch of product made by hydrogenation.

Trans- polyunsaturates occur also in refined oils, and any product made from essential fatty acid-containing oils that have been heated to high temperature during processing.

If the products which we want to buy were required to list both the content of the essential fatty acids and their content of the non-natural polyunsaturates, the consumer would be in a better position to make health-oriented food choices. Manufacturers, who are motivated primarily by profit, take the molecules supplied by nature, subject them to often destructive processes, package them for convenience, and sell us less nutrition for a higher price. Where business interest, to maximize profit, takes precedence over health (so far, that's generally the way it is in our 'modern' fats and oils world), the customer has to be doubly careful in the choices he makes.

Polyunsaturate/Saturate (P/S) Ratio

Oils are often rated for their health value by the P/S ratio, which is the amount of polyunsaturates over the amount of saturated fatty acids present in the oil. A P/S ratio of 2 or higher is considered desirable.

Correcting the P/S Ratio

The biological consideration of the polyunsaturates however, makes it clear that the P part of the P/S ratio should include only the natural polyunsaturates, the essential fatty acids, while the S part of the ratio should also include all of the unnatural polyunsaturates, and the monounsaturated fatty acids as well, since these act in the body much like saturated fatty acids and have no essential fatty acid activity whatsoever. In fact, one group of unnatural polyunsaturates, the *trans-* polyunsaturates, have anti-essential fatty acid activity, and worsen essential fatty acid deficiency.

If we rearrange the P/S ration from this biological perspective, we discover that many of the oils and oil products which we considered valuable are in fact very poor. When the adjustment is made, some oil products change from a P/S ratio of almost 4, which is excellent, to a true P/S ratio of .05, which is 70 times lower, and shows the oil product to be exceptionally poor. Margarines are the products most likely to do poorly when the P/S ratio is corrected to be in keeping with the body's biological requirements, because they generally contain large quantities of non-natural polyunsaturates, and because only small quantities of the natural essential polyunsaturated fatty acids are left when the processes by which they are made are completed.

In a study of Canadian margarines, only 1 out of 100 different samples had a true P/S ratio of 2. The rest were lower. The true P/S ratio of the oils from which these margarines had been made ranged from 3.8 to 6.5 in their natural, unprocessed state. Making margarine thus appears to be a way of ruining a perfectly good oil for the sake of imitating butter's spreadability.

22

Vitamin E and Polyunsaturates

Warnings

One hears or reads regularly in books and scientific articles the warning that an increased intake of polyunsaturates requires an increased intake of vitamin E, and some authors suggest decreasing our intake of polyunsaturates, so that the intake of vitamin E does not have to be increased. What's the reality? We have already looked at the misleading term 'polyunsaturates' (see: Polyunsaturates), and will not repeat that here.

Natural Oils

In nature, vitamin E or other natural antioxidant substances[1] are always found in the seeds and nuts that make oils containing unsaturated fatty acids. The antioxidant substances are always present in the oils in the quantities necessary to protect the oils from being destroyed by light or oxygen-induced free radical reactions both in the seed, and in the human body after consumption of the oil. There is therefore no problem of too little vitamin E, (or, better, antioxidants) if we eat fresh, whole nuts and seeds to supply our nutritional requirements of essential fatty acids and oils to maintain good physical health.

When oil is pressed, the vitamin E and antioxidants contained in it, being oil-soluble, remain in the oil. If you consume fresh oils, simply pressed from seeds or nuts, still there is no problem of getting too little antioxidants to keep the oil from going rancid in your system.

Besides protecting the oils in your body from free radical damage, or perhaps because of this protection, vitamin E is also important in the body to prevent abnormal clotting of blood, and thereby protects us from heart attacks and strokes. It also protects us from cancer, by snagging free radicals which might otherwise get out of control and start free radical chain reactions (see: Free Radicals). Other natural antioxidants in foods also protect us from these free radicals.

Processed Oils

If however, the oil is pressed, then degummed, refined, bleached, and deodorized, many vital substances, including vitamin E are removed from the oil. The oil-refining industry does not throw away the vitamin E. They collect the sludge from deodorization, separate out the vitamin E, and sell it to the health food industry at good profit (vitamin E is the most expensive vitamin on the market).

People who buy their refined (deodorized) oils in the supermarket, may end up short of vitamin E. Without vitamin E, the highly unsaturated fatty acids in their bodies are not protected from free radical damage as well as they need to be. If their diet is also high in other nutrient-deficient, refined foods and non-natural substances, then it is likely that free radical chain reactions are occurring in their body uncontrolled, and causing damage and degeneration (see: Free Radicals).

Refined oils that have been standing around on the shelf in transparent bottles exposed to daylight and oils which have been fried are especially bad. Over time, the consumption of these oils produces brown spots on the skin of older people, especially prominent on head, face, and back of hands. These spots are descriptively called "fleurs de cemètiere", or 'cemetery flowers', and are one sign of fatty degeneration. They also indicate deficiency in vitamin E, as well as selenium. 'Cemetery flowers' contain denatured oils and protein, and are also found glued inside the cells of the heart muscle and brain of older people, where with time, they may take up more and more of the cell's space, and may reach 60% of the cell's total volume. Soon thereafter, they choke the cell, killing it.

Getting Enough

It is a very good idea to take vitamin E supplements to prevent oxidation of oils in our bodies. Many people do, and books have been written on the health benefits of this wonderful vitamin. It is a very good idea to decrease our consumption of refined, denatured, calorie-rich but nutrition-poor oils because they have been altered through processes invented by man out of touch with nature.

If we use oils, it makes sense to switch to oils which still contain what nature put in them, including vitamin E. It makes sense to eat fresh nuts and seeds which contain all the vitamins, minerals, proteins, and fats just the way they were made for us, the way our bodies can best use them to keep vital and healthy. Really, doesn't that make sense? In our food choices we answer that question, each of us, for ourselves.

23

Cold-Pressed Oils

Rumours and Hearsay

Most people are surprised when they hear that there is no such thing as a 'cold-pressed' oil. "But it says so on the label," I am often told. I have found store owners no more knowledgeable than customers, both believing that when oil is cold-pressed, or as the term implies (wrongly), pressed without heat, it is nutritionally superior; and believing also (rightly, in part) that heat destroys oils. What does 'cold-pressed' actually mean?

History of Cold-Pressed

The term 'cold-pressed' is said to have been introduced into the advertising of mass produced oils by one of the large oil distributors strictly for advertising purposes. Oil company spokesmen, when asked today about what the term means, basically say: "Nothing." It means that no external heat has been applied to the seed while it is being pressed. It does not guarantee that no heat has been applied before or after the actual pressing process, and in some cases, oil that has been heated to very high temperatures during deodorization (see: Oil Making) is still called 'cold-pressed', because no external heat was applied to the seed during pressing.

It is almost impossible to press oil commercially from seeds without heat, unless you press your daily supply in a hand-hammered wedge press. This process is very slow. The seed is poured into a wedge-shaped container, and a wooden wedge is driven into it. Every hour or so, the housewife hits the wedge with a wooden mallet (a hammer) and the oil will drip-drip for an hour. Then another whack, and drip-drip. This will carry on all day, and produce the oil needed daily for the household. The original term for the process was 'kalt geschlagen' in German, which translates as cold hammered, and implies no heat applied to the seed or oil, and completely unrefined crude, fresh, high quality oil. The term has been retained in Germany, although no-one today 'hammers' his oil anymore. The term therefore is used to give the sense of the quality of the old method without actually employing that method.

In commercial operations, heat is either applied to the seed from outside, as was the custom in hydraulic presses used 50 years ago, or, as is the custom today in screw presses, the heat is produced by the friction of the seeds and crushed material as it is compressed and at the same time rotated into a squeeze. Heat is needed to make the oil run out of the seed meal faster. The higher the heat, the less oil remains in the pressed seed cake, the more effcient the operation, the better price and profit, and the less waste.

Depending on the kind of operation, however, more or less heat is used. The lowest temperature at which it is possible to press is around 50°C, though the temperature inside the press head is usually higher than that. It is customary to measure the lower temperature of the oil dripping out of the press and call that its pressing temperature, though it would be better to call that the 'dripping' temperature.

In Switzerland, it is illegal to call an oil 'cold-pressed' if the highest temperature which the oil has reached in the entire process from seed to bottle, exceeds 50°C. In North America there is no such restriction, so anything goes. The usual temperature of the oil when it drips out of the press is between 85 and 95°C. Inside the press, the temperature is somewhat higher, and some oils are pressed under so much pressure that the heat created by the friction in the press head scorches the dry seed cake material, and the oil dripping out of the machine may occasionally even have a slightly burnt taste. Some people prefer this taste, and there are oils on the market which contain added burnt flavouring to cater to this taste preference.

Pressing Oil Without Heat

Why should oil be pressed without heat? The first reason stems from the fact that as temperature increases, chemical reactions speed up. The higher the temperature of the oil, the faster it can be broken down and destroyed by oxygen from the air, by light, or by other chemical processes. This can be prevented by excluding air and light from the pressing process. The exclusion of both light and oxygen are easily achieved, but most pressing facilities don't bother to do so.

The second reason is that it is known that internal changes take place in the oil molecules at high temperatures. The unsaturated fatty acids contained in oils may twist, changing the molecule from the natural *cis-* configuration to an unnatural *trans-* configuration (see: Trans- Fatty Acids), resulting in changes in the shape and properties of the fatty acid molecules, and destroying their nutritional and biological value. However, this process does not begin to take place measurably until the temperature of the oil reaches about 160°C. It becomes really serious at about 200°C. These temperatures are far above the temperatures normally reached by oil presses, which only rarely exceed 100°C, and when they do, exceed it only slightly. Thus the heat produced during *pressing* is not really a problem, and the advantage that we ascribe to 'cold-pressed' is not based on fact and does not exist. 'Cold-pressed' oils in this sense are unnecessary. The term is meaningless.

There are however, some processes which do produce dangerously high temperatures, and destroy the nutritive value of the oils. Deodorization during the production of refined, pale, bland oils with a good shelf life is carried out at a temperature of around 245°C, and produces *trans-* fatty acids (see: Oil Making).

Hydrogenation, used to turn liquid oils into semi-solid or solid fats, is carried out at a temperature of 250°C and purposely sets out to create *trans-* fatty acids, because *trans-* fatty acids have higher melting points (are more solid) than *cis-* fatty acids and give the products made from oils (such as margarines and shortenings), body, consistency, texture, and shelf life. Partial hydrogenation is even worse than complete hydrogenation. The former produces *trans-* fatty acids, the latter does not. Both processes result in unnatural and altered oil products. *Trans*-fatty acids are generally considered the worst of the unnatural products (see: Hydrogenation).

Frying with oils, especially if the oil is allowed to sizzle in the frying pan, occurs at temperatures between 160 and 220°C depending on the kind of oil used, and can also produce *trans*-fatty acids, as well as light- and oxygen-induced chemical changes in the fatty acids.

So, while the pressing temperature should be kept as low as possible, to prevent light- and oxygen-induced chemical changes in the oil, the major heat problem in oil manufacture is not the pressing temperature, but the temperature reached during refining and hydrogenating steps in the making of oil products (see: Oil Making; and: Hydrogenation), and in frying (see: Frying).

High temperature does destroy the essential fatty acids required for our health, but because the term 'cold-pressed' is based on misunderstanding, it has no value whatsoever as a term denoting oil quality. We need to look for *unrefined* oils that have been *mechanically* pressed as opposed to chemically extracted. Then we need to make sure that we do not destroy these quality oils in our own frying pans.

24

Containers and Storage of Oils

Exclusion of Light and Air

Just as the process by which the seed is pressed to win the oil should take place in the absence of light and oxygen, so also the 'bottling' and storage operation should exclude light and oxygen from the oil, because both light and oxygen destroy oil very rapidly. Light is worse than oxygen. It destroys oil 1000 times faster than oxygen. Even refrigeration does not prevent this spoilage, but only slows it down to about 1/3 of the rate at room temperature.

Any oil sold in a clear glass bottle is subject to light-deterioration, and contains health-destroying altered fatty acid derivatives. The longer the bottle has been exposed to light while standing on the shelf, the worse the deterioration. The cardboard carton in which the oils are shipped is opaque, and so the oils are fairly well protected from light as long as they stay in the box. But the process of light deterioration begins to take place the moment that the oil is exposed to light, and each ray (photon) of light can begin a free radical chain reaction which goes through an average of 30,000 cycles before it stops, destroying or altering many molecules in the process (see: Free Radicals). Every second that the oil is exposed to light, thousands of photons strike the oil. No light exposure whatsoever is therefore the only guarantee that the oil remains high quality and this is why oils should not be allowed to come in contact with light at any time between the closed, light-and oxygen-excluding seed, and your stomach. Even oils in brown glass bottles are not safe from light deterioration. The brown glass stops some of the light rays from entering and damaging the oil, so brown bottles are better than clear ones, but even a single ray of light can start a chain reaction.

For complete protection, oils should be filled into and stored in metal or completely opaque glass or earthen containers, and nitrogen packed to exclude oxygen. If light and air can be excluded, oils will keep for years without spoiling.

Once Open, Refrigeration and Rapid Use

Once the seal is broken, oils should be kept in the fridge and used up fairly rapidly, because they start to deteriorate on contact with air. Keeping the lid on tightly between uses does not prevent damage, because each oxygen molecule inside the container can induce many cycles of free radical chain reactions without being used up in them. Therefore, only a little oxygen is needed to create a lot of damage. The reactions of oils in which oxygen is used up to produce fatty acid epoxides (rancidity) proceed much slower than the free radical chain reactions mentioned above, in which unstable peroxides are formed which start free radical chain reactions and can then release the oxygen to start another chain reaction. Figure 36 illustrates both types of reaction.

Quantities to Purchase

In order not to waste oil due to spoilage, it should be bought in small quantities, not more than 250 ml for flax oil with its high linolenic acid (LNA, 18:3*w*3) content, 500 ml for safflower, sunflower, and other oils high in linoleic acid (LA, 18:2*w*6) and 1000 ml for olive oil, which is high in oleic acid (OA, 18:1*w*9).

Why the difference in quantities? It has to do with the speed at which the three unsaturated fatty acids react. LNA (18:3*w*3), present in flax oil, essential, and triply unsaturated, is the most reactive of the unsaturated fatty acids commonly found in seed oils, and spoils most rapidly. It reacts with oxygen about 5 times faster than the other essential fatty acid, the doubly unsaturated LA (18:2*w*6), and LA reacts 2.5 times faster than the non-

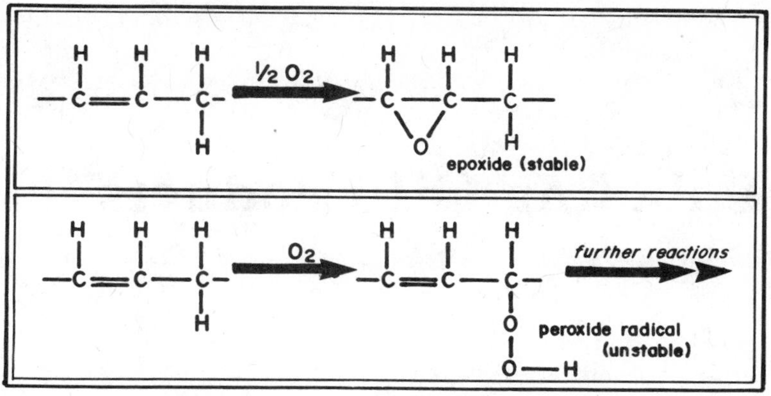

Figure 36. Epoxide and peroxide of a fatty acid.

essential, monounsaturated OA (18:1*w*9).

Because of these differences in reactivity, flax oil will keep about 3 months in the cool and closed container, and after opening, should be used up within 2-3 weeks. Safflower, sunflower, sesame, and pumpkin oils will keep for 9 to 12 months in the cool and closed container, and should be used up within 2 to 3 months after opening. Olive oil will keep for up to 2 years in the cool and closed container, and should be used up within 9 months of opening. Walnut oil and soy oil are less sensitive than flax oil because they contain less LNA, but are more sensitive than the oils containing only LA. The most sensitive LA-containing oils are those which contain the most LA. Fats which contain only or mostly saturated fatty acids are much more stable, although they too spoil, albeit slowly[1].

Nutritionally, flax oil is the most valuable, and the nutritional value is proportional to the rate at which the oil spoils. The best oils spoil fastest. Here is the reason why nutritionist and manufacturer are headed in different directions in the oil trade. The manufacturer wants oils that won't spoil, but which aren't good for us. The nutritionist wants oils which are good for us because they contain the essential fatty acids, but which spoil easily. There is a saying among nutritionists and nutritional therapists, which goes: 'Eat things that spoil, but eat them before they do.' The person who coined that saying was probably thinking of fresh vegetables, but the saying applies equally well to the edible oils.

25

Labeling Oil Products

Introduction

We now know some of the destructive processes to which oils may be subjected on their journey from mother nature to your stomach. As a summary to this section, we will look at how, in the best of all possible worlds, fats and oils products might be labeled to help consumers make informed choices in their purchases of these food items. In the best of all possible worlds, what would the labels tell us?

Essential Fatty Acid Content

Since the essential fatty acids LA and LNA are of prime importance in the maintenance of health, labels of all edible oils and fats and products containing them would list the amounts of all *cis-* LA and all *cis-* LNA in the finished product in grams per 100 grams of fat or oil substance in the product. The consumer would then know that any product containing less LA than 5g/100g of oil or fat is useless, and that any product containing less LA than 8g/100g is nutritionally deficient in LA. A good product has at least 25g of LA per 100g. Thirty-three percent or more of LA is recommended. LNA content should be at least 1/5 of LA content (see: Essential Fatty Acids).

Trans- Fatty Acids and Other Altered Fat Products

Since the *trans-* fatty acids act against the essential fatty acids, interfere with their functions and make essential fatty acid deficiency more severe, each edible product would list the amount of *trans-* fatty acid isomers present in grams per 100 grams of product. The health-conscious consumer would then know to buy only products containing no *trans-* fatty acids (see: Trans- Fatty Acids). Other altered fat molecules, such as positional isomers, dimers and polymers of fatty acids, and breakdown products of fatty acids such as aldehydes, ketones, epoxides, and alcohols are also dangerous, and so it might be a good idea to list the total amount of altered fat substances on the label, in grams per 100 grams.

Maximum Temperature Reached

The highest temperature to which the seed and oil have been subjected during the processing procedures used to manufacture the finished product would be good information to have on the label. The consumer would then be able to choose between oils that have been processed at non-destructive temperatures (below 50° C) and oils processed at higher temperatures resulting in very much higher rates of oil destruction. It is misleading to just call an oil 'cold-pressed' (see: Cold-Pressed Oils). It is important to know exactly how hot that 'cold-pressed' oil has actually been.

Exclusion of Light and Air

Whether light and air were excluded during the whole processing, filling, and storage of the product would be nice to know. The consumer could then choose between natural and deteriorated products. Oils in transparent bottles (even brown ones) are exposed to destruction by light (see: Containers and Storage).

Date of Pressing

The date of pressing (or an expiry date) would be good to have printed on the label. By the age of the product, the consumer would know how fresh the product is, and could avoid age-deteriorated products, if he so desired. Depending on what kind of oil it is, essential fatty acids-containing oils might stay reasonably fresh and edible for 3 months to 12 months in an unopened container, and from 2 weeks to 3 months in an opened one. Skin preparations containing essential fatty acids deteriorate in about 6 months.

Mechanically Pressed or Chemically Extracted

The label, in this best of all possible worlds, would state whether the oil was mechanically pressed or chemically extracted. The consumer knows that mechanically pressed oil contains no traces of chemical solvents (see: Oil Making).

Crude or Refined

The label would state whether the oil was degummed, bleached, deodorized or otherwise refined. The consumer would know that crude oils which are completely unrefined, still contain many of the co-factors required for the metabolism of the oil, and therefore do not rob the body of essential nutrients (see: Oil Making).

Hydrogenation

Whether the oil was hydrogenated is important to keep on the label. The consumer knows that hydrogenated oils and fats contain *trans-* fatty acids and other altered molecules. If health was the consumer's concern, he could stick to non-hydrogenated products.

Organic or Non-Organic

Whether the seeds were organically grown would be stated on the label in this best of all possible worlds. The consumer knows that only oil from organic seeds is guaranteed free of pesticides. Many pesticides are oil-soluble, and can be kept out of foods only if they have not been used on them.

In a free market economy, a manufacturer is free to offer for sale to the public many kinds and qualities of products, and the public is free to buy or to refuse any product available. If the suggested information is present on the label of the oil products, it is then possible for the public to know what kinds and qualities of products are available. With this information, consumers can take full responsibility for their choices and their health. But to make responsible choices, they need that information.

SECTION THREE

Fats And Figures

The Human Body

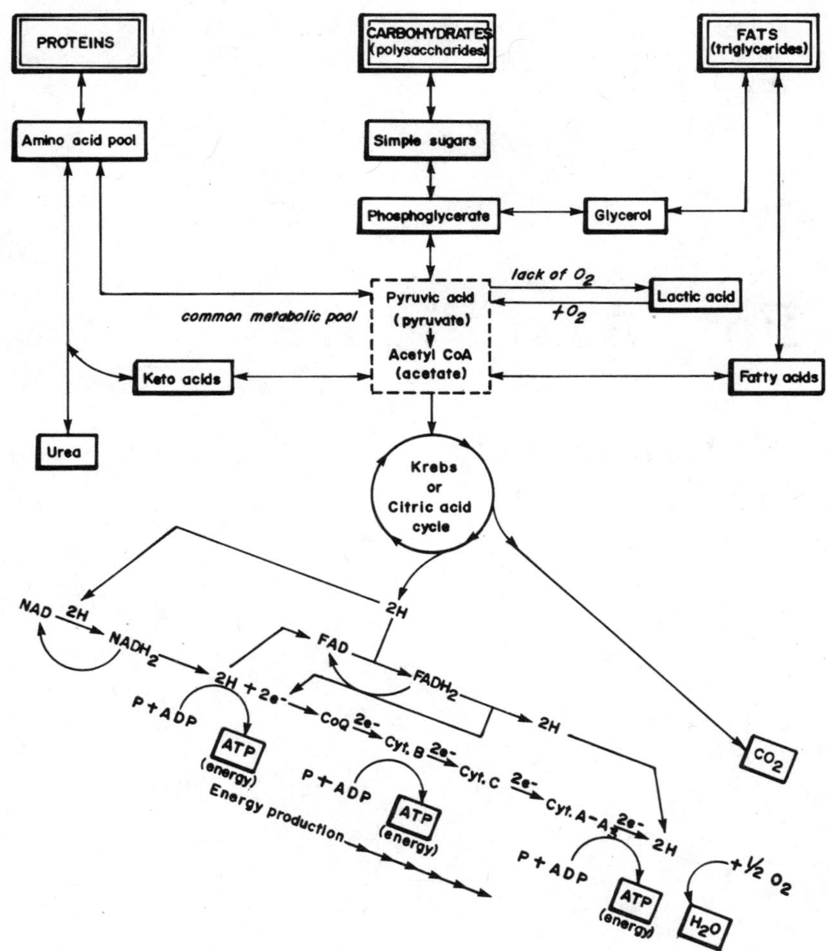

This flowchart shows the main steps (pathways) by which foods release energy. Each step is enzymatically catalyzed. The end products are water and carbon dioxide.

26

Body Fat

Statistics

Next to water, which makes up roughly 70% of the total weight of an adult human being and 84% of that of a newborn infant, fat is the most abundant substance found in the human body. You may not like it, but there it is. However, the exact amount of fat present in the body is influenced by diet, exercise, age, gender, and genetic disposition, and can vary from 5 to over 60%, with an average of 15 to 22%. Degenerative disease is associated with both overweight and underweight.

Diet. Diets high in calories from any source, i.e., diets high in refined sugars, or starches, or proteins, or saturated fats tend to put on fat (the extra 'weight' is plain old fat), whereas diets high in fiber, leafy vegetables, and bulk tend to keep one slim. Concentrated foods of all types increase fat deposition.

Exercise. Athletes like to be more trim than the average, because there's no point in carrying around extra weight during competition. Male swimmers trim down to 12% fat, and runners down to 8%. Women athletes usually trim down to around 15%. Carla Temple, a world class body builder is even more trim, at

12% fat between competitions, and goes down to 6% body fat during competition, for better visibility of muscle profile. Although it is possible for women to lose most of their fat, this may not be desirable from a health point of view, as low body fat may affect female hormonal balance and stop the menstrual cycle. This often occurs in Olympic and other athletes. It is also one of the diagnostic symptoms of the eating disorder known as anorexia nervosa.

Overweight people who want to reduce, can lose their excess fat by building muscle rather than by trying to take off fat. This is the key to successful slimming through exercise. During exercise the muscles consume the fat which surrounds them. The stomach muscles eat the belly fat, the buttock muscles eat the buttock fat, etc. Wherever you want to lose the fat, the muscles in that area of your body need to be exercised. Since muscle weighs more than fat, exercising might increase your weight rather than decrease it, but the exercised body looks and feels better. Your bathroom scales are therefore less reliable than your eyes and inner feeling.

Age. Body fat content tends to increase with age, although this is not inevitable. In some cultures, such as that of the natives of the South Sea Islands, the old are as slim as the young, and as active and child-like. Their unrefined diet as well as their sunny disposition and simple life style has a lot to do with their ability to remain slim into old age.

Sexual Differences. On the average, fat accounts for about 15% of the total weight of a man, and about 22% of the weight of woman. The tendency of woman to carry more fat than man evolved during the ice age or even more primitive times, when one of the primary roles of woman was producing offspring in living conditions characterized by fluctuating food supplies. It was important for her to carry on her body all the energy (stored as fat) necessary to complete the fetus' growth, even if the food ran out. Now that food supplies are more stable, the climate is warmer, and procreation is no longer her main purpose, woman still carries the genes and hormones adapted for survival of the species in the ice age, perhaps in preparation for the next one. The female hormones are responsible for the extra fat that women carry, but these hormones also protect women from deleterious cardiovascular effects associated with excess fat in men. As a result of this hormonal difference, women suffer heart attacks and strokes less than 1/3 as often as men, until the female hormones change after the menopause. After that, women gradually become as prone as men to cardiovascular disease. For men, 23% of the body weight as fat is considered the edge of obesity; for women, 32% is considered the edge.

Genes. Some people, because of genetic mutations, have problems with fat metabolism, which lead to excessive fat deposition. But since such mutations are relatively rare, occurring at a maximum of 5 per 1,000 in the population, most of us cannot hide behind our genes on this one. About 300 to 500 per 1,000 of the adult North Americans are overweight (European figures are comparable), mostly because of poor diet and inadequate exercise.

Comparisons. Compared to fats at 15% of body weight, proteins constitute a fairly constant 12% of the weights of both men and women, less than fat on the average. Excess proteins are converted into stored fat. Carbohydrates make up a mere .5% of body weight. Sugar in the blood and tissues, and muscles and liver stores of glycogen are included in this figure. Any carbohydrates above this low level are turned into fat. Minerals are about 3.5% of body weight.

On the average then, fat is the most abundant body component next to water. Nature chose wisely to store energy reserves in this efficient way. Each gram of fat stores more than twice as much energy as the same weight of protein or carbohydrates. Furthermore, while most cells contain about 70% water, fat cells contain up to 70% fat. Thus fat and fat cells are an extremely economic and efficient way of storing energy for further use. Fat tissue stores more cholesterol than other body tissues, except for brain, whose content of cholesterol is very high.

Fatty Acid Content of Body Fat

The fatty acids contained in body fat varies greatly in different parts of the world, a direct consequence of the differing contents of saturated (long and short chain), monounsaturated, and essential fatty acids found in different diets. Table C1 gives the percentages of linoleic acid (LA, 18:2*w*6) and linolenic acid (LNA, 18:3*w*3) found in the fat tissues of various groups of people.

Three interesting points emerge from this information. First, in both tissue samples from people living in hot, sunny, dry climates (New Zealand, and Africa), low fat tissue levels of LA and LNA occur in keeping with the low occurrence of LA and LNA in their food supply. Neither Maoris or Hottentots are especially prone to degenerative diseases (see: Oil and Sunlight), but, on the other hand, neither are known for longevity, either. We'll have to

	% 18:2w6	% 18:3w3	
New Zealand Maoris	2.6	.93	
Hottentot	5.9	.6	
obese American	8.7	1.1	
normal American	10.2	.58	
American students	17.3	2.0	
Israeli students	22.1	2.4	
Japanese (surgery)	14.8	1.2	+ 2% w3 long
Japanese	16.5	.97	chain fatty acids
Leipzig normal	7.9	1.5	
British omnivores	11.0	2.1	
British vegans	25.4	2.4	

Table C1. Essential fatty acids in human body fat.

reserve judgement on the meaning of these figures until more information becomes available.

Second, in the cooler temperate areas, obese people, who are prone to degenerative diseases, consistently have levels of less than 10% LA in their adipose tissue, and adult American people generally have only about 10% LA in their fat tissues.

Third, the people in temperate regions who have the least degenerative diseases (Japanese, British vegans, strict vegetarians) have much higher than average levels of LA as well as LNA in their fatty tissues. Several present-day popular writers in nutrition warn that high levels of polyunsaturates in the diet may increase the chance of cancer. The evidence does not bear this out. If the polyunsaturates are fried, oxidized by light or oxygen, hydrogenated, or processed at high temperatures — in other words, if the essential fatty acids in the oils are destroyed — then they may indeed increase the incidence of cancer. It is important to distinguish between the health-destroying kinds of polyunsaturates and the essential fatty acids, which are health-enhancing (see: Polyunsaturates).

Changing the Body Fat Picture

How can we change the fat content of the body? To increase the amount of essential fatty acids in our fat tissue, which is desirable for both beauty (they soften the skin) and for health (they decrease our risk of degenerative diseases), we simply decrease our intake of excess calories, especially refined sugar, refined starches, and saturated (hard) sticky fats, and increase our intake of essential fatty acids from sources such as fresh flax, pumpkin seeds and walnuts, as well as soy beans or their fresh oils which have not been destroyed by heat in processing, by light on the shelf, or by oxygen or by frying in the home. Sunflower and sesame seeds, in combination with fatty cold water fish, also provide both essential fatty acids. Increasing the bulky foods in our diet provides an easy way to cut down on the calories we consume. Bulky foods are less concentrated in calories, and spend less time sitting around in our intestines. Our very efficient digestive mechanism therefore absorbs less unnecessary calories.

When I start putting on fat, I don't cut out entirely any of the foods that I like. I just change proportions. I go easier on cheese, meat, bread, sugar, and pasta, and hit the salads harder. Instead of using the sprig of parsley to garnish the meat, I use a little meat to garnish the salad. It works like a charm. More natural fiber-rich foods, and less processed, concentrated foods. For example, it is impossible to gain weight on a diet of broccoli and supplements. It requires over 6 kg (or over 13 lbs) of broccoli to get 2,000 calories, and hardly anybody can eat 6 kg of anything. We can also get 2,000 calories from 4.75 kg of carrots, 7.7 kg of spinach, over 14 kg of lettuce, 7.4 kg of cauliflower, or 13 kg of cucumbers. But less than 1 kg of cheese (.571 kg), chocolate chip cookies (.378 kg), beef (.476 kg), wheat (.606 kg), pork (.371 kg), beans, peas or lentils (.588 kg), soy beans (.497 kg), or peanuts (.355 kg) give the same 2,000 calories, and these amounts are easy to 'put away' in a day. The average adult U.S. male eats about 2.7 kg, and the average U.S. female eats about 1.8 kg of food per day.

Since the essential fatty acids increase the metabolic rate, they are preferable to the saturated fats, which slow down the metabolic rate, depositing more fat, and making us feel lazy and unenergetic. A good supplement of vitamins and minerals also helps to increase metabolism and increases vitality, so these are highly recommended. Perhaps a little fiber added to the foods is also in order.

Exercise burns off calories, speeds up metabolic rate, and invigorates. It is easier to exercise if we feel like exercising, but this should be no problem if the nutritional balance is up to scratch. Diet and exercise go hand in hand. Each one builds the other and each makes the other both fun and worth maintaining. Together, they make us feel energetic, adventurous and full of pep.

Overweight is associated with every kind of degenerative disease. Too little body fat also makes us prone to disease, because our reserves run out sooner in times of stress. The middle road leads to health.

27

Fat Consumption and Daily Requirement

Statistics

According to 1979 figures, the average person in the U.S. ate 135 lbs (61 kg) of fats that year, about 168 grams per day. The consumed fat was made up of 34% saturated, 40% monounsaturated, and 15% polyunsaturated fatty acids. The information did not distinguish between the essential fatty acids (EFAs) and non-essential, altered, denatured, and toxic polyunsaturates (see: Polyunsaturates). The amount of EFAs left after hydrogenation, exposure to destruction by light, and frying in the home may be as low as 2 to 3% and even some of this is unavailable for its important functions in the body because saturated and monounsaturated long-chain fatty acids, *trans-* fatty acids, and sugars present in the diet interfere with the ability of the EFAs to function. The rate of fat consumption has been increasing by about 1 pound per person per year for the last 10 years.

According to Nutrition Reviews (1984), fat calories make up about 42% of all the calories consumed in the Western diet, but 168 grams per day is closer to 56% of the average daily calories (168 grams fat, multiplied by 9 calories per gram is 1,512 calories, which is over half of the 2,500 calories consumed daily by the average adult person). High fat diets result in faster growth, earlier sexual maturity (from 17 years old at first menstruation in the 17th century, down to 13 years now), and earlier aging and death.

Nutrition Reviews also states that 15 to 25 grams of fat, or 5 to 8% of total calories, is all that is required daily, if it is the right kind of fat. The author does not say what the right kind of fat might be.

In some countries such as Thailand (27g/day), the Philippines (30g/day), Japan (40g/day), and Taiwan (45g/day), fat consumption is indeed, very much lower than it is in Western countries such as Denmark (160 g/day), New Zealand (155g/day), U.K. (142g/day), the U.S. (168g/day), and Canada (142/g/day). The people in the nations consuming a low fat diet have a low incidence of fatty degeneration, and the high fat diet nations, a very high incidence of fatty degeneration.

Recommendations

Several official bodies in the U.S., including the National Academy of Sciences, the Senate Select Committee on Health and Nutrition, the American Heart Association, and the National Research Council have all recommended decreasing our consumption of fats in order to improve our health. Their general recommendation is that only 30% of our calories should come from fats, and that the fats should be divided equally between saturated, monounsaturated, and essential fatty acids, at 10% each. No doubt this change would bring an improvement in the health of the people of Western nations. But the people in the nations with the lowest incidence of fatty degeneration, like Japan, consume only about 15% of their calories as fat, indicating that 30% of calories as fat is still too high.

Researchers at the Loma Linda School of Nutrition, less bound to the fats and oils industry, and inclined toward vegetarianism by their Seventh Day Adventist heritage, have studied the diets of vegetarians and other groups of people around the globe, and have concluded that 15 to 20% of total calories as fats is the optimum, and that this should be made up of no more than 4% saturated fatty acids, that linoleic acid (LA, 18:2*w*6) should be around 6% and that the remaining 5 to 10% should be monounsaturated. They give no figures for linolenic acid (LNA, 18:3*w*3) which is also essential. They have found that fat consumption at around 5% or less of total calories compromises the absorption of the fat-soluble vitamins A, D, E, and K and leads to increased occurrence of blindness and cancer, both probably the result of lack of vitamin A, and possibly E in the body.

Individual researchers have recommended that as much as 20% of total calories should be the essential linoleic acid (LA, 18:2*w*6). This seems high, except for people with severe cardiovascular problems stemming from atherosclerosis. In this case, the high intake of LA appears to help to take down the fatty deposits in the arteries. But more highly unsaturated fatty acids including linolenic acid (18:3*w*3), eicosapentaenoic acid (20:5*w*3), and docosahexaenoic acid (22:6*w*3) are even more effective for this purpose.

Dr. Nathan Pritikin, who directed the Centre for Longevity in California, recommends that 10% of calories as fats is the absolute maximum allowed. His experience comes from treating people with obesity and cardiovascular problems, and his diet, which contains only 7% of calories as fat, is quite effective for restoring his type of patient to health. In the long run however, as a regular diet to maintain health, this diet is too low in fats[1] and too low in vitamins and minerals (he does not use supplements). Many of his former patients cheat. His program of diet (80% complex carbohydrates, 10% protein, and 10% fat) and exercise (a lot of walking) is calorie-restricted, and lowers blood cholesterol levels by 25%. But his diet contains only 10 units of vitamin E, which is less than the very low recommended minimum daily requirement of 15 units set by the government (vitamin E is required, among other things, to protect the highly unsaturated fatty acids in the brain). Furthermore, when Pritikin claims that even lettuce contains 7% fats and that therefore getting enough fats cannot be a problem (we know every food contains more fat than lettuce!), he is stretching the point. According to the U.S. Dept. of Agriculture's Handbook on the Composition of Foods, lettuce contains about .2% (between .1 and .3%) fats, depending on the variety. Common sense tells us that lettuce is extremely low in fats[2]. To get our *minimum* daily requirement of fats (15-25 g/d) from lettuce, we'd have to eat between 15 and 25 kg of this vegetable. Only a cow could do that.

Other research reported in the scientific literature, and adopted by the World Health Organization, sets the requirement for LA at 3% of calories for children and adults, at 4.5% during pregnancy and at 6% during lactation, but makes no recommendation about the intake of saturated and monounsaturated fatty acids, nor about the intake of the essential LNA.

No one, except the manufacturers of fat-containing products, encourages us to increase our consumption of fats; and of course, our health is not the motive in this case.

The fact that overweight is one of the major factors which increases the risk of cardiovascular disease, cancer, and diabetes, and that overweight is almost always fat (Arnold Schwarzenegger is also overweight, but *his* overweight is muscle, and he is healthy) makes it clear that we need to decrease our consumption of fats and of calories from sugars and starches in order to come down to our ideal weight, and in order to enjoy our ideal health. 15-20% of calories as fats, with 1/3 of this as LA, and not more than 1/3 as saturated fatty acids is a strong step in that direction. 20% of calories as fats is only 10% of the weight of our food, since fats store twice as many calories as an equal weight of protein and carbohydrates.

There is also a good reason for decreasing our consumption of (saturated) fats from land animal sources. Fat tissue contains more cholesterol than lean body tissue and therefore increases the cholesterol load carried in the 'dangerous' low density lipoprotein (LDL) fraction in the blood. The body's capacity for metabolizing the LDL appears to be limited, and by present-day nutritional standards, the body requires 2.5 days after the meal to remove the cholesterol from the blood stream. This suggests that unless other aspects of our diet (e.g. vitamin and mineral intake) change, we should eat our usual kinds of cholesterol containing foods only about every 3 days, in order to give the body time to metabolize it completely and to avoid the build-up of cholesterol in arterial linings.

Requirement for the Essential Fatty Acids

LA (18:2*w*6). About 1% of daily calories (about 3 grams in a 2,500 calorie diet) as LA is enough to relieve the symptoms of LA deficiency, and therefore constitutes a minimum daily requirement for LA. But this is not the optimum dose, which is probably around 6% (or 18 grams/day), with a range between 5 and 10% for different individuals (see: Individuality).

LNA (18:3*w*3). The daily requirement for LNA is less well known. The only case of LNA deficiency described in the journals is that of a 6-year-old girl, who required .54% of daily calories as LNA in order to reverse the symptoms of LNA deficiency. The optimum for LNA is unknown, but can be guessed at. Eskimoes consumed 2% or more of their daily calories as EPA (20:5*w*3) and DHA (22:6*w*3), both of which are made from LNA. The optimum for LNA may be around this figure. Several other traditional diets associated with good health also contain around 2% of calories as LNA, and so this figure has been suggested as optimum. People taking fresh flax oil in the treatment of cancer according to Dr. Budwig's method (see: The Oil-Protein Combination), may easily consume 100 grams of fresh flax oil (mixed with 250 grams skim milk kwark, containing 40-50 grams protein) daily for a while, until the tumour is dissolved. This much flax oil contains about 60 grams of LNA, or about 20% of daily calories. No side effects are seen at this dosage. As health is re-established, the urge to eat this much flax oil slowly subsides.

Other required factors. A well balanced diet, containing selenium, vitamin E, cysteine, and other antioxidant vitamins and minerals is important to keep the LNA from oxidizing. Supplements are advisable, although Dr. Budwig does not use them. Instead, she insists that her patients adhere to a *very strict* diet of at least 50% fresh, raw, vegetables, fruits, and nuts, a restricted selection of especially high-nutrient foods, only whole grain products (whole wheat flour is not whole grain), and complete avoidance of fats and oils other than flax and trout until their health is re-established.

28

Digestion of Fats and Oils

Mouth to Bowel

What happens in our bodies to the fats and oils we eat? In the mouth, nothing, and in the stomach almost nothing happens. There is an enzyme in the stomach which can split fats into their components, but this enzyme is inactive under the normal acid conditions of the stomach. The small intestine can digest about 10 grams of food fats every hour. That's its maximum capacity. Figure 37 shows where in the human digestive system digestion and absorption of fats take place. Fat digestion occurs in several stages.

Bile

First the churning action of the intestines mixes the fatty food material with bile, which the liver made out of cholesterol, then stored and concentrated in the gall bladder[1]. The bile emulsifies the fatty material, breaking it into tiny droplets. This increases the surface area of fat exposed to fat-digesting enzymes, and speeds up the rate at which the fatty material can be digested by these enzymes. The fat-digesting enzymes are made by the pancreas and released into the food mixture in the first part of the small

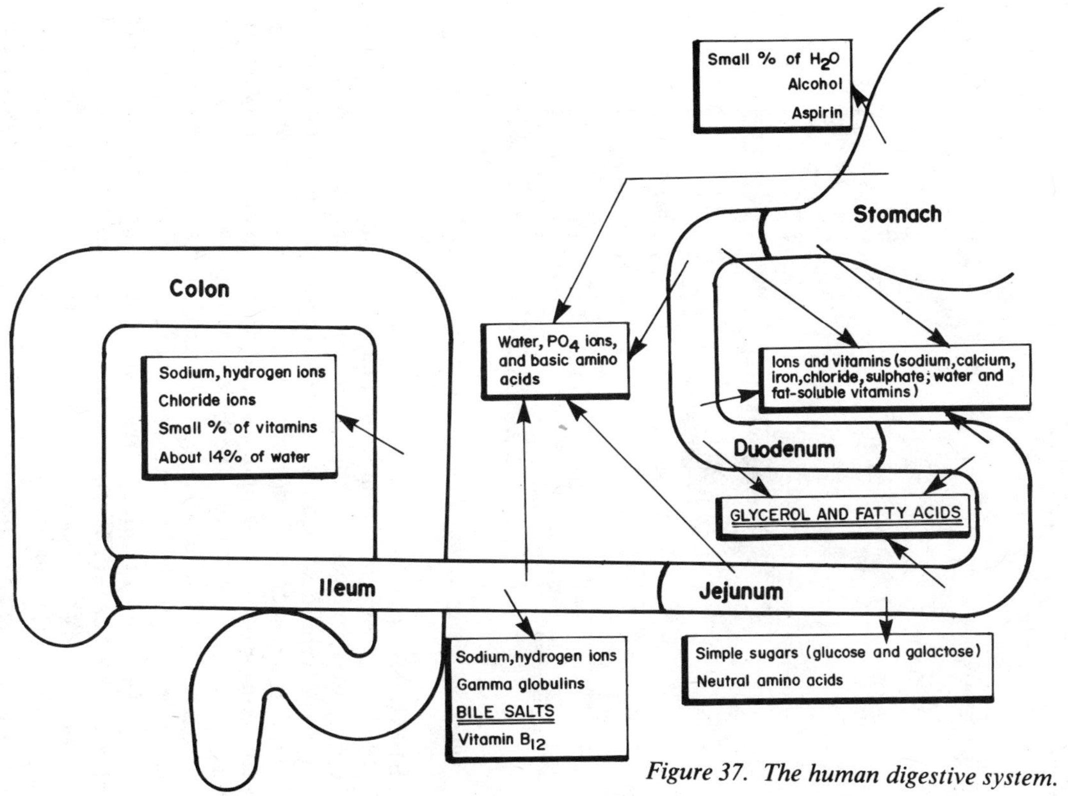

Figure 37. The human digestive system.

intestine, the duodenum. Digestion and absorption of fats takes place as the food passes through the small intestine. Figure 38 shows a cross-section through the intestinal wall.

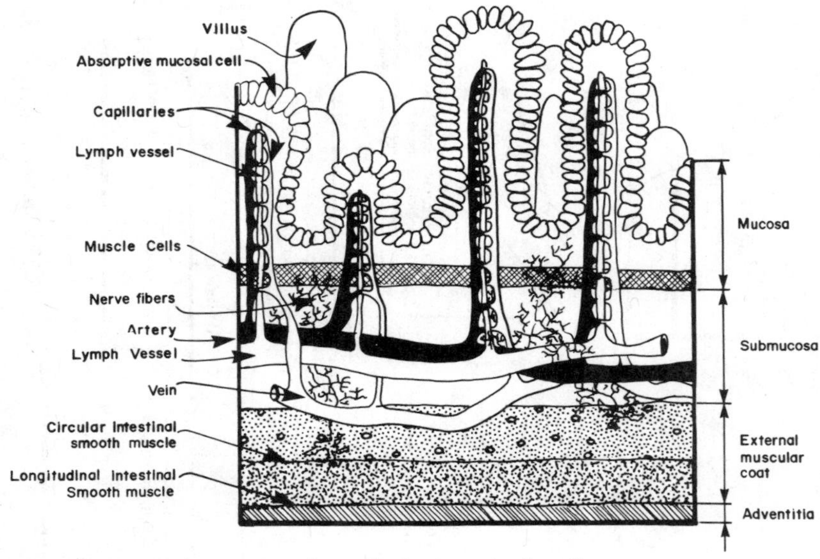

Figure 38. Cross-section through the intestinal wall.

Enzymes

Different enzymes contained in the alkaline pancreatic juice digest the triglycerides, the phopholipids, and the cholesterol esters present in the food fats[2]. These enzymes split the fatty acids from the outside carbon positions of the glycerol molecules in triglycerides and phospholipids, and they remove fatty acids attached to cholesterol. The bits and pieces are then absorbed separately into the cells lining the intestinal tract (mucosal cells), where they are put back together. Free fatty acids may also be hooked up with albumin protein, and taken directly to the liver for further metabolism. Figure 39 summarizes the steps by which fats are digested, absorbed by mucosal cells, re-assembled and carried into the lymph and blood fluids.

It might seem pointless to take apart the food fats, just to put them back together, but it is really quite clever. By breaking down the molecules, the body makes sure that complex chemical substances[3] from other species of animals or plants don't get into

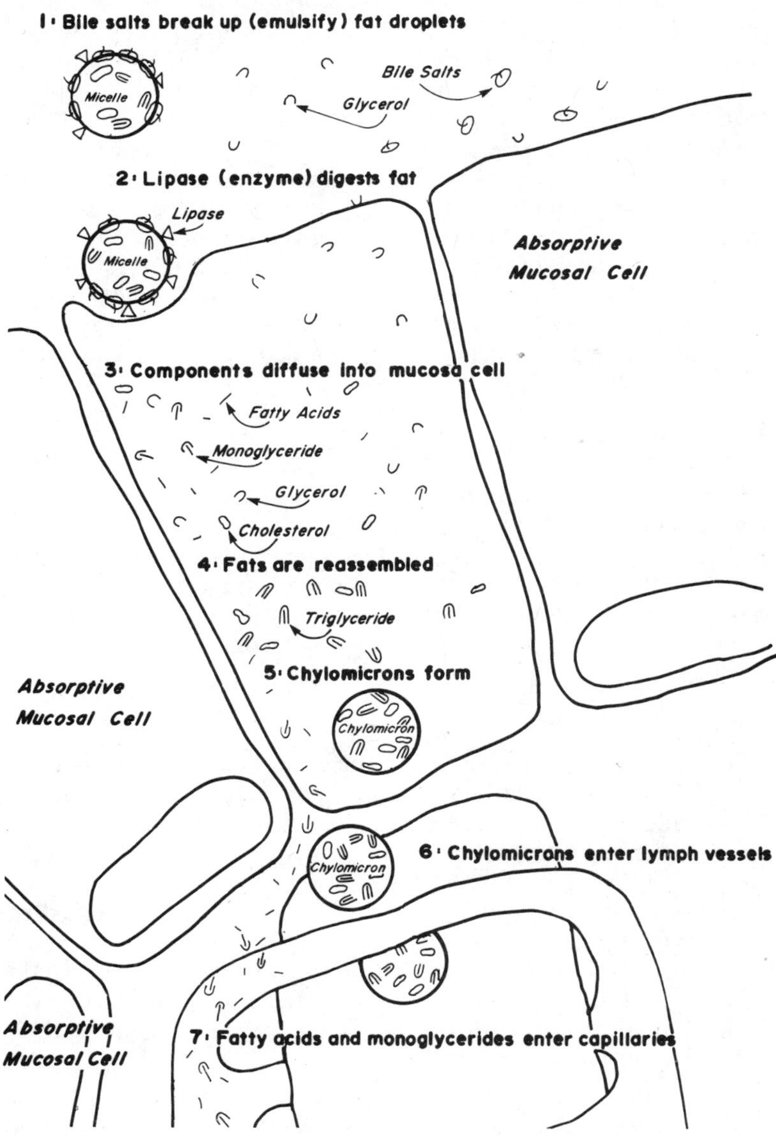

Figure 39. Digestion and absorption of fats.

our blood. Were this to happen, an alarm reaction would be set off, and several different kinds of white blood cells, the soldiers among our cells, would mobilize and destroy the 'intruder' molecules. It would be wasteful to call out the army every time we eat something, and so the precaution taken is to disassemble the molecules into their component parts to avoid such a problem from occurring. When, due to mechanical or biochemical injury or biochemical (nutritional) deficiency, foreign substances do get into our bodies, our immune system makes war on these substances, and builds a standing army of antibodies against future intrusions by the same foreign substance. The result? Anytime we eat the food or synthetic substance in question, we break out in hives, manifest various physical and mental symptoms, or in extreme cases, go into anaphylactic shock, which can be fatal. These reactions can occur in food allergies and other allergic conditions.

Chylomicrons

In the mucosal cells, transport vehicles called chylomicrons (fat droplets) are built. Out of proteins and phospholipids, a membrane or bag is made, and the reconstituted food fats are stuffed into this bag. The loaded bags, now called chylomicrons, are dumped into the lymphatic vessels[4], which ship them to a large vein close to the heart, where they merge into the blood stream. The heart then pumps the blood containing the chylomicrons to all parts of the body.

Lipoproteins

The chylomicrons never reach the cells. They transfer their fat material to the high density lipoproteins (HDL) circulating in the blood, and both HDL and empty chylomicron remnants are taken to the liver. The liver makes smaller transport vehicles called very low density lipoproteins (VLDL). These too, exchange material with HDL, or they can be transformed into other vehicles called low density lipoproteins (LDL), which still can exchange material with the HDL (see: Blood Cholesterol). VLDL and LDL, containing fats and cholesterol, are carried by the blood to the cells. Figure 40 illustrates the transport vehicles and their relationships to one another.

Each one of the body's 3 trillion cells has on its membrane, several 'docks' for receiving and unloading from the VLDL and LDL, the fats and cholesterol the cell requires for its functions.

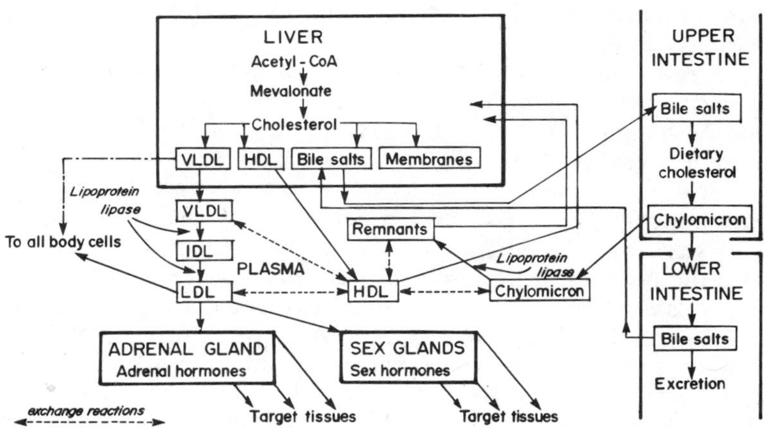

Figure 40. Transport of and interaction between fat and cholesterol carrying vehicles.

When the requirement is filled, the docks are shut down. Excess fats and cholesterol from foods continue to circulate in the blood (high blood triglyceride and cholesterol levels are the measurable result) until they are metabolized by the liver or taken to fat cells for storage.

Fatty acids serve as the fuel for the mitochondria (the cells' energy-producing factories); phospholipids and cholesterol are incorporated into the membranes according to need; some triglycerides are kept in reserve as fat in the cells. Excess fats not needed by the cells are transported to the fat depots around the organs or the body, and stored there for later use.

The fats that the HDL pick up from the other transport vehicles are taken to the liver and further metabolized. HDL is the 'good', and LDL the 'bad' component of the 'blood cholesterol', and both are important in cardiovascular health and disease (see: Blood Cholesterol).

Regulation and Control

This extremely complex lipoprotein system makes sure that the fats are digested, absorbed into the body, get transported to the cells, that the cells get supplied with the fats they need, and that excess fats don't build up in the blood stream. This system is also responsible for removing excess cholesterol from the cells to the liver. The liver converts cholesterol into bile salts, pours the bile into the intestine to aid in fat digestion, and by this route gets rid of excess cholesterol through the stool.

There are many points of regulation and control that ensure the proper functioning of the lipoprotein system. It is sensitive to the body's changing needs for fats and cholesterol, and balances these needs against the fluctuating food intake of these two substances.

The lipoprotein system works very effectively except when it is continuously being overloaded with excess fats, sugars, or cholesterol, overloaded or disrupted by substances that interfere with the system's operation or by deficiency of the vitamins and minerals required for the many steps involved in the processes of fat, sugar, and cholesterol metabolism.

There are some oils, such as castor oil and mineral oil, that the body does not digest or absorb at all. Rancid oils have toxic effects, from which the body protects itself by not digesting and absorbing them well. Rancid and spoiled oils cause problems in our intestines on the way through, by irritating the delicate intestinal lining and perhaps feeding unfriendly organisms in our intestines.

In one sense, it is the marvellous efficiency of the system for digesting and absorbing fats that causes the problems which we experience when we eat over-rich, over-fat, over-sweetened, and over-processed foods. Realistically, we cannot blame the digestive system for digesting what we put into our mouths. Digestion is, after all, its purpose. If we are dissatisfied with the results of the work that the digestive system is doing, then we, as its employer, can change what we give it to work with.

29

Metabolism of Fats and Oils

Definition

The chemical changes which food molecules undergo in all of their functions in the body, for energy production, growth, maintenance, and repair of body structures, are included in the study of metabolism. We have already looked at digestion, absorption, and transport, all of which are aspects of metabolism (see: Digestion). A discussion of fat metabolism includes how fats and oils are broken down for energy, how fats are made, what other substances useful to the body they are transformed into, and how finally they are destroyed and discarded. Thus, the study of fat metabolism concerns itself with the birth, life, death, and disintegration of fat molecules.

The components of fats: glycerol, saturated fatty acids, mono-unsaturated fatty acids, and essential fatty acids, are each used differently in the body, so we will consider the metabolism of each separately.

Glycerol

The glycerol backbone of the fats can be used to make glucose when the body's supply runs down. All that is required is to modify the molecule slightly (to something called pyruvate), and then to hook 2 of these together.

In the opposite direction, glucose can be split in half to make 2 glycerol molecules. These are produced when the body needs to make triglycerides for storage out of excess sugars absorbed from the diet.

Saturated Fatty Acids (SFAs)

The body breaks down saturated fatty acids to produce the energy necessary for the chemical reactions that maintain life. Besides their presence in membranes, where they help to form the basic membrane structure, this is the main function of SFAs. An enzyme within the cells snips successive 2-carbon fragments (called acetates) off the acid end of the SFA molecules (the process is called beta-oxidation), and injects these fragments into the cells' main energy-producing factory (scientists call it the Krebs or tricarboxylic acid cycle), which 'burns' them into carbon dioxide, water, and energy. The energy drives the bio-chemical reactions which build and maintain our body structures, or it dissipates as heat, which keeps us warm. Too little fuel in the Krebs cycle 'fire' gives the signal for beta-oxidation of fats to begin, to supply added fuel to keep the fire going.

Short chain SFAs such as those found in butter and coconut oil, 'burn' better than long chain (16 or more carbon atoms) SFAs found in beef, mutton, and pork. The latter also interfere with important reactions involving the essential fatty acids, and lower the metabolic rate and our vitality.

When there is too much protein or, more usually, refined sugars or starches in the diet, excess 2-carbon acetate fragments are formed, and must be taken out of the energy factory to prevent the Krebs cycle 'fire' from burning too hot. SFAs are synthesized out of the excess acetate fragments, by hooking them end to end, and are stored as body fat.

The body makes enzymes which can insert a *cis*- double bond into long chain SFAs, and at the same time, removing two hydrogen atoms. The molecules are bent at the *cis*- double bond carbons, and because they now stack together less well, their melting point goes down, which makes them more liquid than SFAs (see: Unsaturated Fatty Acids). For example, stearic acid (SA,18:0) an 18 carbon SFA is changed into oleic acid (OA, 18:1*w*9) by inserting a *cis*- double bond between carbon atoms 9 and 10 and removing a hydrogen atom from each of these carbons. The result? SA, which melts at 70° C, is hard at room (20° C) and body (37° C) temperatures. OA melts at 13° C, and is liquid at both temperatures. SA makes platelets more sticky and more likely to form flow-impeding clots in blood vessels, and therefore increases the risk of stroke or heart attack. OA does not have this effect. Thus, the body's ability to insert that *cis-* double bond into SA can save your life. The double bond also gives each OA molecule a slight negative charge and since like charges repel, this prevents the oil molecules from aggregating, further helping to prevent clots.

The enzymes in the human body which insert double bonds in fatty acid chains insert them only into positions *w*7, *w*9, *w*12, *w*15, etc., but are unable to insert double bonds into positions *w*6 and *w*3 (where double bonds are found in the essential fatty acids). These enzymes therefore cannot turn SFAs into essential fatty acids. Because of this inability of the human enzymes, and because, nevertheless, our bodies require them, linoleic acid (LA, 18:2*w*6) and linolenic acid (LNA, 18:3*w*3), with the double bonds at *w*6, and *w*6 and *w*3[1] respectively, are essential fatty acids. It is necessary that they be present in our diet.

As double bonds are inserted into saturated fatty acids, hydrogen atoms are released into the system. The body has mechanisms to snag these hydrogens.

Although exact measurements have not been published, the body's ability to insert double bonds into the long chain SFAs may be limited. A high rate of consumption of the sticky saturated fatty acids (and the longer the chain, the stickier they are) leads to blood vessel degeneration, clots, heart attacks, and strokes, as well as pulmonary embolism, circulatory problems of the extremities, and blindness in diabetes (see: Saturated Fatty Acids).

Monounsaturated Fatty Acids (MUFAs)

Monounsaturated fatty acids can also be chopped down to produce energy in the same way and by the same enzymes that do this with the saturated fatty acids.

MUFAs can be made by inserting a double bond into a saturated fatty acid built out of 2-carbon fragments, as explained above. When there is a deficiency of essential fatty acids, several double bonds may be inserted into the 16 or 18 carbon MUFAs to make them up to 3 or 4 times unsaturated. At the same time, they are also lengthened to 20 carbon fatty acids. Mead acid (20:3*w*9) is the most common of the products made from MUFAs. They pinch-hit for the missing essential fatty acids, but are unable to do so successfully. The presence in the body of a high concentration of these pinch-hitting molecules compared to the concentration of essential fatty acid products is the most commonly measured indicator of essential fatty acid deficiency (see: Essential Fatty Acids).

The fibers (called axons) of brain and nerve cells contain enzymes which lengthen 18 carbon MUFAs up to 24 carbon atoms without inserting any more double bonds. The insulation around each axon is made from these long chain MUFAs[2]. Nervonic acid (24:1*w*9) is one such fatty acid.

Essential Fatty Acids (EFAs)

Unless the body has sufficient EFAs for its needs and the diet provides a lot of them, more than 12 to 15% of total calories, the body uses EFAs for special functions and it does not burn them for energy. EFAs stimulate metabolism, increase the metabolic rate, and speed up the rate at which fats and glucose are burned in the body. In this way, they help to burn off excess fats, and help a person to stay slim.

EFAs are required to make the phosphatides, which are the main structural components of the cell membranes. In the very active tissues (brain and nerve cells, synapses, retina, inner ear, adrenal, and testis), and also in muscle, enzymes insert several extra double bonds into EFAs and lengthen them to 20 or 22 carbon chains. Alternately, these long and highly unsaturated fatty acids can be supplied by eating the oils of certain fish, among them trout, salmon, and fresh sardines.

EFAs interact with proteins which, in ways not fully understood, are involved in the transfer of electrons and energy in biological systems. These interactions, just beginning to be studied, are as complex as they are fascinating. EFAs take part in so many vital biochemical reactions and biological functions, that so far, they defy description. The elusive nature of energy and electrons makes their transfer reactions difficult to pin down, since life is a movement of energy, dancing via electrons from one molecule tip to another, and not an array of static molecular chunks. A whole book could be written on the nature and importance of these transfer reactions. Much, much work remains to be done (see: Essential Fatty Acids).

The metabolism and use of the different kinds of fatty acids in the body is very different. The kinds of reactions in which they take part are also very different. Nutritional fats are not all alike. Some harm, and some heal. Some enhance metabolism, and some hinder it. Some bring oxygen to the tissues, and some choke us. Some are vital, and some are fatal. The interactions of the different kinds of fatty acids with one another, the chemical changes they undergo, the functions they have in the body, and the regulation of all of their functions are precise, specific, and fascinating.

30

Vitamin and Mineral Co-Factors in Fat Metabolism

Enzymes

Each step in each chemical reaction in metabolism, (see: Metabolism of Fats and Oils) requires the presence of a specific enzyme, without which the chemical reaction cannot occur.

What are enzymes? Enzymes are proteins, made according to our genetic DNA (deoxyribonucleic acid) templates, via RNA (ribonucleic acid) blueprints, in response to need. Enzymes encourage chemical reactions to take place, reactions that could not happen without them. They are catalysts, facilitators. Like the host at a party who introduces strangers and facilitates social intercourse, resulting in deals being made, friendships begun, or couples formed, enzymes facilitate social interaction between molecules. And like good hosts, who have specific kinds of talent to facilitate specific interactions in specific situations, specific enzymes facilitate specific interactions between specific molecules in a very precise way, resulting in very precise chemical changes leading to precise, predictable, and reliable results.

Minerals

In order to carry out their functions, enzymes are usually allied with essential mineral factors, which we must get from our diet. For instance, over 80 zinc-requiring enzymes have been found so far. Without this mineral, these enzymes can't do their job. Several other enzymes require copper. Still other enzymes must have magnesium to function. Several need iron. Hemoglobin requires iron to carry oxygen. There are about 20 minerals which take part in functions in the human body. Specific enzymes are allied with specific minerals, and these minerals are the co-factors, or prosthetic groups, or helpers, in their functions. There are about a dozen minerals involved in enzyme functions.

Vitamins

The second group of substances essential for the proper functions of enzymes are the vitamins, which must also come from the diet, since the body can't make them. The vitamins are more complex than the minerals, and are associated more loosely with the enzymes than are minerals, which are often bound to their enzyme molecule. There are about 20 vitamins, and without them, the enzyme-catalyzed interactions between molecules cannot take place.

Co-Factors in Fat Metabolism

In the metabolism of fats, several minerals and vitamins are known to be involved. The involvements of many others is not yet certain. This field of study, important as it is, is just in its infancy.

Vitamins A and E are necessary to keep essential fatty acids intact in the body, to protect them from destruction by oxygen and free radicals, and to keep them capable of fulfilling their important duties.

In order to break down saturated fatty acids into 2-carbon fragments (beta-oxidation), several co-factors are required, because many different enzyme steps are involved. Vitamins B2, B3, pantothenic acid, sulphur, and potassium are all required in different steps of the break-down process of these saturated fatty acids.

There are other ways in which saturated fatty acids can be broken down. These alternate methods of fatty acid oxidation may require vitamin B12, pantothenic acid, biotin, sulphur, and magnesium in order to take place.

To synthesize fatty acids out of 2-carbon fragments, vitamins B2, B3, and biotin are necessary co-factors. In burning the 2-carbon fragments into carbon dioxide and water, vitamins B2, B3, and iron act as co-factors. Inserting *cis-* double bonds into saturated fatty acid molecules also requires vitamins B2 and B3, and iron as co-factors.

To change linoleic acid (18:2*w*6) into prostaglandin E1 (see: Prostaglandins), several enzymes are involved, and each enzyme has its own co-factor requirement. The first step requires zinc, and is blocked by excess fats, cholesterol, saturated fatty acids, processed vegetable oils, and alcohol. The second step requires vitamin B6. The third step requires zinc, vitamin B3, and vitamin C. If any of these co-factors are missing, some step in the manufacture of prostaglandin E1 is blocked. If any of the co-factors are in short supply, the production of prostaglandin E1 is slowed down. Lack or low level of prostaglandin E1 is a factor in many physical and several mental ailments (see: Prostaglandins), and its symptoms are similar to those of essential fatty acid deficiency (see: Essential Fatty Acids) and degenerative diseases (see: Fatty Degeneration). Other prostaglandins require copper for their formation. Still others may need folic acid and gluthathione[1].

For transport in the body, cholesterol needs to be hooked (esterfied) to a fatty acid, preferably an essential fatty acid. Esterification requires vitamin B6. To change cholesterol into bile acids, vitamin C is required. Vitamin B3 is involved in regulating blood cholesterol level, though the exact role B3 plays in regulation is not yet known.

From this short, partial list of examples, we can see that many essential nutritional factors are required for fat metabolism. These have to be supplied through the diet in sufficient, or even better, in optimal quantities. If we don't get them, the metabolism of fats and oils cannot take place the way it should, and when that happens, we lose health and vigour.

Deranged fat metabolism lies at the root of most degenerative diseases. This derangement may be caused by too much of the wrong kinds of fats in our diet, too much total fat, or deficiency of the right kinds of fats. It may also be the deficiency of any of the necessary co-factors that deranges fat metabolism. That's why all of the nutritional factors have to be in place, working together.

One example will illustrate this point. Cancer is the enigma of our time, eluding every attempt at pin-pointing its exact cause, which is often assumed to be a *single* cause. It clearly is a form of fatty degeneration, something gone haywire with the way the cells handle fats and energy production.

There may be changes in the fat composition of cell membranes, these may be fat droplets within the cells, or there may be fats surrounding the tumour. In separate animal experiments, it has been shown that cancer can be induced by an imbalance in any one of many factors. Deficiency of essential fatty acids, too much saturated fatty acids, too many calories, deficiency of zinc, iron, oxygen, vitamin A, vitamin C, vitamins B1, B2, B6, pantothenic acid, vitamin E, sulphur, protein deficiency (especially the amino acid methionine), and perhaps choline deficiency can lead to cancer. The list may not be complete. Similarly, it has been shown that a diet rich in these factors protects animals from radiation-induced and chemically-induced cancers.

Co-factor Deficiencies

Surveys of human nutritional states have uncovered that the most common deficiencies among humans are vitamins C, E, and A, and the minerals iron, zinc, calcium, and magnesium. Essential fatty acid deficiency and deficiencies of the B vitamins are widespread. Iodine and manganese deficiencies are also common. Nutritional surveys in America showed that between 60 and 80% of the population is deficient in one or more essential nutrients. Over 75% of the people die from degenerative diseases.

It does not take much imagination to put these pieces of information together. The vitamin and mineral co-factors of fat metabolism deserve more attention. Our diet needs to be complete, needs to contain all of the essential elements of nutrition working together to maintain health, and a vigourous, long life.

31

Individuality

How Unique!

"When God made me, he threw away the mold." The same is true for each and every one of us. From the shape of our noses, the fullness of our lips, the curve of our necks, the colour of our eyes, and the shape, size and structure of our bodies, we are individual and unique, and our uniqueness extends to the shape and capacity of our hearts, the length and strength of our bones, the weight of our brains, the placement and structure of our inner organs, the distribution and attachment points of our tendons, and the pattern and distribution of hair follicles. Our physical individuality and uniqueness finds expression in our unique athletic abilities, our sensory capabilities, our mental and intellectual prowess, our social skills, our artistic talents, and our aesthetic sensitivities.

Biochemical individuality

In a similar way, we are all biochemically unique. We differ in our ability to digest, to assimilate, and to metabolize foods. We differ in the chemical structure of our enzymes, and we differ in the efficiency of our enzyme systems. We differ in our nutritional requirements. We differ in our food preferences, and often our food preferences reflect our genetic and biochemical differences.

Because we are unique, no one diet will be right for everyone, and so it is each individual's personal task to find their own optimal diet. It requires some experimentation with our foods and with supplements to discover the kinds and amounts of these which make us feel our physical and mental best.

Experimenting With Foods

To experiment with our foods: the quantity, the quality, the combinations, the timing, and the brands is safe, provided we listen to what our bodies tell us. It is foolish to cut out food entirely for a month just on a whim. It is foolish to decide to eat nothing but fried carrots for a year. But to try different kinds of foods and food combinations, and to try different concentrations and brands of supplements in an open-ended way, where we respond not just to an idea or a taste but also to how our bodies feel, is wise. We do this anyway, beginning from childhood, with our food preferences and experiments, when we balk at eating parsnips or steaks; when we insist that our carrots must be cooked; when within the same family, our food preferences diverge as much as those of Jack Spratt and his wife; when we get tired of certain foods we used to like; or when we turn green from our first smoke, dizzy from our first drink, and so on.

To help us in our careful experiments with what we feed ourselves, there are several books available which, while they cannot prescribe exactly what our optimal individual diet will be, can give guidelines to follow, regarding types and concentrations of nutrients to try. These guidelines have been worked out by doctors and researchers who themselves have carefully experimented with the effects of nutrients on health, and who successfully treat patients with nutritional therapy, also called orthomolecular nutrition (see: Orthomolecular Nutrition). The titles of some of these books are listed in the references on nutrition. Using these guidelines, your own ability to do, feel, and think, and a little patience, you too can arrive at the individual diet on which you feel and function at your personal best.

Examples of Individuality

Let's have a look at some examples of individuality. There are some people who cannot digest fresh salads without rice, and who get diarrhea on the same salads which I consider a gift straight from heaven. Others cannot tolerate whole grains. Two spoonfuls of whole grain cereal will send them into severe depression, with crying spells, confusion, and blackouts. Yet such a grain-based diet has helped people with extreme cases of cardiovascular disease and obesity back to health. Some people on a 'cleansing diet' of raw vegetables and fruit may get cancer, even though cancer is usually associated with diets high in saturated fats and processed foods, and the 'cleansing diet' usually helps to free people from cancer and degenerative diseases. If the intake of essential fatty acids was too low in the first place, it would need to be increased rather than decreased.

Some people get nausea, headaches, and depression from eating any kind of oil, but are able to tolerate quite well the seeds of flax, walnut, sunflower, and pumpkin, all of which contain 35% or more of their weight as oil. Others are unable to digest any kind of fat, until they discover flax oil, which becomes their new delicacy. Still others can digest all fats. All of these are examples of biochemical individuality, based either on genetic differences or on environmental influences, but individuality in either case.

There are many, many other possible examples. Inability to digest lactose (milk sugar) or phenylalanine (an amino acid involved in phenylketonuria) are examples of nutritional individuality based on genetics. Other genetic conditions such as sickle cell anemia, hemophilia, Hapsburg lip, or hairy ears are examples of individuality experienced by a part of the population and not by others. These result from single mutations (changes) in the genetic material. The number of points of possible changes in the genetic material run into the millions or billions, and the possible combination of possible changes run into astronomical figures. These are the genetic roots of individuality.

Individual Differences in Nutrient Requirements

Dr. Roger Williams, who has done more work on biochemical individuality than any other living scientist, found that in animals, the requirements of specific essential nutrient substances can vary 10-fold or more for different animals. One animal may thrive on 1 mg/kg/day of vitamin C, whereas another might need more than 16 mg/kg/day in order to thrive as well as the first animal.

Each of the essential nutrient substances shows a range similar to that given for vitamin C. In human subjects, it has been shown that people suffering from certain types of schizophrenia require much more vitamin C and vitamin B3 than the average person to be able to function normally. The normalizing effect of high doses of these 2 vitamins on the behaviour of some schizophrenics is so striking that it has been suggested that schizophrenia is a deficiency disease brought on by an inordinately high requirement for these vitamins, which is not met by the usual Western diet.

Individual Differences in Essential Fatty Acid Requirements

Studies to determine individual differences in the requirement for the essential fatty acids in humans have not been carried out. It has been suggested that the requirement for males may be 3 times higher than that for females of our species. Further studies will likely show that the range of optimum amounts of these substances will show a spread similar to that shown for other essential nutrients, perhaps 10-fold or more. This may explain in part why different writers have come up with widely diverging 'daily requirements' for the essential fatty acids. Again, each individual needs to find their optimal level by careful observation and experimentation.

Minimum. While 1 or 2% of daily calories as linoleic acid (LA, 18;2*w*6) prevents the symptoms of LA deficiency for most people, some people may have higher requirements for LA to prevent deficiency. Conditions of stress or disease may modify the requirement, and sugars, saturated fatty acids, and other substances in the food supply may increase the essential fatty acid requirement.

Optimum. As with most essential nutrients, it appears likely that the optimum requirement for the essential fatty acids is higher than the minimum requirement. 5 to 10% of daily calories as LA, 2% as LNA and a combined total of essential fatty acids of at least 1/3 of the total fat consumed has been suggested as optimal. What exact level is *your* optimum is something which you can best determine for yourself.

32

Orthomolecular Nutrition

Introduction

The nutritional advice given by government agencies, taught in schools, passed on in medical practice, and adhered to by people, is clearly inadequate for physical health, as attested to by our poor national state of health. The foods we eat at home, in cafeterias, restaurants, and hospitals are factors leading to the growing incidence of degenerative disease, which has risen to epidemic proportions in just 80 years. The fact that there are other people who eat other kinds of diets and are not prone to degenerative disease strongly suggests that our food habits are to blame. The observation that healthy people from healthy dietary backgrounds become prone to degenerative diseases soon after they adapt our dietary ways[1], very strongly underlines that suggestion. Existing evidence that people can be cured by nutritional means of their degenerative afflictions adds the exclamation point to the strong suggestion very strongly underlined.

Defining 'Orthomolecular Nutrition'

What is orthomolecular nutrition? Twice a Nobel Prize winner (Chemistry and Peace), Linus Pauling coined the term orthomolecular, which means 'with the right molecules'. The word is used in combinations such as orthomolecular nutrition, orthomolecular medicine, and orthomolecular therapy. Dr. Pauling defined orthomolecular medicine in 1968 as the "preservation of good health and the treatment of disease by varying the concentration in the human body of substances that are normally present in the body and are required for health".[2] Orthomolecular nutrition and orthomolecular therapy fit that definition exactly. The definition distinguishes this approach from toximolecular medicine, which is the introduction into the body of alien chemicals or drugs, the standard practice in established medicine.

The difference in approach is shown by the difference in results. In the last 80 years, using the orthodox medical or toximolecular approach, deaths from fatty degeneration have risen from 15% of the population to 75%, an increase of 500%. Nutritional medicine has not gained the acceptance of the medical establishment, but in the hands of a few courageous doctors it is chalking up an impressive record of healing successes in the treatment of fatty degeneration.

Nation-wide Nutritional Deficiencies

Nation-wide surveys in North America have shown that the diets of more than 60% of the people tested are deficient in one or more of the essential nutrients. The surveys tested only 10 of the 45 known essential nutrients, and used as their standard for adequate nutrition the ridiculously low Recommended Daily Allowances (RDAs). At best, the RDAs give the minimum requirements of these substances, and at worst, they are the official standard of accepted levels of substandard nutrition, inadequate to maintain optimum health for almost everyone. Other major surveys have obtained similar results and the present trend is toward increasing malnutrition.

The most common deficiencies found in these surveys were iron, calcium, zinc, magnesium, vitamins C, A, E, B6, B2 and folic acid. Other surveys have turned up frequent deficiencies of iodine, manganese, chromium, and selenium.

Studies carried out in several hospitals have discovered that over half of the patients became nutritionally deficient and more ill *after* entering hospitals, from eating hospital foods, and not as a direct result of their illness. The trend toward hospital-induced malnutrition too, is worsening across the continent. Even the diets of the hospital dieticians were found to contain inadequate amounts of vitamin B6, when measured by the already-low standard of the RDA for that vitamin.

Orthomolecular Medical Practice

When a person visits a doctor practising orthomolecular medicine, the first step the doctor takes is to assess that person's nutritional status, using simple tests for blood and tissue levels of the essential nutrients. Such tests are already available and are simple to carry out[3]. Frequently, some deficiencies are found. When the deficiencies are corrected either by oral or injected supplements of the missing essential nutrients, usually a change for the better occurs. If not, larger doses of certain nutrients may be tried, because some people have much higher requirements of these nutrients than others.

Orthomolecular nutrition cures diseases such as scurvy (lack of vitamin C), pellagra (lack of vitamin B3), beriberi (lack of vitamin B1), rickets (lack of vitamin D) and so on, because these diseases are the direct result of lack of these vitamins. Deficiency of each of the essential nutrients has its particular set of disease symptoms. The symptoms of deficiency of each of the two essential fatty acids are varied and severe (See: Essential Fatty Acids). Prolonged severe deficiency of any single essential nutritional substance is fatal. Deficiency states which are less severe than those which result in the classical symptoms of scurvy, beriberi, etc. are also possible. For instance a less severe (sometimes called sub-clinical) deficiency of vitamin C results in tissue weakness, because vitamin C is necessary for building collagen, which is the major protein component of connective tissue. Connective tissue holds the body together. A sub-clinical deficiency of zinc slows down wound healing, because zinc is required in the healing function. A sub-clinical deficiency of vitamin A results in proneness to infection and poor skin condition, because this vitamin has important functions in the making of healthy skin. Sub-clinical deficiency of essential fatty acids lowers the ability of the body to withstand stress. Each essential nutrient has its own set of sub-clinical symptoms. These symptoms do not result in definable disease, but rather in sub-optimal functioning of the whole organism, lowered vitality, and feeling of malaise. Over the course of many years, and often precipitated during periods or in situations of high stress, clinically definable diseases do occur, and these diseases, such as the diseases of fatty degeneration are then termed 'of unknown origin' by the medical profession, because the medical profession has not been knowledgeable about nutritional states and optimal nutrition. Happily, the medical profession is changing — slowly. Orthomolecular nutrition attempts to bring the levels in the body of all essential nutrients up to the minimum required level for health, and beyond that, to their optimum level for well-being, vitality, and accomplishment.

Orthomolecular nutrition also concerns itself with lowering the concentration of substances natural to the body which may be present in excessive quantities. Examples of such substances are glucose and saturated fats. The concentrations of these substances are reduced by decreasing our dietary intake of foods which are high in them, and by increased exercise.

Orthomolecular nutrition also addresses itself to genetic metabolic diseases, such as phenylketonuria, which can be prevented by designing a diet low in the natural amino acid phenylalanine, whose presence in the diet of susceptible people causes mental deficiency and other problems. Some genetic diseases of fat and cholesteral metabolism, which result in very high blood levels of these substances and carry high risk of cardiovascular disease and death can also be helped by diets which minimize the food content of fats and cholesterol.

Orthomolecular nutrition provides natural substances such as insulin, thyroxin, and other glandular products in the treatment of patients who have defectively functioning glands.

Another aspect of orthomolecular nutrition is megavitamin therapy, in which high doses of vitamins are taken by people who for some reason of disease or biochemical individuality (See: Individuality) require far higher than average amounts of certain vitamins for normal functioning, or who, because they consume diets deficient in vitamins and/or minerals, need to supplement these diets in order to maintain or regain health.

There is plenty of evidence which links different disease states, both physical and mental, with deficiencies of essential nutrients, with excesses of some nutrients, and with imbalances of the levels of various nutrients in the body. This is why orthomolecular nutrition and therapy are effective. They treat nutritional problems at their nutritional source, with nutritional substances, altering the concentrations in the body of these natural substances.

Toximolecular Medical Practice

Medical science has made tremendous progress in the control of certain diseases. Smallpox, diphtheria, typhoid, yellow fever, rabies, polio, and malaria have been virtually eradicated by medical science through vaccinations. The childhood diseases have been stopped. Antibiotics have taken the threat out of the infectious diseases. We still get infections, but the use of antibiotics keeps most of them under control. The medical technology has taken huge strides. Surgical techniques, life support systems, diagnostic tools, and lab tests are amazing in their sophistication, and doctors have become very skillful in their application.

On the other hand, these medical triumphs have brought with them some problems. One problem is that our reliance on medical technology has made us less inclined to take care of ourselves, to keep strong from within, so that our bodies are capable of fighting infections and other threats to our health. Another problem, related to the first, is that our reliance more on doctors and technology than ourselves, has resulted in what is often called 'the passive patient syndrome' and a giving up of personal responsibility for health. This is an unfortunate change, because health is a personal responsibility. My disease hurts me the most. Because my heart attack kills me, and not my doctor, it is most important for me to be responsible for my health.

Probably the greatest problem with the way medicine has evolved is our overwhelming reliance on synthetic drugs. The evidence for the effectiveness of these toximolecular medicines to actually cure diseases is small. No-one has been found so far to be suffering from aspirin, tranquilizer, or pep pill deficiency. Logically, these drugs would truly cure only such deficiency states, but since the substances are unnatural, natural organisms never suffer such deficiencies. Drugs may remove, mask, or 'bury' the symptoms of diseases caused by other factors, and because the symptoms are thus removed, the use of drugs destroys the incentive for finding the real cause and cure of the disease state. Drugs may cause many diseases themselves (called 'side effects'), because they are alien molecules introduced into the very delicate and precise architectural design of the body. An example of side effects from drugs are diuretics which cause potassium depletion, resulting in heart beat abnormalities. Another is the birth control pill which results in water retention and behavioural changes, and also depletes the body of vitamins B6, B12 and folic acid. A third example is tranquilizers, which separate the fatty parts of the membranes from proteins, resulting in lowered vitality, sleep without rest, and increased risk of cancer. Some of the drugs used for other conditions such as rheumatoid arthritis can have serious and wide-ranging side effects. Antibiotics can cause rashes, nausea, vomiting, anemia, joint pain, and yeast infections, as well as failure of I.U.D.'s for birth control. The list of detrimental effects of other pharmaceutical drugs is very long. Even the 'harmless' aspirin can cause internal bleeding, and each year about 40 deaths are attributed to it.

Returning What's Missing

A major factor in the cause of the degenerative diseases rampant today are nutrient deficiencies and imbalances. Changes in the content of nutrients in our food have resulted from 'refining' essential nutrients out of the natural raw materials (See: Oil Making), from processing, from nutrient losses which occur naturally during storage and transportation, from unbalanced farming methods which leave soils depleted, and by the addition of artificial, non-natural ingredients to our foods. Our food choices have been influenced by a constant barrage of advertising (See: Advertising). Ultimately, the only effective treatment for these diseases is a return to the simple food habits of our 'preprocessing' ancestors, a return to food choices which adequately cover our (now) known nutrient requirements, a return to a way of eating more in harmony with the ways of nature. Orthomolecular nutrition attempts to move us in that direction, returning to our bodies, often in concentrated form, the biochemical nutrients which are missing from our diets.

33

Stress and the Battery of Life

Stress

Hans Selye received a nomination for the prestigious Nobel Prize and world-wide recognition for his inquiries into the nature of stress. He (and later, other scientists as well) showed that many different kinds of stress — cold, heat, noise, overexertion, mental and emotional stress, forced physical restraint, injury, sensory overload, toxic chemicals, x-ray and other radiation, deprivation of food or love, overeating, even pregnancy — produce a common set of response symptoms. From his observations, he suggested that one underlying adaptive mechanism deals with all of the various kinds of stress. Selye named this common set of symptoms which occur in response to stress the General Adaptation Syndrome (GAS), and divided the GAS into 3 distinct stages.

During the first stage, which he called the alarm reaction, the animal (Selye worked with chicks, rats, hamsters, and rabbits, but similar observations have also been made with human beings) displays restlessness, 'the jitters', nervousness, and other non-specific and non-directed behavioural signs of agitation.

During the second stage, the stage of resistance, the animal actively uses its inner resources (we'll see below what the biochemical components of these resources are) to deal with the stress. Directed activity and specific biochemical functions within the animal are the characteristics of the stage of resistance, and if the inner resources are sufficient to overcome the stress, the animal adapts.

If the stress is greater than the animal's adaptive resources, these resources are depleted, and the third stage, exhaustion occurs. The diseases of adaptation (or better, diseases due to the failure to adapt) characterize exhaustion, and additional minor stresses can then kill the animal or human. The most noticeable organ changes during exhaustion include enlarged adrenal glands and atrophied (shrunken) lymph and thymus glands. The diseases of maladaptation include high blood pressure, water retention, arthritis, heart enlargement, strokes, ulcers, kidney disease, eclampsia and toxemia of pregnancy, allergies, diabetes, neurological problems, and cancer. These disease symptoms closely resemble the symptoms of essential fatty acid deficiency (see: Essential Fatty Acids). They also resemble the modern-day degenerative diseases (see: Fatty Degeneration).

The 'Life Battery'

It appeared to Selye that there was within each organism a sort of 'life battery' which stores life current in the same way in which an electric battery stores electric current; a battery with a limited capacity, which, under stress, runs down. Selye wondered what might be the bio-chemical basis of this 'life battery', and whether there might be a way to recharge the 'life battery' when it has run down.

Selye did his major work in the 1940's. He was not a biochemist but a doctor, and many biochemical techniques now available were not known then, so he had no way of answering his own question, and it remained for others who followed to elucidate the biochemical and molecular mechanisms underlying the fascinating experimental observations that Selye made on tissue, organ, and organism levels.

The analogy of the 'life battery' turns out to be a very good one. A battery has two poles, a positive and a negative, between which a current of energy will flow under suitable conditions, i.e. when the circuit is completed. This happens to be true for the human 'life battery' as well. It too, is a battery containing two poles, and between these, the life current, the life energy flows, when the circuit is completed. It was Dr. Budwig who, in the early 1950's, discovered and explained the biochemical nature of the poles of the 'life battery' working together in synchrony.

What are these two poles? In nutritional terms, the poles of the battery are 'good' oil and 'good' protein; flax oil and skim milk protein; oil rich in the essential fatty acids, and sulphur-rich protein; oil containing many slightly negatively charged *cis*-double bonds and protein containing many slightly positively charged sulphydryl groups. 'Good' oil is the negative pole; 'good' protein, the positive pole of the life battery. Between these two poles, the life current flows when the circuit of essential nutrients is complete. In biological terms, perhaps it would be even better to call 'good' oil the female pole, because the egg, as well as the female form contains a preponderance of these oils, and the 'good' protein the male pole, because the sperm as well as the male body contains a preponderance of these proteins[1].

The more we are stimulated and stressed, the more life current flows between the poles of the battery, the more 'good' oil and 'good' protein is used up, the sooner the life battery runs down. The oil and protein must be replaced through the diet to continually recharge the battery, starting from the moment of birth and ending at the moment of death.

More stress requires more oil and protein; less stress requires less. Whenever the demand by our body for 'good' oil and 'good' protein exceeds that supplied through our food, the battery begins to run down, and we slowly develop a deficiency as the reserves of these substances in the body are used up. With the deficiency comes sickness. The severity of the sickness depends on the severity of the deficiency. We require rest then, a chance to reorganize our resources, and good nutrition to replenish our low supplies. The cure for the rundown life battery, the deficiency, the sickness, is to increase the intake of 'good' oil and 'good' protein through our food. The maintenance of health requires the maintenance of optimum intake of 'good' oil and 'good' protein to provide for the fluctuating demands of our bodies in a changing environment with fluctuating levels of stress.

Protein and oil are the two most abundant and important structural and functional substances in human, and, for that matter, all living cells of all bodies: animal, plant, and single-celled. We find them together in the cell membranes, in the lipoproteins that carry fats and cholesterol in the blood, in the membranes of subcellular organelles (see: Essential Fatty Acids); in short, they form the main structures and functional components of the entire body.

Completing the Circuit

What completes the circuit of the life battery, so that the current can flow? The vitamins and minerals, as well as other substances which the body itself produces out of essential nutrients complete the circuit (see: Co-factors of Fat Metabolism). They are the supporting cast, oil and protein the stars in the drama of life. Vitamins C, E, and A, and the minerals zinc, selenium, and iron are especially important, but all other essential nutrients are also necessary. The absence of any one of them is itself an intolerable internal stress.

The effect of the fast pace at which we live is to run down our life battery. Life in the fast lane is faster, but it is also shorter. The better our nutrition is, the better or longer we can stand up to this pace; the worse our nutrition, the sooner we fall apart. The degenerative diseases, fatty degeneration, the 'diseases of civilization', Selye's 'diseases of adaptation' or Budwig's 'fat syndrome', all refer to the same conditions, characterized by a run-down life battery, and are all worsened by increased stress and by poor food choices, the latter being one of the major stresses to which we subject our bodies. These degenerative diseases share many of the same symptoms, the same aggravating factors, and the same alleviating factors (see: Fatty Degeneration).

The Relationship of Oil and Protein

We can get too much oil or too much protein if either is taken by itself (see: The Oil-Protein Combination), and we can get too little. But together, it is difficult to get too much, because oil and protein belong together, work together, and protect each other. The protein protects the oil from free radical formation, and the oil protects the protein from breakdown.

People who are deficient in these nutrients often crave the oil-protein combination for a few weeks, and then slowly reduce their intake in response to a natural decrease in their body's need for the combination. The body knows its needs. Hunger signals us to begin to eat, or to search for something to eat; satiety signals us to stop eating. Were this signal not effective, our eating would get out of proportion and so would we.

When the natural composition of foods has been altered through refinement, processing, artificial flavours, and additives, our hunger signals become imbalanced, and our eating gets out of proportion. This is one of the reasons for obesity. No wild animal on a diet of natural foods ever gets abnormally, unhealthily fat.

Domesticated animals, who share our nutritional habits and stresses, also share our degeneration.

The average diet of people living in industrialized countries contains ample good protein, because we live in a protein-conscious time. We are protein-, muscle-, and male-conscious. The meat, egg, and dairy industries have successfully convinced us of the need for protein in our diets. Besides, protein occurs in all living tissues, and so whatever natural foods we eat, all contain protein. Protein foods are easy to store, because they can be dried or frozen, and keep well for long times[2].

Destruction of the Female Partner

'Good' oil however, the equally necessary female partner of good protein, is systematically destroyed by our methods of preparation and storage (see: Hydrogenation). Oil does not keep well, because light, oxygen, and heat destroy the delicate *cis*-double bonds (see: Essential Fatty Acids). Even cold temperatures do not protect oils from destruction by light and oxygen.

Exclusion of light, air, and heat throughout the entire process of pressing, filling, and storing, up to the point of consumption keeps 'good' oils intact. Such methods are possible, but are not yet being used by the oil industry.

Destroyed oil is foreign to the body. It cannot couple with 'good' protein, cannot recharge the life battery, and even worse, interferes with the action of the oils that can recharge the life battery. When the female, softening, receptive partner to the protein is absent, the life battery, like a man without a wife, ends up with only one pole. No life current flows, because the circuit is interrupted, and thus the current has no place to flow.

The deficiency of essential fatty acids-containing oils is one of the greatest stresses in our technological way of life. We don't need huge amounts of them, but they are extremely important. This book is about fats and oils rather than about proteins. Dr. Budwig's oil-protein combination is effective in alleviating the suffering from degenerative diseases, because it supplies the missing oil ingredient.

34

Calories and Fats

Introduction

Energy contained in foods is measured in calories. It is the energy released for body functions when foods are oxidized or 'burned' in the body. Proteins, carbohydrates, and fats are the food sources of calories. Calories in excess of the body's needs are stored as fat, and therefore, all calories are potential sources of fat.

An adult person consumes about 2,500 calories daily. The rate for men is a little higher than that for women, and varies from 1,500 to 4,000 for most males, and from 900 to 2,500 for most females. The extremes are wider still, and go from 0 on a water fast (with loss of weight) to over 8,000 calories for a logger, who burns them all up in the work he does without gaining an ounce, and even as high as 12,000 calories per day for professional weightlifters.

Calories are provided by each of the 3 main food types: fat, carbohydrate, and protein. Fat stores more than twice as much energy at 9 calories per gram as does an equal weight of carbohydrate or protein, each of which stores 4 calories of energy per gram. Logically, the body prefers to carry its energy reserves as fat, because this is the most efficient way to carry energy reserves, both in terms of volume and in terms of weight.

Vitamins and minerals, although essential to health, contain no calories at all.

Food Sources of Calories

Where do the calories come from? The food groups which supply the calories in a typical Western diet are as follows: meat supplies about 20% of the calories; refined cereals and flour add 18%; refined fats, another 18%; sugar, 17%; dairy products, 12%; eggs and alcohol, 2% each; and high fiber foods, including whole grains, vegetables, and fruit make up the remaining 11% of calories.

Broken down according to food constituents, the typical Western diet is made up as follows: Fats provide 42%[1] of the total calories consumed. Of these, 18% are visible refined fats such as butter, margarine, shortenings, and oils. The other 24% are hidden in various foods and may be natural or refined. 46% of the calories come from carbohydrates. Of these, 17% are refined sugar, 20% are refined cereal products such as breakfast cereals and refined flour bakery products, 3% are alcohol, and only 6% come from complex unrefined carbohydrates. 12% of daily calories come from proteins.

According to the figures given above, at least 58% of all the calories in the typical Western diet (refined fats, refined sugar, refined cereal products, and alcohol) come from 'empty calorie' foods, that is, foods whose minerals, vitamins, and fiber have been removed in the processes used to refine them.

Calories as a Source of Fat

Refined, 'empty calorie' foods are the most likely kind of foods to cause us to gain fat, for several reasons. 'Empty calorie' foods cause us to overeat. One of the mechanisms that turns off hunger is the feeling of fullness, and by the time we've filled up on these concentrated calorie foods, we've eaten more calories than we need. The excess turns to fat.

Because they lack fiber and bulk, high calorie refined foods slow down intestinal activity, too. They take up to 3 times longer to pass through the intestinal tract than do natural, unrefined, high fiber foods, (75 hours compared to 24) and the body absorbs calories during the entire time of their constipated passage.

Foods cannot be metabolized properly without minerals and

vitamins. The energy that 'empty calorie' foods contain becomes unavailable to our bodies and is stored as fat until (or, in the hope that) we get the necessary minerals and vitamins at some later time. In the meantime, we feel hungry, and eat more. This too, turns into fat, unless minerals and vitamins are also provided.

Minerals, vitamins, and essential fatty acids are systematically removed from foods during refining. Their absence lowers the metabolic rate; we become lethargic, and feel less like exercise and activity. Then, even if we eat less, we don't burn up the little we do eat, and get fat even on low calorie diets.

Calorie-counting Doesn't Work

Calorie-counting as a way of keeping weight down does not work. It is easy enough to count the calories, but there are so many other important factors that modify the rate at which our bodies use calories, that simply regulating the number of calories we consume is ineffective in the battle against the bulge.

What are some of these factors? The theoretical measure of the caloric values of foods, printed in books, assumes that foods containing them are completely burned or oxidized, but in practice, in the body, this often is not the case. The caloric value of fats is often overrated, because fats, especially when present in large amounts in the diet, may not be completely burned to carbon dioxide and water by the body. Instead, they oxidize partially and produce ketones, which are like the charcoal left when wood burns incompletely (or carbon deposited on the pistons of an engine whose fuel-air mixture is unbalanced). While they are in the blood, and until the kidneys get rid of them, ketones suppress appetite, and this is one reason why fats are used in reducing diets. Long term presence of ketones produced from such diets damages kidneys and other internal organs, so care has to be taken in the use of high-fat reducing diets. The essential and other highly unsaturated fatty acids all contain 9 calories per gram, but the body does not use them for energy production, because they are more valuable for structural and electrical functions.

Another objection to calorie-counting is that the metabolic rate differs from person to person, and from time to time in the same individual. Genes, hormones, nutrition, exercise, and state of health affect the metabolic rate. Some people are born with a high metabolic rate and never gain weight, no matter how much they eat. Thyroid activity affects metabolic rate over a wide range, from hyper (over-active), which increases metabolic rate, all the way down to hypo- (under-active), which lowers it. The slower the rate, the less calories are burned, the easier it is to put on weight. The essential fatty acids, the B-complex (especially B3) vitamins, vitamin C, and completely adequate and balanced nutrition all increase the efficiency of oxidation, and raise the metabolic rate, and with it, the energy and activity level. Finally, the state of health alters the metabolic rate. During fevers and infections, much more energy is burned than when a person is healthy. In the late stages of cancer, the tumour eats most of the body's stores of energy, resulting in loss of weight.

After injury, proteins and fatty acids are used to rebuild cellular structures and new tissues rather than just for energy, and the metabolic rate is also increased. During childhood too, calorie-containing protein and fat molecules are built into body structures. These examples underline the false assumptions made by calorie-counters, which is that calorie-containing foods are useful only for energy production.

A third objection to calorie-counting looks at levels of activity. Exercise burns many more calories than sedentary living. An hour of exercise keeps the metabolic rate elevated for many hours (12 or more) after the exercise has finished. The length of time per day spent awake makes a difference, as more calories are burned in the waking than in the sleeping state. The level of mental activity affects calories use. The brain, although it is only 2% of the body's weight, may use up to 20% or more of the total calories burned by the body.

Environmental conditions affect the rate at which calories are used. The body responds to changes in temperature, season, and climate, increasing or decreasing the rate of metabolism to keep the body temperature constant. Also, clothing conserves more or less of the heat calories produced by the oxidation of food. The body loses more heat swimming in water than when surrounded by air of the same temperature, because air conducts body heat away less rapidly than does water.

Hunger and satiation factors are a 5th influence that determines whether the foods we eat keep us fit or fat. Different foods are digested, absorbed into the body, and made available for use at different rates, and therefore have different hunger-stilling values. Fats may take as long as 5 to 8 hours to be digested, proteins take about 3 to 5 hours, and complex carbohydrates about 2. Refined sugars take about 30 minutes. Even though fats contain twice as many calories as carbohydrates, they keep hunger satisfied 3 times as long, and therefore result in less weight gain. On the other hand, refined sugars are absorbed so rapidly that they flood the blood, and to prevent toxic reactions, the body quickly turns them into fat. This begins a vicious cycle of hunger, overeating, fat deposition, and more hunger. Hunger usually wins hands down over our strongest resolutions to restrict our caloric intake. A built-in drive, it demands that we eat until we get whatever food substances our bodies need for their functions. If this drive were weak, we would get absorbed in some of our other pursuits, would forget to eat, and would starve to death. Refined foods being short of many essential nutrients, lead us to overeat until we get the vitamins and minerals we need. If a major part of our diet is refined foods, we need to overload on calories in order to satisfy the minimum requirement for these essential factors, and we can get very fat in the process.

Finally, calorie-counting doesn't work because who's got the patience to systematically weigh out their food portions without cheating? We eat for enjoyment — far more with our eyes, our noses, and our palates[2] than we do with our rational minds. Feast today, and fast tomorrow. Even better, feast today and feast again tomorrow. We prefer the pleasure of eating to the pain of restricting ourselves. We people of the Western nations live in a century of plenty, uninterrupted by hunger pangs, and eating is one of our great passions. It may even be our greatest passion. And on top of all this, many people eat out of habit at regular, clocked intervals, and never actually experience hunger. One writer who counsels the obese claims that the difference between slim and overweight is this: the slim eat when hungry, eat whatever they like, and stop when the hunger subsides. The overweight eat when they see food, think about food and dieting all the time, and stop eating when all the food is gone. According to this counsellor, to lose weight one needs only to learn to think like those who are slim.

Calorie-counting and Health

Aside from overweight, which is an important risk factor in many forms of degenerative disease, there is another aspect of calories and health. The energy value of foods has some importance in diets. There have to be enough calories for the body's energy requirements. But about 20 vitamins and 20 minerals and fiber, all of which contain no calories whatsoever, are also essential to health. Calorie-counting does not take into consideration our need for these vital nutrients.

In the 20th century with its fad and junk foods, it is very easy to get the perfect number of calories every day and at the same time to suffer from malnutrition, which sets the stage for the degeneration of cells and tissues. The body literally falls apart, molecule from molecule. The fabric of life unravels. Degenerative disease bridges our journey from the refined food feast to the graveyard.

Several nation-wide nutritional surveys reveal that over 60% of the North American population is deficient in one or more vitamin or mineral. The surveys tested for only 10 of the 45 known essential nutrients. If all of them had been measured, the incidence of malnutrition would have been shown to be even higher (see: Orthomolecular Nutrition).

In the midst of plenty, people are starving. It is possible to be fat and starving at the same time. It is possible to be getting plenty of calories and to be starving at the same time. People in poorer nations, who can't afford refined foods and are still eating the primitive fare of pre-industrialized man are often better nourished than we are.

When the foods we feast on are natural and we eat when we are hungry, then hunger by itself takes care of our caloric needs, our vitamin and mineral requirements, and our taste buds; at the same time, hunger takes care of maintaining our ideal body weight and physical health, through all of the changes and conditions through which we pass in our lifetime. When the nutrient content of our foods is altered, is out of balance, it follows that the hunger mechanism and our bodies will also be out of balance. And in that case, all our calorie-counting will not help us.

35

Blood Cholesterol: The Plasma Lipoproteins: HDL and LDL

Introduction

The 7 grams of cholesterol present in the blood stream[1] is found, together with triglycerides, phospholipids (see: Triglycerides; and: Phosphatides), and proteins in carrier vehicles. There are several different kinds of vehicles or fractions with different functions, called, collectively, the plasma lipoproteins.

One fraction, made up of 4 sub-fractions, the most important of which is called the low density lipoproteins (LDL)[2], carries cholesterol from the food and liver to the cells to be used there. The other fraction, called the high density lipoproteins (HDL), carries cholesterol from the cells back to the liver, where that organ changes some of the cholesterol to bile acids and excretes bile acids and cholesterol through the intestine into the stool[3]. The total blood cholesterol, then, is all the cholesterol in transit to and from the cells, being carried by the different vehicles.

Measuring Blood Cholesterol Levels

There are different ways of measuring the blood cholesterol or plasma lipoprotein level. The most common method used by doctors is to measure total blood cholesterol level. This measurement lumps the 'good' HDL and 'bad' LDL fractions together. Total blood cholesterol is considered to be a general indicator of the risk of cardiovascular disease (CVD), but it can be inaccurate. For example, a low total cholesterol level which consists of a low protective HDL coupled with a high 'bad' LDL might inaccurately indicate low risk of CVD. On the other hand, a high total cholesterol level consisting of a high protective HDL coupled with a high 'bad' LDL would inaccurately indicate a high risk of CVD. Another, perhaps better indicator of CVD risk is to measure the HDL level. Most doctors will take this measurement only if they are specifically asked to do it. A third measure of CVD risk is the ratio of total cholesterol to HDL cholesterol. A ratio of 3.5 or lower indicates low risk of CVD.

Medical experts, including Dr. William Castelli of the famous Framingham Heart Study, estimate that CVD could be detected and prevented 5 years before it occurs by simply measuring the cholesterol ratio and the blood pressure regularly, because these two indicators are said to be about 98% accurate in predicting CVD. If the blood cholesterol ratio was found to be high, treatment could be started, and early death could be avoided.

According to Dogma

Both the HDL and the LDL fractions have vital functions to fulfill, but in opposite ways. According to the 'cholesterol theory' of cardiovascular disease, which is the accepted dogma of the medical establishment, a high 'good' HDL level (50-75 mg/dl) in the blood indicates that the system for getting rid of excess cholesterol is functioning well, and preventing the accumulation of cholesterol in the body and blood. We are therefore protected from cholesterol deposits in our arteries and from cardiovascular disease. A high 'bad' LDL level (above 120 mg/dl), on the other hand, indicates that our system is being overloaded by cholesterol from our food, and the cholesterol is backing up in our blood. This excess cholesterol is being deposited in our arteries, and is increasing our risk of death from heart attack, stroke and high blood pressure.

According to Nutrition

According to nutritional theory, the measurement of blood cholesterol is a fad. Cholesterol consumption has remained about constant over the last 80 years, while CVD has sky-rocketed. Factors which appear to be more closely related to CVD than cholesterol levels are consumption of sugars, oils, additives, *t*-fatty acids, and drugs which lower cholesterol without reducing heart attacks (exception: high doses of *niacin*, which protects the heart not by its cholesterol-lowering effect, but against toxic effects of adrenochrome, according to Dr. A. Hoffer). Even the Framingham study is open to interpretations.

CVD appears nutritionally linked to vitamin, mineral, and essential fatty acid deficiency, and to any conditions which impair the biochemical orchestra from playing the symphony of life. Using this analogy, we can imagine what would happen during the trumpet solo if the trumpet were missing, or the first violin, the bass, or the drums. Or even, perhaps the conductor. The blend, the harmony, the balance, the cohesion, the co-operation between parts, in short, the quality of the music would suffer. If the instruments necessary to play the crucial parts of the symphony were absent, the piece of music could not be performed. This is like the nutritional deficiency.

If someone who was not a member of the orchestra were to get up on the stage and start yelling loudly, or put his hands on the strings of the cello, his fist into the mouth of the horn, or were to try to play an instrument which he was not competent to play, or to bring into the orchestra several exotic instruments like a hammer, a cannon, or a hot rod for which there were no parts and to start playing randomly, or were to occupy the chair belonging to an orchestra member, preventing the member from playing, that would be like drugs' effect in the biochemistry of life.

To the nutritionists, the cholesterol 'problem' is secondary to disruptions in the biochemistry of life, and probably there are many different kinds of disruption which can lead to high cholesterol levels, cholesterol deposits, high blood pressure, and other symptoms of CVD.

When the emphasis is put on obtaining foods that contain all the essential nutrients in ample quantities, then, according to orthomolecular nutritionists, we can forget about the blood cholesterol levels and their measurements. Just like all the animals which live in nature and all generations of humans until the last 2 or 3, the blood cholesterol levels will take care of themselves, if we eat wholesome foods.

But let's be on the safe side. Since cholesterol is not essential, we can *both* lower our food intake of cholesterol *and* increase our intake of vitamins and minerals. That way, neither side of the theoreticians, nor our own bodies, can argue.

SECTION FOUR

Fat Options

Fats in Food Products

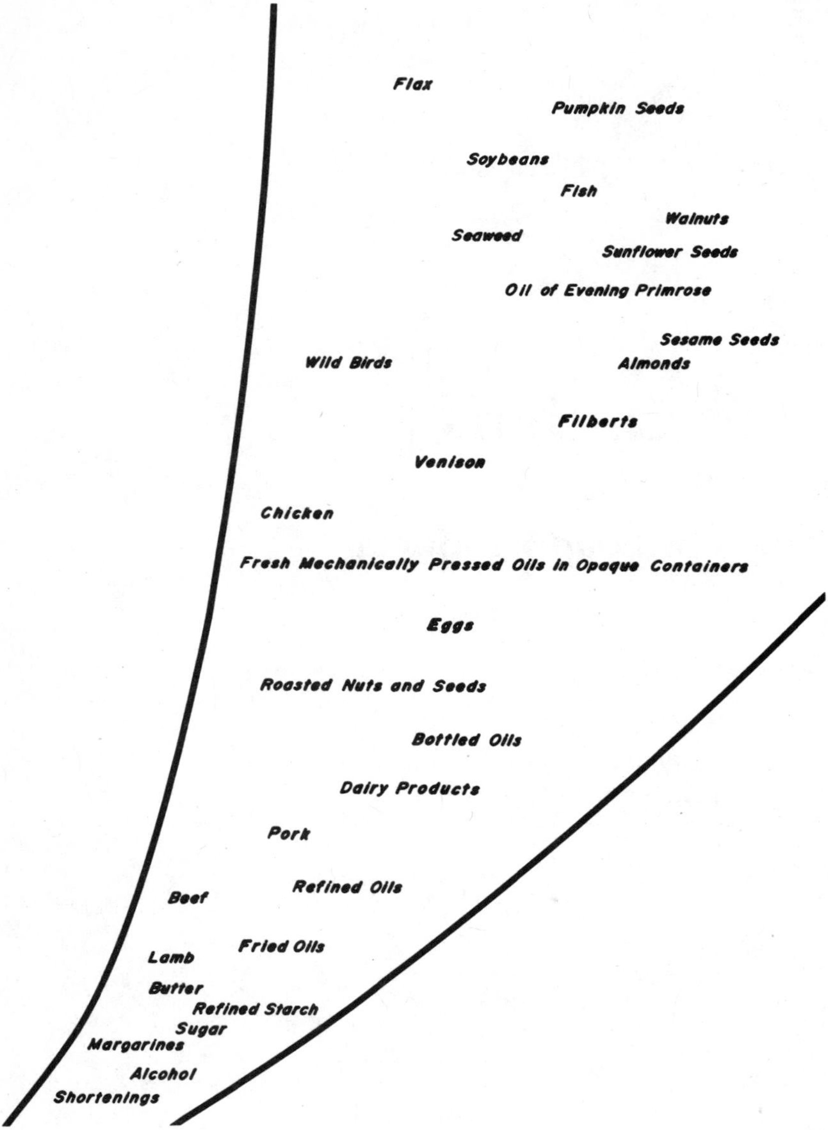

Flax

Pumpkin Seeds

Soybeans

Fish

Walnuts

Seaweed

Sunflower Seeds

Oil of Evening Primrose

Sesame Seeds

Wild Birds

Almonds

Filberts

Venison

Chicken

Fresh Mechanically Pressed Oils in Opaque Containers

Eggs

Roasted Nuts and Seeds

Bottled Oils

Dairy Products

Pork

Refined Oils

Beef

Fried Oils

Lamb

Butter

Refined Starch

Sugar

Margarines

Alcohol

Shortenings

36

Diet Controversy

Introduction

Some writers in nutrition express the opinion that by nature man is a hunter who, since the dawn of our species, has lived on a diet high in animal proteins and fats. These writers, mostly North American or European and affluent, cite as evidence the primitive hunting spears, arrows, and other weapons, animal bones, and other artifacts of the hunt and kill found around the remnants of fire pits in archeological sites on all the continents. They also take their stand on the basis of the North American and European preference for diets high in meats from beef, mutton, and pork, as well as lesser amounts of birds and fish. But probably more than anything else, these opinions are based on the writers' own personal preferences, which they justify with selected evidence from historical records.

Equally vociferous, and marshalling a similarly impressive set of evidence, are the writers who claim that man was always a gatherer of seeds, grains, roots, nuts, berries, and herbs. Seeds and implements for crushing and preparing seeds have also been found in archeological digs. Furthermore, 3/4 of the world's population today is mainly vegetarian, with a diet based around the grains (rice, millet, corn and beans, buckwheat, wheat, rye, oats, barley). Animal products (eggs, meat, blood, and milk products) are consumed rarely, often only on festive or religious occasions.

It is not clear why these two sets of writers insist that man should have been rigidly one or the other. Survival is a practical matter, and it makes sense that during a million years of history, climatic changes, and migrations, man ate whatever he found in his environment and climate to sustain him physically. Only in a state of affluence can we afford the speculations. In a state of hunger, we eat what is available.

Climatic Differences and Diet

In tropical climates, fruits and vegetables were the foods easiest to obtain, and so tropical people tended to favour them. The plains grew grasses and grains, and here the people became gatherers and later, farmers. The plains also provided animals such as buffalo, antelope, gnu, and wild cattle, and so we find on the early plains both hunters who followed the animals, and herders who tamed these grazing animals and lived on meats, blood and milk, as well as vegetation. The people of the North depended mainly on animal foods, since the winters were long and cold, and the vegetation was sparse. The people on coasts, lakes and rivers included fish in their food supply. In each area, man adapted himself to the foods available, and learned the skills required to live.

Seasonal Differences in Diets

Seasonally too, there were differences. Summers provided man with the juicy, fresh, perishable fruits and vegetables, which provide minerals and vitamins, and replace the water lost in the sweat of summer heat. During winters man relied on the storeables: seeds, roots, grains, and dried, smoked, and frozen meats. Many of these storeable foods contain highly concentrated energy, the fuels that keep us warm in cold weather: starches, and fats.

Animal-based Diets

The traditional Eskimo and Northern Canadian Indian diets come close to being completely animal-based, but these people ate virtually the whole animal, including the stomach contents of animals living off vegetation, and much of it raw. Organ meats such as liver, eyes, gonads, and brain were preferred to muscle meats, and on nutritional analysis (which became possible only in recent history), it turns out that organ meats are nutritionally superior to muscle meats. The stomach content (lichens, mosses, seaweed, and plankton) of the animals were eaten, and in summer, these people collected herbs from the almost barren land. These bits of vegetable matter provided fiber and vitamin C, both of which are difficult to obtain in sufficient quantities from animal sources, especially if they are cooked, dried, or stored.

Plant-based Diets

Completely vegetarian diets are also rare. One tribe, adapting a diet which lacks animal products, got its supply of calcium from limestone. Many other peoples relied on the grains and greens for their main meal, but could occasionally get their hands on meat, or eggs, or fish, or milk, or blood. Grain eaters got some of their nutrition from dried insects, crushed in the grain, or insect eggs. This was important, because vitamin B12, which is required, but only in minute quantities, is not present in grain, but is present in insects.

Changes in Dietary Preferences

Many changes have taken place over the history of civilization in man's food habits, and many traditional and time-tried healthful food habits have been lost.

Organ meats have taken a back seat in our present day consumption of animal products; we prefer the muscle meats, which are deficient in many mineral factors, low in several vitamins, and quite low in essential fatty acids.

After the domestication of wild animals, breeding, changes in feeding, and commercialization of certain stocks have resulted in changes in the quantity and quality of the fats in our animal foods. Processing of food substances has brought about changes in the fat, mineral, and vitamin content of these foods, as well as introducing into our food supply many substances foreign to body biochemistry. Transportation and storage have resulted in nutrient losses. Farming methods have depleted soils, bringing further decreases in the nutrient content of our foods.

Food consumption has been influenced by moral, ethical, philosophical, and religious considerations. In times of plenty, man can afford to indulge in the speculations (and he loves to!), and on these speculations he can, in times of plenty, base his food choices. Statements such as: 'Taking the life of conscious creatures is wrong!', and 'I don't think that anything that died in agony can be good food for humans!', are valid ethical notions, but don't usually stand up in the face of famine, nor do they necessarily stand up under the rigours of nutritional science which, at least at its best, deals in an objective fashion with the essential components of human nutrition, the amounts of each essential nutrient necessary for minimal or optimal health, and the sources of these essential nutrients in nature and our food supply. Nutritional science does not take the side of the vegetarian or the side of the meat eater, but can improve the health of both through better food choices based on nutritional information.

In this section, we will look at the different kinds of foods and their fat contents. We will observe how the fat content of the human diet has changed over history. It may give us some insight into why diets which *appear* to be the same, then as now, did not then, but do now, result in the diseases of fatty degeneration.

37

Fats in Foods

Fats in Membranes

Everything that lives contains some fats and oils. This is so because everything that lives is made up of cells, and all cells are surrounded by a membrane containing phosphatides; phosphatides, as we learned in Chapter 8, contain fatty acids.

All cells contain within them smaller sub-units called organelles which are the 'little organs' specialized for particular functions. These sub-units too, are surrounded by membranes containing phosphatides, which contain fatty acids.

Membranes contain between 20 and 80% phosphatides, depending on the type of cell or organelle under consideration. Red blood cells for instance, contain about 45% phosphatides and 55% proteins in their membranes, whereas the nerve cell membranes (the myelin sheath) contain 80% phosphatides and only 20% proteins. Membranes of some of the organelles, such as nuclear membrane, inner membrane of the mitochondria, and lysosomal membranes contain 25% phosphatides and 75% protein. Liver cell membranes and membranes of endoplasmic reticulum contain about 50% each of phosphatides and protein.

Membranes account for 1 to 3% of the cell's total weight, and the fats contained in low-fat green plants and fruits are found largely in their membranes.

Plants: leaves, stems, and roots. The cells of green plants contain 1% or less fats. According to the U.S. Department of Agriculture's Handbook #8 on the Composition of Foods, the lowest amount of fats is found in cucumbers, potatoes, beets, celery, kohlrabi, and squash, at .1% each. Cabbage, carrots, lettuce, and garlic are .2% fats. Kale, collard, and lamb's quarters are .8% fats, and dandelion greens and water cress are .7% each. The rest of the vegetables fall between .1 and .8% fats, except for seaweeds, which run between .3 and 3.2% fats.

The fats in the green parts of plants are of high quality, especially if eaten raw rather than cooked. More than half of the fatty acids of dark green leaves are the essential and triply unsaturated linolenic acid (LNA, 18:3*w*3), which is especially concentrated in the membranes of the green organelles, the chloroplasts. Here, LNA takes part in the process of photosynthesis, by which the plant captures sunlight energy and stores that energy in the bonds of the molecules that it makes — sugars, starches, proteins, and fats. The energy stored in the bonds of these molecules is the energy we need to live. We eat leaves, stems, roots, or seeds of these plants, and in our bodies the sunlight energy stored in the plant's molecules is slowly released through the process of respiration or oxidation, and this energy powers the molecular motors of our life. Indirectly, all life on earth depends on the ability of chlorophyll to trap, harness, and store sunlight. The meat we eat is either made from plants or made from flesh made from plants.

The membrane material of the other parts of plants contains up to half of its fatty acids in the form of the other essential fatty acid, the twice unsaturated linoleic acid (LA, 18:2*w*6). Both essential fatty acids in all living plant material are in the all *cis*- state. The essential fatty acids degenerate rapidly when the cells die, and so it is most healthful to eat as much as possible of our plant material fresh; if our vegetables are cooked and eaten immediately, that is still okay, but the leftovers, eaten the next day have lost much of the nutritional value due to oxidations processes by this time. Cooking itself often destroys more than half of the vitamin C present in fresh, raw vegetables.

Fruits. Fruits are similar to vegetables in fat content, except that the seeds are usually fairly high in fats.

Peaches and grapefruit are .1% fats each. Apples, apricots, gooseberries, and oranges are .2% fats. Lemons, figs, crabapples, and cherries are .3%. Pears and mangoes come in at .4%; blueberries at .5%; and blackberries at .9%.

The fats in fruits are similar to the non-green parts of plants in their fatty acid content. They contain less linolenic acid (18:3*w*3) than the green parts of plants, but contain both essential fatty acids, and are therefore highly nutritious, although obviously, their total fat content is low.

Because of their higher sugar content, fruits tend to put more weight on us than green vegetables, since fruit sugars are converted into fat in our bodies if we eat more fruit sugar than we can burn off in immediate activity.

Fats in Fat-Storing Cells

Besides the phosphatides found in the membranes of all cells, triglyceride fats may also be found in special fat-storing cells, found in the seeds of plants such as grains, legumes, and nuts, as well as in animal tissues. Figure 41 shows some of the major sources of different kinds of fatty acids.

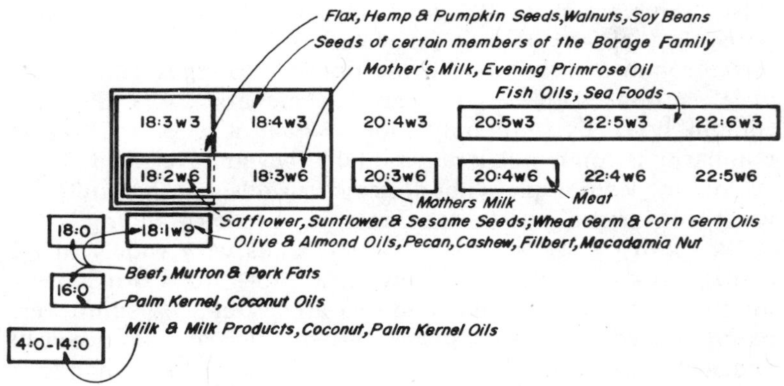

Figure 41. Major food sources of different fatty acids.

Depending on what percentage of the total number of cells are fat cells, a seed or tissue can contain from less than 2 to over 70% fats and oils. Let's take a look, beginning with the grains.

Grains. Grains usually contain between 1 and 3% fats. Amaranth is lowest, at .5% fats, followed by wild rice at .7%.

Barley is 1%, rye is 1.7%, and rice is 1.9% oils. Then comes wheat at 2%, buckwheat at 2.4%, millet at 2.9%, and sorghum grain tops the list at 3.3% oils.

The oils contained in the grains are about half LA, and so are good quality oils. The oils spoil rapidly when the grains are broken, pressed, or ground into flour. For this reason, store-bought rolled oats are often rancid during the summer months.

To keep flours from going rancid during the very long time that they sometimes spend on shelves and in warehouses, the oils are extracted from the seeds in modern milling practices (along with many other mineral and vitamin nutrients) to avoid the spoilage problem. Even insects cannot live on this flour anymore, and so refinement also protects against infestation by vermin. Whole grains can be cooked without destroying the valuable fatty acids, but once cooked, the nutrient value deteriorates rapidly with time. That's why old porridge tastes so limp.

Legumes. Among the legumes, there is a wide range of oil content. Lentils contain the least at 1.1% oil, followed by peas at 1.3%, mung and lima beans at 2%, chickpeas at 4.8%, and soybeans at 18% oils. Peanuts, which are not nuts but legumes (more pea than nut), top the list at 47.5% oils.

Soybeans are especially good, because soybean oil contains both essential fatty acids in fairly high quantities. Peanuts grow underground, and are prone to infection by the fungus *Aspergillus,* which produces the highly carcinogenic aflatoxins. Peanuts contain no LNA, and only modest quantities of LA. Their popularity is commercial; nutritionally they are overrated.

Cooking legumes does not destroy their oils, but their nutrient value is lost rapidly if after cooking, they are left standing.

Nuts and oil seeds. Nuts and oil seeds vary widely in oil content also. Chestnuts are lowest, at 1.5% oil. Corn is next lowest, at 4% oil. Coconuts and flax are about 35%, sunflower, pumpkin seed, cashew, safflower, and sesame seed are between 40 and 50% oil. Almonds, pistachios, and pine nuts are around 55% oil; brazil nuts, walnuts, and filberts go up to 60%; and macadamia nuts top the list at 71.6% oil.

The oil content of nuts and oil seeds varies quite a bit from year to year and with area of cultivation (northern plantings produce more oil in their seeds, to ensure adequate energy for sprouting seeds in colder climates). The figures given in the Handbook appear a little on the high side, perhaps because they are taken from seeds grown further north.

The kinds of fatty acids present in the oils of these seeds and nuts also vary widely. Some have no LNA, and some have very little LA in their oils. Others contain one or both in varying proportions (see: Oils in Seeds). Whole nuts and seeds are nature's way of excluding light and air from oils, and keep for a long time without spoiling. Broken nuts and seeds have lost this protection. Olives, whose oil is pressed from their flesh rather than their seed, contain 12 to 20% oil. This oil is low in essential fatty acids. The olive seed also contains oil, but this is not used in olive oil. Oils from all plant sources contain virtually no cholesterol. A few oils contain traces of it, but for practical purposes, the amount is so small that it can be ignored as a source of cholesterol in human nutrition.

Eggs. Whole eggs contain about 11% fats. The yolk contains about 30% fats and oils by weight. The egg white is fat free. An egg also contains about 250 mg of cholesterol. One third of the fats in *natural* free range eggs is essential fatty acids.

The fats found in eggs vary with the foods the chicken eats. If it forages for its own food, the yolk contains both LNA and LA, but if it is fed man-made chicken food which contains none of these two fatty acids, then the egg yolk will not contain them, either (see: Eggs).

Dairy Products. Among the dairy products, dry cottage cheese contains only .3% fat. Cow's milk contains about 3.5% fat, and goat's milk, about 4% fat. The milk of reindeer, domesticated by the Lapps of Northern Finland, contains a whopping 19.6% fat, similar to their body fat content. Human milk (not exactly a dairy product) contains about 4% fats (see: Fats in Milk and other Dairy Products). Cheeses vary widely. Some low-fat cheeses are less than 10% fat. Most normal cheeses and processed cheeses run between 20 and 30% fat. Fancy cheeses may contain over 30% fat, and cream cheeses, over 35% fat. Butter tops the list at 81% fat. The fatty acids in dairy products are mostly saturated, short chain, and easily digestible. From butter, about 500 different fatty acids have been isolated, many of them present in only trace amounts.

Dairy products contain *trans-* unsaturated fatty acids (up to 6% in summer and 3% in winter) produced from the LNA and LA present in grass by bacteria which live in the stomachs of cattle. The main *trans-* fatty acid component present in dairy fat is the *trans-* isomer of the monounsaturated vaccenic acid (t18:1*w*7), with its double bond between *w* carbons 7 and 8. This isomer is easier to digest than most of the *trans*- fatty acid isomers found in margarine.

Dairy products contain very little essential fatty acids (see: Butter vs. Margarine).

Sea foods. Among the sea foods, the shell fish are the lowest in oils. Scallops (and frog's legs) are .3% oils. Abalone are .5%, shrimp and octopus are .8%, mussels are 1.4%, and lobster, crab, oysters and clams are 2% oils.

Fish range in their oil contents between 1 and 15%. Cod, ling cod, and red snapper are the leanest fish, containing less than 1% oils. The roe (eggs) of cod, pike, shad, haddock and herring are about 2.3% oils. Whales are 7.5% oils, sardines 8.6%, and salmon, sturgeon, steelhead, lake trout, shad, and herring contain about 10% oils, and mackerel is up to 15% oils. The roe of salmon and sturgeon are also around 10% oils. Eel is about 18% oils.

In general, the warmer the water, the lower the fat content of the same kind of fish. Herring from the Atlantic, cooled by the Arctic current, have 11.3% oils, while Pacific herring, warmed by the Japanese current, have only 2.6% oils. The fat content of fish can also vary greatly with age, season, and spawning activity.

The oils of some fish and sea foods are very high in the highly unsaturated oils, and these find uses in ailments such as cancer, arthritis, and heart disease. The highly unsaturated fish oils lower the blood triglycerides, lower cholesterol slightly, and protect against fatty degeneration of inner organs. These oils are very sensitive and easily destroyed, and need protection from being attacked by light, oxygen and heat.

Not all marine animals and fish contain the highly unsaturated fatty acids. Sharks for instance, and the slower fish contain other fatty acids. Some fatty acids found in fish are toxic (see: Toxic Products).

Among the highly unsaturated fatty acids found in sardines, trout, salmon, and mackerel are two of special note: the 5 times unsaturated, 20 carbon eicosapentaenoic acid (EPA, 20:5*w*3), and the 6 times unsaturated, 22 carbon docosahexaenoic acid (DHA, 22:6*w*3). These have very low melting points (between -40° and -50°C), and are found in fish and marine animals living in very cold waters. The animals and humans of the far north, who live on these fish and marine animals incorporate these fatty acids into their own body fat. These oils keep the bodies of fish and marine animals fluid so they don't freeze solid at low temperatures. The oils supply a source of high energy at low temperatures; this energy is needed for fast getaway from danger. The oils also attract into the body the oxygen necessary for life functions, from water which does not contain all that much oxygen; the oils are extremely oxygen-loving, and are vital in many reactions involving oxygen[1] in these animals.

In humans, these oils are beginning to find use in the prevention and reversal of degenerative diseases resulting from overconsumption of the saturated and monounsaturated fatty acids (16:0, 18:0, 16:1*w*7, 18:1*w*7, and 18:1*w*9), which interfere with oxidation, and choke us to death by interfering with 'breathing' or respiration on the cellular level. EPA and DHA, and the other highly unsaturated fatty acids are extremely oxygen-loving, and in our bodies are able to overcome the choking effect of the 'bad' fatty acids. (see: Oils from Fish). EPA is also the precursor of the series 3 prostaglandins (see: Prostaglandins), which have beneficial effects on the state of health of our arteries, platelets, and triglycerides.

Meats from land animals. Wild animals carry less fat than their domesticated equivalents, and wild animals have a higher percentage of the essential fatty acids in their fat (see: Fats in Meats). Wild rabbit is 5%, and domestic rabbit is 8% fat. Venison carries about 3%, moose about 1% fat. Beef, their man-bred equivalent, is between 18% and 41% fat, almost all saturated and monounsaturated fatty acids. Some northern animals such as the domesticated reindeer of Lapland, average 19.6% fat. Their wild northern counterpart, the caribou, are only 3% fat. Mutton and lamb is 20 to 40% fat. Wild sheep are about 5% fat. Pork is between 35 and 60% fat[2], whereas wild pig has only 1.3% fat. Beef and lamb fats contain almost no LA. Pork fat contains up to 10% LA (see: Fats in Meats).

Fowl. Goose and duck are around 30% fat, chicken around 20 to 25% fat. Most of the fat of birds is just under their skin. The meat itself is only 7% fat. This is why doctors recommend fowl over beef, lamb, and pork for people who need to decrease their fat consumption, and the doctors always specify not to eat the skin. Fowl fat contains up to 25% LA, which helps to metabolize the saturated fats more than do beef, mutton or pork.

Organ meats. Organ meats are lower in fat and higher in essential fatty acids than muscle meats. Liver contains about 4% fat, brain about 9%, heart about 6 to 10%, kidney about 6%, etc. Organ meats are also richer in essential vitamins and minerals than muscle meats, and are therefore preferable to muscle meats from a nutritional point of view.

Meat Concoctions

Sausage meats vary in fat content, from 20 to 38% for salami, 27% for bologna, 37% for blood sausage, and 50% for some pork sausages. Weiners are about 43% fat. Most of the fats in these products are saturated. Some of these products also contain starch as fillers or 'extenders', and the starch, converted to saturated fat, adds to the load of saturated fats that the body must manage.

Processed Foods

A potato contains .1% oil, which is very low. If the potato is cut into sticks and french fried, the product now contains 13.2% oil, almost all of which has been picked up from the heated oil in which it was fried. A potato cut into thin slices and turned into a crunchy potato chip contains 39.8% partially hydrogenated fat, containing up to more than one third *trans-* fatty acids. Clearly, the natural composition of the potato has been changed drastically by these simple processes. A 'natural' potato chip is anything but natural, if 'natural' is used to mean the way nature made it.

There are literally hundreds of products on the market that contain hidden fats, sugars, starches, salt and of course, colourings, flavourings, preservatives, and other additives not found in nature. They interfere with the very delicate workings of natural biological systems, because they do not fit the highly specific structural or functional requirements of these systems. These hidden and unnatural substances comprise an unwelcome addition to the human diet, from the standpoint of health.

38

Cholesterol in Foods

Introduction

Both saturated, sticky, 'land animal' fats and cholesterol, and especially the combination of both in foods increase the unfriendly low density lipoprotein (LDL) cholesterol level in the blood, when their quantity in the foods consumed exceed the cells' capacity to absorb and the liver's ability to metabolize[1] these cholesterol-carrying transport vehicles from the blood. As a result, the amount of cholesterol carried in the blood remains high, and a high LDL level appears to enhance the slow build-up of the atherosclerotic plaque that narrows our arteries, and in time, kills us by what is known as a 'cardiovascular accident' (stroke, embolism, or heart attack), a combination of narrowed arteries and sticky blood cells and platelets. The 'cardiovascular accident' is really no accident.

For this reason, it is good to know which foods contain cholesterol, and how much, so that we can more carefully choose the level of cholesterol in our foods, to prevent or reverse the build-up of atherosclerotic plaques in our cardiovascular systems.

All cholesterol comes from animal sources, so if you want to be sure of minimum (zero) cholesterol intake, strict vegetarianism is your ticket. No meat, no eggs, no dairy products.

Worst and Best

The worst kind of animal product for raising LDL level in the blood is the kind which contains both saturated fats in high quantities and cholesterol. Although cholesterol consumption has remained about constant during the last 100 years, and therefore cannot be the *primary* cause of the increase in cardiovascular disease (350%) and cancer (600%) in that time period, it does worsen the problems caused by the 'sticky' saturated fats, and in the later stages of CVD, is involved in the deposits which narrow the arteries. Beef and mutton muscle meats are the highest in saturated fats. The inner organs of these animals are higher in cholesterol, but they are also higher in the essential fatty acids, which hook up with (esterify) cholesterol and aid to some extent — the exact extent has never been measured accurately enough to be agreed upon — in the metabolism and transport of cholesterol.

Because many cold water fish and other marine animals contain large amounts of the highly unsaturated fatty acids which tend to spread out (disperse) rather than stick together, these foods do not lead to cardiovascular problems, although they also contain cholesterol.

Cholesterol Content of Foods

Here are some figures, from highest cholesterol content to lowest, among animal foods. A 100 gram portion of brain contains over 2,000 mg of cholesterol. Next is 100 grams of egg yolk, with 1,500 mg of cholesterol (550 mg for 100 grams of whole egg). 100 grams of kidney contains 375 mg cholesterol; liver and caviar, 300; thymus and butter, 250. Then come oyster and lobster at 200, followed by heart at 150, shrimp and crab at 125, cream at 120, cheese at 100, lard at 95, veal at 90, beef, pork, and fish at 70, mutton at 65, chicken at 60, ice cream at 45, cottage cheese at 15, and milk at 11 mg cholesterol per 100 grams.

Supplements and Fiber

Unless you are taking a high potency vitamin and mineral supplement and/or the kinds of fiber[2] which binds bile acids and cholesterol in the intestine and removes them out of your body, you are wise to indulge in these items far less than is the custom in Western industrialized nations.

Sea Foods

Of all the cholesterol-containing foods, cold water animals and fish are the least troublesome for your heart, arteries, and immune system. While saturated 'sticky', hard fats and cholesterol are especially bad in combination, and are involved in every type of fatty degeneration, high levels of the highly unsaturated, 'dispersing' (anti-sticky), liquid fatty acids found in fish like salmon, trout, mackerel, and sardines protect against fatty degeneration, fat aggregation, and cholesterol deposits (see: Oils from Fish...).

39

Fats in Meats

Introduction

No aspect of nutrition illustrates as clearly as does meat production the influence that man's taking control of his food supply (by domestication, breeding, and commercialization) has had on its nutritional content and his physical health.

The diseases of fatty degeneration afflict mainly the people who eat diets high in beef, mutton and pork, and spares those people who live on diets high in the complex, unrefined carbohydrates made up of mostly grains and vegetables. Fatty degeneration also passes by those people who eat meat from wild animals or fish. Beef, mutton, and pork are not the only sources of fatty degeneration, however.

Some writers, who evidently like their steaks, lamb, and pork chops, suggest that meat and fats cannot possibly be the problem since man has been a hunter from the beginning. Even accepting man's hunting ancestry as true (which is open to debate), and notwithstanding the fact that man today does not exactly 'hunt' for his steaks in the old sense of the word, at great expense of energy and exercise with bow and arrow, spear, or stone implements, there is another important factor which is usually overlooked by the meat-loving writers: a comparison of the kinds and amounts of fats present in modern-day and wild meats.

Fat Content of Meats

If we compare the fat content of the domesticated animals with that of their wild counterparts, we discover that the domesticated animals have far higher fat content than the wild ones which our ancestors hunted. If we compare the types of fatty acids contained in the domestic animals and their wild counterparts, we find important differences in these as well. Let's look at some figures.

Beef is between 24 and 45% fats, mutton is between 20 and 40% fats, and pork runs between 35 and 60% fat. In comparison, venison and moose run a maximum of 5% fat, and are usually about 2-3% fat. Wild sheep too, are muscular and sleek; they could not survive for long in nature if they carried a lot of fat around. Wild pig carries only 1 to 3% fat. Even wild animals which live in the far north carry little extra fat, in spite of cold winter conditions. Wild caribou have only 3% fat, but the domesticated reindeer go up to almost 20% fat. In short, the 'hunter's' diet has increased in fat content with the domestication and breeding of animals. Beef over the years was specifically inbred for a marbled appearance, which results from fat deposits within the muscle tissue, and which is said to improve both the taste and the moistness of the meat. Rabbit has increased from 5% or less in the wild, to 8% in the domesticated. The same trend of increased fat is observed in all food animals which man has tamed.

Table D1 shows the results of one study which compared the fat content (in %) of several species of animals.

Of special note is the finding that the nomad cattle of East Africa, which are domesticated, but not inbred, are as low in fat content as their wild counterparts. When writers claim that the high meat diet of Africans does not predispose them to degenerative diseases, this is true. But when in the next breath they claim that therefore beef does not predispose us to these diseases, that is not true. The fat content in these two diets is very different.

Fatty Acid Composition of Meats

What about the kinds of fatty acids present in the fats of animals? Beef and mutton contain mostly the sticky, saturated fatty acids, which explains why their fats, such as tallow, are hard. Pork also contains mainly saturated fatty acids, but more of the essential, anti-sticky linoleic acid (LA, 18:2*w*6) is present, so

Table D1. Total fat content of domestic and wild pigs and cattle.

	Domestic		Wild
	Pig	Heavy Hog	Warthog
Fat (%)	38	46	1.3
Lean (%)	50	44	82
* Protein/Fat ratio	1/3	1/4	10/1

	Western			East African		
	Domestic Beef		Wild	Dom.	Wild	
	Fat	Lean	Venison	Zebu	Eland	Buffalo
Fat (%)	35	25	2	1.8	2	3
Lean (%)	50	55	76	71	79	75
* Protein/ Fat ratio	1/3	1/2	7/1	7/1	6/1	5/1

* Protein/fat is not the same as lean/fat because
  a) both fat and lean contain both protein and fat
  b) muscle tissue contains 80-85% water; fat tissue contains 30-50% water.

pork fat is softer and preferable in that regard to beef and lamb fats.

Let's look at some figures. Table D2 shows the results of another study, in which researchers measured the content of the different fatty acids present in cattle and pigs, both wild and domestic.

Cattle. Domestic cattle animals contained 40% saturated fatty acids: 28% palmitic acid (PA, 16:0) and 12% stearic acid (SA,

Table D2. Fatty acid content of wild and domestic animal fats.

	Fatty Acids (percent of total fat)						
	Non-Essential			Essential		Derivatives of Essential	
	Saturated		Mono-unsat.				20:5*w*3
	16:0	18:0	18:1*w*9	18:2*w*6	18:3*w*3	20:4*w*6	22:6*w*3
Cattle							
Wild	16	20	21	16	5	8.2	3.2
Domestic	28	12	40	2.1	.8	.7	.8
Pigs							
Wild	18	9.6	9	32	5	8.7	3.6
Domestic	24	13	34	10	.5	.4	.5

18:0); 40% monounsaturated oleic acid (OA, 18:1*w*9); only 2.1% of the essential linoleic acid (LA, 18:2*w*6), and only .7% of the other essential linolenic acid (LNA, 18:3*w*3), plus 1.5% of the highly unsaturated derivatives of both essential fatty acids. Since both the saturated and monounsaturated long chain fatty acids in the human body compete for enzymes which metabolize the essential fatty acids (see: Fatty Acids), we might guess that a ratio of 80% non-essential fatty acids to 2.1% of the essential fatty acids LA (or a ratio of 80:2.1) is not ideal for health.

Sure enough, tests have shown that in an oil containing oleic acid (OA, 18:1*w*9) and linoleic acid (LA, 18:2*w*6) in a ratio of 69 OA to 3.5 LA, the non-essential fatty acid OA completely inhibits the activity of the roughly 5% essential fatty acid LA present in the oil. This is the 'Critical Ratio'. From table D2 we can see that the ratio of OA:LA for beef fat is 40:2.1 or 69:3.6, which is very close to the critical ratio. Beef fat therefore contains almost no functional LA. But that's not the end of the bad news. There's more. The body can convert the saturated fatty acids into unsaturated ones. 16:0 is converted into 16:1*w*7 and 18:0 into more 18:1*w*9. These then compete with the essential fatty acids 18:2*w*6 and 18:3*w*3 for the enzymes which normally elongate and desaturate the essential fatty acids and make prostaglandins and other vital long chain derivatives from them. Although the enzymes prefer to work on the essential fatty acids, large quantities of the long chain non-essential fatty acids compete successfully for enzyme attention. Thus the ratio of OA:LA for fat is not just 40:2.1, but potentially 40(18:1*w*9) + 12(18:0) + 28(16:0) to 2.1 or 80:2.1, which is much lower than the critical ratio of 69:3.5. This means that the effect of eating beef fat is worse than getting no LA at all. Its long term consumption inhibits the function of the essential linoleic acid in the body. Beef fat might therefore be called an essential fatty acid robber.

In wild animals, the ratio of non-essential fatty acids to LA is 57:16, or 69:19, which is more than 5 times more LA than the critical value of 69:3.5. Clearly, there is enough LA in the fat of wild cattle to be active in humans, and not so much non-essential fatty acids to cancel out the ability of LA to function.

Pigs. Domestic pigs have a ratio of 71:10 or 69:9.7 (usually the LA content of pork is 10% or less), whereas the same ratio for free living warthogs is 37:32 or 69:59.7. Although some LA activity still occurs in the body of humans eating a diet high in domesticated pigs[1], the ratio found in wild members of the species is far better. Wild pig fat therefore has far higher LA activity. Refined sugars, and refined starches in desserts and confections, and saturated and altered fats in junk foods add further to the load of the non-essential fatty acids in the body and lower even more the amount of LA still able to function. For this reason, the domestic pig diet might be considered close to marginal in LA., e.g., pork chops with sweetened apple sauce followed by dessert.

Essential fatty acids are involved in regulating the muscle tone of the arterial walls and thereby the blood pressure, via the prostaglandins formed from them (see: Prostaglandins). They are important in keeping the blood vessels elastic. Essential fatty acids are also required for the metabolism of cholesterol (see: Essential Fatty Acids).

It is easy to see that cholesterol metabolism will be hampered, the arteries will harden, and the blood pressure will rise, when there is a functional deficiency of LA. From our consideration of the fat content of the three most commonly eaten meats, such a deficiency appears to be quite likely on the normal, affluent, Western diet.

The traditional Eskimo diet is high in both meat and fat, and yet these people are completely free of degenerative diseases. This finding is easy to explain when we understand the quality of the fatty acids found in their foods (see: Oils from Fish and other Sea Foods).

A Hopeful Note

We can end this chapter on a hopeful note. With the volume of information emerging on the role of the saturated fatty acids in heart and arterial disease, stroke, high blood pressure, and kidney failure, the meat industry is starting to listen and to think. The American Heart Association, the American Academy of Science, and several other official and government bodies have all recommended decreasing our consumption of red meats because of their high content of saturated fatty acids. There is talk in the beef industry of growing leaner red meat animals, or breeding the fat back out of beef. One of the ways to do this would be to cross the lean East African Cattle with beef, or perhaps one could import and grow East African Cattle here. Beef crossed with buffalo, and called 'beefalo' is beginning to appear on restaurant menus. If customers keep asking the butcher for extremely lean, red meats (3-5% fats), they can help, from their end, to encourage the meat industry to produce red meats which won't kill us.

40

Fats in Milk and Dairy Products

History

Mother's milk is primordial. Its origin reaches back through the dark shadows of the past, to a time when reptiles evolved into mammals and began to hatch their eggs within the safety of their own bodies instead of just laying the eggs, running off, and leaving the hatchlings to fend for themselves. The young mammals were better protected than young reptiles, and had a better chance of survival with the extra maternal care. Mother's milk goes back to the time when the cold-blooded reptiles began to warm up, an adaptation that made them able to move faster even in cold climates, at a time when the earth's climate was cooling off.

Human Milk

As time progressed, the little reptiles-cum-mammals changed, through many new forms, to give rise to... us. That's if you believe in evolution. If not, then mother's milk has been around since Eve begat. In either case, mother's milk as human food has been around as long as we have, and only the last few generations in recent civilized history have worshipped the breast as an anatomical ornament while feeding their children ersatz out of a bottle.

According to figures published by the World Health Organization, mother's milk contains about 4.4% fat, of which an average of 8% is the essential linoleic acid (LA, 18:2*w*6). It also contains gamma-linolenic acid (GLA, 18:3*w*6) and traces of dihomogamma-linolenic acid (DGLA, 20:3*w*6), both of which are intermediates in the production of the different members of the PG1 family of prostaglandins (see: Prostaglandins). DGLA may also be converted to arachidonic acid (AA, 20:4*w*6)[1], which is the parent substance from which the prostaglandins of the PG2 family are made. GLA and DGLA are absent from most other human foods, and are not present in dairy products. Mother's milk, by ensuring the newborn of a plentiful supply of prostaglandins, gives the baby a healthy cardiovascular start into its new world.

Several studies have measured the content of the different fatty acids present in the fats of mother's milk. The studies show wide variations in fatty acid content, depending on the kind of diet the mother eats. Table D3 shows the pooled results of the studies.

Table D3. Fatty acid composition of human breast milk.

Fatty Acids (percent of total fat)

	10:0	12:0	14:0	16:0	16:1	18:0	18:1	18:2	18:3	*w*6 long	*w*3 long
*	2.5	8	11	25	2	6.2	30	9.2	.9	.9	1.3
**omnivore				$\underline{27.6}$		$\underline{10.8}$	$\underline{35.3}$	(6.9)	(.8)		
**vegan				(16.6)		(5.2)	31.3	$\underline{31.7}$	1.5		
**Japanese				22.2		(5.5)	(27.9)	13.0	$\underline{2.5}$		
**American				21.9		7.6	$\underline{37.7}$	14.5	1.9		

Numbers in brackets are lower than average.
Numbers underlined are higher than average.

* Average from studies carried out by FAO/WHO
** Values reported by Tinoco

It is especially interesting that breast milk of a strict vegetarian mother is very high in the essential fatty acid LA (18:2), and low in the sticky saturated fatty acids 16:0 and 18:0. Strict vegetarians have less than 1/4 the average rate of death from cardiovascular disease, and it looks like their protection from this disease starts early in life.

Japanese (and Eskimoes) have a higher content of the *w*3 fatty acids in their milk than North Americans. This results from their high intake of the oils of fish, marine animals, and seaweed, and protects these people too, against cardiovascular disease, starting from an early age.

Cow's Milk

Cow's milk averages about 3.5% fat, a little less than human milk, and its history as human food is quite old. It is praised in East Indian scriptures over 5,000 years old, and cheese-making equipment has been unearthed in old Stone Age dwellings in Switzerland, also from about 5,000 years ago. It is likely that the actual use of dairy products goes back much further than that. A typical milk fat sample has the fatty acid composition shown in Table D4.

Table D4. Fatty acid composition of cow's milk.

Fatty Acids (percent of total fat)

4:0	6:0	8:0	10:0	12:0	14:0	16:0	18:0	18:1	18:2	18:3
3	2	2.5	1	5	10	30.6	12.5	26.9*	3.1	1

* Includes 3 to 6% *trans*- vaccenic acid (t18:1*w*7)

The fatty acid content of cow's milk too, can be modified by diet, to increase its content of 18:2 and 18:3. However, this is more difficult to achieve in cows than in humans, because bacteria in the cow's four stomachs automatically destroy these two essential fatty acids by hydrogenating (saturating) them. To prevent this bacterial destruction of the essential fatty acids, the cow's food has to be specially coated and processed, an expensive and time-consuming procedure which is economically unfeasible. Besides, the milk which results from this endeavour, though high in LA, tastes rancid, due to the presence of formaldehyde, a preservative and carcinogen which is fed to the cattle to knock out the bacteria in the cow's stomachs which normally saturate the essential fatty acids the cow gets from its food. For this reason, cow's milk is almost always low in essential fatty acids.

Cow's milk contains many different types of fatty acids, and about 500 have been isolated so far. Most of them are present in only minute quantities. Only the major fatty acids are shown in table D4. Cow's milk fat contains many short chain fatty acids, which are easy to digest, but is higher than human milk in both 16:0 and 18:0, the sticky, saturated fatty acids.

Other Milks

Goat's milk contains about 4% fats, and these fats are higher than cow's milk in the short chain fatty acids, making goat's milk easier to digest than cow's milk. Goat's milk, like cow's milk, is low in the essential fatty acids, (EFAs), because goats too, have the bacteria in their four stomachs which destroy the EFAs.

Other animals which have been used for the production of milk as human food include sheep, camels, asses, water buffaloes, llamas, zebu, reindeer, and mares.

In Russia, mare's milk was fermented to make the original kefir, and an analysis of the milk shows why it had such a good reputation for enhancing health. Mare's milk contains a whopping 38.4% of its fatty acids in the form of the second essential fatty acid, linolenic acid (LNA, 18:3*w*3)[2], and almost none of the sticky 18:0. The figures are given in Table D5.

Table D5. Fatty acid composition of mare's milk.

Fatty Acids (percent of total fat)				
16:0	18:0	18:1	18:2	18:3
19.9	1	18.6	7.4	38.4

The famous name 'kefir' was imported to North America, but the mare's milk remained in Russia. You may be relieved to know that the kefir sold here is a cow's milk product, but on the other hand, the mare's milk would have been a lot better for you. The high content of LNA in horses is also reflected in the makeup of their serum, their blood fluid, where it is found associated with sulphur-containing proteins. Dr. Budwig used horse serum in some of her experiments, and found that it dissolves hard cancerous tumours. This is part of the research that led her to the flax oil — sulphur-rich protein combination which she uses successfully to dissolve tumours in humans (see: Oil-Protein Combinations).

Milk from animals that live in the cold far north has a very high milk fat content, and the milk fat is high in the *w*3 long chain fatty acids, which are required by these animals to supply the energy they need to keep warm. Polar bear milk contains 31% fat, dolphin milk is 19% fat, and harp seal milk is 50% fat, almost the consistency of soft margarine, but a whole lot more nutritious.

Dolphin milk contains almost 15% of its fats as the natural long chain *w*3 polyunsaturated 20:5*w*3 and 22:6*w*3 and another 1.2% as the *w*6 polyunsaturated 20:4*w*6 and 22:5*w*6; harp seal milk contains about 10% of its fatty acids as *w*3 and *w*6 polyunsaturates. Both dolphin and harp seal milk contain a very low level of the sticky saturated stearic acid (18:0). All these pieces of information are in line with the requirements for living in the northern climate which these mammals call home, and their need and ability not to curdle in cold weather. You probably will never get to drink much of any of these kinds of milk. Polar bears, dolphins and seals won't stand still to be milked, except by their cubs.

The above information is useful for a different reason. It shows that the fatty acid profiles of the fats in the food supply, the fats in the fat tissues, and the fats in the milk of any particular type of animal are similar. It shows that both fat tissue and milk are adapted to the needs of the climate (see: Oils and Sunshine), and that they differ from one species of animal to the next. Finally, it shows that all the information we can gather from studying the fat composition of the milk of these different animals lines up nicely with our notions of which fats cause fatty degeneration, and which fats prevent and heal it, or, why the traditional Eskimoes were free of these diseases, and why we are not.

Dairy Products Other Than Milk

Not much remains to be said about the other dairy products made from the milk of sheep, goats, and cows. By extracting the water or removing all or part of the fat from milk, man makes products whose fat content varies from less than 1% fat in skim milk and dry cottage cheeses, to close to 50% fat, in some of the gourmet and cream cheeses (see: Fats in Foods).

The fatty acid profile of the fats in dairy products are similar to the fatty acid profile of milk, and all dairy products are quite low in the essential fatty acids. They add nothing to help alleviate the fat problems of human beings, and taken in excess, even enhance these fat problems. They raise triglyceride and cholesterol levels, and increase platelet stickiness. Although they contain good protein, calcium and other minerals, and many dairy products taste delicious, from the fats and oils point of view, they leave a lot to be desired.

The cholesterol content of dairy products, combined with the sticky fatty acids creates a burden for the body, that has to be carried by the fat-dispersing *w*3 and *w*6 acids, which must come from another source. Human milk, although it also contains cholesterol, also contains the dispersing essential fatty acids which help to keep cholesterol from settling in the walls of our arteries. Human milk is therefore much better adapted for human consumption than the foods that the cow (or any of her relatives) produces.

41

Fats in Poultry

Introduction

In contrast to beef, whose meat is marbled with fats throughout the muscle tissues (beef was bred by man especially for this effect), birds carry the bulk of their fat just under the skin. For this reason, it is easy to separate the fats from the meats, should this be desired.

Fat Content

Table D6 gives the fat content of the different parts of the birds most commonly eaten.

According to these figures, turkey meat without the skin is the leanest meat from poultry. Because this is true, turkey is also the driest meat. More fats make meats more 'moist'. White meat contains less oil than dark meat, and is therefore drier. We know this from our own experience.

The skin of poultry is loaded with fat. For people on low-fat diets, doctors recommend that they eat only the meat and leave the skin. The figures in Table D6 show the difference in the fat contents of meat and skin.

Young birds are more lean than older ones. Domestic turkeys

Table D6. Fat content of common fowl.

	Fat Content (percent of total weight)					
	Total Fat	Skin	White Meat	Dark Meat	Innards	Linoleic Acid (18:2*w*6)
Turkey - young	14.7	39.2	.4	2.6	6.6	15-20%
- old	14.7	39.2	1.2	4.3	6.6	15-20%
Chicken	17.9	28.9	1.9-3.7	4.7-7.5		20-25%
Goose	31.5		7.1			
Duck - domestic	28.6		8.2			
- wild	15.8		5.2			

get middle aged spread, just like humans. Inner organs contain higher fat content than muscle meats, but less fat than skins.

Fowl contains more of the essential linoleic acid (LA, 18:2*w*6) than either beef fat, which has only about 2% or pork fat, which has up to 10% LA, but far less than the good oil seeds. Oily fish contain far more of the other, *w*3 essential fatty acid family. Goose and duck contain more oil in their meats and skins than do chicken and turkey. Goose grease was used traditionally in much the same way as lard, for frying.

Domestic birds are higher in fat content than wild birds, as usual. This is also true for other birds such as pheasant, quail, and pigeon. Fat wild animals perish quickly. Changes in feeding and commercial poultry raising practices have resulted in increases of the fat content of the birds sold to customers.

Nursery Wisdom

Most of us are familiar with the nursery rhyme about Jack Spratt and his wife:

Jack Spratt would eat no fat.
His wife would eat no lean.
So twixt them both,
They cleared the cloth
And licked the platter clean.

However, how many of us realize the practical wisdom in the verse? Jack Spratt and his wife had a useful arrangement. He avoided the fat, and she wasted no food. He kept his arteries clean and so avoided a coronary or stroke, and she could eat the fats, because her hormones (estrogens) protected her from cardiovascular disease at least until her menopause. This old traditional nursery rhyme is based on sound understanding of fats.

In practice however, men consume slightly more fats than women, and women avoid eating fats, more for mistaken cosmetic reasons[1] than for health. This is unfortunate, because men are 3 times more prone than women to get fat clogging their arteries, and they die of cardiovascular disease 3 times more frequently.

42

Eggs

Wild Birds' Eggs

The egg is primarily the bird's way of making other birds, and not primarily for man's culinary pleasure. To make a whole bird out of an egg, the egg has to contain within it all the nutritional factors necessary for the task of creating a fully formed, hatchable, living chick, and that is why the egg is (or was) such a good source of nutrition for man, whenever he succeeded in stealing it from the bird before the latter brooded and hatched it and it flew away.

Eggs contain about 11% fats. The yolk contains about 30% fats by weight; the white is fat-free. An egg contains about 250 mg of cholesterol. For primitive man, eggs were a delicacy. Since he did not keep birds, he had to find and then pilfer the hidden nests of birds, and so eggs for him were a rare treat. Birds laid only a few eggs every year, and these eggs were nutritionally rich.

Domestication

As man domesticated birds, a number of changes occurred. First, he fed them grains and other household discards. Second, he sheltered them, so their egg laying capacity increased, and his consumption of eggs became more regular. Even then, winters were eggless, a time of rest for the chicken, to gather its resources for the next breeding, laying, and hatching season.

Commercial Egg Production

When commercial egg production became a 'scientific' business, several other changes took place. One of these was the introduction of chicken feeds scientifically formulated to maximize egg production. It is called 'getting everything out of the chicken'. These feeds replaced grains, insects, and plant materials that the birds obtained in the wild.

There were other commercial considerations — how to keep the chicken alive and producing in the least labour-intensive situation. This resulted in the 'battery', where the chickens spend their life indoors, eating and laying, till they die. Antibiotics were added to the feed to keep the cooped up chickens 'healthy'.

The feed make-up was changed to increase its shelf life. Grains and seeds are nature's way of packaging nutrients for long 'shelf' life; and to obtain fresh greens, free chickens foraged in the barnyard. When the nutrients were formulated into commercial feeds which lack nature's packaging genius, these feeds or at least some of their ingredients, were not protected from spoiling. Of course, feeds that spoil are unsuitable as commercial products, because commercial products need to be stable during their long time in transport, in the warehouse, and on the retail shelf. To accommodate this commercially valid consideration, some of the most easily spoilable of the nutrients had to be taken out. Guess what they were? You guessed it. The easily spoilable but essential (to humans at least) linoleic acid (LA, 18:2*w*6) and linolenic acid (LNA, 18:3*w*3), which are present in the natural chicken diet of grain, seeds and greens, were replaced by the much more stable but non-essential oleic acid (OA, 18;1*w*9). The result of this change in the composition of chicken feed is eggs high in OA, but low in LA and LNA, eggs with the same amount of cholesterol, but less of the fatty acids required to metabolize and transport it properly in the human body.

Another change occurred in eggs. With the 'refinement' of commercial chicken feeds, plant sterols, which are found naturally in all vegetables and which reduce the cholesterol content of eggs by up to 35%, were removed from the chickens' diet. Commercial eggs therefore contain more cholesterol than home grown, barnyard eggs. This is why eggs, considered for centuries a most nutritious food, have been attacked during the last 35 years as a source of cardiovascular disaster[1].

Over the course of the years, 'improvements' in commercial methods have resulted in the ability to produce cheaply by the millions, eggs whose yolks are almost colourless, almost tasteless, and unhatchable. Not exactly a 'good egg' anymore. Chickens in concentration camps, like humans, don't perform at their best, because they are not in a healthy situation. Like humans, they require for health, sunshine, fresh food, fresh air, and room to move.

Free Range Eggs

Health-conscious consumers have created a market for a return to more 'primitive' small-scale methods of egg production, the free range eggs, or eggs from free ranging chickens. These chickens are also fed some commercial mash — without it, with just what the chicken can scratch for itself, egg production would be too low, and the price therefore too high — but free range chickens are allowed to run around and forage for themselves as well. The difference in the taste is amazing. Although precise biochemical analyses to compare the nutritional merits of the two types of eggs have not been done (no one has been willing to support such research), the difference in taste points to differences in nutritional content. To compare the nutritional qualities of battery and free range eggs would be a worthwhile project for a budding young scientist.

Where I live it is illegal to advertise free range chicken eggs. If such advertising were allowed, the Egg Marketing Board might have to explain the difference and they don't want to have to do this. The colour of the egg shell is not an indicator. Brown eggs are not a sign of better nutritional quality. The colour of the egg shell depends on the kind of chicken which laid the egg. The nutritional value of the egg depends on what the chicken ate.

It is possible to 'doctor' the colour of the egg yolk with beta-carotene, but this is not usually done because beta-carotene is expensive (bottled oils are sometimes doctored with B-carotene or other dye). Perhaps artificial dyes might be used. So it is wise for the consumer to know the source of his eggs. Free range eggs are usually found only in health food stores and on farms. Since free range eggs cannot be advertised and there is no government control, someone might sell you battery eggs as free range. The surest way is to keep your own chickens, because then you know what you have, and you don't have to feed them commercial preparations. The chicken can only make eggs as good as the feed it gets, so a bad egg is not the chicken's fault. When it is free to pick its own food, it makes great tasting, and nutritionally superior eggs.

Free ranging chickens lay few eggs in winter, because it is their time of rest. Winter is not a good time to hatch eggs, so in keeping with the flow of nature, between November and February, such eggs are hard to find. This is another way of telling whether your eggs are free range. The custom of pickling or 'jelling' was used traditionally to make the eggs go round when the chickens quit for the year.

43

Oils in Seeds

Introduction

The seeds of most plants contain oils[1], which serve as the high energy starter for the seedling. Just like the chicken's egg, the plant seed has to contain enough energy for sprouting a whole plant, and for growing the first root, first stem, and first leaves, which then take over the functions of drawing water and minerals from the soil, drawing sunshine from the sun, and conducting the former up and the latter down. The oil in the seed is the mother's breast for the seedling until the new plant becomes independent.

The tougher the conditions, the more oil the seed needs to store. The colder the climate, the more of the highly unsaturated fatty acids it contains in its oils to increase its metabolic rate. For this reason, the amounts of the various fatty acids contained in oil from different seeds varies greatly.

Oil Content

The amount of oil found in the different kinds of seeds varies from 4% for corn to over 70% for pecans. There are wide variations in oil content of seeds from the same plant in d. years and from different locations, so that tables giving t.. values are only typical, and not firm values.

Fatty Acid Composition

Table D7 lists the common (and some not so common) oil seeds and their fatty acid composition.

The best oils for human nutrition are flax, hemp, pumpkin, soy, and walnut oils, because all of these oils contain both essential fatty acids.

Table D7. Fat content and fatty acid composition of different seed oils.

<table>
<tr><th></th><th>Fat Content</th><th colspan="5">Fatty Acid Composition (% of total oil)</th><th></th></tr>
<tr><th>Name</th><th>(%)</th><th>18:3w3</th><th>18:2w6</th><th>18:1w9</th><th>18:0</th><th>16:0</th><th>Problems</th></tr>
<tr><td>flax</td><td>35</td><td>58</td><td>14</td><td>19</td><td colspan="2">9</td><td></td></tr>
<tr><td>hemp</td><td>35</td><td>25</td><td>55</td><td>12</td><td>2</td><td>6</td><td>illegal</td></tr>
<tr><td>pumpkin</td><td>46.7</td><td>15</td><td>42</td><td>34</td><td>0</td><td>9</td><td></td></tr>
<tr><td>soy bean</td><td>17.7</td><td>9</td><td>50</td><td>26</td><td colspan="2">15</td><td></td></tr>
<tr><td>walnut</td><td>60</td><td>5</td><td>51</td><td>28</td><td>5</td><td>11</td><td></td></tr>
<tr><td>evening prim.</td><td></td><td></td><td>81*</td><td>11</td><td>2</td><td>6</td><td></td></tr>
<tr><td>safflower</td><td>59.5</td><td></td><td>75</td><td>13</td><td colspan="2">12</td><td></td></tr>
<tr><td>sunflower</td><td>47.3</td><td></td><td>65</td><td>23</td><td colspan="2">12</td><td></td></tr>
<tr><td>grape</td><td></td><td></td><td>71</td><td>17</td><td colspan="2">12</td><td></td></tr>
<tr><td>corn</td><td>4</td><td></td><td>59</td><td>24</td><td colspan="2">17</td><td></td></tr>
<tr><td>wheat germ</td><td>10.9</td><td></td><td>54</td><td>28</td><td colspan="2">18</td><td></td></tr>
<tr><td>sesame</td><td>49.1</td><td></td><td>45</td><td>42</td><td colspan="2">13</td><td></td></tr>
<tr><td>rice bran</td><td>10</td><td></td><td>35</td><td>48</td><td colspan="2">17</td><td></td></tr>
<tr><td>cotton</td><td></td><td></td><td>50</td><td>21</td><td colspan="2">25</td><td>toxic ingreds.</td></tr>
<tr><td>rape (canola)</td><td>30</td><td>7</td><td>30</td><td>54**</td><td colspan="2">7</td><td>toxic fatty acid</td></tr>
<tr><td>peanut</td><td>47.5</td><td></td><td>29</td><td>47</td><td colspan="2">18</td><td>(toxic fungus)</td></tr>
<tr><td>almond</td><td>54.2</td><td></td><td>17</td><td>78</td><td colspan="2">5</td><td></td></tr>
<tr><td>olive</td><td>20</td><td></td><td>8</td><td>76</td><td colspan="2">16</td><td></td></tr>
<tr><td>coconut</td><td>35.3</td><td></td><td>3</td><td>6</td><td colspan="2">91</td><td></td></tr>
<tr><td>palm kernel</td><td>35.3</td><td></td><td>2</td><td>13</td><td colspan="2">85</td><td></td></tr>
<tr><td>beech</td><td>50</td><td></td><td>32</td><td>54</td><td colspan="2">8</td><td></td></tr>
<tr><td>brazil</td><td>66.9</td><td></td><td>24</td><td>48</td><td colspan="2">24</td><td></td></tr>
<tr><td>pecan</td><td>71.2</td><td></td><td>20</td><td>63</td><td colspan="2">7</td><td></td></tr>
<tr><td>pistachio</td><td>53.7</td><td></td><td>19</td><td>65</td><td colspan="2">9</td><td></td></tr>
<tr><td>hickory</td><td>68.7</td><td></td><td>17</td><td>68</td><td colspan="2">9</td><td></td></tr>
<tr><td>filbert</td><td>62.4</td><td></td><td>16</td><td>54</td><td colspan="2">5</td><td></td></tr>
<tr><td>macadamia</td><td>71.6</td><td></td><td>10</td><td>71</td><td colspan="2">12</td><td></td></tr>
<tr><td>cashew</td><td>41.7</td><td></td><td>6</td><td>70</td><td colspan="2">18</td><td></td></tr>
</table>

* Includes 9% of 18:3w6, gamma-linolenic acid.
** Includes up to 5% erucic acid.

The Best Oils

Flax oil is the best seed oil for people with fatty degeneration, because the oil contains the largest amount of the most strongly dispersing essential fatty acid, the three times unsaturated linolenic acid (LNA, 18:3*w*3)[2]. LNA helps to disperse from our tissues deposits of the saturated fatty acids and cholesterol, which like to aggregate and which make platelets sticky. The oil has to be fresh, and not exposed to light, oxygen, and heat, because these three agents destroy the essential fatty acids very rapidly. Flax oil should be in opaque containers and fresh, not older than 3 months after pressing.

Hemp oil is an excellent oil but it is illegal, because it comes from the seeds of the marijuana plant. When my parents were children in Russia, they remember huge, lush fields of dark green hemp plants. The fiber of the plants was used to make hemp rope; the seeds were used to make delicious 'hemp butter' that puts our peanut butter to shame for nutritional value; the leaves were ploughed back under for organic fertilizer. No one cared to smoke the plant!

Pumpkin seed oil is dark green and delicious, but hard to obtain in North America. Walnut oil has a delightful flavour, but is difficult to find fresh. Soy oil is high quality, except that the yield is low (only 18% of the bean), and it is often refined, so it is better to eat the bean than the extracted oil. Also, breeding experiments to make strains of soybean with lower LNA content are under way. If such strains become commercial — they have better shelf life — we will have succeeded in lowering the quality of another excellent food. It would make a lot more sense to keep the nutritional value of the oils intact and invent better methods of pressing, preserving and storing and to improve the technology of transport, so that good oils reach the customer fresh. The technology for making and keeping oils is already available. It just has to be applied.

All of these oils need to be pressed and treated with care, and stored in opaque containers, away from light, oxygen and heat. All of them are nutritionally superior, but must be consumed fresh. So far, in North America, there is no fresh oil from these superior seeds available to consumers, pressed, packaged, and delivered in such a way that the customer gets it unspoiled.

Good Oils

The next 3 oils in the table are good oils, but they don't contain any of the essential LNA. They therefore are not as good as the first 5. However, the body's need for the other essential fatty acid, the twice unsaturated linoleic acid (LA, 18:2*w*6), may be even higher than its need for LNA, and these oils supply good quantities of the major essential fatty acid.

Both safflower and sunflower seed oils are available unrefined in health food stores alongside the refined oils. Generally they are sold in transparent bottles, and this means that they are exposed to light while waiting for you to come and get them. These oils too, should be in metal containers, safe from light, air and heat.

None of the oils considered so far are good oils for frying, baking and cooking, because the essential fatty acids are destroyed by heat (see: Frying). These oils are great in salads, dressings, mayonnaises, and in any dishes prepared and eaten fresh, using the oil-protein combination (see: Oil-Protein Combination). To improve our health, some of our preferred habits, such as frying with oils, may have to be changed. Obviously, some of these habits, either handed down or learned from recent food trends, are not giving us the present day health we'd like to enjoy.

Evening primrose oil is a special oil. It is used therapeutically only, and is sold in small capsules in health food stores. It is more expensive than bottled oils, because the seeds are extremely small and must be hand-picked several times during each season, as they don't all ripen at the same time. The oil contains gamma linolenic acid (GLA, 18:3*w*6) which is triply unsaturated, but not to be confused with linolenic acid (LNA, 18:3*w*3) by healthy individuals, and is found in mother's milk as well. In certain conditions of illness and dietary deficiency in which the body becomes unable to make GLA, evening primrose oil capsules can be taken to compensate for this inability. GLA is a necessary step in the production of certain prostaglandins (see: Prostaglandins), which have important functions in maintaining cardiovascular health, and whose absence results in diverse diseases affecting the arteries and heart, the menstrual cycle, the glands, the joints, mental function, and metabolic rate (see: Oil of Evening Primrose).

More Good Oils

Sesame seed oil has a pleasant natural flavour, and is easy to press without heat. It therefore does not need to be refined.

Grape seed oil is also a good oil, but rarely available, and fairly intense heat is required to express the oil, because the seeds are so hard. You'd have to eat a lot of grapes to collect enough seeds to get a teaspoon full of oil, but it might be a good idea to buy seeded grapes instead of seedless ones[3], and to crunch up the nutritious seeds instead of throwing them away. Your digestive system will extract the high quality oils contained in the seeds, without destroying their quality or losing the vitamins and minerals they also contain.

Corn oil is usually chemically extracted and refined, but occasionally one can obtain mechanically pressed, unrefined corn oil pressed from corn germ. This latter oil has a nice flavour and is good quality oil. Wheat germ oil is also good oil, and contains octacosanol[4], which protects the heart and improves heart function. It also contains large quantities of vitamin E. Rice bran oil is the last member of the good oils.

Skin Oils

Almond and olive oils are nice, but too low in essential fatty acids to be a good oil for people on a diet which also contains large quantities of saturated animal fats. Olive oil was used traditionally for liver flushes when the human diet contained a lot less fat, but its usefulness has declined in recent years, and increasingly often it is found to be ineffective in relieving overworked livers. Both almond and olive oils can be used in massage, but fresh oils containing more essential fatty acids are better.

Seed Oils That Can Be Heated

Coconut and palm kernel oils may be used for cooking, baking, and frying, but contain only very small quantities of the essential fatty acids which the body needs for health. These oils are preferable to the essential fatty acids-containing oils for heating purposes, because heat does not turn them into poisonous breakdown products which interfere with essential fatty acid functions in the body. The saturated fatty acids contained in coconut and palm kernel oils are inert and therefore heat-stable. They are best when they are not hydrogenated, nor should a lot of them be eaten, as they are the sticky types of fat.

Some Not So Good Oils

The rest of the oils on the list have one or more of several possible problems. Cotton and rape seed oils contain toxic natural ingredients, and peanut oils may contain carcinogenic substances made by a fungus which grows in damp peanuts (see: Toxic Products). Most of the remaining oils on the list are refined, bland, nutritionally questionable, pesticide-containing oils. Many natural ingredients of the raw oil, including lecithin, carotene (provitamin A), vitamin E, essential minerals and other vital substances have been removed from these oils. Aromatic substances responsible for the pleasant bouquets of oils such as almond have also been taken out. They contain *trans-* fatty acids (see: Trans-Fatty Acids) and other altered oil products.

If they are not refined or sprayed with pesticides, the oils as far down the list as rice bran are okay. An oil should contain at least 1/4 of its fatty acids as essential fatty acids (LA and/or LNA) to be passable, and at least 1/3 of its fatty acids as LA and/or LNA to be good; 2/3 or more of their fatty acids as essential fatty acids is desirable in a superior nutritional oil, but such an oil must be unrefined. When refined and thereby unprotected, superior oils become dangerous to health because of their tendency to form free radicals when they come in contact with light or oxygen.

Whole Seeds

If it is not possible to get good, fresh oils, the seeds are nutritionally the most completely balanced way to get these good, fresh oils. The seeds also contain vitamins, minerals, proteins, and fiber.

In view of the nutritional value of some of these seeds, you might reconsider throwing away the seeds of squash and other members of the pumpkin family, and of watermelon and other members of the melon family. Of course, the seeds of apple, pear, prune plum, apricot, and nectarine can also be eaten with the fruit. This is customary practice in many older cultures, including traditions which are famous for their health and long life, like Hunza, and parts of Russia. In India, even the seeds of papayas are eaten for their nutritional value and their tonic effects on nerves. They have a slight peppery nip, reminiscent of radishes or watercress. Perhaps we need to re-examine our habit of throwing away the seed, that most nutritious parts of many of our foods.

44

Butter Versus Margarine

Background

Is butter better than margarine? This question began a popular battle in the media, created by the dairy board and the oil processing industry. Everyone loves a good controversy, and this one has become a good advertising tool for both sides. Let's look at the nature of butter and margarine in light of what we know about the fatty acids and their metabolism in the body.

Butter

About 500 different fatty acids have been isolated from butter so far. Butter contains butyric acid (4:0) and other short chain fatty acids (6:0, 8:0, 10:0), which are easy to digest. Score 1 point for butter. But butter is quite low in the essential fatty acids, containing only about 2% linoleic acid (LA, 18:2*w*6) and virtually no linolenic acid (LNA, 18:3*w*3). Human milk fat, in contrast, contains between 7 and 14% LA and up to 2% LNA. The milk fat of vegetarian mothers contains up to 32% LA and 3% LNA. Since the composition of human milk provides a natural standard for humans, and butter fails to meet that standard, take 1 point from butter.

Butter contains about 9% stearic acid (SA, 18:0) 19% oleic acid (OA, 18:1*w*9), and 38% palmitic acid (PA, 16:0), a total of 66% of its total fat content. These three, because they compete for the same enzyme systems that metabolize LA and LNA, can interfere with the functions of the essential fatty acids if the latter make up less than about 5% of total fat content; therefore take 1 point from butter.

Butter contains cholesterol, about 1 gram per pound. Cholesterol is required for the proper functioning of every body cell, but the average North American diet, severely deficient in the vitamins, minerals, and fiber required for the metabolism of cholesterol and fats, becomes overloaded with cholesterol which we find deposited in arteries and associated with cardiovascular problems and deaths from heart attack, stroke, and kidney and heart failure. It is not the fault of butter that the North American diet is so poor in vitamins and minerals, but butter itself does not contain the factors required for its own metabolism (oil seeds and fresh seed oils do contain these factors). Take 1 point from butter.

Butter concentrates pesticides about 5 to 10 times more than oils of vegetable origin. Therefore, take 1 more point from butter.

Present dairy practice uses antibiotics[1], both in feed and by injection, and these find their way into butter. Some antibiotics encourage the growth of yeasts and fungus (including candida) in humans, and these can produce allergies, tiredness, sugar craving (which feeds candida), hypoglycemia, skin afflictions which resemble psoriasis, and other conditions. In addition, the use of antibiotics kills only susceptible types of bacteria and thereby encourages the growth of bacteria which have developed resistance factors to antibiotics. These resistance factors can be transferred by benign bacteria to disease-causing ones. The findings are only just beginning to get attention. The implications are ominous. Take 1 point from butter.

Butter contains up to 6% *trans-* fatty acids, but usually about 3%. The *trans-* fatty acids are produced by bacteria in the stomachs of cows, and are mainly the *trans-* vaccenic (t18:1*w*7) acid isomer, which is more easily metabolized in the body than most *trans-* fatty acid isomers found in hydrogenated oils, fats, shortenings and margarines; therefore they constitute only a small risk to health. Take 1/2 point from butter.

Butter can be used for frying, baking, and heating because it is mainly saturated fatty acids which are relatively stable to light, heat, and oxygen. Score 1 point for butter. Total score for butter: plus 2, minus 5½ = minus 3½.

If the butter is from an organic farm, it contains no antibiotics or pesticides. Then it scores -1.5. If your diet contains the factors necessary for fat metabolism, cholesterol is not a problem. Then butter almost breaks even. And that's what butter is. A neutral fat, not good, not bad. Useful for frying and easy to digest. But not necessary. And dangerous in excess.

Margarine

Margarine does not contain much of the short chain, easily digestible fatty acids. The oil from which margarine is made usually contains a good proportion of essential fatty acids. But in the process of partial hydrogenation, much of the content of the essential fatty acids is destroyed or changed into other substances, and the finished product is much lower in essential fatty acids. Take 1 point from margarine. Margarine's high content of non-essential 18-carbon fatty acids competes with the essential fatty acids still present, further lowering the functional amount of essential fatty acids in the product. Take 1 point from margarine.

Margarine contains no cholesterol. Score 1 point for margarine[2]. But the metabolism of fats requires mineral and vitamin factors which the seed contained, but which were 'refined' out of the oil, and are not present in margarine. Take 1 point from margarine.

Margarine contains less pesticides than butter. Take ½ point from margarine. Margarine contains no antibiotics. No point for or against.

Margarine contains *trans-* fatty acids in substantial amounts. Some samples of Canadian margarine tested contained as much as 60% *trans-* fatty acids[3]. The *trans-* fatty acids have properties different from the natural *cis-* fatty acids, interfere with the functions of the essential fatty acids, are concentrated in heart tissue, burn slower than *cis-* fatty acids and may for this reason be involved in the cause of cardiovascular disease. Take 1 point from margarine.

Margarine also contains dozens of other non-natural chemicals produced in the process of hydrogenation. Many of them have not been adequately studied, and so their effects on human health are not known. But altered fat substances make up almost 10 pounds per year in the average diet, more than twice the amount of all other food additives combined. Take at least 1 point from margarine.

Margarine is not good for frying, because the unsaturated fatty acids which it still contains are further denatured by heat, light, and oxygen. If you fry with margarine, take 1 point from margarine; if you don't use margarine for frying, no point for or against.

Margarine is often advertised in a misleading way as high in polyunsaturated fatty acids, which the public equates with good health because the essential fatty acids are also polyunsaturated. However, some of these poly's are not essential fatty acids, but non-natural, chemically altered poly's, which are in fact, bad for health. Take 1 point from margarine.

The water present in margarine[4] (margarine is almost 20% water[5]) slowly destroys the double bonds, creating altered products while the margarine is in storage, in transit, or on the store shelf, waiting to be bought. Take 1 point from margarine. Total score for margarine: minus 7.5, at the least.

It is theoretically possible to make margarine without pesticides. It is difficult to make margarines without *trans-* fatty acids because *t-* fatty acids are one of the substances that give body and spreadability to the margarine made from a liquid oil. It is possible without hydrogenation to make a spreadable product that is good for health and high in essential fatty acids, but no such product is yet on the market in North America. When it appears, it will be found in health food stores. Margarines the way they are now manufactured are dangerous to health, especially when consumed to excess.

In some countries such as Spain, people do not spread butter or margarine on their bread. They cut a tomato in half, squash the open face of the tomato into the bread to close the holes, and then pour fresh oil directly onto their slice of bread. That solves both the margarine and butter question for them.

In terms of taste, digestibility, usefulness for frying, and naturalness, butter wins easily. Lower cost is the main factor in favour of margarine. But with margarine, you never know what you are getting. Even different batches of the same brand of margarine may contain substantially different amounts of *trans-* fatty acids and other altered fat derivatives, and so far, the manufacturer is not required to disclose the exact composition of his product on the label.

But the key issue is not butter, or margarine, but how to get an optimal quantity of the essential fatty acids. Neither butter nor margarine are reliable sources of these.

History of Butter and Margarine

The story of butter and margarine would not be complete without an historical perspective. Butter has been a part of man's diet ever since cows became domesticated, thousands of years ago. Degenerative diseases on a large scale are more recent in origin, having risen from rarity to epidemic proportions in the last 100 years, so it is unlikely that either butter, or the cholesterol that it contains or the cows that provide us with both are to blame for the meteoric rise of degenerative disease.

The history of margarine is shorter. It began in France under Napoleon III, who was looking for a cheap source of nutritional fat to feed the 'cheap' classes of people in his country: the army, the navy, and the poor. He announced a contest in 1867, inviting inventors to submit recipes and samples. The contest was won by Professor Hippolyte Mege-Mouris, who mixed beef fat (suet) with skim milk to create the first margarine. The concoction tasted so awful that as late as 15 years later, in 1882, poor working housewives were being dissuaded from using this 'artificial butter' because its 'taste is disagreeable, and it is harmful for health'. Since then, the history of margarine has been twofold: experiments were done to concoct tastier mixtures; and a huge image-making campaign was created to free margarine from its image as the 'poor people's butter'.

The experiments led to changes in the starting materials used in the making of margarine. The most common sources today are oils from seeds, usually the cheapest, and most inferior kinds: cotton seed, rape, and refined corn oils. Sometimes fish oils and whale oils were also used. Some margarines are made from mixtures of these. The process of hydrogenation makes it possible to chemically 'harden' these liquid oils to the consistency desired in a product that can be spread on bread. In the chemical process employed, many changes take place (see: Hydrogenation).

The image-making campaign has been largely successful. Margarine is far cheaper to make than butter, and can be sold at a price below that of butter, still leaving a large profit, part of which can be used to continue the image making (see: Advertising).

SECTION FIVE

RESEARCHING THE FATS

Findings, Breakthroughs, and Applications

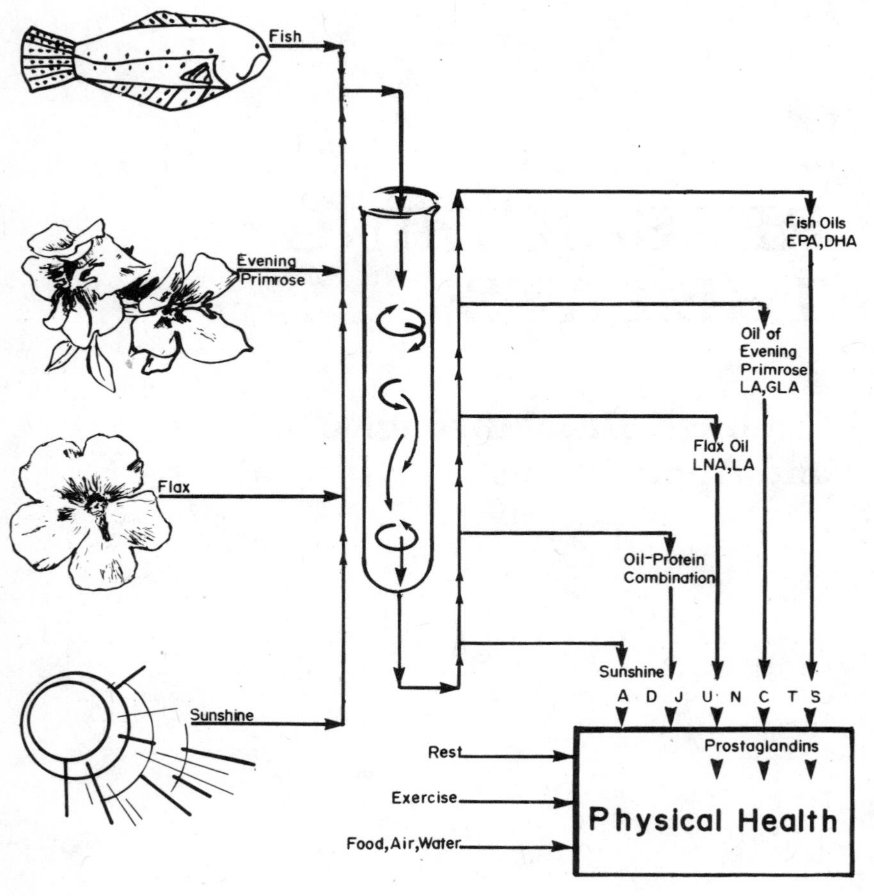
Fish
Evening
Primrose
Flax
Sunshine
Fish Oils
EPA, DHA
Oil of
Evening
Primrose
LA, GLA
Flax Oil
LNA, LA
Oil-Protein
Combination
Sunshine
A D J U N C T S
Prostaglandins
Rest
Exercise
Food, Air, Water
Physical Health

45

Oils from Fish and Other Sea Foods: EPA and DHA

Introduction

Oils from fish brings to mind the tablespoon of cod liver oil we used to get in winter when I was a kid. It's hard to forget the fishy smell (which was actually caused by rancidity), and the fishy taste, and the battle nearly every night with my parents, and finally the tearful surrender to fate, as I swallowed yet another slug of that hideous stuff, and gagged on it yet once again.

We've come a long way from those days. At least the cod liver oil is now in capsules, and only the occasional burp reminds one that it is still the same rancid fish oil. But we've come a long way in our knowledge of other fish oils as well.

Toxic Fish Oils

First, not all fish oils are special, at least in the sense of their health-enhancing capacity. The oils of many fish contain fatty acids which are not good for us at all. An example of such a fatty acid is cetoleic acid (22:1*w*11), which is found in herring and capelin oils, and makes up between 12 and 20% of the oil these fish contain. Cetoleic acid is also found, though in lower quantities in the oils of menhaden and anchovetta, and to some extent also in cod liver oil (maybe the child sensed something that the parents missed). Cetoleic acid is toxic (see: Toxic Fat Products), and causes fatty degeneration of heart tissue until the body makes enzymes which shorten this long-chain fatty acid.

So-so Fish Oils

There are many fish oils which are neither toxic, nor especially beneficial. Many low fat and warm water fish fall into this 'kettle of fish'. While these fish are very nutritious foods, their oils have no special nutritional merits. Oolichan oil, prized by the Indians, was their equivalent of olive oil from the sea. It does not contain special oils, but keeps well, and was therefore a stable and useful staple for them to dip their foods in.

Wonderful Fish Oils: EPA and DHA

But there are some fish oils which are associated with clean arteries and virtually complete absence of fatty degeneration diseases. The health secret that these oils contain was discovered only recently, and revolves around the content of these fish oils of two *w*3 fatty acids called eicosapentaenoic acid (EPA, 20:5*w*3) and docosahexaenoic acid (DHA, 22:6*w*3), respectively.

What makes these oils so special? Both EPA and DHA are normal constituents of some human tissues, including brain cells, synapses (nerve relay stations), retina, inner ear, adrenals, and sex glands — all the most active tissues in the human body.

Both EPA and DHA can be manufactured by the healthy human body, albeit slowly, from the essential *w*3 fatty acid, linolenic acid (LNA, 18:3*w*3), which is found in flax seeds, pumpkin seeds, soybeans, and walnuts. However, many degenerative conditions, listed in Chapter 46 (see: Oil of Evening Primrose), impair the body's ability to make the *w*3 long chain fatty acids EPA and DHA from LNA, for the same reasons that these degenerative conditions impair the body's ability to make the *w*6 long chain fatty acids[1].

Because of our degenerate habits, lifestyle, and diet, fish oils containing EPA and DHA, made for us by cold water fish and other northern marine animals, come to the rescue, and allow us to continue to live in our chosen (unnatural) way, without reaping the grim consequences which would otherwise await us. All we need to do is add to our diet a capsule (or several — the label on the container says how many) of fish oils containing these wonderful fatty acids, or even better, eat the fish containing oils with EPA and DHA.

EPA and DHA, being highly unsaturated, have a strong urge to disperse. They have extremely low melting points (-54° and -44°C., respectively), and will not aggregate. So strong is their tendency to move away from other molecules of the same kind, that they help to disperse aggregations of the saturated fatty acids, which like to stick together. EPA and DHA thus keep deposits of saturated fatty acids and cholesterol from glueing up our arteries, and they also keep the platelets from getting sticky. The result? Clean arteries. No clots. No cardiovascular disease. No problems. They also lower blood pressure by about 10 points.

Dr. Budwig uses fresh rainbow trout in her treatment of cancer, because the *w*3 oils which these fish contain help to dissolve tumours. Dr. Budwig has been using these oils successfully for years. In North America, the *w*3 fish oils are just beginning to be valued for their tumour-dissolving capacity. As well as trout, salmon, mackerel, sardines, tuna, and eel are good sources of *w*3 fatty acids.

EPA is important for another reason. It is the fatty acid out of which the body produces the third family of prostaglandins, the PG3 family (See: Prostaglandins). The members of the PG3 family have very potent anti-clotting properties. They prevent the occurrence of strokes and heart attacks, as well as other problems of the circulatory system which involve clot formation, such as pulmonary embolism. They also prevent the cardiovascular complications which accompany diabetes, which can result in gangrenous limbs and blindness.

The presence of EPA and DHA lowers triglycerides in the blood very dramatically, (from 75 to 50 mg/dl in one study), lowers cholesterol level and LDL slightly, and lowers VLDL by half (from 12 to 6 mg/100 ml in the same study). Exactly how or why they have these effects is still a mystery. High cholesterol, triglycerides, LDL, and VLDL levels in the blood are associated with cardiovascular disease: high blood pressure, atherosclerosis, heart and kidney failure, stroke and heart attack.

Conversion of LNA to EPA

The rate per day at which the average North American body can convert LNA to EPA has been measured in one study to be 2.7% of the LNA administered. People who consume only small amounts of saturated, monounsaturated, and *trans*- fatty acids in their diet (these all interfere with the conversion), are likely to convert LNA to EPA at a higher rate. If cholesterol, which also interferes, is kept at a minimum, and the rest of the essential nutrients are also present in adequate amounts, the rate of conversion of LNA to EPA is likely to be even higher and quite adequate for human needs. If the diet contains an ample and regular supply of LNA (most Western diets don't), the body will manufacture more of the enzymes necessary to make the conversion more efficient. Studies to show that this is true in the particular case of converting LNA to EPA have not been done, but the body's ability to increase its enzyme production in response to demand has been observed in many cases, and can be generalized. The body adapts to changing conditions in amazingly competent ways.

However, since most people don't get much LNA in its natural state in their diet — the only reliable source of substantial amounts of LNA is flax or flax oil, and *fresh* flax oil has not yet made its debut in the North American marketplace — the enzymes which convert it to EPA are not present in large amounts in most people's bodies, and so it is wise for these people to get their EPA and DHA directly from fish or fish oil preparations.

Government 'Protection'

In spite of all the information available from scientific studies on the beneficial effects of EPA and DHA on cardiovascular health, the 'health protection' Branch of the Canadian Health and Welfare Department has removed EPA and DHA supplements from stores, classifying them as drugs rather than foods, because it turns out that foods are the 'drugs' which can cure degenerative diseases whose origins lie in nutritional deficiencies. Until this confusion is dealt with (which may take years), Canadians can get their EPA and DHA supplements from the U.S., or they can eat fish containing these oils, which luckily for us, are still classified and considered foods.

Which Fish?

The fish which provide the best source of EPA and DHA include both fresh and salt water, cold water fish. High fat (10 to 15%) fish like fresh salmon, sardines, mackerel, trout, and eel are especially good. Low fat (1 to 4%) fish like pike, carp and haddock, also contain EPA and DHA, but in much smaller quantities. The amount of EPA and DHA in the fats of these fish ranges between 15 and 30% of total fat content. The *w* fatty acid content of different types of salmon has been measured between 18.9 and 31.4% of total fat content[2].

How Often?

The EPA and DHA from fish sources lasts about 2 to 3 weeks in the human body after it has been eaten, so its lowering effect on the blood triglycerides, its unstickying of the platelets, and its protective effects on the arteries lasts about the same length of time. In order to maintain this protective effect, such fish should be eaten at least every 2 weeks. The Catholic custom of eating fish on Fridays may have had some real health benefits before it degenerated to deep fried fish and chips. It has to be fish containing the right kind of oils, and not fried in saturated butter or coconut fats. The best way to prepare them is to bake them whole, so that the oils are not exposed to oxidation or light, and stay fresh. Even better, they can be eaten fresh and raw as the Japanese sashimi[3], served in sushi bars which are becoming popular everywhere. This best preserves the oils to give maximum health benefits. Unlike chicken, these fish are best eaten with their skins on, because most of the oils, which in this case we want, are found just under or in the skin, especially around the gills, the fins, and the belly.

Other Sources of EPA and DHA

Seals contain about 3.5% EPA and 7.5% DHA in their fat tissue. Dolphins and whales have between 1 and 3% of each in their blubber. Penguins carry about 3% EPA and 9% DHA in their body fats.

The tiny animals called krill and copepods and the tiny plants called phytoplankton, which live in the ocean and provide the food for fish and marine animals are also high in EPA and DHA content. And the polar bears who eat the marine animals that live on the plankton contain about 7% of each EPA and DHA in their fat.

The fats of scallops, clams, oysters, and squid are 1/4 to 1/2 EPA and DHA, but since the total oil content of these sea foods is only 2% or less of their weight, they are not a major food source of these fatty acids.

Functions of EPA and DHA

Besides the functions which keep the arteries clean and the

animals in the cold ocean from freezing, and besides EPAs function as starting material for making PG3 prostaglandins, EPA and DHA have some other functions. In the retina, these highly active fatty acids are involved in ways which are not yet completely understood, with the conversion of the light energy entering the eye into the chemical energy of nerve impulses.

In the brain, they have neurological functions that, although not yet clearly understood, have something to do with energy conversion, with electron transfer, and with the attraction of oxygen to the brain cells for their very intense level of functioning. In the ear, they likely take part in the conversion of sound energy to chemical energy. In the adrenals and sex glands, their function is similar to that in the brain.

EPA and DHA are extremely sensitive to destruction by light, air, and heat — even more sensitive than LNA, which is considered the 'prima donna' of the essential fatty acids because it is so emotional, so labile, so reactive. For this reason, EPA and DHA should be sold in completely opaque capsules, and the capsules made under conditions which exclude light, air and heat. Their sensitivity is also the reason why the best way to eat fish is fresh from the sea and fast to the table.

If these precautions are taken, EPA and DHA are a valuable addition to the human diet. They provide one of the main reasons why the traditional Eskimo, whose diet contained 39% fat (of which up to 1/10 or more was EPA and DHA) and very little fiber, could maintain virtually complete immunity from the diseases of fatty degeneration.

Fish Farming

It is one thing to eat your fish straight from the sea, but another to buy your fish from the fish farm. Salmon and trout are being raised in tanks or shallow ponds, much like chickens in the chicken coop. Since the fat content of the fish depends on what it eats, and since its food in the fish coop is not fresh, live animals and vegetation (krill, copepods, and plankton), it is likely that its fat content is not the same as that of the free-swimming ocean or fresh water lake fish, and the process of changing the type of fat and its content in the fish has begun, similar to the changes in quantity and quality of fat that have occurred in beef farming (see: Fats in Meats) and egg production (see: Eggs). In preparing commercial fish foods, there are problems with the contents of vitamin A, vitamin C, and the *w*3 fatty acids. All three spoil rapidly, and all three are essential to fish[4]. Commercial fish foods have a fairly short shelf life of about 2 months for dry foods and 3 months for refrigerated wet foods.

According to experts in the fish farming field, farmed salmon are lower quality than fresh ocean fish. This difference in quality is offset by some advantages. Farmed fish are often transported to the consumer within 48 hours, much faster than ocean fish, which may sit around in the boat for a week or two before the boat comes in. Farmed fish are available fresh all year round, while ocean salmon are fresh only in season, and must be frozen the rest of the year. Market surveys indicate that buyers prefer fresh ocean salmon to fresh farmed, but prefer fresh farmed to frozen ocean salmon. This preference actually mirrors the nutritional quality.

46

Oil of Evening Primrose

History

The value of the oil from the seeds of evening primrose is a recent discovery, although the plant itself was used traditionally for medicinal purposes by the Indians of North America long before the white man reached these shores. After the discovery of America, the Pilgrims learned of its healing properties from the natives, and sent the plant back to Europe, where it became known as the 'king's cure all'.

The Mother's Milk of Oils

What is so special about the oil of evening primrose? Besides containing 72% linoleic acid (LA, 18:2*w*6), which is the major essential fatty acid, and containing only small amount of non-essential fatty acids (11% of oleic acid, 18:1*w*9, 6% of palmitic acid, 16:0, and 2% of stearic acid, 18:0), oil of evening primrose also contains 9% gamma linolenic acid (GLA, 18:3*w*6), which is present in only a few other plant seeds[1]. The other main nutritional source of GLA is human mother's milk, and so one might say that oil of evening primrose is the mother's milk of oils.

The Magic of GLA

What is so special about GLA? GLA is the result of body's first biochemical step in the transformation of the main essential fatty acid, LA(18:2*w*6) into the PG1 family of prostaglandins (see: Prostaglandins).

When GLA is Missing

A healthy human being's body transforms LA into GLA by removing one hydrogen atom each from carbons 12 and 13, and inserting a double bond between these carbons, but there are several dietary deficiencies and disease conditions which block the enzyme[2] that catalyzes this chemical reaction, and these conditions prevent the transformation of LA into GLA from taking place.

Excess cholesterol, very common in Western diets high in meat, eggs and dairy products interferes, in ways not well understood, with the transformation of LA to GLA. Excess saturated fats and monounsaturated long chain fatty acids, which make up between 85% and 93% of all the fatty acids contained in Western diets, interfere with essential fatty acid function. Processed vegetable oils, which make up over 90% of all oil sold to customers, contain *trans-* fatty acids which interfere with the enzyme that changes LA to GLA. Alcohol, whose use is widespread, also interferes with this enzyme. Aging, which catches up with all of us, makes all of our enzyme systems less efficient. Zinc deficiency, which is widespread, slows down the conversion of LA to GLA, because zinc is a required factor in this conversion. Common viral infections, a result of weak tissues and weak immune systems brought about by poor nutrition, also interfere with the transformation of LA into GLA. Finally, diabetes and pre-diabetic conditions, which affect 10-20% of the population, involve a functional deficiency of essential fatty acids. High sugar consumption, which is the rule in the Western diet, prevents the proper mobilization of these fatty acids from fats stored in our bodies, and also interferes with the work that the EFAs do.

This means that in a large part of the population, the conversion of LA to GLA does not take place efficiently. Since GLA is available as a nutritional supplement, produced for us by the evening primrose seed, we can take the oil containing it, bypass our own blocked enzyme, and go merrily on our way to produce the prostaglandins our bodies need, without having to make drastic alterations in our diets and lifestyles.

Therapy With Oil of Evening Primrose

Oil of evening primrose has been extensively tested in double blind trials in hospital settings on several continents, and an impressive list of its therapeutic successes in many diseases has accumulated. Almost all clinical studies have been done on Efamol, a variety of evening primrose specially bred to produce oil of constant quality and composition.

Oil of evening primrose has been used successfully to lower blood pressure, to lower blood cholesterol level, and thereby to decrease the risk of cardiovascular accident (stroke and heart attack).

It has been used to normalize fat metabolism in diabetes, and to decrease the amount of insulin required by diabetics. It is not a cure for this disease, but a valuable part of the treatment of diabetics.

Oil of evening primrose prevents liver damage due to alcoholism, prevents the withdrawal symptoms when the habitual use of alcohol is discontinued, and prevents the hangovers which so often spoil the morning after the party. Salted pickled herring, which contains highly unsaturated fatty acids was used in Europe for this purpose before evening primrose came along, but oil of evening primrose is more effective.

Oil of evening primrose is a useful adjunct in the treatment of schizophrenia, because schizophrenics have very low levels of prostaglandin E1, the most important of several prostaglandins made from GLA. When the level of prostaglandin E1 was increased by the administration of oil of evening primrose, some improvement was noted, especially in schizophrenics whose disease had been of less than 5 years' duration.

Oil of evening primrose has been used by overweight people for losing weight. Because it increases metabolic rate, it increases the burn-off of fat, without special dieting.

Oil of evening primrose has been used to relieve premenstrual breast pain (mastalgia) in women. It is so effective and so safe, that the doctors who did the studies in Britain and Wales now use it as the treatment of first choice for this painful condition. Related to breast pain, studies in England have shown oil of evening primrose to be highly effective in relieving premenstrual syndrome, which involves bloating, breast pain, irritability, and depression, often leading to aggressive behaviour. Oil of evening primrose completely relieved 2/3 of the women in the trial, and improved the condition of almost 90% of them, suggesting that this condition has its origin in nutritional deficiency, and its cure in nutritional therapy.

In Scotland, researchers have found oil of evening primrose to be effective in conditions of atrophy of tear and salivary ducts. In Pennsylvania, a doctor is using oil of evening primrose to prevent arthritis in animals, based on the known fact that increasing the level of prostaglandin E1 prevents arthritis. Studies with humans are under way. In Scotland, the oil of evening primrose was shown to improve the condition of hair, nails, and skin. Certain kinds of eczema, and poor nail and hair condition are often an indication of essential fatty acid deficiency. In Britain, oil of evening primrose is used by multiple sclerosis patients to slow down or stop the deterioration of their condition. The sooner the program is started after the initial diagnosis of MS is made, the better the results.

Comparing Gamma linolenic acid (GLA, 18:3w6) and Alpha linolenic acid (LNA, 18:3w3)

Before continuing with the discussion of oil of evening primrose, we need to clear up some confusion which exists about GLA (18:3*w*6) and LNA (18:3*w*3). Some writers have made no distinction between them, while others have confused the functions of the two, and still others think there is only one form of linolenic acid. What is the truth?

GLA and LNA are almost identical. Both are fatty acids. Both have 18 carbon atoms in their fatty acid chain. Both have 3 double bonds. Both have double bonds in the *w*6 and *w*9 positions. All of the double bonds of both are methylene interrupted (see: Fatty Acids). Both are used in the treatment of degenerative diseases. The only difference between them is the position of the 3rd double bond. In GLA, the 3rd double bond is in the *w*12 position on the fatty acid molecule, whereas in LNA, the 3rd double bond is in the *w*3 position. This means that the shape, and therefore the properties of these two fatty acids are different.

GLA (18:3w6)

GLA is found in mother's milk and evening primrose oil, and is a member of the *w*6 family of fatty acids, to which the major essential fatty acid LA (18:2*w*6) belongs, as well as arachidonic acid (20:4*w*6), the precursor of the prostaglandin PG2 family.

GLA is the precursor of the prostaglandin PG1 family (see: Prostaglandins).

LNA (18:3w3)

LNA, found in flax, and in smaller quantities in pumpkin seed, soybean, and walnut, as well as in dark green leaves, is a member of the *w*3 family, to which EPA (20:5*w*3) and DHA (22:6*w*3) also belong. LNA is the other (the second) essential fatty acid required for human health that must be supplied in foods.

GLA and LNA are not interchangeable. They have completely different functions in the body. Both are very important, but neither can replace the other.

Co-Factors With Oil of Evening Primrose

Zinc, vitamin C, and vitamins B3 and B6 are taken with oil of evening primrose, because they are co-factors in the body's conversion of GLA to prostaglandin E1 (see: Vitamin and Mineral Co-Factors of Fatty Acid Metabolism). These co-factors should accompany therapy with oil of evening primrose.

Biochemical Engineering

Therapy with oil of evening primrose is an example of the use of biochemical engineering for the control and prevention of diseases, using knowledge of nutrition, biochemistry, and medicine to improve human health. The health food industry was recommending beta-carotene for the prevention of cancer prior to the medical profession recognizing its use. They were recommending vitamin C to strengthen connective tissues, bones, gums, and teeth; and for fighting virus and bacterial infections before medical practice began to look at vitamin C seriously. And now the health food industry is pioneering the importance of fats and oils in human nutrition.

47

Prostaglandins

History

Prostaglandins were named for the prostate gland, from which they were first isolated in 1930. Later, they were isolated from many other tissues as well, and they are now known to be present in every organ in the body. The study of the prostaglandins is still in its infancy, and is another one of the most fascinating fields developing in fat and oil biochemistry.

Description

What are prostaglandins? There are several ways to describe the prostaglandins. Functionally, they are short-lived, hormone-like chemicals which regulate cellular activities on a moment-to-moment basis. Chemically, they are products of the controlled oxidation of several different highly unsaturated fatty acids. Enzymes, made specially for that purpose, oxidize specific fatty acids in just one particular way to make a particular type of prostaglandin. This accuracy and control of chemical reactions stands in stark contrast to the processes of oxidation in air and hydrogenation, which are random and unpredictable, and which produce different substances in uncontrolled amounts from any specific fatty acid. But the body, through the enzymes, has this amazing precision.

Kinds of Prostaglandins

About 30 different prostaglandins have been isolated and identified. Each has a highly specific different function, and some are stronger in their function than others. The prostaglandins fall into 3 families or series, depending on which fatty acid they were made from. All prostaglandins have 20 carbon atoms, a 5-membered ring, and 2 side chains. They differ in the number of double bonds in the side chain.

The series 1 and 2 prostaglandins come from the *w*6 family, with the essential fatty acid linoleic acid (LA, 18:2*w*6) as the starting point. LA is changed in the body to gamma linolenic acid (GLA, 18:3*w*6)[1], then to dihomogamma linolenic acid (DGLA, 20:3*w*6)[2], and then to arachidonic acid (AA, 20:4*w*6)[3]. The series 1 prostaglandins are made from DGLA and have 1 double bond in their side chains. The series 2 prostaglandins are made from AA and have 2 double bonds in their side chains. Figure 42 shows the chemical sequence by which LA is converted to AA and what one member of the series 1 and 2 prostaglandins look like.

The series 3 prostaglandins are made from the *w*3 family, with the essential fatty acid linolenic acid (LNA, 18:3*w*3) as the starting point. LNA is first changed to stearidonic acid (SDA, 18:4*w*3)[4], then to eicosatetraenoic acid (ETA, 20:4*w*3), then to eicosopentaenoic acid (EPA, 20:5*w*3)[5]. The series 3 prostaglandins are made from EPA and have 3 double bonds in their side chains. Figure 3 shows the chemical sequence by which LNA is converted to EPA, and what series 3 prostaglandins look like.

Functions of the Prostaglandins

The series 1 prostaglandins made from dihomogammalinolenic acid (DGLA, 20:3*w*6) are the most famous, because they have been studied in the most detail. The most famous member of the series is prostaglandin E1, or PGE1. PGE1 has several important functions in different tissues in the human body. It keeps blood platelets from sticking together, and thereby helps to prevent heart attacks and strokes caused by blood clots in the arteries. In the kidneys, it helps to remove fluid from the body, acting as a diuretic. It opens up blood vessels, improving circulation and relieving angina. PGE1 slows down cholesterol production. It

Figure 42. Prostaglandins of the PG1 and PG2 series.

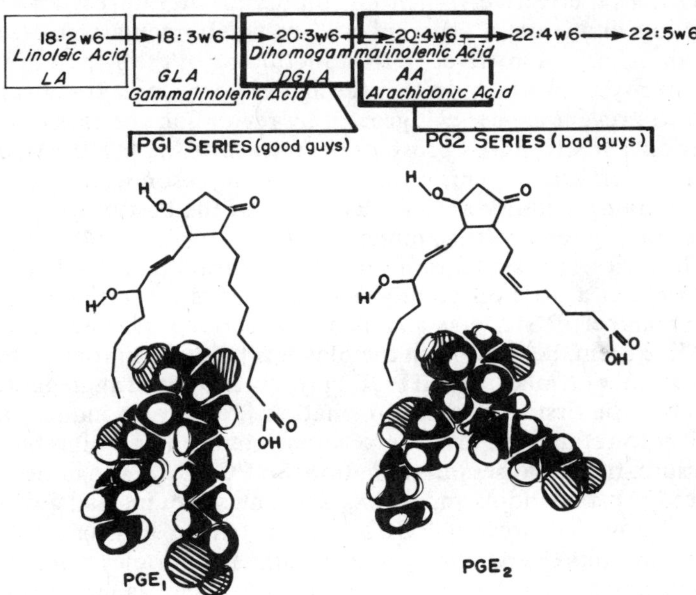

Figure 43. Prostaglandins of the PG3 Series.

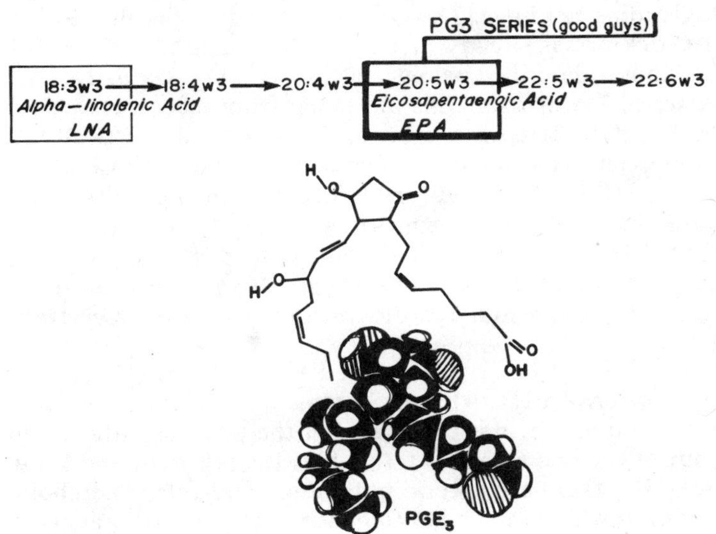

prevents inflammations and controls arthritis. It makes insulin work more effectively, helping diabetics. It improves nerve function and gives a sense of well-being. It regulates calcium metabolism. It is involved in the functioning of the T-cells of the immune system, which destroy foreign cell invasions. It may also help to prevent cancer cell growth by regulating the rate of cell division. Finally, PGE1 prevents the release of AA (20:4*w*6) from the cell membranes. This is important for a reason which we will see in the next paragraph. PGE1 is one of the best of the 'good guys' among the prostaglandins.

The series 2 prostaglandins, made from arachidonic acid (AA, 20:4*w*6) act a little differently from the series 1 prostaglandins. One member, PGI2, acts similar to the series 1 prostaglandins, and like them, helps to keep the platelets from sticking together, but another member, called PGE2 promotes platelet aggregation, which is the first step in clot formation. PGE2 also induces the kidney to retain salt, leading to water retention and high blood pressure. It also causes inflammation. So PGE2 works against the series 1 prostaglandins and is considered an all round 'bad guy' for this reason. To prevent PGE2's bad act from getting started, PGE1 inhibits the release of AA from the membranes where it is stored, and since AA remains tied up in the membranes it cannot be converted to series 2 prostaglandins[6]. This prevents all of the bad effects which PGE2 and other members of the series 2 prostaglandins can have. The good effect of PGI2 in preventing platelet stickiness is already covered by PGE1 and also by series 3 prostaglandins described below.

The series 3 prostaglandins are made from eicosapentaenoic acid (EPA, 20:5*w*3). One member of this series, called PGE3, has potent platelet anti-stickiness effects which are like those of the series 1 prostaglandins, and further decrease the likelihood of a person dying from a clot formed in an artery to heart or brain. Another, PGI3 also has very potent platelet anti-aggregating effects. This is why the fish oils are so effective in preventing degenerative changes in the cardiovascular system (see: Oils from Fish).

Prostaglandins in Health and Disease

Healthy human beings can make all the prostaglandins they need out of the two essential fatty acids LA (18:2*w*6) and LNA (18:3*w*3), but there are several nutritional and other metabolic conditions in which the ability to convert essential fatty acids to prostaglandins is blocked (see: Oil of Evening Primrose) at the first (the delta 6 desaturase) step[7]. In these conditions, the block can be bypassed by giving nutrient supplements. The GLA (18:3*w*6) contained in evening primrose oil bypasses the block that prevents the series 1 prostaglandins from being made, and fish oils which contain EPA(20:5*w*3) bypass the block that prevents the series 3 prostaglandins from being made. If these nutritional supplements are given, the production of prostaglandins by the body can proceed properly, and health can be re-established and maintained.

Production of prostaglandins from essential fatty acids also requires several vitamins and minerals, which can also be taken as supplements. Vitamins C, B3, B6, and the minerals zinc and magnesium are involved, and there may be others not yet discovered. The relationship between the prostaglandins and health is complex, and research in the field is just beginning to take off.

In large doses, pharmaceutical preparations of prostaglandin-like substances are being used to induce abortions, to lower high blood pressure, and to decrease platelet stickiness. But the pharmaceutical use of the prostaglandins is extremely crude. Because they are so short-lived, much of an injected dose of prostaglandins breaks down before it reaches target tissues. Comparatively huge doses have to be administered, far larger than the body would normally produce. If they are given orally or added to the diet, they are destroyed during digestion.

By by-passing the known biochemical block with more basic nutritional supplements, i.e. the fatty acids from which the prostaglandins are made, the body is given the material it needs to make its own supply of the prostaglandins, where and when and how much it needs, according to its own internal requirements for health.

48

Flax

History

Flax may be new to the generation born after the Second World War, but its known history is very old, and its use is likely much older. It is one of the oldest known cultivated plants, probably originating in the Orient.

According to archeological authorities on the subject, flax was already being cultivated in Babylon around 5000 B.C. Flax seeds and seed pods, wall paintings depicting its cultivation, and cloth made of flax fiber were found in the oldest known burial chambers of the Egyptians, around 3000 B.C. Late Stone Age archeological digs in Switzerland, dated 3000-4000 B.C., turned up flax seed and flax fiber cloth.

References to the healing properties of flax are found in Greek and Roman writings dating around 650 B.C. Hippocrates, in the 5th century B.C., mentions the use of flax to relieve inflammation of mucous membranes, for relief of abdominal pains and diarrhea. Theophrastus recommends the use of flax mucilage against coughs. Ancient East Indian scriptures state that in order to reach the highest state of contentment and joy, a yogi must eat flax daily. The Roman writer, Tacitus, in the 1st century A.D. praises the virtues of flax in his writings. The 8th century emperor Charlemagne considered flax so important for the health of his subjects that he passed laws and regulations requiring its consumption. The 15th century abbess, Hildegard von Bingen, used flax meal during the middle ages in hot compresses for the treatment of both external and internal ailments.

In Europe, flax has been cultivated on a large scale for hundreds of years, both for its seeds and its fibers. The seeds found many uses in folk medicine, for the treatment of ailments in both humans and livestock. So highly regarded was flax oil in Europe, that the hero of Ehm Welk's autobiographical novel exclaims: "Truly, flax oil lubricates our way into eternal life." Mahatma Gandhi once observed: "Wherever flax seed becomes a regular food item among the people, there will be better health."

After the Second World War, flax was almost forgotten in Europe. Large oil mills chose to press oil seeds inferior in health value but with longer shelf life; the textile industry went to synthetics; the paint industry turned to man-made drying oils. But flax has made a strong comeback in all three areas.

Today flax is grown in every part of the world except the tropics and the arctic. The world's main suppliers of flax are Argentina, India, and the U.S. It is also grown in Canada, many European countries including both Germanies, Hungary, France, Holland, Austria, and Poland. It is cultivated in the U.S.S.R., China, Egypt, and Morocoo.

Flax has been used since antiquity to maintain healthy animals. Its uses include: correction of digestive disturbances, especially common in calves, where losses can be very high due to these diseases; feeding of pregnant cows with flax to make calving easier and to produce healthier calves; to prevent, in cattle, infectious diseases such as hoof-and-mouth disease, which often took very heavy tolls; to make horses' coats glossy (my father, born in 1907, remembers as a young man using flax to treat respiratory infections in horses); it is also added to the diets of pets to improve their coats, prevent distemper, and improve their general health; people who raise show dogs use flax to make their coats full, shiny, and luxurient, and to improve their dogs' general health.

The Plant

What is flax? Flax is an annual plant which grows only in good soil — it will not grow on depleted soils — and may reach a height of 1 metre, though it usually gets only half that high. It has small, green, pointed (lanceolate) leaves on a tough stalk, and small deep blue flowers. In tropical climates, the flowers are deep red. Ornamental varieties of flax also exist, with white, gold, and red flowers.

The Latin name for flax is *Linum usitatissimum.* My mother remembers that where she grew up, people used to soak flax stalks in shallow ponds for 2-3 weeks to rot the flesh off the fibers. They spread out the fibers to dry, then danced on them with rubber boots to break the remaining debris off the dry fibers. The clean fibers were collected and subjected to further processing. No doubt more sophisticated methods are now available, but the principle remains the same. It is the first step in making the high quality cloth called linen, its name derived from the Latin name *Linum. Usitatissimum* means 'the most useful', and the other 'most useful' part of flax is the seed, which is harvested by a threshing method similar to that used for harvesting other grains.

The seeds come in golden and brown varieties and they can be large or small. Dr. Budwig prefers to use the golden flax, while others find the brown more useful, but all varieties are nutritious.

Nutrients Contained in Flax

What is in these brown and gold seed packages? Though the contents vary slightly from year to year and from different growing regions — northern latitudes produce seeds with higher oil content — a sample of 100 grams or seed will give about 45 grams of oil, 22 of protein, 12 of fiber, 10 of mucilage, 4 of minerals, and 7 of water. Let's look at these in turn.

Oil. The fresh oil of the very useful flax seed is the very best oil there is, in every way. It looks good: a rich, deep golden colour like fresh, liquid sunshine — which by the way, it is. The aroma is a gentle, pleasant, nutty bouquet. It has a light and unique taste that is delightful. Its texture is so light that it is hard to believe that it is oil at all. We usually associate oil with a 'heavy', 'oily' texture. Not so for flax. People who have tried it once (good quality flax oil is sold in European health food stores) get hooked on it, and sometimes go to great lengths to get it air-shipped from the European manufacturer to this continent. But a warning is in order. Fresh flax oil spoils when exposed to light, oxygen and heat, and therefore care needs to be taken in pressing, filling, and storing operations. In North America, this care is not taken, and the oil (called linseed oil) found in health food stores is highly refined and often completely spoiled. The same is true for oils imported from Europe. The time taken in transit and storage usually exceeds the safe shelf life of fresh flax oil, which if the oil is kept cool, is about 3 months. The oil gets bitter, or acrid, and scratchy. Whenever someone tells me that they have tried flax oil and don't like it, I know that they have not tried *fresh* flax oil.

The oil in the flax seed is very rich in both essential fatty acids, the twice unsaturated linoleic acid (LA, 18:2*w*6) and the three times unsaturated linolenic acid (LNA, 18:3*w*3), both of which are necessary for physical health (see: Essential Fatty Acids). Flax seed oil is the richest of all food sources of LNA, containing between 50 and 60% of this fatty acid. It contains between 15 and 25% LA. The remainder of the oil is about 18% of the once unsaturated oleic acid (18:1*w*9), and about 10% saturated fatty acids (16:0 and 18:0) neither of which are essential, although all oils contain them. Other oils which are high in LA are safflower, and sunflower oils, but neither of these contains any LNA. LA and especially LNA are useful in the treatment of the diseases of fatty degeneration — cardiovascular disease, and especially cancer (see: The Oil-Protein Combination), and flax oil is traditionally well known as a therapeutic tool in the treatment of these diseases, and is gaining popularity in medical practice, where doctors are beginning to prescribe it for their patients as the best oil for good health.

A unique feature of flax seed is that it contains a substance which resembles the prostaglandins, which may well be a part of its therapeutic value. Prostaglandins regulate blood pressure and arterial function, and have an important role in calcium and energy metabolism (see: Prostaglandins). No other vegetable oil examined so far can match this property of flax oil.

Flax seed oil is rich in lecithin and other phosphatides. These aid in the digestion of fats and oils, and are also known for their contribution to physical health. It contains carotene (pro-vitamin A) and vitamin E when unrefined, and these vitamins are necessary for the stability of the oil both in the container and in the body. When oil is refined, vitamins and lecithins are removed, and the oil loses its stability and many of its health-giving components (see: Oil Making).

Fresh flax oil is used in high-quality European sun-tan and skin oils which nourish the skin with essential fatty acids. These preparations are better for the skin than other commercial preparations, but will not keep as long.

Dr. Budwig, the world's leading expert on the therapeutic uses of flax oil, uses it with good success for enemas in cases of colon cancer and bowel obstruction. Research in North America is only just beginning to discover the value of flax oil's LNA in the treatment of cancer. The first papers hinting renewed interest in this direction were presented at the annual Oil Chemists' Meetings in 1984 and 1985.

Protein. The flax seed contains high quality, easily digestible, and complete protein. It contains all of the amino acids essential to human health. The essential amino acids — by name they are lysine, leucine, isoleucine, valine, threonine, methionine, phenylalanine, and tryptophan — cannot be made by the human body and must therefore be provided through the diet. If all the essential amino acids are supplied, our bodies can manufacture from them the other dozen or so amino acids required to make all of our proteins. If any one or more essential amino acids is missing from the diet, protein deficiency disease develops. The text book example of protein deficiency disease is kwashiorkor, which occurs in African children on a diet of bean protein which is low in the essential amino acid methionine[1]. The children are emaciated, with protruding bellies. The disease is fatal if the diet is not improved. But the flax seed has all of the essential amino acids, and in good balance. For infants, one more amino acid, called histidine, is also essential, and yes, the flax seed has that one, too.

Fiber. A lot has been written about fiber. It keeps the digestive tract from being clogged with mucus; it keeps it swept and moving. It is necessary for intestine and colon health, and to maintain a healthy intestinal flora, those friendly little bacteria and yeasts which make some of our vitamins and protect us from unfriendly intestinal organisms. A healthy colon means no toxins in our blood and liver, and healthy blood and liver means that you may reach a ripe and healthy old age.

Fiber is also famous for its effect of lowering cholesterol, probably because it prevents cholesterol and bile acids from being reabsorbed into the body. Instead, they attach to the fiber and are carried out of the body with the wastes. Finally, fiber is known for its ability to soften the stool, prevent constipation, and maintain regularity. Flax is an excellent source of fiber.

Mucilage. Its content of mucilage makes the flax seed the best natural laxative available. It soothes and protects the delicate stomach and intestinal lining, prevents irritation, and keeps the contents moving smoothly along. Because it absorbs water and swells (it reaches about 3 times its dry volume so this much fluid should accompany its consumption), the stools don't become hard and dry. Considering that between 30 and 50% of the North American adults have problems with constipation, flax could offer a great service here. It has no side effects. This alone makes it the laxative of choice.

Flax mucilage also has the ability to buffer excess acid. This makes it ideal for people with acid or sensitive stomachs, and ulcers. Mucilage from flax is capable of lowering the blood cholesterol content, by preventing reabsorption of bile acids, decreasing absorption of cholesterol from foods, increasing the amount of cholesterol excreted, or a combination of these three possibilities. Finally, mucilage helps to stabilize and modulate blood glucose, which is useful in diabetes.

Minerals. The flax seed contains just about every known major and trace mineral. According to one laboratory analysis, 100 grams of flax seed contains: .74g potassium, .70g phosphorus, .38g magnesium, .21g calcium, .21g sulphur, .046g sodium, .043 chlorine, .0077g iron, .0057g zinc, and adequate trace amounts of manganese, silicon, copper, fluorine, aluminum, nickel, cobalt, iodine, molybdenum, and chromium. The only trace minerals not present are selenium and vanadium. Their absence may be the flax seed's only flaw, but it's more likely that the laboratory chemist did not test for these most recently discovered trace minerals.

Vitamins. Besides this almost complete array of minerals, the flax seed also contains the fat-soluble vitamins E, A (as the non-toxic carotene), and the 'sunshine' vitamin D. It also contains the water-soluble vitamins B1, B2, and C.

The Uses of Flax

First of all, it is excellent food, because it contains almost a complete diet all by itself. Secondly, its components are used in the treatment of many ailments which, if it were a regular part of the diet, would not occur in the first place. The solid part of the seed is used in all of the digestive, eliminative, toxic diseases of the stomach, intestines, and colon. They include inflammation of stomach (gastritis), intestinal tract (ileitis), or colon (diverticulitis). It is useful in the treatment of constipation. It increases the bulk of the stool, speeds up the movement of the stool out of the body, and thereby prevents the buildup of toxins in the bowel. The stool smells less foul, the liver is relieved of toxic stress, and the breath sweetens. The whole body becomes healthier. Many disease conditions have their beginning in the colon through constipation. Externally, hot compresses of flax swelled with hot water draw toxins, and soothe and heal boils, bruises, and other skin afflictions.

According to East Indian medicine, flax creates heat. Translated into Western terms this says that flax increases metabolic rate or stimulates oxidation, by which energy is produced, which we experience as warmth. Flax therefore enhances all life processes, because all life processes depend on energy production. The oil can be used successfully in the treatment of degenerative diseases, in combination with proteins, as we will see in the following chapter.

49

The Oil-Protein Combination

Introduction

Is there evidence that oil and protein belong together in the diet and the body? Yes there is. There is plenty of evidence, both from experience and the laboratory, that links oils with proteins in nutrition.

Observations Close to Home

Here are some simple common observations close to home, which any of us can verify for ourselves.

Dry skin. The human skin is made largely of collagen, which is protein. On a diet low in fats or for other nutritional reasons, the skin may become dry, flaky, and hard. And what do we do with such skin? We oil it. The kind of oil that works best is one that the skin absorbs. Human skin absorbs oils containing the essential fatty acids very easily, and to a smaller extent, the less unsaturated oleic acid. Saturated fatty acids are poorly absorbed, and a non-organic, artificial grease like petroleum jelly is not absorbed at all.

Infant eczema. Some children get an eczema-like skin condition over many parts of their bodies when they are weaned from the breast, because they change from a diet of mother's milk which contains 8% or more of its fatty acids as essential fatty acids, to a diet of 'baby foods' which contains ample protein, but little or no essential fatty acids. This rash can be eliminated by rubbing oil containing essential fatty acids on these children's wrists. The oil is absorbed through the skin and transported to wherever it is needed in the skin and elsewhere in the body.

Skin creams. All active skin preparations and cosmetic skin creams have an oil base, plus a number of substances to give them smooth texture, fragrance, and other desirable external properties.

Manufacturers of the common skin preparations prefer to use oils which will not spoil. These preparations can protect the skin against the drying effects of sun, wind, and rain by covering the skin, but do not actively support the healthy glow of the skin, because they are lacking in the (spoilable) essential fatty acids.

Better types of skin creams and oils nourish the protein skin, with oils. The best ones, those which are sold with *real* guarantees of improvement, and which *do* really work wonders for skin health and complexion, always contain essential fatty acids. Sesame oil is the oil base most often used, because it resists spoilage best. Since the essential fatty acids are sensitive and spoil easily, the better preparations have a shelf life of only around 6 months even when special stabilizing ingredients are used, and are therefore quite expensive. They make the skin supple and soft, and prevent lining and wrinkles. Several such preparations are available in Europe, where the knowledge of skin health through natural substances is more advanced than in North America, but there are also a few on the North American market. In Europe, flax oil is used in some face and body oils. It is the best oil, by far, for this purpose.

In the long run, the skin-beautifying essential fatty acids must be present in the diet, and must oil the skin from within. Then the skin becomes velvety, smooth, and radiant, without the need for external creams and at a small fraction of the cost.

Many people who begin to use the oil-protein combination are amazed that oils can make such an amazing difference to their skin. The hardness of the skin, as well as greasy pores and bumps disappear, and they find that their skin feels creamy, supple, soft, and lovely to touch. This is one of the first changes that many people notice on the oil-protein combination diet, along with an enhanced feeling of general well-being.

Diet. Many people on a high protein diet suffer from constipation. Athletes who follow such a diet because they know that protein builds muscle, and because they've heard that fat is bad (fat has a bad reputation in this age of muscle consciousness), often report constipation. Much of the constipation, estimated at 30 to 50% of the population, can be relieved simply by the inclusion of the stool-softening oils, the oils containing essential fatty acids.[1] The oil of evening primrose, is well known for its stool-softening effect. It is sold in health food stores. A little oil goes a long way. Flax oil also has this stool-softening effect. Just by changing the type and amount of oil in one's diet, one can obtain just about the precise stool consistency one wants. Oil enemas to relieve constipation and bowel obstruction are traditional and work very well[2].

Problem skin. When a working person's hands are cracked from physical labour, solvents, or detergents, oils are used to soften the hands. Oils also speed up the healing processes. The proteins of our hands need to be oiled to stay supple and soft.

People with dry skin, eczema, and psoriasis, and also older people and those with arthritis, find that when they use soap, their skin gets dry and rough, and their skin condition worsens. They discover for themselves, or sometimes the doctor advises them, that it is better for their skin to use less soap. This is good advice, because soap emulsifies and removes oils, leaving the skin's proteins oil-less. Organic solvents in household cleaners and gasoline products also remove oils from our hands, leaving them chapped, hard, and prone to cracking. An equally good piece of advice given by nutrition-conscious doctors is to eat more of the essential fatty acid-containing oils, which replenish from inside, the body's own supply with which to oil the skin.

Scientific Evidence

Early hints. The scientific evidence that links oil and protein in nutrition goes back many years, and includes work carried out by some of the best scientists of their time. Liebig in 1842, Pflueger in 1875, and Hoppe-Seyler in 1876 had shown that a clear connection exists between oil and protein nutrition on the one hand and oxygen uptake and biological oxidation in tissues on the other.

Lebedow in 1888 showed that if starved dogs are given either high protein or high fat diets, they die even faster than if they are given no food at all, i.e. continue to be starved. However, if they receive good protein and good fat *together*, they recover from starvation very quickly. 'Good' fat in this experiment was fresh flax oil, which is the richest source of both essential fatty acids. 'Bad' fats were animal fats (which are high in saturated fatty acids).

Rosenfeld in 1899 showed that the consumption of animal fats (high in saturated and low in the essential fatty acids) causes obesity and fatty degeneration of the inner organs.

Of course, at the time that the above experiments were carried out, the difference between the saturated and the essential fatty acids had not yet been discovered. Still, the results are in line with what we now know about the effects of these two different classes of fatty acids on the health of animals and man.

The essential nature of what we now call the essential fatty acids was not known until 1930. In that year, Burr and Burr discovered them, and showed that if protein is given to animals deficient in the essential fatty acids, they die very quickly.

In 1902, Rosenfeld showed that a high carbohydrate, low protein diet results in fat deposition. So does a high carbohydrate, high protein diet. But when 'good' fats are added, less fat deposition occurs and better food utilization and energy production takes place. In other words, the 'good' fats help one stay slim. Contrary to popular opinion, not all dietary fats make us fat.

The biological reasons behind these observations took longer to work out, but are now better understood. For one thing, fats are digested slowly and prevent hunger from recurring for up to 5 or 8 hours after a meal, whereas proteins and carbohydrates are digested in about 2 to 5 hours, and hunger recurs much sooner, possibly encouraging overeating. For another, the essential fatty acids increase metabolic rate, thus helping to mobilize and burn excess saturated fats. A third reason is found in the loss of craving for more food when the body's need for essential fatty acids is satisfied. The hunger mechanism is set up to shut off only when the nutrient needs of the body are fulfilled. A poor diet, lacking in essential substances leads to continuing hunger, overeating, and weight gain.

More findings. Several other researchers obtained results in their experiments which consistently showed that protein and oil belong together in nutrition, and work together in the body. Sensitivity to toxins increases if oil and protein are not given together, and in the right proportions. Researchers also found that too much protein causes disease. If in addition, oil is withdrawn from the diet, the disease is made worse. In all tissues which are intensely active, an increased amount of sulphur-rich protein is found. This is *always* paralleled by an increased concentration of essential fatty acids in these active tissues.

In Italy, where flax oil consumption is high, sulphur-containing proteins are effective in the treatment of severe liver disease, skin afflictions, eclampsia[3] of pregnancy, and other toxic conditions. These proteins are also used to wake patients from anesthesia. In the U.S.A., (where flax oil is not commonly consumed and the essential fatty acid content of the diet is generally low), the same proteins fail in these same medical applications, to the surprise and dismay of the doctors. The combination of oil with protein is very important in these clinical applications.

By the 1920's, the synergistic (co-operative) action in the body of sulphur-rich protein and fatty substances was already firmly established, though the identity of the fatty substances was still unknown.

Nobel Prize-winning Scientists. Thunberg in 1911 knew the importance of the sulphur-rich proteins, and knew that these proteins work in combination with a functional partner in biological systems. He was searching for that partner, but ran into technical difficulties, and was unable to isolate the partner, because the methods to do this had not yet been invented.

Meyerhof in 1920 found that the fatty acid called linoleic acid (now, but not then, known to be essential) and sulphur-rich proteins work together to help fatigued muscle recover from exercise and exertion very rapidly. He did not recognize the far-reaching significance of this finding.

Szent-Gyorgyi in 1924 discovered that the sulphur-rich protein-and-linoleic acid system takes up oxygen. He lacked the biochemical techniques to prove the identity of the components of this system conclusively.

Warburg in 1926 showed that a fatty substance was required to restart oxidation when it was low, as is the case in cancer and diabetes. He didn't know which substance it was, and he tested a number of different fatty acids, including the saturated butyric acid (4:0) and the once unsaturated oleic acid (18:1*w*9) (see: Fatty Acids). He was surprised and disappointed when the expected increase in oxidation did not occur. It did not dawn on him that it might be linoleic acid (18:2*w*6), although he was familiar with this substance. So close, but yet so far!

All four researchers named above were Nobel Prize winning

scientists, who, stumped by the insurmountable technical difficulties, missed the solution they were close to. They turned their attention to other scientific questions of their time, and the almost solved problem was shelved and forgotten for years.

Specialization. With increasing specialization, scientists developed tunnel vision. Protein scientists studied proteins in detail. Oil chemists studied oils. Both fields grew enormously, especially protein biochemistry. There was little overlap of these fields into each other.

The breakthrough. Then Dr. Johanna Budwig appeared. She was a meticulous woman of genius, with a broad perspective. She knew physics, chemistry, biochemistry, pharmacology, and medicine. She recognized the loggerhead in research that had stopped previous scientists. It was the lack of techniques for separating and accurately identifying the different fatty components present in a mixture of biological material. Because of the lack of techniques, problems of fat metabolism could only be identified after the patient had died. Dr. Johanna Budwig undertook painstaking, meticulous, and time-consuming work to develop new techniques. Night after night she worked in the laboratory. Different substances had to be systematically tested under different conditions of temperature, concentration, and acidity in different solvents. The breakthrough techniques she developed are so sensitive that the fatty substances from a single drop of blood can be accurately separated and the substances in it identified. Her work allowed the earlier scientists' leads to be followed. Pieces of the unsolved puzzle began to fall into place.

Clinical application. Thousands of blood samples from healthy and sick people were systematically analyzed, and the findings were tabulated. Blood samples from people who have cancer, diabetes, and some kinds of liver disease (a frequent forerunner of cancer) consistently lack one of the essential fatty acids, the doubly unsaturated linoleic acid. These blood samples also consistenly lack the substances of which linoleic acid is a part: the phosphatides, which are necessary for the development and integrity of the cell membranes; and a type of blood lipoprotein, now identified as fatty acid-carrying albumin.

The lack of phosphatides helps to explain the polyploidy of cancer, the fact that cancer cells often have multiple sets of chromosomes. The genetic material divides, but the cell membranes can't be produced, due to the lack of the material from which they are made. Cell division remains incomplete.

The lipoproteins in the blood, which contain linoleic acid combined with sulphur-rich protein are missing. Dr. Budwig found instead a yellow-green protein substance in the blood. When linoleic acid and sulphur rich protein are added to this substance, the yellow-green colour disappears, and the red blood pigment, hemoglobin, appears. This explains the anemia of cancer. The lipoprotein which makes hemoglobin, (the blood's oxygen carrier) is missing, so hemoglobin is low and the blood can't carry enough oxygen. It also explains the lack of vitality associated with cancer. Oxidation, the process which produces the energy for the life functions, requires oxygen and linoleic acid. Oxygen is low because of lack of hemoglobin, and there's too little linoleic acid present to make more hemoglobin or to fulfill the other energy functions of that essential fatty acid.

It appeared to Dr. Budwig that cancer, diabetes, and some liver diseases involve a deficiency of the essential fatty acids. Since these must be provided in the diet — the human body cannot make them — the cause of its absence in the body is a diet deficient in essential fatty acids. Blood from people with any of the other diseases Dr. Budwig tested do not show this severe deficiency, and healthy people's blood always contained essential fatty acids.

If cancer is a deficiency disease brought on by lack of essential fatty acids, she reasoned, then we should feed cancer patients a diet high in essential fatty acids. This should alleviate at least some of the cancer patient's problems.

The Oil-Protein Combination

Based on the information she knew about oil and protein working together, Dr. Budwig fed cancer patients a mixture of skim milk protein (because it is a good source of sulphur-containing proteins), and essential fatty acids in the ratio: 100 grams skim milk protein[4], 40 grams fresh flax oil, and 25 grams milk (the milk to liquefy the whole mixture, to make it easier to work with), and monitored the changes which occurred in the blood of these patients.

Dr. Budwig found that the yellow-green pigment slowly disappeared; the phosphatides returned; the lipoproteins re-appeared. She also found that tumours receded and disappeared; anemia was aleviated; vital energy increased and vitality returned; the patient recuperated. It took about 3 months for these changes. During this time, the symptoms of cancer, diabetes, or liver disease also disappeared.

Further Findings

In other experiments, Dr. Budwig demonstrated that the lipoproteins of all very active tissues (buds, liver, brain, glands, skin) always contain highly unsaturated fatty acids and sulphur-rich proteins. The association between these two substances can be broken by oxygen from the air.

She discovered that anesthetics and many other drugs, among them barbiturates, sleeping pills, and pain killers separate the highly unsaturated fatty acids from their association with sulphur-containing protein. They destroy that system.

Her research showed that the blood lipoproteins migrate into the skin and there break into their components: linoleic acid and sulphur-containing proteins. Usually, the linoleic acid is conserved, but if the diet contains plenty of linoleic acid, some of it appears in the skin oils.

She discovered that linoleic acid reacts with sulphur-containing proteins to form a new product with new properties. The product is water-soluble (linoleic acid is not water-soluble) and attracts oxygen from the air.

She proved that hard carcinoma tumours can be dissolved by cysteine or insulin (both of which contain sulphur groups) and linoleic acid (18:2*w*6), or by horse serum, which is high in both linolenic acid (18:3*w*3) and organically bound sulphur.

She isolated fatty substances from soft tumours which contain polymerized fats of marine origin. Such substances are formed when highly unsaturated fish and whale oils are subjected to high temperatures. These oils and high temperatures are used in the making of margarine. She immediately recognized the danger to the health of consumers.

In her capacity as government spokesperson for the use of fats and fat products in health and nutrition, she made statements to that effect.

A Conflict of Interests

Then Dr. Budwig found herself in the midst of conflict. The head of the institute where she worked had a financial interest in margarine. He held patents for some of the processes used to make margarine, including hydrogenation processes, which produce toxic polymers found in tumours. He feared that her discoveries, if made public, would destroy margarine sales. He tried to bribe her, offering her money and ownership of a drugstore if she promised not to publish her findings. When she refused the bribe, she was threatened. She lost her laboratory facilities at the fat research institute. When she tried to find another institute in which to continue her research work, she found her way blocked. Her laboratory work came to an abrupt halt, and she could not publish her further discoveries in the fat research journals. However, she copyrighted her work, and later published it in book form.[5]

Practical Application and Experience

Dr. Budwig opened a country health practice. She has said, "This is the best thing that could have happened. It forced me to apply my theoretically sound knowledge practically, on humans, on the cases doctors had given up as hopeless." She uses no drugs, surgery or x-ray treatments. Her treatments are entirely nutritional. The oil-protein combination is the basis of her treatment, and the diet includes plenty of carrots (for carotene, the precursor of vitamin A), fresh greens for their content of vitamin C, whole grains, fresh, natural, unheated flax oil, skim milk protein, nuts, and a few herbs such as stinging nettles and celeriac for their diuretic effects. She also recommends rainbow trout for its high content of *w*3 fatty acids. And she demands very strict adherence to the recommended regimen when she counsels terminal cancer patients.

Dr. Budwig does not consider the oil-protein combination to be a special diet. Rather, she says, it is a return to the way we should have been eating in order not to get sick in the first place. And once sick, the return to a natural, nutritious way of eating supplies the life force within us with the materials it needs to repair and rebuild our bodies. Once healthy, it is also the kind of nutrition that will keep us that way.

Epilogue

In the last 2 or 3 years, researchers have begun to become *seriously* interested in the effects of linolenic acid (LNA, 18:3*w*3) on cancer. It will probably be several years before they make any daring statements, but for someone who knows Dr. Budwig's work, it is clear that these researchers are just following in the footsteps that this courageous woman took over 30 years ago.

In several of her books, Dr. Budwig describes cases that she has successfully treated using her oil-protein combination and whole foods. These cases include: cancer — her specialty (colon, brain, lung, stomach, breast, lymph, liver, melanoma, and leukemia), cardiovascular disease, diabetes, acne and other skin conditions, weak vision and hearing, constipation, sterility, dry skin, difficult birth, menstrual problems (cramps, foul odours, breast pain), glandular atrophy, fatty liver and other liver complaints, gall stones, pancreas malfunction, kidney degeneration, heart dysfunction, blood dyscrasia, anoxia, arthritic conditions, childhood diseases such as mumps, measles, and swollen tonsils, immune deficiency, and low vitality. References to her books (all of which are in German) are given in the bibliography.

50

Recipes

The Basic Oil-Protein Mixture

The basic recipe for the oil-protein mixture is very simple. To 100 grams of skim milk cottage cheese or baker's cheese or kwark (contains about 17 grams of protein), one adds 40 grams of fresh flax oil, 25 grams of milk (to produce a more liquid consistency) and stirs or blends these ingredients together until the oil is no longer visible. That's all there is to it.

The mixture can be eaten as is, or we can add other ingredients. And this is where the fun begins, because the oil-protein mixture lends itself to just about any kind of dish we'd like to make.

Breakfast

To start the day, a touch of honey added to the mixture makes a very tasty and nutritious breakfast that stays with you all morning. We could mix into the oil-protein combination rolled oats, sprouted grains, cooked cereal, or fiber, if we like these or they are important to us. I personally don't like grains in my oil-protein breakfast and prefer to eat my grains separate from my oil-protein meals. Ground flax stirred into the oil-protein mixture gives a delightful nutty taste and is supernutritious. A touch of honey or maple syrup (just a touch, though!) makes this breakfast incredibly yummy.

Fresh fruit slices on top are delicious. Peaches, apples, pears, mangoes, oranges, papaya, grapes, pineapple, kiwi — just mouth-watering! Or berries: strawberries, raspberries, blueberries, blackberries, or any of the wild berries are good. Chopped almond, crushed filberts, walnut pieces, ground sunflower or pumpkin seeds go great in this breakfast. Or nuts and fruit together....

Main Dish

For a tasty main dish for lunch or supper, we could use a little salt (or potassium-sodium salt to keep the blood pressure down), and/or any number of spices fresh from our window sill garden, or in winter, dried spices. We could chop, slice, or blend onions, parsley, carrots, garlic, green onions, green and red peppers, or just about any fresh vegetable into the mixture. We could eat the oil-protein mixture with spices and baked potatoes, as they do in Silesia, where oil-protein and potatoes is the national dish. A little soy sauce, a little cayenne, a touch of dill, or celery seed, a snip of sage, or thyme, or oregano, or rosemary, or anything else that we fancy in spices; some yeast. Cucumbers and peppermint are cool in this mixture when the summer gets hot. We could... it's as endless as the human imagination, as endless as the colours, fragrances, and shapes of nature. People who cannot chew can let the blender do the chewing for them. That way, they can eat much of their food fresh and raw. This is a really good idea, since cooking makes digestion more difficult and destroys some of the vitamins, while vitamin requirements actually increase with age.

Salad Dressing

To make salad dressing, I add a little vinegar, lemon juice, or vitamin C powder, tamari, and various spices to the basic mixture. To bring out the taste I want, I would emphasize the vinegar for sour, a little honey to sweeten, more spices or yeast for a bitter tinge; for salt, I use a vegetable mineral mix from the health food store (it contains less sodium and more potassium and other minerals than does table salt); and for a hot salad dressing, cayenne. Besides these tastes, the nuances of flavour that can be made with various mixtures of ingredients and spices are endless. For colour, fresh spinach leaves or parsley will give you a 'green goddess', red peppers and tomatoes give a bright red, and carrots an orange salad dressing.

Fresh salad dressings are tastier than the store-bought ones, and are far more nutritious. Because you make them in your own kitchen, you can cater to the taste preferences of the members of your family, as well as their nutritional needs. Even various vitamin and mineral supplements can be added to the salad dressing to boost nutritional value or to compensate for some of the low nutrient or junk food items consumed by our children (and ourselves).

Mayonnaise

For mayonnaise, mustard, horseradish, apple cider vinegar, lemon, perhaps some soysauce, and various spices are added to the basic mixture.

Dessert

A dessert to tickle the palate as well as heal the body can be made by adding fruit, berries, nuts, or a little honey to the basic mixture. Mint, carob, ginger, vanilla, clove, cinnamon, cardamon, licorice root powder, and other natural flavours can be used to provide a tasty variety.

There are literally thousands of tastes and taste combinations possible using the flavours of nature. A real taste adventure out of our own gardens, combined in our kitchens according to our understanding, as an expression of our hearts, to feed and heal the ones we love — isn't that what 'cooking' is really supposed to be all about?

Flax Butter

Flax butter is better than both dairy butter and margarine because it contains ample essential fatty acids. Until there is a suitable similar product on the market, we can make flax butter ourselves. Here's how:

Melt 250 grams (1/2 pound) of coconut fat to boiling. At the same time, put 100 grams of fresh flax oil into the freezer compartment of the fridge. When the coconut fat boils (160°C), add finely chopped garlic or onions. Let them sizzle until they begin to turn brown, but take out the pieces before they're crisp. Let the coconut oil cool. Before it hardens, pour the coconut oil into the cold flax oil, mix, and return the mixture to the freezer compartment until it hardens. Voila! Flax butter. Tastes great. No cholesterol. No *trans*- fatty acids. Spreads like butter. Better than both butter and margarine, because it contains about 25% essential fatty acids. If a softer butter is desired, add more flax oil. If a harder product is desired, increase the amount of coconut fat.

If you hate the taste of onions and garlic (which are good for you) oats, peppers, or buckwheat may be substituted. The flax butter tastes more bland with these ingredients. The foods listed above provide organic sulphur groups, which protect the essential fatty acids from destruction by oxygen, and provide the body with the sulphur needed to make sulphur-rich proteins. With the protection of the sulphur, flax butter keeps fresh longer.

Specific Recipes for Beginners

For those of you who hate cooking without recipes, and love cooking by the book, here's just a few recipes to get you started.

Breakfast. 1) To the basic mixture (100g baker's cheese, and 40 grams fresh flax oil) add 2 or 3 tablespoons of freshly ground flax (flax should be dry-ground just before using). Then add one fresh rasped apple, a little honey, a little cinnamon, and eat. 2) To the basic mixture add 2 tablespoons of freshly ground flax, a drop of vanilla, and mix. Layer this over sliced fresh peaches. Top with crushed walnuts, almonds, or coconut flakes.

Main Dish. To the basic mixture add finely cut parsley and a clove or two of finely cut garlic, a little soy sauce, and a little thyme or oregano. Add a baked potato and a fresh salad made of lettuce, shredded carrots, cucumbers, and tomatoes. These can be mixed in with the oil-protein, if desired. Perhaps a pea or lentil and barley soup to start the meal.

Salad Dressing. 1) To the basic mixture, add the juices of half a lemon, 1 teaspoon of tamari or soy sauce. To this, add 1/4 teaspoon of cayenne, and a pinch of oregano, or sage, or rosemary or your favourite spice, and 1/3 teaspoon of dill, nettle, or mint. Then add a handful of fresh parsley and blend the whole mixture thoroughly. Taste the product and then adjust the taste with more lemon, more cayenne, more soysauce, some vegetable salt, or a little honey, depending on the taste you want to emphasize. 2) To the basic mixture add 4 grams of vitamin C or 2 tablespoons of apple cider vinegar, then 1 teaspoon of tamari or soysauce. Spice with 1/4 teaspoon of paprika, turmeric, or cayenne. Caraway or cumin brings out a nice flavour. Add 1/2 of one fresh large red pepper (not the hot type) cut into pieces, and blend all of these items together thoroughly. Taste. Adjust the taste as in previous recipe. If it tastes too strong, or you want more body to your salad dressing, add soybean curd (tofu) until the desired body or blandness is reached (tofu is very bland in taste, but very nutritious). Some people like to add an egg.

Mayonnaise. To one ounce each of baker's cheese, fresh flax oil, and milk, add the juice of half a lemon, a teaspoonful of mustard, a teaspoonful of dill, marjoram, or other spice, half a teaspoonful of vegetable salt, and perhaps a little soysauce. Blend. Green onions cut fine can then be added, or dill pickles.

And now, start to experiment with whatever suits *your* fancy. Be creative, and happy eating!!

51

Oil and Sunshine

Different diets

It is difficult to resist the temptation to prescribe one diet for everyone, and that is why so much controversy exists about how much fat a diet should contain. One set of writers insists that man has always been a hunter, eating meats high in animal fats; another set insists that man has always been a fruit and vegetable eating monkey; a third set can prove that man's natural diet is high in complex carbohydrates, mainly grains, with greens.

Whom are we to believe? From studying the natural diets of different people living in different areas, it appears that man adapts to the food which grows in the area in which he happens to live, and this in turn, depends on the climate and environmental conditions of the area, because the plants and animals are adapted to the natural condition of the area in which they live.

For instance, Eskimoes who live in the far North, traditionally consumed a diet very high in meats from fish, marine mammals, and arctic wildlife. Their diet contained few vegetables, and very little fiber. Their foods contained a large amount of fat, and was especially high in the very highly unsaturated fatty acids which some writers suggest as the cause of cancer. Yet the Eskimoes on this diet were free of cancer. They were also free of heart disease, arthritis, multiple sclerosis, diabetes, appendicitis, colitis, gall stones, dental caries, and acne, on this diet extremely high in fats and meats.

People living in regions with a temperate climate seem to do best on a diet of high complex carbohydrates. If they consume foods high in animal products from beef, mutton, and pork (and in the affluent nations, they do), they set themselves up for all the degenerative conditions which the traditional Eskimoes didn't get[1]. The program that Dr. Pritikin suggests, of high complex carbohydrates and exercise, and a fat intake of maximum 10% of calories (he considers all fats poisonous above this level) is successful in reversing many of the degenerative conditions brought on by the beef, mutton, pork diet.

In tropical areas, the ideal diet comes closest to the fresh fruit and vegetable diet that the monkeys are accused of having popularized. This diet is low in fats, containing perhaps a little coconut fat, which contains mostly saturated fatty acids, and the fats found in the cell membranes of plants. A high fat diet does not sit well in the tropics.

Seasonally too, there is a shift in food consumption, based on sunshine and warmth, at least in the temperate regions. In winter, our consumption naturally turns more towards the northern diet, and in summer, more towards the tropical diet.

The Oil-Sunshine Connection

There is a relationship between sunlight and fats. Excessive sunlight can destroy unsaturated fatty acids, causing skin spots, free radical-induced oxidation, and perhaps cancer. The more highly unsaturated the fatty acid, the more sensitive it is to destruction.

Geography. In wonderful adaptation to the amount of sunlight present in an area, we find that where sunlight is least, the wild animals carry the largest amount of the most highly unsaturated fatty acids (5 and 6 times unsaturated 20:5*w*3 and 22:6*w*3) in their tissue, and the humans who live there and eat these wild creatures, do too. Because there is so little sunlight, the highly unsaturated fatty acids cause no problems for Eskimoes.

As we go south we find that the foods that grow wild contain less of the highly unsaturated fatty acids, but contain the 2 and 3 times unsaturated (18:2*w*6 and 18:3*w*3) essential fatty acids instead. These are less sensitive than the 5 and 6 times unsaturated, but still very sensitive to destruction by sunlight. We find also that seeds of the same type of plant grown further north contain more oil and more essential fatty acids than the seeds grown further south.

By the time we get to the mediterranean where it's warm, olive oil, which contains mostly monounsaturated (18:1*w*9) fatty acids is the common natural oil. And in the tropics, we find coconut oil, which contains almost completely saturated (12:0, 14:0, 16:0) fatty acids.

Anatomy. Every animal, as well as man, contains within its tissues, saturated, monounsaturated, essential (2 and 3 times unsaturated), and 5 and 6 times unsaturated fatty acids. The most highly unsaturated fatty acids are found mostly in the inner organs such as brain, adrenal, inner ear, and reproductive glands; all are well protected from direct light (in the retina, these highly unsaturated fatty acids have a special function in vision, which requires them to be exposed to indirect light; exposure to direct sunlight destroys the fatty acids, and blinds us).

The oils which oil the skin and are exposed to direct sunlight, are mostly the less sensitive monounsaturated fatty acids and the saturated fatty acids, which are the least sensitive to destruction by light.

The essential fatty acids and even more highly unsaturated fatty acids store a great amount of readily and easily useable sunlight in their chemical bonds (*cis-* methylene interrupted, *pi-* double bonds), and these, in the absence of sunlight, provide the body from within, with stored 'sunlight' energy during the winter months darkness. The Eskimoes were not depressed and suicidal during the winter time of total darkness, because their diet of fish and marine animals provided them with large quantities of the most highly unsaturated fatty acids (EPA, 20:5*w*3 and DHA, 22:6*w*3), large quantities of the 'liquid' sunshine contained in the oils of these animals. Europeans living north of the Arctic Circle, eating the typical Western diet high in saturated fatty acids (16:0 and 18:0), suffer severe winter blues — neurotic, psychotic, and suicidal behaviours — and often have to be flown out to 'see the light.' EPA and DHA are required for the functioning of brain cells and synapses, and in winter, European brains become depleted of these substances, resulting in depressed brain function and behavioural depression.

In summer, sunlight absorbed through eyes and skin of healthy people can be conducted into the body and stored in chemical bonds for future (or immediate) use. The essential fatty acids are required for the absorption of sunlight to take place. The saturated and monounsaturated fatty acids cannot substitute for the essential fatty acids in this function, and in fact, they interfere with this function of the essential fatty acids when the diet contains excessive quantities of saturated and monounsaturated fatty acids, as does the Western diet.

Science. The theory of light absorption through human skin has been worked out by Dr. Budwing, using principles established by Nobel Prize winning researchers in physics, chemistry, and biology.

The physical properties of light waves and the electrons of the double bonds in the essential fatty acids make such a relationship plausible and likely. The wave lengths of sunlight resonate with (vibrate at the same frequency as) the pi-electrons of the double bonds; these electrons can therefore capture light energy. In practice, it is known that the essential fatty acids absorb light (they are part of the photosynthesis mechanism by which plants absorb sunlight), and are chemically very sensitive to light. They are also known to react with oxygen, and a part of their function in the brain and other extremely active tissues is to attract the required high supply of oxygen and energy which enables these tissues to be active. The lack of oxygen in tissues always decreases their metabolism, and leads to depressed function. Low tissue oxygen and depressed function are two symptoms common to all degenerative diseases.

Finally, the essential fatty acids react weakly with sulphur-containing proteins; the physical details for this have also been worked out by Dr. Budwig. The essential fatty acids and sulphur-rich proteins form an association within which the sunlight energy stored in foods is released, oscillates, and dances. They also attract oxygen, which is needed to keep the dance of life energy going.

Conclusions

Sunlight and highly unsaturated oils are twins, and each can substitute for the other to some extent, though both are necessary. Their partnership explains why diets in different latitudes may be drastically different in fat content, and fat type, yet each be health-giving and life-sustaining for the consumers living in the area where it is naturally found.

Every region of the globe gets at least a little light, and every area grows organisms which contain at least a little of the essential fatty acids. The more light, the less essential fatty acids seem to be needed. The less light, the more of these fatty acids appear to be necessary in the diet, and the more unsaturated they may be.

If an Eskimo ate just fruits and vegetables during the Arctic night, he would die. If the Samoan ate the Eskimo's fish oils in the hot tropical sun, he would fry. Each in his place and on his native diet, thrives.

52

Rating the Diets for Oils

Introduction

Not every diet is capable of building and maintaining healthy bodies. In this section we will look briefly at the most common types of diets, and rate them for their oil content and their ability to maintain or rebuild health.

The Pritikin Diet

The Pritikin diet is the most popular of the high complex carbohydrate (80%), low fat diets. Another high complex carbohydrate diet is the Airola diet, which is too low in protein, but similar to the Pritikin diet in the rest of its make-up.

The Pritikin diet is good for people who have overeaten themselves sick on the typical Western or North American diet, which is high in protein and super high (over 40%) in mostly saturated fats. Pritikin's diet is mostly a grain and vegetable diet with a little fruit, and with meats used mainly as condiments. Such a diet is able to reverse many of the degenerative changes which occur in cardiovascular disease, obesity, diabetes, rheumatoid arthritis, hypertension, and senility.

Once a person is healthy however, the Pritikin diet is dangerously low in fats. The absorption of the fat-soluble vitamins A, D, E and K is seriously impaired when total fat intake is 5% or less, and the Pritikin diet comes too close to that lower limit (at the Pritikin Longevity Center, the diet is 7% fats). Diets lower than 5% fats are also correlated with cancer in places like the Philippines, most likely due to impaired absorption of vitamin A, which is known to protect against cancer.

Deficiency in essential fatty acids is also correlated with the occurrence of cancer, and the Pritikin diet may be somewhat low in these vital nutrients, although the fats that this diet does contain are adequate in essential fatty acid content. There may just not be quite enough of them.

In a place like California, and for people who spend time outdoors in sunny, warm climates, the sunshine may compensate to some extent for the low supply of essential fatty acids, but in winter, more northern latitudes, and for people indoors, more essential fatty acids are required, and 15 to 20% of calories as fat with 1/3 to 1/2 of that in the form of essential fatty acids is a more realistic (or health-ensuring) estimate. In more southern hot climates, the grain content may be too high, and the lighter fare of fresh fruits and vegetables needs to be emphasized. People in the tropics who spend their time indoors under air-conditioning and artificial lights may need more essential fatty acids than the Pritikin diet supplies.

Still, the Pritikin diet is a step in the right direction for this generation's over-fat, over-processed way of eating. Excluding of course, those people who are carbohydrate-intolerant or allergic to carbohydrates, and those who are not overfed.

Dr. Atkins' Diet

Dr. Atkins' diet is the best known of the high protein, high fat, low carbohydrate diets. Other diets in this category are the Stillman and Drinking Man's diets. Dr. Atkins' diet assumes that man has always been a hunter, which is open to debate, and that he has always eaten a diet high in protein and fat, which is not true (see: Fats in Meats). A high protein, high fat diet is necessary for some people who are intolerant, sensitive, or allergic to carbohydrates.

The Atkins diet is largely a weight reduction diet, promising the loss of pounds and inches while eating all we want. It works, because fats are digested slower and suppress appetite for much longer than carbohydrates (especially refined carbohydrates), and because they produce ketones, which reduce hunger even more. Refined carbohydrates, which are usually a large part of overweight people's diets, are either omitted completely from the menu or allowed only in small quantities.

The Atkins diet is basically the Western meat and potatoes diet without the potatoes. For weight reduction, it works, but it has come under criticism as leading to kidney damage, cardiovascular disease, and other degenerative conditions. The essential fatty acid intake is not even considered in the Atkins diet, and the diet is usually high in saturated fats.

The Traditional Eskimo Diet

Eskimoes, adhering to their traditional diet[1], consume mostly animal foods which are high in fats and proteins, but they are completely free of degenerative diseases. The fats in these diets come from fish and other marine animals, and contain large concentrations of the very highly unsaturated fatty acids derived from the essential fatty acids. When these people adopt the Western diet, they lose their immunity to degenerative disease.

The 'Western' Diet

The Western diet is world-famous for causing degenerative diseases. It contains over 40% mostly saturated fats, 40% refined carbohydrates, and only 6% complex carbohydrates. Any member of any national group who consumes this diet becomes susceptible to all the degenerative diseases. People who move to the West from a place and diet which is free of degenerative disease and people who adopt the Western diet wherever they live, become prone to degeneration soon after they adopt the Western lifestyle.

Sorting Out the Details

Here we have four different diets. Two of them, one high in complex carbohydrates and low in fats, the other high in fats and low in carbohydrates, both prevent and reverse the symptoms of degenerative diseases.

How can we reconcile the fact the one high fat diet protects against degeneration, while the other high fat diet fosters it? The answer lies in the kinds of fats that these diets contain, the kinds of fats they omit, and their content of other essential nutrient factors.

Both the Pritikin and the Eskimo diet are free of refined sugars and refined starches, which rob the body of the vitamins and minerals necessary for their digestion and metabolism, and which the body turns into saturated fatty acids (see: Sugars and Starches). Both diets are free of refined oils and altered oil products. Both diets are low in the saturated fatty acids which can interfere with the functions of the essential fatty acids in the body. Both diets are free of the processed foods which are deficient in many of the vitamins and minerals, and which contain de-natured fat products. Both diets contain natural amounts of the vitamin and mineral co-factors which the body requires to maintain health. There is some evidence that a deficient diet can be prevented from leading to degenerative diseases if appropriate amounts of vitamins and minerals are taken in the form of supplements (see: Orthomolecular Nutrition). Both diets contain the essential fatty acids or their derivatives in adequate amounts, although Pritikin's diet borders on being deficient in them.

The Atkins and Western diets are high in saturated fatty acids, which interfere with the functions of the essential fatty acids. The Western diet contains refined carbohydrates, which add to the load of saturated fatty acids. The Western diet is also deficient in vitamins and minerals.

The Atkins diet is low in refined carbohydrates, and therefore is an improvement on the average Western diet. Neither diet is high enough in the essential fatty acids, and neither diet is a good diet for health. For people who are allergic or intolerant of carbohydrates, a fat and protein diet is necessary, but the fats have to be chosen to contain 1/3 to 1/2 of their fatty acids as essential fatty acids or their derivatives. These required fatty acids are found in flax, safflower, sunflower, pumpkin, sesame, and fish oils. Beef, mutton, pork, cheese, and butter are not good sources of the essential fatty acids, nor are margarine or shortenings reliable sources of essential fatty acids.

A good fat-and-protein diet for people who are carbohydrate-intolerant or hypoglycemic can be made using skim milk solids and flax oil (see: The Oil-Protein Combination).

53

Wholesome Nutrition

The Major Components

Good oil combined with good protein is the basic and major structural component of a wholesome diet, in which complex carbohydrates provide the major energy component. The oil needs to be high in the essential fatty acids, and needs to contain both linoleic acid (LA, 18:2*w*6) and linolenic acid (LNA, 18:3*w*3) to be complete. The protein needs to be complete (contain all 8 essential amino acids), and high in sulphur, since sulphur is attracted to the double bonds of the essential fatty acids, thereby protecting them from damage and free radical formation. The protein and oil, associated together, play the key part in the structures of cells. The structures provide the framework on which the energy, made available for life functions by the oxidation of carbohydrates and other food stuffs, moves. Oil and protein form an association, like the points of the spark plugs, between which the life energy, the spark of life, jumps. Good oil is one major aspect of our nutrition that is systematically destroyed by commercial processing methods (vitamin C is the other). Good oil also spoils easily in storage, if care is not taken in packaging (see: Essential Fatty Acids).

Since the essential fatty acids are major nutrients (along with proteins and carbohydrates), it makes sense that deficiencies of essential fatty acids result in *major* health problems.

The Minor Components

The minor nutrients, the vitamins and minerals, are also essential to good physical health, but are required in smaller concentrations. Carotene, vitamins C and E, the B-complex, and zinc are especially important in helping the oil-protein combination fulfill its functions, but the other minor nutrients must be present as well for physical health. For complete nutrition, all the essential nutrients must be present in the foods we eat and in their appropriate amounts.

Nutritious Foods

Fresh root and leafy green vegetables, nuts, seeds, grains, and fruits, plus herbs and spices are the basics of wholesome nutrition. Garden-fresh and sun-ripened, organic, from rich soils, grown without pesticides and artificial fertilizers are best, of course, and are worth seeking.

Soils

Artificial fertilizers are not evil. They are merely deficient. The plant takes 20 minerals out of the soil, and we put back only 3 to 6. Fertilizers are often high in nitrogen, which 'drives' the plant to suck up extra water, but not extra nutrients. For these reasons, composting is recommended over artificial fertilizer. Good composting practice returns to the soil all the ingredients that plants take out.

Raw Foods

The more of our food that is consumed in its natural raw state, the higher the vitamin content of our diet. However, there are some limits. Raw potatoes are good nutritionally, but not palatable for most of us. Raw beans contain the protein factor phaseolin, which causes indigestion. This is inactivated when beans are sprouted, and destroyed when they are cooked. Raw egg whites contain avidin, a protein which interferes with the absorption of the vitamin biotin. Cooking destroys avidin.

There are as usual, several opinions on the subject of raw foods. They range from 'everything raw', through 80%, to 50% raw, to 'doesn't make a difference'. Research done in Europe discovered that when cooked (or dead) food is eaten, a defense reaction occurs in the tissues of the stomach and digestive tract. This reaction is similar to the reaction we find in infections and around tumours, and involves the accumulation of white blood cells, swelling, and a fever-like increase of temperature of the stomach and intestinal tissues. We experience tiredness after the meal. The same reaction takes place when half of the food eaten is raw, but the cooked part is eaten first. When the raw part of the food is eaten first, however, this reaction does not take place.

The explanation? Raw foods contain livng enzymes in their cells which help to digest the food material which we have eaten. This makes it easier for our digestive glands because they need to secrete fewer enzymes to do the work of digestion. When foods are cooked, the enzymes in the living food, being protein, are destroyed, and as a result, our digestive systems carry a far heavier load.

It is surprising how much better we start to feel when we eat this way. According to Dr. Budwig, who uses wholesome nutrition to cure cancer (see: The Oil-Protein Combination), carrots, garlic, and dark green leafy vegetables are especially good for us. Peppers (both hot and sweet, both green and red), radishes, horse radish, onions, and oats are good sources of sulphur. Sauerkraut, yogurt, and other lactic acid-fermented foods are easy to digest. Whole grains and milk, with sunflower seeds or nuts and a taste of honey are great for breakfast. Fresh ground golden flax with milk, nuts, or fruit are scrumptious. Flax should be ground or blended dry not more than 15 minutes before eating, as it spoils very rapidly once the seed is opened to air (if it is ground or blended wet, it gets very sticky). Ground flax meal sold in plastic containers in stores is usually rancid. Flax swells up to 3 times its dry volume by soaking up water, so ample liquid should accompany its consumption.

Avoiding Garbage Foods

You must be getting tired of being told that sugars, starches, commercial flours, pastas, and white rice do not support your health, so I won't say that, although it's true. Only whole grain breads, which have whole grains in the bread, are good. Whole grain flour such as whole wheat flour has also had many nutrients taken out, and is not okay for health. In Europe, it has become popular to buy a little grain mill and to buy whole grain one knows to be genuinely organic by the sack-full from a farmer, and to grind one's own flour just before baking. The bread tastes great. Grain mills are reasonable in price, and thus affordable. Unfortunately, household oil mills are more complicated, because they need parts that can stand up to several tons of pressure, and would therefore be quite expensive to buy. There are none on the market.

Margarines, shortenings, hard fats except butter, refined oils and products containing it (mayonnaise, salad dressing, etc.), non-dairy creamers, are out. Roasted seeds and nuts should be avoided, because they are often very, very old.

Commercial meats, sausages and other processed meats are to be avoided, because they contain preservatives, fillers like refined starch, and saturated fats, all of which interfere with vital biochemical functions in our bodies.

Supplements

Since even the best foods we get are not garden-fresh, sun-ripened, organic, and since we live in an environment polluted with lead, cadmium, smoke, carbon monoxide, plastics, pesticides, and other toxins, and especially if we smoke and drink, we would be wise to augment (but not substitute) the best balanced fresh diet we can get, with a good vitamin and mineral supplement. Good preparations contain both chromium and selenium. They usually contain more than the minimum daily requirement of the vitamins, but usually contain less than optimal carotene and vitamins C and E, so extra carotene and vitamins C and E might be wise. Optimum dose of vitamin C is usually between 2 and 10 grams per day, and for E is between 400 and 800 units for most people (people with rheumatic heart disease usually cannot tolerate more than 150-200 units).

A large body of clinical evidence attesting to the value of supplements of various vitamin and mineral co-factors in the treatment of diseases has accumulated, and the results are extremely exciting and encouraging.

The value of fresh air and sunshine cannot be overemphasized. While we don't *eat* either, both can be considered food for the body. Both are essential for health.

Sunshine

According to Dr. Budwig, when flax oil (or both essential fatty acids in their natural state) are a regular part of the diet, they are present in the skin, and act as an 'antenna' for the photons of sunlight energy. They absorb sunlight into the body, and can store this energy in chemical bonds for future use in vital biochemical reactions. Light absorption, according to her, is not limited to plants.

Cancer patients often lack these oils in their skins, and are allergic to the sun. It burns their skins, makes them nauseous, dizzy, and faint. A few days on the oil-protein combination enables these patients to sit and enjoy the sun without any problems, and the sun helps to cure their cancer.

Sun-caused skin cancers too, are the result of deficiency of the necessary oils in the skin, and of other nutritional deficiencies, such as vitamins A and B6. Dr. Budwig uses the oil-protein combination and a wholesome diet; she also uses the essential fatty acid-containing oils on the skin, and is working with laser light of visible wave lengths and its cancer-curing powers. The wave length most in keeping with the biological oil-protein system and its quantum properties is ruby red (6,900 angstroms) light; this wave length, according to Dr. Budwig, is absorbed best by the pi-electrons of the double bonds in the highly unsaturated oils. The energy of x-rays and other forms of 'hard' radiation is far too intense for the biological system and destroys the delicate pi-electron systems of the double bonds in the essential fatty acids and their more highly unsaturated derivatives. For this reason, she avoids using radiation treatments in her therapy. She says that one should not expect to cure cancer with rays known to *cause* cancer, and adds that the idea of rays to cure cancer is right, but that the wave lengths employed in medical practice are the wrong ones.

Activity

Although it is not food, activity along with a wholesome diet is absolutely necessary for health, because the body is made for activity. Playing and exercise, or activity while having fun. The fun may be more important than the exercise, but the exercise is important also. Chasing the chickens around the barn yard. Climbing trees and mountains, even stairs. Bouncing on the bed. Swimming in lakes or rivers, canoeing, rafting, tobogganing, skiing, chasing balls, rebounding. Laughing[1]. Dancing. Stretching. Yoga. Kung Fu. Whatever you like!

Faith

And finally, to have faith in life, to love it, to get close to it, to get to know it, to be it. Faith in life, and enjoyment of life is really first in importance, because it makes all the other aspects of wholesome living easy and worth the effort.

SECTION SIX

FATS AND FATES

Fats and Disease

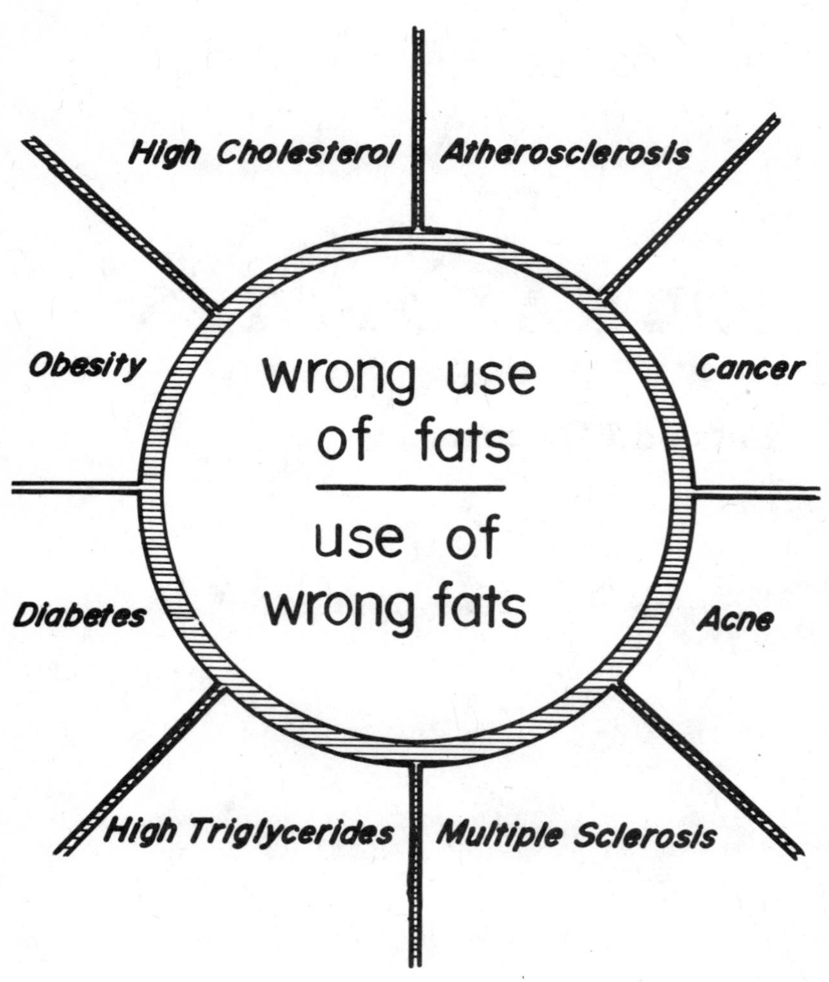
High Cholesterol
Atherosclerosis
Obesity
Cancer
wrong use of fats
use of wrong fats
Diabetes
Acne
High Triglycerides
Multiple Sclerosis

54

Changes in Fat Consumption and Degenerative Disease

Fat Consumption

Between 1910 and 1980, many changes took place in the kinds and amounts of fats and oils that people ate. Total consumption of all fats increased by 35%. Fat consumption rose from 32% of daily calories to 42%, and is still rising every year. The average daily fat consumption in Western countries ranges between 140 to 170 grams per person[1].

Fats and oils (shortening, margarine, refined salad and cooking oils) account for 57% of the total increase in fat consumption, dairy products account for 7%, and meat, poultry and fish account for 31% of the increase.

In 1911, the first shortening (Crisco), made by the hydrogenation of oils, hit the supermarket shelves. The average intake of *trans*- fatty acids in hydrogenated products has risen from zero in 1910 to close to 10% of all fats consumed today, or between 10 and 15 grams per day per person.

Vegetable fat consumption has increased from 21 to 70 grams per day, while consumption of animal fat decreased slightly, from

104 to 99 grams per day.

The consumption of beef has gone up, while that of pork, especially since 1947, has gone down. Poultry consumption has gone up, the use of fish has remained essentially stable, and the use of other meats has diminished.

The use of butter has declined to 1/5 of its 1910 level, while the use of margarine has increased by 9 times. The use of lard has gone down to about 1/5 of its former level, while the use of vegetable shortenings has almost doubled in the same time span. The consumption of edible beef fat has gone up 2.5 times. The consumption of salad and cooking oils has increased by about 12 times.

Consumption of whole milk is less than 1/2, and of cream less than 1/3 of its level in 1910, whereas cheese consumption has almost tripled, ice cream and frozen desserts have increased 5 times, and low-fat milk has increased by a factor of 3.

The annual consumption of sugar has risen from about 90 lbs per year to about 120 lbs per year per person. Cholesterol intake from foods has remained essentially constant during the last 70 years.

The consumption of saturated fatty acids has increased 16%, that of oleic acid (18:1*w*9) has gone up by 33%, and that of linoleic acid (LA, 18:2*w*6) has increased by 170%. But, it is important to note that these figures do not take into account how much of the LA was altered or *trans*- or other breakdown products, how much LA was denatured by processing and frying, or how much LA was destroyed by light in transparent bottles, i.e. how much LA was still LA when it was finally consumed. Nor do these figures take note of decreases in the diet of the vitamin and mineral co-factors required for the metabolism of LA. Between 1900 and 1980 many products deficient in vitamins and minerals were introduced into the marketplace. The figures are theoretical, based on the fatty acid content of the oil sources in their natural state. The figures for LA, taken at face value, are therefore not very helpful in determining correlations between nutrition and disease trends.

Poultry fat content has increased. And men consume more fat than women, but not a lot more. From these figures, it seems clear that cholesterol is not the primary cause of cardiovascular disease, that *trans*- fatty acids and altered vegetable fats deserve suspicion, that butter is *not* to blame for the increase in fatty degeneration, but that total fat intake may be beyond the human body's capacity for fat metabolism.

Degenerative Disease

In 1900, cancer killed one person in every 30. Today it kills one in 5. Around the turn of the century, cardiovascular disease accounted for 1 death in every 7. Today, it accounts for 1 death in every 2. Diabetes has risen at a similar rate, and the other diseases of fatty degeneration, like multiple sclerosis, liver and kidney degeneration have risen equally rapidly.

55

Fatty Degeneration

Definition

What is fatty degeneration? Dr. Budwig, probably the most knowledgeable person in the world today on fats and oils in nutrition and their relation to the causes and cures of degenerative diseases, defines fatty degeneration as "the appearance of fatty materials in cells...in places in which fats are not normally found."[1] What are some examples of fatty degeneration?

Cardiovascular Disease

Deposits of fatty materials in our arteries and heart (atherosclerosis) provide one example of fatty degeneration. The deposits contain more cholesterol than other fatty materials. This is easy to understand, because cholesterol is the stickiest and hardest of the fatty materials, and so forms aggregations most easily. The deposits in the arteries also contain saturated fatty acids, which are also sticky, and they contain protein and unsaturated fatty acids. When there is too much saturated fat and cholesterol in our diet, these deposits are inevitable. If there is too little of the highly unsaturated fatty acids present in their natural state, then deposits will occur, because the highly unsaturated, natural fatty acids are necessary to keep the saturated fatty acids dispersed, keep them from aggregating. They are also necessary for proper transport of cholesterol. In this function, the fatty acids are first hooked up (esterified) with cholesterol.

From atherosclerosis, because the arteries lose their elasticity and become narrowed, high blood pressure develops, and this in turn, leads to heart and kidney failure; therefore these are also conditions of fatty degeneration.

High blood cholesterol level and high blood triglyceride level precede atherosclerosis, since they supply the material being deposited in artery walls, and result either from excessive dietary intake of cholesterol, fats, and sugars, or from lack of adequate supplies of the vitamins and minerals needed to metabolize sugars, fats and cholesterol properly. Sometimes, but only rarely, high triglyceride or cholesterol levels result from genetic deficiency. High blood cholesterol and triglycerides may also result from the use of unnatural chemicals such as drugs, which interfere with the metabolism of these important substances. High blood cholesterol and triglycerides are fatty degeneration.

Sticky platelets occur when the diet contains too much saturated fatty acids, cholesterol, and sugars, and too little of the highly unsaturated fatty acids. Sticky platelets lead to blood clots which may lodge in any artery going to any part of the body. They precede the occurrence of coronary heart attacks, strokes, lung clots, clots in the limbs, the eyes, or wherever. Sticky platelets are therefore problems of fatty degeneration.

Cancer

Cancer is fatty degeneration. Microscopic studies have revealed that the common feature of all types of cancer cells is the presence of fatty materials within the cell plasma and the nucleus. These findings have been confirmed by electron microscopic examinations in France. The fats do not appear to take part in cell functions. Healthy cells are free of them.

Hard tumours have a hard, rubbery, sulphur-containing proteinaceous core, surrounded by oils which cannot form associations with the proteins. These two essential elements which belong together are separate because the oils are denatured, altered, unable to fulfill their biological functions.

Dr. Budwig considers cancer to be not cell growth out of

control, but retarded. Her basis for saying so is that in rapidly growing tissues, one always finds high concentration of essential fatty acids and high oxygen consumption, whereas in tumours, essential fatty acid concentration and oxygen consumption are always depressed. The pile-up of tumour material is the result of debris which the cell cannot take away because it lacks the energy necessary to do so. This energy is supplied by essential fatty acids and oxygen (along with the other essential nutrients).

Cancer represents the most extreme form of nutritional collapse. The metabolic rate is decreased. Oxygen uptake is inhibited. Cell division often remains incomplete. The polarity of the cells is disrupted and all the cell's functions are crippled. The membranes are defective. The red blood cells fall apart. The cell is in a severe state of disorganization.

Long chain saturated fatty acids interfere with oxygen use in the cell, as do altered fatty acids and fat products created by processing seed and marine animal oils. Heat, hydrogenation, light, and oxygen all produce chemically altered fat products which are toxic to the cell. Products altered by processing include margarines, shortenings, partially hydrogenated oils, deep fried oils, refined, deodorized oils, oils exposed to light in transparent bottles on store shelves, oils fried in the home, and oils gone rancid from exposure to oxygen after opening the bottle.

Fatty acids which enhance oxygen use in the cells and which help to dissolve tumours are the essential fatty acids found in the fresh seeds of flax, pumpkin, soy bean, and walnut, or their fresh oils from these seeds. These fatty acids are also found in the fish oils of some of the fatty fish, while those fish are fresh (see: Oils from Fish).

Deficiency of the co-factors required to protect the highly unsaturated fatty acids from damage, or required to metabolize the fatty acids and sugars also interferes with oxygen use in the cells. Co-factors include several B-complex vitamins required for the production, by oxidation of energy within the cell, the vitamins E and A, which protect the integrity of the highly unsaturated fatty acids and the cell membranes, and vitamins C, B3 and B6, the minerals zinc, selenium, and iron, and sulphur-containing amino acids, which facilitate the production of prostaglandins. Deficiency of any one of these can disrupt metabolism enough to cause the fatty degeneration called cancer. The immune system, vital for destroying cancer cells, requires essential fatty acids, vitamin C, B6, A, and zinc to function.

Finally, many man-made synthetic drugs, which interfere with the functions of the essential fatty acids, and deficiencies of the fatty acids themselves, can also create the conditions of fatty degeneration collectively known as cancer.

Obesity

Obesity, which increases the risk of cardiovascular disease, cancer, and diabetes, is another condition of fatty degeneration. Here, low metabolic rate, excess fats in the fat depots, and low tissue content of the essential fatty acids, all occur together. Consumption of diets high in refined sugars and starches, (which turn to saturated fatty acids), and low in vitamins and minerals, are often part of the cause of the fatty degeneration.

Diabetes

Diabetes, resulting from the consumption of improper fats, refined sugars and starches, and associated with a diet severely deficient in the vitamins and minerals, is a disease of fatty degeneration. It is almost always accompanied by cardiovascular complications, and these complications are the usual cause of death among diabetics. Blindness, blocked circulation of the extremities (leading to gangrene in extreme cases), and heart attack, the results of impaired circulation, are symptoms of fatty degeneration.

Diabetics suffer from linoleic acid (LA, 18:2*w*6) deficiency partly because high sugar levels make the LA present in the fat tissues unavailable to the body for the important functions it needs to fulfill. The old name for diabetes was sugar diabetes, in honour of its connection with sugar: high sugar consumption, high blood sugar, and sugar in the urine. LA given to diabetics has an insulin-sparing effect, indicating that the effectiveness of insulin in some way depends on LA.

Rheumatism

Fat droplets found in muscle cells are the only microscopic feature that distinguishes rheumatic from normal cells, and these fat droplets appear to be the factor which by distorting the cell, set off the nerve endings whose activity cause the excruciating pain of rheumatism. The fat droplets contain fats which are saturated or unreactive, and are unable to take part in the cell's metabolic activity. When excessive fat, usually from pork or beef is consumed and the body can't use the fat, it dumps the extra fat somewhere. In rheumatism, that place is the muscles. Rheumatism is a symptom of fatty degeneration.

Acne

Acne and several other skin afflictions like blackheads, whiteheads, and dry skin conditions are examples of fatty degeneration, resulting from the consumption of fats that will not associate with proteins and fats that are not able to flow. These include the hard, saturated fatty acids and chemically altered unsaturated fatty acids. Fats and horny (hard) protein debris clog the narrow pores and invite infection. The liquid and freely flowing essential fatty acids are required for the health of the skin. Teenage diets, often lacking in several other essential nutrient factors besides the essential fatty acids, especially vitamin A, zinc, and vitamin E are behind the appearance of acne. Acne is not an inevitable teenage condition, and can usually be ended with proper nutrition.

Other Conditions of Fatty Degeneration

Multiple sclerosis is fatty degeneration. In places where essential fatty acid consumption is high, multiple sclerosis does not occur. People with MS use essential fatty acids to arrest or slow the deterioration of the nerve fibers that slowly destroys their nervous systems. The sooner after diagnosis the treatment with essential fatty acids and diet begins, the better the outlook for the sufferer. In one study, people who got MS were eating diets high in bread, biscuits, cheese, pies, and prepared foods. None ate liver and only 2 out of 67 ate fish and fresh green vegetables more than once a month.

Cystic fibrosis is fatty degeneration. The body is unable to properly change the essential linoleic acid (LA, 18:2*w*6) into more highly saturated fatty acids, and there appears to be interference with the production of prostaglandins.

Fatty degeneration conditions of the liver (cirrhosis), the kidneys, the heart, and other internal organs results from the same causes as the other members of the group, and have similar cures.

Glandular atrophy, arthritis, and asthma result from deficiency of the essential fatty acids, which are necessary to produce the secretions of the glands, the mucus which lines the air passage to the lungs, and the lubrication for the lining of the joints. These conditions, therefore belong to fatty degeneration.

High fat diets increase the proneness to food allergies, probably by overworking the pancreas. On the other hand, a tablespoon of safflower oil can help to lessen the allergic reaction, because it slows down stomach emptying time and gives the pancreatic enzymes a chance to fully digest the substances which, absorbed into the body undigested, give rise to these allergic reactions.

Premenstrual syndrome and breast pain may be symptoms of fatty degeneration and are often taken care of by nutritional means.

Many liver and gall problems, and the most common type of gall and kidney stones result from diets too high in the hard, sticky saturated fats together with cholesterol. It is common knowledge that a person with these problems needs to avoid saturated and altered fats: animal fats, butter, shortenings, and margarine. The stones are slowly dissolved by a reduction in these fats and an increase in the use of the essential fatty acids. Amazingly, a weak liver tolerates essential fatty acids wonderfully well, because it needs them to function. However only small doses should be given at first and gradually increased, until the liver becomes strong again.

Calcium metabolism is closely linked to essential fatty acid metabolism. This makes calcium problems at least a first cousin to the diseases of fatty degeneration.

Cellulite is sluggish fat, and another member of the family of fatty degeneration. It is the result of both poor diet and lack of exercise.

Various problems of sense organ function result from lack of the high energy fatty acids which the senses need for their very active metabolism. Use of the proper fats in nutrition improves both vision and hearing in such cases.

Every organ in the body is bathed in its own supply of liquid high energy oils when it is healthy. The eyes are floating in an oil bath, the kidney sits in its 'oil can', the heart is surrounded by its oil supply of linoleic acid, the ear's source of energy sits in close proximity to the inner ear, the marrow cells carry their fat supply in the bones, etc. Lack of the essential fatty acids in the diet impairs the functions of these organs, resulting in diseases of fatty degeneration.

Brown spots on the skin called aging spots or 'cemetery flowers' are an indication of fatty degeneration. These become especially pronounced on parts of the body which are exposed to direct sunlight frequently, like the back of the hands, the bald spot, and the face.

Depositions of fatty material under the eyes and on the white of the eye ball are signs of fatty degeneration. They indicate the kind of fatty degeneration condition the person who carries them has. There are several different types of these deposits, depending on the dietary or metabolic 'crime' the patient has committed.

This list of fatty degeneration conditions includes many of the most widespread diseases in our society, including the major killers, cripplers, and torturers. Many are the diseases that modern medicine has not been able to control.

One Cause?

Can it be possible that so many different conditions have one underlying cause? The common underlying factor is the excess saturated fats and sugars in our diets, excess altered fats and fat-like substances, and an inadequate supply of essential fatty acids in their natural state. Figure 44 illustrates some causes for fatty degeneration in summary form.

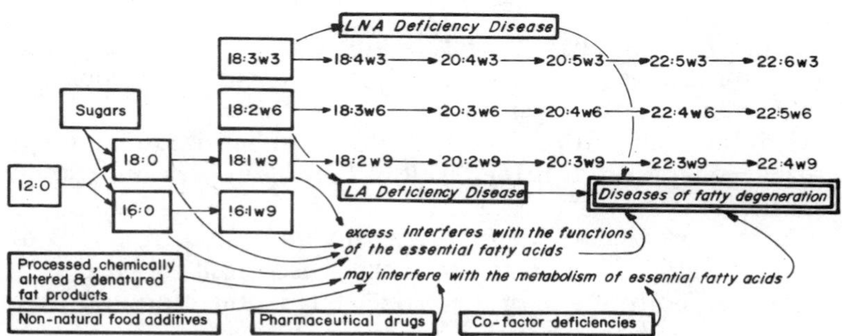

Figure 44. Some nutritional factors in fatty degeneration.

The reason for this common underlying problem rests in the consumption of refined foods in which the essential fatty acids have been systematically destroyed, removed, or altered during processing practices. The essential fatty acids would spoil (and do spoil) on the shelf if left in the food. The blame for the consumption of deficient foods, although these are offered to us by producers, processors, and manufacturers, lies with us, the consumers. We buy and eat these foods. We make the choices, and we change the choices when they no longer work for us, and when we know better. There are, after all, people living in this society, who do not acquire, and who do not live in fear of acquiring, any of the afflictions of fatty degeneration. Their immunity lies in their food choices and lifestyle. There are, furthermore, people who, having become ill with one of the degenerative diseases, have had the will to stop, to search, to learn, to change, and to heal themselves. This too, is possible.

Differences, Too

On the other hand, the underlying causes for the diseases of fatty degeneration are not all the same. Besides the common denominator of the faulty consumption and metabolism of fats, there are also differences. Other nutritional deficiences come into play. Deficiency of zinc will cause degeneration in a way that is different than deficiency of vitamin C, but both will cause disease. That is why, beyond the fatty part of the degeneration, the different members of the degenerative family also show differences in their symptoms and treatment.

Individual differences also determine whether a person gets one kind of fatty degeneration or another. Every person has some stronger and some weaker organs. The weaker organs are the first to be affected by deficiency. People are also different in their requirements of different nutrients.

Finally, other factors, such as different drugs that people take, the kind and amounts of alcohol, cigarettes, fresh air, and sunshine they consume, how much exercise they get, how much joy they have, what their mental program is, all determine how well a particular person's body will cope with living in the world, with stress, and with challenge.

56

Cholesterol and Disease

Introduction

Stroke and heart attack are the leading cause of death in the Western world, accounting for approximately 50% of all deaths, and killing many people prematurely. Cancer is next, at about 20% of all deaths, and deaths from diabetes adds another 5%.

Cholesterol Theory

For over 30 years now, cholesterol has been blamed for the fatal diseases of the heart and arteries, the cardiovascular diseases (CVD) which include heart attack, stroke, heart failure, kidney failure, and high blood pressure. According to the cholesterol theory, high blood cholesterol levels predispose us to CVD, and many studies have been done which seem to support this theory. For instance, the average blood cholesterol level in the American population is 220mg/dl. At 240 mg/dl, the death rate from CVD is 4 times higher than average; at 260 mg/dl, it is 6 times the average rate. People in poorer countries, who live on a simpler diet containing mostly grains and vegetables, and very little food of animal origin, have cholesterol levels in the 120-160 mg/dl range, and CVD is virtually unknown. Strict vegetarians present a similar picture, and their rate of CVD deaths is 1/4 that of the average North American population. Furthermore, CVD was rare before 1900; and during the second world war, when less animal products and more grains and vegetables were eaten, the CVD death rate fell dramatically. From the evidence given so far, it does look like high blood cholesterol levels predispose us to death by CVD, and low cholesterol levels seem to protect us. It also appears that animal foods, which contain our dietary cholesterol, are under question, along with the cholesterol they contain.

Cardiovascular disease afflicts 2/3 of the North American population. Doctors have had very little success in preventing, curing, or even predicting this epidemic. 40% of fatal heart attacks and strokes[1] were the first (and only) indication of cardiovascular disease; there were no early warning signs to either victim or doctor.

It has also been shown that Greenland Eskimoes, living on their traditional diet high in meat and fats, and also high in cholesterol, are free of CVD, as well as a cancer, diabetes, arthritis and other degenerative disease. And there are tribes in Africa that eat a diet high in meat, dairy products, and blood, and they are free of CVD too. And actually, there are many groups to be found around the world who do not kill themselves on cholesterol-rich food the way we do.

In search of an explanation to this riddle, diets have been analyzed, and many substances have been tested for their cholesterol-lowering capacity. More plausible explanations for the real cause of CVD and other degenerative diseases have been sought. It looks like in the end, cholesterol will be excused as the *primary* cause of CVD, although it is clearly involved in the later stages.

Triglyceride Theory

A number of other theories to explain the cause of degenerative disease are beginning to gather momentum. For example, the triglyceride theory is based on the finding that the blood triglyceride level (see: Triglycerides) is as well correlated with CVD as the cholesterol level, and that the triglyceride level is related to the intake of refined sugars, starches, and fats, whose increased use in our diets parallels the increase since 1900 of CVD and other degenerative diseases, whereas the intake of cholesterol has remained constant.

Deficiency Theory

Another theory, the deficiency theory, suggests that the cause of degenerative disease is deficiency of vitamins, minerals, fiber, and essential fatty acids which are necessary for the metabolism of cholesterol and fats in the body, but which have been systematically refined out of our foods by processing methods which came into widespread use since just before 1900. Refined sugars, refined oils, and refined starches are all deficient in minerals and vitamins.

The finding that increasing the vitamin and mineral intake lowers cholesterol and triglyceride levels in the blood lends weight to the deficiency theory. The fact that just cutting down our consumption of refined sugars and fats stops many degenerative conditions and increases vigor and longevity[2] lends weight to the triglyceride theory.

Lowering Cholesterol Levels

Since the correlation between high cholesterol levels and CVD and other degenerative diseases is high, it would be beneficial to know how to lower (or normalize) high cholesterol levels. There are many nutritional changes that will lower it.

Decreasing the intake of animal products, and replacing them with foods from plant sources lowers cholesterol levels. A person with a cholesterol level of 260 mg/dl can lower that level by as much as 100 mg in one month if he switches to a strict vegetarian diet. Of course, such a diet also increases the vitamin, mineral, and essential fatty acid content, and also lowers the fat (especially saturated) intake. Conversely, 2 quarts of milk per day can raise the cholesterol level from 180 mg/dl to 400 mg/dl in less than 2 months. Again, milk is low in several vitamins, minerals, and essential fatty acids, and relatively high in saturated fatty acids.

Excess body fat increases blood cholesterol levels and CVD. Losing weight lowers the risk and the cholesterol level. Excess refined sugars, refined starches (white flour, white rice, pastas), and refined or altered fats and oils raise cholesterol levels and CVD. Return to natural complex, high fiber carbohydrates and natural unrefined fats and oils lowers cholesterol and CVD risk. Just removing the refined items from the diet is surprisingly effective in lowering cholesterol levels. Smoking raises cholesterol level and CVD. So does coffee. Quitting reverses the trend. Abstinence from food lowers cholesterol level. This is not a method of choice, since fasting burns up proteins rapidly, and someone deficient in minerals and vitamins might easily die during a fast. Vitamin C, niacin (B3), zinc, magnesium, chromium, selenium, thyroid, fiber, and fresh, natural, highly unsaturated oils from fish or flax: all these lower cholesterol levels. The fish oils are the secret of the Eskimoes'[3] good health on their traditional diets. A happy disposition, inner peace, laughter, and freedom from fear, anxiety, worry, and depression also lower cholesterol levels.

Increasing the Protective HDL Cholesterol Fraction

The protective HDL fraction which aids in cholesterol removal, can be increased by such delicacies as garlic, onion, brewer's yeast, ginseng, fish, lecithin, and vitamins C and E. The HDL fraction is also increased by aerobic exercise, any exercise which increases cardiovascular fitness. Walking, dancing, swimming, running, cycling, laughing, and any other exercise that brings out a little sweat, that is active and prolonged, qualifies.

The Reversal of Atherosclerosis

Can atherosclerosis be reversed? Although the medical profession has always claimed for years that atherosclerosis is irreversible and at best can only be arrested, there is increasing evidence that it *can* be reversed. It makes sense that the energy of life within us, which built the human body out of water and a handful of dust, can also repair the body, if given the materials it needs to do so. Pritikin, using dietary manipulations and exercise, a low-calorie, low-fat, high complex carbohydrate diet and a lot of walking (but no vitamin or mineral supplements) has succeeded in rehabilitating many cases of severe arterial disease. Of course, he did not section the arteries of his still living subjects, so the evidence is indirect. Such work has however been done in monkeys. On a natural and unrefined diet without vitamin or mineral supplements, atherosclerosis was decreased from 90% occluded arteries to 60% occluded. The change took almost 4 years. No exercise was included in the experiment.

There is at least one report in the medical literature of a man who, by increasing the content in his diet of the essential fatty acid linoleic acid (18:2*w*6) to over half (54%) of total fat consumed (he made safflower oil 2/3 of his fat calories), was able to resume a normal working and walking life within less than 1 year after being wheelchair-bound because of almost completely atherosclerosis-obstructed leg arteries.

Finally, in the last few years, doctors using the orthomolecular approach of high doses of vitamins and minerals (see: Orthomolecular Nutrition), have had impressive successes in the treatment of atherosclerosis-clogged circulation. Although the studies are individual histories and not double-blind controlled, their results are consistent and reproducible.

57

Fats and Aging

Earlier Maturity

Diets high in fats speed up the rate at which children mature. The average age of first menstruation in girls during the 17th century was 17 years old, on a diet containing about 20% fat. The present average age of first menstruation is 13 years old, on a diet containing 42% fat.

Faster Growth Rate

High fat diets also increase the growth rate and adult body size of the people who consume these diets. This explains why the physical stature of human beings has increased over the last 100 years. It also explains why Japanese people living in Japan are shorter on the average than Caucasians. Their diet is less than 15% fat, compared to ours at over 40%. When Japanese people come to North America and adopt the Western diet, their offspring become taller, and the same phenomenon holds true for other racial groups around the world.

Shorter Life Span

Earlier maturity and taller stature are balanced by shorter life span. People on a high fat diet burn out quicker. The most recent theory to explain this is that free radicals (see: Free Radicals) produced from fats in the body cross-link the genetic material, cross-link proteins, and produce toxic chemical compounds in the system, which hinder metabolism. Other people suggest that aging is the result of the accumulation of breakdown products of metabolism and these clog up the body chemistry, making enzymes less efficient and slowing down the wheels of life until they stop. Still others talk about biological aging clocks, which run down like the spring in a watch. In practice, the more fanciful the theory, the less concrete evidence there is to sustain it. Probably free radicals are involved. Probably, metabolites are also involved. Either enhances the production of the other; and neither came first, just like the chicken and the egg.

Sugar

Besides fats, refined sugars (perhaps through their tendency to produce fats), also shorten life span. Therefore exclusion of refined sugars from the diet will also slow aging and lengthen life span. Restriction of calories also slows aging. But nobody knows for sure what mechanisms in the body determine aging.

Diet Manipulation

If you want tall children who will live for a long time, feed them a high fat diet until they are adults, and then teach them to eat a low fat (and low sugar) diet for the rest of their lives. My mother says this is the way they used to feed their livestock to keep them healthy. The calves were fed high fat foods, and when they were mature, they were switched to a low-fat (grass) diet. And that's apparently the way nature does it. If you want children to stay children longer then keep them on a low-fat, low sugar diet from the time you wean them off your breast.

Dietary manipulation is common in nature, and works for the bees. Bee larvae fed one kind of food become sterile workers who die after 6 weeks. Queen bee larvae, fed royal jelly, live up to 8 very productive years. Dietary changes can also work for humans.

58

Recommendations

Lower Total Fat Consumption

A large body of research indicates that if we want to remain healthier longer, we need to change our eating habits. We need to decrease our total fat consumption, from over 40% down to 30% of total calories. Even better would be to bring our fat consumption down to between 15 and 20% of total calories. At this level, our chances of dying from cardiovascular disease, cancer, or other diseases of fatty degeneration become relatively smaller.

How do we lower total fat consumption? The easiest way to decrease fat consumption is to decrease consumption of foods which contain more than 20% fats, and to increase our consumption of foods with lower fat and higher fiber content. Therefore, obvious sources of fat such as margarine, shortening, butter, and refined vegetable oils which are 80 to 100% fat need to be avoided or minimized. Visible fats on beef, lamb, and pork, and perhaps even skins on birds need to be removed and discarded.

Consumption of foods containing large amounts of hidden fats, such as sausages, hamburgers, cheese (except low fat cheeses which contain less than 10% butter fat), salad dressings, potato chips, and fried foods need to be minimized, or avoided altogether. Increased consumption of fish and sea foods, beans and grains, low fat dairy products, fresh vegetables and fruit, all of which contain less than 20% fat, can replace the high fat items.

Increase Essential Fatty Acid Consumption

We need to increase our consumption of essential fatty acids up to at least 1/3 of our total fat intake, no matter how high or low our total level of fat consumption is. The best sources of essential fatty acids are flax, soybeans, pumpkin seeds, and walnuts. All of these sources contain both essential fatty acids.

Fish like salmon, mackerel, rainbow trout, sardines, and eel contain large quantities of one of the essential fatty acids; the seeds of safflower, sunflower, and sesame contain large quantities of the other essential fatty acid. We need both in our diet.

Sea weed and shell fish also supply both essential fatty acids, but in smaller quantities, and dark green vegetables such as spinach, parsley, and broccoli contain small quantities of the essential fatty acids also.

The essential fatty acids are extremely important for health and vitality. Deficiencies of these fatty acids are related to such diverse diseases as cancer, cardiovascular disease, multiple sclerosis, cystic fibrosis, premenstrual tension, behavioural problems, failure of wound healing, arthritis, glandular atrophy, weakened immune functions, and sterility (especially in males).

Under proper conditions, it is possible to mechanically press[1] oils from the seeds which contain both of the essential fatty acids: flax, pumpkin seed, and walnut. These oils, in order to retain their biological value, have to be pressed at low temperature with light and oxygen excluded (the label will say if this has been done), have to be unrefined, and have to be kept in completely opaque metal, earthen, glass, or plastic[2] containers (Soybean oil can not be made in this way. Because its oil content is too low for the low heat mechanical pressing, soybean oil is chemically extracted from the soybean). If these conditions have not been fulfilled, the essential fatty acids are likely to have been at least partially destroyed, and are no longer good for the maintenance of health. It would not be wise to buy such deteriorated oils.

Even given the proper care, good oils keep fresh for only about 3 months, so the 'best before' date should be checked on the bottle. Health food stores carry oils which have been made by the procedure which keeps the essential fatty acids intact. In Europe, these oils are quite popular, but in North America, they are just beginning to make their appearance.

Lower Refined Sugars and Starches

We need to decrease our consumption of refined sugars and refined starches. The body transforms these into the saturated, hard, sticky, kind of fats that the body doesn't need, and this kind of fat interferes with the functions of the essential fatty acids in the body. Sugars also increase the level of triglycerides in our blood, and increased triglyceride levels increase our risk of cardiovascular disease: stroke, heart attack, high blood pressure, kidney failure, and heart failure.

In 1865, human beings consumed about 40 pounds of sugar per year[3]. By 1900, sugar consumption had risen to 85 pounds per person per year. Today, sugar consumption alone is about 120 pounds per person per year, and sugars and starches are found in the majority of processed foods on the market, including ketchup, which contains more sugar than does ice cream, processed meats which are extended with starch or sweetened with sugar, canned vegetables which are sweetened, and non-sweet bakery products which contain added sugar. So besides just the sweet, refined junk foods and refined starches such as cornstarch, macaroni, refined (called enriched) flours, noodles, and pastas, there are other, less obvious sources of refined sugars and starches to watch for. Refined sugars and starches lack the essential vitamin and mineral factors which are necessary for their digestion and proper use in the body.

Cardiovascular disease, diabetes, and obesity are some of the results of our increasing use of refined sugars and starches. In the 1800's, death from cardiovascular disease was extremely rare; it rose to 1 in 7 deaths by 1900, and today accounts for 1 death in every 2. The occurrence of diabetes has risen at a similar rate, and today accounts for 1 death in 20. Obesity affects about 30% of the adults in Western society today, and is highly correlated with cardiovascular disease, diabetes, allergies, cancer, and a host of other ailments.

Human societies which consume the traditional unrefined, natural fare rarely suffer from these afflictions. Returning to the use of natural foods: whole grains, fresh vegetables and fruits, and unprocessed meats and animal products eliminates many of the problems that refined sugars and starches bring on.

Lower Hard Fats and Cholesterol

We need to decrease our consumption of cholesterol and saturated (hard, land animal) fats, because we consume far more of this combination than our bodies can handle by our present day nutritional standards. Hard fats which are sticky such as those found in beef, lamb, pork and dairy products, combined with the cholesterol they contain which is also sticky, are especially bad combinations, and it appears that it is not the cholesterol, but the *combination* that mediates the cardiovascular problems which have been blamed on cholesterol. Fish and other sea foods, which contain cholesterol combined with anti-sticky oils, do not cause problems, even when eaten in large quantities.

Over several years or decades, the consumption of cholesterol and hard fats together results in the accumulation of these substances in the linings of our arteries, narrows these blood vessels, causes circulation problems, and increases our risk of cardiovascular disease: stroke, heart attack, blindness, high blood pressure, kidney failure, heart failure, and other problems associated with insufficient circulation to various parts of the body.

One month on a strictly vegetarian diet (no meat, no eggs, no dairy) can bring down the blood cholesterol level from 260 mg/dl to 160 mg/dl. The death rate from cardiovascular disease of strict vegetarians is only 1/4 that of meat eaters. The average blood cholesterol level of a heart attack patient is 244 mg/dl. A level of 160 mg/dl or less is associated with virtually complete absence of cardiovascular disease.

Increase Fiber, Vitamins, and Minerals

We need to increase our intake of fiber, vitamins, and minerals. Certain kinds of fiber called pectins, mucilages, and gums, which are found in apples, potatoes, beets, carrots, okra, bananas, beans, and oats tie up and carry bile acids and cholesterol out of the body, thus lowering blood cholesterol levels and reducing the risk of cardiovascular disease. Other kinds of fiber help to prevent constipation, weight gain, colon cancer, and gall stone formation, and increase glucose tolerance.

Several vitamins and minerals are required for the metabolism of cholesterol, and their presence in the body lowers blood cholesterol levels, while deficiency of these vitamins and minerals raises cholesterol. Vitamin C, niacin (B3), and zinc are the best known examples.

Several vitamins and minerals are required to protect the

essential fatty acids from destruction by oxygen and free radicals (loose, and extremely damaging unpaired electrons). Vitamins A (or carotene), C, and E, and the minerals zinc, selenium, and sulphur (contained in the amino acid cysteine) are some of the essential substances involved in this protection.

Several vitamins and minerals are required for the metabolism of sugars and starches. They include the vitamins of the B-complex, and the mineral chromium.

Since much of the original content of fiber, vitamins, and minerals has been refined out of many of the fats, oils, and carbohydrates we consume (the essential fatty acids often are also removed or altered), we need to augment our foods by supplements of vitamins and minerals. The easiest way to ensure adequate supply of all the known vitamins and minerals is to take a high potency multi-vitamin, multi-mineral supplement. Additional vitamin C and additional vitamin E may be advisable, since the multi-vitamin, multi-mineral supplements contain less of these two vitamins than most people find optimal for health. Health food stores carry good preparations of these supplements and can give information.

Avoid Altered Fats.

We need to minimize our intake of altered fat substances, because such substances do not fit into the very precise molecular architecture of our bodies. This architecture is the framework on which the life energy flows, keeping us alive and healthy. Altered fat substances are linked with the occurrence of cancers, are found in tumour cells or around tumours, and take part in uncontrolled free radical chain reactions within the body, which result in toxic metabolic by-products.

The easiest way to avoid altered fat substances is to avoid hydrogenated oil products. Shortenings and margarines make up the bulk of hydrogenated and partially hydrogenated oil products in our food supply. Other sources include bakery products, candies, fries and other deep-fried foods, and processed convenience foods such as potato and other bagged 'chips'. Refined oils also contain altered fat substances. Human beings consume an average of almost 10 pounds of altered fat substances per year. This is more than twice their consumption of all other food additives put together.

Fresh raw seeds and nuts, the raw materials from which the shortenings, margarines, and other altered fat products are made, do not contain any of the altered fat products, and are the prime choice for health-giving fats and oils. Health food stores carry some oils which have been changed minimally from their natural state. Oils are destroyed by light and air during processing and storage and on the shelf, by heat during processing, and by frying in the home. They are best eaten in their natural, unaltered state, mixed with sulphur-rich protein, such as skim milk yogurt.

Minimize Drugs and Avoid Food Additives

We need to minimize our intake of synthetic drugs and food additives, many of which have not been adequately tested for safety of consumption, and many of which clearly have side effects which are full-blown diseases themselves. Many cause cancer in animals, and many have been used on human subjects for years before their very serious side effects became sufficiently known to force them off the market. Arsenic, thalidomide, and the carcinogenic food dyes (butter yellow and sudan red) are just a few examples.

To reduce our need for these drugs, we need to strengthen our bodies' innate resources and ability to resist disease by increasing the quality of our food intake, and by ensuring that we get all of the 45 presently known essential nutrients in sufficient quantities. In this way our body's needs are met: for proper growth and activity, for the maintenance of physical health, for the healing of sicknesses, and for resistance to stress, pollution, and toxic influences from the environment.

To reduce our intake of food additives, research suggests that we avoid the man-made, highly processed, artifically coloured and flavoured foods, and return to the fresh fruits and vegetables, whole grains and seeds and the wild meats (especially fish). These foods kept our ancestors free of the diseases of fatty degeneration and still keep the 'primitive' people of the world and the wild animals healthy.

Exercise

We also need exercise. The body is made for activity. If our only exercise is the grinding movement of the jaws, the movement of our hands from plate to mouth, and the push away from the table, that's not enough. Lack of exercise results in stagnation and poor metabolism of fats, carbohydrates and proteins. Regular activity which brings out a little sweat is extremely important for the maintenance of health. If our nutrition is up to par, then exercise too, comes easily.

59

Health

Dialogue

In this closing chapter, I would like to take you on a personal journey in which we will look at the nature of health and of human nature. I feel that an expanded perspective is necessary, because the bulk of this book is concentrated on a limited (though extremely important) part of only one of several aspects of health, the physical-nutritional aspect. Of the 45 known essential nutrients that make up this aspect of health, we focused on only two, the essential fatty acids. While it may be tempting to focus on just one narrow aspect of health and to expect this limited focus to solve all our health problems, this is, of course, an unrealistic expectation which leads to disappointment.

My personal journey to an understanding of health and human nature began in medical school, but let's start here with the word itself. The word health is derived from the Old High German root word for whole or hale, but common usage does not reflect this meaning. We use the word more in the sense of 'freedom from disease, pain, or defect'. We are healthy when we are not sick. But if you examine it, this way of using the word is misleading. Health has to be the presence of something (wholeness, haleness) and when we lose that presence, disease results. We need to search for, find, and embrace that presence.

I enrolled in medical school because I wanted to learn about health. I discovered that modern medicine teaches the use of medicines for fighting illnesses, but medicines do not necessarily establish health. We consult a doctor when we are ill. Doctors diagnose and treat illnesses, mainly by prescribing the 'medicines' of drugs, surgery, and radiation. Modern practice of medicine also concerns itself with disease prevention, but disease prevention is not health, either. I wanted to learn about the nature of health. Whom do we consult when we want to know about health? I was dismayed. I took my dismay to the Dean of my medical school, and this conversation ensued.

"What is health?" I asked him.

"We don't know," he answered. "We're working on it."

"Health must be something more than just not being sick!" I suggested. He agreed, adding that the World Health Organization has been saying so for years. Encouraged by this remark, I went on.

"It's really important! If we *know* what health is, curing illness becomes easy. We know that illness is a departure from health. So we just turn a sick person who wants to get well back in the direction of health."

"Yes, but we don't know what health is," he reminded me.

The Dean was open and friendly. "How about life itself?" I suggested. "The life energy creates, maintains and repairs our bodies, using the nutrients present in our foods. It knows (though we don't know) exactly where to take each nutrient molecule and how to use it. Therefore it must also be the ultimate standard of health." His eyebrows rose, but I went on. "Whatever brings us closer in harmony with life will bring us closer to health. All *we* need to do is discover it, get to know it, and live according to its nature."

Later, reflecting on the conversation, I realized that I should have stopped after the first sentence, because the moment I used the term 'life energy', I lost the Dean. For me, that conversation was the beginning of a long search to discover the nature of health in relation to human nature.

Life and its energy is a fact. It is less controversial than new drugs and organ transplants; it has been around far longer than both, and will still be around when both have been abandoned for something not yet imagined by medical scientists. Life energy[1] is within everything that lives. While it is present, so much is possible. We walk, talk, eat, work, heal, digest, think, reproduce, feel, laugh and play. Without it, nothing! We might as well have a look at it, get to know it, and maybe even become friends with it. We might as well look at the other components of human nature as well. Our refusal to look reminds me of a story.

Galileo's Apple Cart

Up to Galileo's time, the earth was considered the center of the universe, and the stars, moon, and sun were thought to revolve around the earth. Along came Galileo, and by the use of a telescope, he charted the movements of the celestial bodies. He discovered that the earth revolves around the sun.

Scientists and theologians of his time were outraged at his proposition. It contradicted what they'd learned, believed, and taught. Galileo upset their conceptual apple cart, and the apples were rolling everywhere. We laugh at these learned men because though Galileo had the telescope and the mathematical proofs, and he put everything at their disposal when he invited them to see for themselves, they wouldn't even look. Their minds were closed on the subject.

We too, are sometimes like the learned minds of Galileo's time, though not about the earth and sun anymore. That issue was settled in Galileo's favour. We all believe him now. Our preoccupation with disease and crisis intervention, and our refusal to take the time to look for the nature of health is the modern version of Galileo's apple cart. We believe in disease, but not in health. Countless sincere men and women have dedicated their lives to study and describe diseases in greater and greater detail. Huge institutions have been built around disease, such as hospitals, research centres, and community organizations. Enormous amounts of time, money and effort have fostered the growth of the monster of disease, while health has been left to grow without nurture. A turnaround in our way of thinking is necessary if health *is* really what we are after. Health is not the absence of disease. Disease is the absence of health.

Health and Human Nature

If we want to know what health is, we need to know more about the parameters of human nature. Why? Because health, like human nature, has several different aspects, all of which are important in the establishment and maintenance of health. Health is something within us which we feel and radiate when we are living in alignment with all aspects of our own nature. I'd like to share with you a model for understanding health, one which I derived from observation, experience, study and common sense. My way of expressing this model, or view, is biased by my background in the sciences.

Human nature can be said to consist of three distinct aspects: what our bodies are made of, what we've learned, and what keeps us alive. In healthy people, all three aspects of human nature are integrated and working together in harmony. Each of the three aspects differs from the others in its composition, its function, its properties, and its relationship to health. To establish and maintain health, we must work with each aspect in accordance with its distinctive nature.

Body

In my view, the essence of physical health is comprised of food and activity. The physical body is made out of food, air, and water. Since this is so, physical health depends on the quality of these. Besides air and water, about 45 different essential food substances have been discovered so far. Physical health depends on the presence in our foods of ample quantities of all of these. Absence or deficiency of any one of more of these 45 results in less than optional functioning, and over time, in gradual degeneration, degenerative disease, then death. A good nutritional program includes optimum quantities of all essential food substances from fresh foods grown in the most natural ways possible, supplemented if necessary by concentrates of these substances in pill, powder or liquid form.

The body is made *from* food, and *for* activity. If the body is inactive, it serves no purpose and degenerates. Thus for physical health, besides food, air and water, activity is also necessary.

Finally, the body is created out of smaller units such as atoms, molecules, cells, organs, and tissues and will one day be destroyed again. Therefore, physical health can be described as a worthwhile but losing proposition! But within this restriction, nutrition and exercise help to ensure quality time and physical health so that we can live fully functional, active lives.

Mind

According to the psychologists Alfred Adler and Rudolf

Dreikurs, the essence of mental health is a sense of belonging and constructive contribution to the well-being of the whole of which we are a part (self, family, humanity, nature, life). We are social creatures throughout our lives, and through learning we acquire concepts that adapt us to live harmoniously in a complex social world. I find this view practical and optimistic. We *choose* the views we hold, and if we find them unsuitable, we can choose to learn others that work better for us. Improving mental health is a matter of educating and re-educating ourselves toward better social integration, co-operation, and contribution.

People who lose their sense of belonging lose their feeling of kinship and equality with others. They become discouraged, can develop inferiority feelings, can become pre-occupied with having power over others, and can behave in socially useless and destructive ways. Helping discouraged people toward better mental health requires acceptance, encouragement, and acknowledgment of socially useful contributions.

The mind is located in the surface of the brain, that part known as the associative cortex. The mental-emotional-social aspect of human nature is extremely complex, and my above description is a mere hint or summary of our social workings.

Energy

According to physicists, the essence of energy is energy itself: it is stable, constant, unchangeable, indestructive, and indivisible. It cannot be burned, drowned, broken or dried. Energy pervades the entire body, enlivens every cell, and powers us. It catalyzes the chemical changes that make life possible, but remains itself unchanged. It is beyond health and illness, beyond concepts, beyond learning.

Besides these more obvious and scientifically verifiable attributes, there is also a more subtle experiential attribute to energy. Experienced directly, the essence of life energy brings a feeling of contentment, completion, fulfillment, radiance, and well-being. Regardless of the circumstances, an individual can still know this life energy and feel contentment. This experience however, will not bring about social changes or eliminate physical or mental illnesses. Only through decisions and actions can such changes be brought about. If we are unable to connect ourselves to the life energy within us, we may feel incomplete, discontent, or frustrated, even in situations which (we think) are ideal and should make us feel content. If our own attempts to reach contentment are unsuccessful, we have another option. There are some people who are competent in this aspect of human nature, who may be able to provide guidance.

Integration

In order to be fully human, a person needs to be both healthy and content. Our problems find their solutions in that aspect of human nature in which they originated. Physical problems have physical solutions. Mental problems have mental solutions. Energy problems have energy solutions. When we embrace the essence of each aspect of our nature, we maximize our possibilities for complete well-being and health.

We have to be open to learn, because there is a lot to learn, a lot to experience, a lot to enjoy. We can learn to be quiet and observe our habits and our ways of thinking — to become sensitive to ourselves.

We learn best, not by blindly following rules or opinions, but by relaxed attention; by watching with open heart and calm mind the ways of nature and of life. In this calm state of being, we can see clearly, and learning becomes discovery, easy and natural. It is a state to nurture. Life is a flow with its own texture, melody, and beauty.

To a lover, the whole world vibrates with love. It can be seen everywhere. Love is not an opinion or concept projected on the world, as cynics out of touch with love claim. A lover has discovered the depth of life's nature, and sees that depth in everything.

If we expect to succeed in our quest for health, we need to get to know, to respect, to trust, to love, and to merge in our own nature. And this is really the basis of holistic health — trust in life, in nature, in human nature. Holistic health is discovering our own human nature and harmonizing with it, to all the way deep inside.

Notes

SECTION ONE

Chapter 1

1. The other commonly used system called the delta (d) system, starts at the acid end, and numbers the carbon atoms in reverse direction. To avoid confusion, we will not use the delta system in this book.

Chapter 2

1. If a double bond in a fatty acid is in the *trans-* configuration, that has to be specified by a t in the nickname. For instance t18:1*w*9 has 18 carbons with a *trans-* double bond between carbons 9 and 10.

Chapter 3

1. The complete story of plaque formation is more complex. First, there appears to be injury to the lining of the artery. This is followed by the body's attempts at repair, and involves proteins, fats, and cholesterol. Special cells called macrophages gobble up the excess fats and cholesterol, dig their way into the arterial lining, and accumulate there. Many of these fat and cholesterol gorged cells, now called foam cells, form the plaque which narrows the arteries. The stickiness of the saturated fats and cholesterol is one important factor in the accumulation of plaque.

Chapter 4

1. Wheat and corn allergy, for instance, are quite common.

2. Glycogen, also called animal starch, and stored in liver and muscle, is many glucose molecules hooked end to end in a chain.

Chapter 5

1. This placement of the hydrogen atoms is called the *cis*- configuration. Both hydrogens on the carbons involved in the double bond are on the same side of the carbon chain. The other way of placing the hydrogens on the double bond carbons is called the *trans*- configuration.

Chapter 6

1. The saturated fatty acids, though also able to react with oxygen, do so at a rate very much slower than the rate of reaction of the essential fatty acids. They react at 1/125th and 1/25th of the rate of reaction of LNA and LA, respectively.

Chapter 10

1. The pharmacological doses used, much higher than what the body itself normally manufactures, produce some very powerful side effects, and are not recommended for prolonged use.

2. Depending on which source supplies the statistics, between 20 and 60% of first heart attacks are fatal.

3. Vitamin B6 is required for this step.

4. Fiber from oats, apples, beans, and peas lower cholesterol. Wheat bran does not.

SECTION TWO

Chapter 12

1. The hydrogenation process was patented in 1903, and the first commercial hydrogenated shortening, made by Procter & Gamble, and called Crisco, went on sale in 1911.

Chapter 15

1. *Trans*- fatty acids have received most of the attention of researchers, because they make up a large part of the altered substances. They are not necessarily the most important altered fat products in terms of toxicity to biochemical processes, and therefore, health of consumers.

2. The Dutch, incidentally, enjoy the longest life expectancy among industrialized nations, 5 years more than Americans.

3. The experimental work behind these figures is described in more detail in Chapter 42: Fats in Meats.

4. See G. J. Brisson, *Lipids in Human Nutrition* (New Jersey: Burgess, 1981), p.39.

5. Ibid, p.39.

Chapter 16

1. Imagine what kinds of problems you'd have if your head or the top half of your body were back to front. You'd never know whether you were coming or

going. On the molecular level, *trans-* fatty acids have their head screwed on backwards and don't know whether they are coming or going.

Chapter 18

1. Electrons provide the basis of all chemical activity, since they form 'chemical' bonds between atoms, thereby creating molecules. Their need to be paired is expressed in the strength of the bond that an unpaired electron from one atom forms with an unpaired electron from another atom.

The number of unpaired electrons found around an atom is always constant for a particular element, and determines the number of bonds that an atom of that element will form. A hydrogen atom always has 1, an oxygen 2, a nitrogen 3, and a carbon, 4 unpaired electrons. These elements, therefore, always form 1,2,3 and 4 bonds, respectively, when they share electrons with other atoms to form the bonds that hold these atoms together in molecules.

2. Saturated fatty acids do not catch photons as readily as unsaturated fatty acids, because their electrons are less active, more stable in their pairing.

3. The human body also requires daily more LA than any other essential substance. Nature must have had a good reason for arranging it this way.

Chapter 20

1. But corn oil contains no linolenic acid (18:3*w*3), which is also essential.

2. T. J. Weiss, *Food Oils and Their Uses*, 2nd Ed. (Connecticut: Avi Publishing Co., 1983) p.40

Chapter 22

1. There are literally hundreds of natural antioxidant substances known, besides vitamin E. Sesame oil contains an antioxidant factor called sesamol, and many of the kitchen spices including rosemary, celery, sage, oregano, and cloves, as well as the more exotic herbs myrrh and frankincense contain potent antioxidant factors. Even vanilla contains antioxidants. In addition, there are the more familiar normal antioxidant vitamins A, C, B1, B5, and B6, the minerals selenium and zinc, the amino acids cysteine and tyrosine, and various combinations of these elements. In fact, just about every kind of food, including potatoes, cabbage, broccoli, cauliflower, brussels sprouts, bananas, grapes, and other fruits, contains its own brand of natural antioxidant substances to protect their (and our) life.

Chapter 24

1. The protein impurities in fats can also spoil. Butter, for instance, will spoil if left out during hot summer weather, but if the butter is 'clarified' to remove the protein and other 'impurities', leaving 100% butter fat (or ghee) then it will keep quite well. This custom is an East Indian tradition, adapted to a hot climate without the technology of refrigeration.

SECTION THREE

Chapter 27

1. Nothing more than a slightly defective nutrient absorption, common with

age, brings fat absorption to the critical 5% level at which cancer increases and fat-soluble vitamin absorption is impaired.

2. The confusion between 7% and .2% results from different measures being used. 7% of the *calories* in lettuce come from fats, but fats make up only .2% of the *weight* of the lettuce.

Chapter 28

1. Bile actually consists of bile salts, phopholipids (lecithin), and cholesterol in a ratio of 12:2.5:1.

2. Pancreatic juice also contains the enzymes required to digest starch and protein.

3. Allergy-producing substances are usually proteins, but sometimes complex fatty or carbohydrate substances may also cause allergic reactions.

4. After a fatty meal, the lymph fluid turns milky white from the presence of millions of fat-filled chylomicrons being transported in that fluid.

Chapter 29

1. Both LA and LNA also contain a *w*9 double bond.

2. The nerve cell bodies and synapses, however, contain enzymes which transform the essential fatty acids into very highly unsaturated fatty acids.

Chapter 30

1. Glutathione is made within the body from three amino acids: glutamic acid, cysteine, and glycine.

Chapter 32

1. Healthy people become prone to degenerative diseases soon *after* they adopt our dietary ways, because degenerative diseases need some time to develop. Thus there is usually a time lag of 2 to 20 years before a person's health is destroyed by poor food habits.

2. Natural substances include vitamins, minerals, essential amino acids, essential fatty acids, hormones, and enzymes.

3. Many of these tests are so simple that kits are being marketed which enable people to measure and monitor their own tissue, serum, and urine levels of vitamins and minerals. Hair samples can also be sent to laboratories for a fairly accurate mineral analysis.

Chapter 33

1. Of course, each gender contains both biochemical poles, as well.

2. Protein deficiency can occur and is increasing, mainly due to food allergies and digestive (usually pancreas) malfunction, in which the proteins consumed are not broken down properly, and are poorly absorbed. This kind of malfunction occurs in hypoglycemia and diabetes, which are often the long-term results of poor food choices.

Chapter 34

1. The percentage of calories supplied by fats is probably higher now, because fat consumption is increasing, largely due to increasing consumption of fried, deep-fried, processed and fast foods.

2. We also eat for many social and psychological reasons that have nothing to do with hunger, health, or survival. Much recent attention in weight loss clinics

focuses on discovering the social-psychological reasons behind overweight. The question is: What goal is overweight serving? If the goal can be identified and another way to reach it found, then the person becomes free to "drop that weight."

Chapter 35

1. The total body content of cholesterol is 150 grams.

2. The other 3 sub-fractions are called the very low density lipoprotein (VLDL), the intermediate density lipoprotein (IDL), and the chylomicrons. Their interrelationships are complex. They exchange material among themselves, and also with the HDL fraction.

3. This is the major route by which the body gets rid of excess cholesterol.

SECTION FOUR

Chapter 37

1. Oxygen is 8 times more soluble in fats than in water, and far more attracted to the highly unsaturated than the less unsaturated or saturated fatty acids.

2. Pork gets so fat that on the train ride to slaughter houses in Europe, up to 10% or more of the animals die of heart attacks. They literally choke on their own fat. Dr. Budwig quotes the Japanese as saying that Western civilization will choke itself to death. The Japanese don't say how, but in our choices of the kinds and amounts of fats we consume, we are fulfilling that prophecy.

Chapter 38

1. The liver's capacity to metabolize cholesterol is also influenced by the presence or lack of the minerals and vitamins required.

2. Examples of fiber which binds cholesterol are: *pectin,* found in apples, potatoes, beets, and carrots; *gums* and *mucilages* found in beans and oats; and *lignin*, found in whole grains, cabbage, peas, tomatoes, strawberries, and pears. Cellulose, however, does not bind cholesterol. Seaweeds are excellent foods for binding cholesterol as well as good sources of all the minerals and vitamins.

Chapter 39

1. There are other compelling reasons for avoiding domesticated pork, which involve both parasitic contamination and toxic chemical compounds found in their meat.

Chapter 40

1. Rats convert LA into AA readily, but it appears that humans, under normal circumstances, do so only very slowly, if at all. Since much of the experimental work was done with rats, some confusion resulted in scientific circles when these were automatically assumed to also apply to humans.

2. Horses, unlike cows, have only one stomach, and no saturating bacteria in it. Their diet, of course, is the same grass. What a difference a bacteria makes!

Chapter 41

1. The underlying notions are that fats make you fat, and that slimness is

attractive. The first notion is not true; the second is a matter of taste. Rembrandt, Michelangelo, and the Renaissance painters, as well as many less artistically gifted, present-day men prefer their women 'pleasantly plump'!

Chapter 42

1. Despite its high cholesterol content, egg use and cardiovascular statistics seem to exonerate the egg from blame in the rise in deaths from cardiovascular disease. In the years from 1950 -1965, egg consumption dropped from 390 to 315 per person per year, while deaths from heart disease rose 215 to 292 per 100,000 population, suggesting that *not* eating eggs causes cardiovascular death. One has to be careful, however, with these statistics, since many factors besides egg consumption, including time lag between consumption and disease development, need to be taken into account.

Chapter 43

1. Seeds also contain protein, fiber, minerals, vitamins, and water, but our focus here is on their oils.
2. 18:3*w*3 or linolenic acid is sometimes called *alpha*-linolenic acid, to distinguish this essential fatty acid from *gamma*-linolenic acid (GLA, 18:3*w*6). A fuller explanation is given in Chapter 46.
3. Castrated grapes are another of man's 'improvements' on nature.
4. Octacosanol, like EPA, is considered a drug by the Canadian Health Protection Branch, but the wheat kernel, the wheat germ, and the wheat germ oil, all of which contain it are considered foods.

Chapter 44

1. Before the advent of antibiotics, farmers kept their cattle healthy by feeding them cooked flax mash.
2. Actually cholesterol is not a problem for a normally active person on a diet containing all the essential nutrients.
3. Some of these margarines contained less than 5% of the essential linoleic acid (18:2*w*6).
4. Butter also contains about 20% water, but since saturated fatty acids are not altered by water, butter loses no points on this count.
5. Water is cheap, and is therefore added to the hydrogenated oil.

SECTION FIVE

Chapter 45

1. *W*3 and *w*6 essential fatty acids use the same enzyme system to make their corresponding long chain derivatives.
2. Their *w*6 content was measured between 1.6 and 3.6% of total fat content.
3. Fish which might be carriers of parasites are not eaten raw by the Japanese. Such fish include cod and other bottom feeding fish which live close to the shore, where both hosts — fish and human — in whom these parasites grow, have regular contact. Open ocean fish, because they lack contact with humans, do not carry parasites active in humans, and can therefore be eaten raw. As an added precaution, they freeze the fish before sashimiing, which would also kill any

parasites present in the fish.

4. *W*6 fatty acids, which are essential in human nutrition, are not essential to fish. Fish can convert *w*3 fatty acids, which *are* essentiald for them, into *w*6 fatty acids.

Chapter 46

1. GLA is also found in the seed oils of several members of the Borage family (up to 20% of total fatty acids), in black (18%) and red (12%) currant seed oils, in gooseberry seeds, in poplar seeds, seed oils from several species of the Liliacea family (12-30%), a blue-green alga (21.4%), and several fungi, mosses, and protozoa. Some of these seeds are not edible, and only evening primrose has been developed commercially.

2. The enzyme is called delta 6 desaturase.

Chapter 47

1. GLA is also found in human breast milk and evening primrose oil.
2. DGLA is also found in human breast milk.
3. AA is also found in meats.
4. SDA is also found in seeds of the borage family.
5. EPA is also found in certain fish oils.
6. For added protection from the PG2 prostaglandins and their damaging effects, the human body converts DGLA (20:3*w*6) only very slowly to AA (20:4*w*6). This minimizes the amount of AA available for making the 'bad guy' series 2 prostaglandins (in rats, DGLA is converted rapidly to AA, and their prostaglandin metabolism differs from that of humans). Since meats contain AA, however, a high meat diet works against this added protection. This is another reason why high meat diets tend towards cardiovascular disease, inflammatory diseases like arthritis, and kidney disease.
7. The step blocked in series 1 prostaglandin formation is:

   LA (18:2*w*6) ————▶ GLA (18:3*w*6).

   The step blocked in series 3 prostaglandin formation is:

   LNA (18:3*w*3) ————▶ SDA (18:4*w*3).

Chapter 48

1. Beans are low in methionine, but high in lysine. Most grains, on the other hand, are low in lysine and high in methionine. Beans and grains together supply a good balance of all essential amino acids. Their complementary nature is the basis of the bean-and-grain dishes which keep Mexicans and many vegetarians healthy.

Chapter 49

1. Increasing the fiber content and increasing the intake of water may also help to reduce constipation.

2. Oils have widespread uses in industry, machinery, and engines because of their lubricant properties.

3. Eclampsia, or toxemia of pregnancy is a convulsive disorder occurring near the end of pregnancy; a serious toxic condition which endangers the life of both mother and child.

4. Skim milk protein is also called kwark. It is prepared by souring skim milk with acidophilus (yogurt) culture, and then dripping off the whey. The white protein remainder, which is smooth in texture because it has not been 'curded' by heat, is kwark.

5. To make her findings accessible to interested people, both scientific and general public, Dr. Budwig has published 11 highly informative and most interesting books.

Chapter 51

1. Modern Eskimoes, on modern diets: white sugar, white flour, alcohol, canned foods, and refined oils, are prone to all the degenerative conditions of the white man.

Chapter 52

1. Japanese fishermen and West Coast North American Indians on their traditional fare, are also free of degenerative disease.

Chapter 53

1. Laughter is such a healthy form of exercise that it is also known as 'inner jogging'!

SECTION SIX

Chapter 54

1. The U.S. tops this list.

Chapter 55

1. Johanna Budwig, *Fette als wahre Hilfe* (West Germany: Hyperion Verlag, 1972), p.7-8.

Chapter 56

1. 20% die within 60 minutes of the onset of symptoms; another 20% die a little slower, but as a consequence of their first heart attack.
2. When sugar is cut from the diet, rats live almost twice as long as when their diet contains it.
3. Traditional Japanese fishermen too, owe their good health and absence of fatty degeneration to fish oils, as well as to seaweed.

Chapter 58

1. As opposed to chemically extracted, which leaves solvent residues in the oil.
2. Polyethylene is suitable for oil, but many plastics are not.
3. In 1815, sugar consumption was only about 15 pounds per person per year.

Chapter 59

1. Life energy uses our hereditary or inherited material, the genetic DNA blueprint, translates this into RNA, and uses the RNA to manage the production of proteins, both structural and enzymatic. These proteins catalyze the building and assembly of molecules into the superstructure that we call the human body. But without life energy, the entire genetic program, the RNA, and the enzymes are all lifeless.

Glossary

AA (20:4w6): See arachidonic acid.

acetate: 2 carbon molecular fragments containing an organic (carboxylic) acid group; the basis of acetic acid, which is vinegar; the building block for fatty acids and cholesterol; the breakdown product when sugars and fatty acids are 'burned' to produce energy for the body.

adipose: the scientist's name for fat tissue or body fat.

all cis-: in a fatty acid, the arrangement where the single hydrogens on both carbons involved in a double bond are found on the same side of the molecule.

alphalinolenic acid: see linolenic acid.

amino acid: the building block of proteins; there are over 20 different amino acids present in nature.

antioxident: any one of a large group of natural or synthetic substances whose presence slows down the deterioration induced by oxygen of other substances such as fatty acids.

arachidonic acid; a 20 carbon, 4 times unsaturated fatty acid made from the essential linoleic acid by enzymes in the body, and also found in meat foods. It is the parent compound from which the series 2 prostaglandins are made.

which the series 2 prostaglandins are made.

beta-carotene: an orange plant pigment; 2 vitamin A molecules hooked end to end. While too much vitamin A can be toxic, beta-carotene is not. The body stores it, and makes vitamin A from it only as it needs the latter.

bile acids: made from cholesterol in the liver and stored in the gall bladder, bile acids are emulsifying agents (detergents) which break up fat droplets into smaller droplets, expose a larger surface area of the fats to the action of fat-digesting enzymes and speed up fat digestion.

blood cholesterol: all of the cholesterol in transit from the bowel to the liver and body cells, and all the cholesterol returning from the cells to the liver to be turned into bile acids and discarded into the intestine.

bond: see chemical bond.

carbon chain: carbon atoms linked to one another in a chain by bonds formed when atoms share electrons.

catalyst: a protein molecule made from the genetic material, which facilitates a specific chemical reaction which would not otherwise take place.

cell membrane: a double layer of fatty material (phosphatides) and proteins which surrounds each living cell of all organisms.

chemical bond: atoms held together by the sharing of electrons with one another to form molecules. The shared electrons constitute the chemical bond.

cholesterol: a complex fatty substance which has many important functions in the body. It can be made in the body or supplied through foods of animal origin. Excess cholesterol may be deposited in artery linings.

choline: a vitamin involved in the proper metabolism of fats and in nerve function, and found in ample quantities in lecithin (phosphatidyl choline).

chylomicron: fat and cholesterol carrying vehicle, made in the intestine's cells and transported by the lymphatic system into the blood stream. It is the body's way of getting digested food fats into the blood stream for distribution to the billions of cells which need these fats.

cis- configuration: see all *cis-*.

cold-pressed: an advertising term used to imply quality in edible oils.

complex carbohydrate: sugar molecules linked together in various ways to make digestible molecules such as starch and glycogen or indigestible molecules of 'fiber' which include cellulose, bran, pectin, lignin, mucilage and gum.

cross-link: bonds which form across molecules and result in complex molecular structures.

deficiency disease: the effect on health of shortage or lack of any one or more of the 45 or so essential nutrients.

degenerative disease: loss of the capacity of cells, tissues and organs to function normally. Causes include deficiency of essential nutrients, presence of interfering substances, excess of substances or imbalance in the relative concentrations of substances.

desaturation: the enzymatic process by which 2 hydrogen atoms are removed from neighbouring carbon atoms in a fatty acid chain and at the same time, an additional bond is created between these 2 atoms.

DHA (22:6w3): see docosahexaenoic acid.

docosahexaenoic acid: a 22 carbon fatty acid with 6 double bonds in its chain. It is found in high concentrations in cold-water fish and marine animals, and also in retina, brain, adrenals and testes. It can be manufactured in healthy human tissue from the essential linolenic acid (18:3*w*3).

double bond: in fatty acids, a linking of adjacent atoms in the carbon chain, which is characterized by the sharing of 2 pairs of electrons between the carbons instead of the usual 1 shared pair.

EFA: see essential fatty acid.

eicosapentaenoic acid: a 20 carbon fatty acid with 5 double bonds in its chain. It is found in high quantities in cold-water fish and marine animals. It is the parent substance from which the body makes the series 3 prostaglandins.

elongation: the enzymatic process by which a fatty acid is lengthened by 2 carbon atoms.

emulsify: to break up into smaller droplets by the action of detergents.

enzyme: a protein produced by the body to catalyze (facilitate) particular chemical reactions. The enzyme which catalyzes the reaction is not itself changed thereby.

EPA (20:5w3): see eicosapentaenoic acid.

essential amino acid: any one of 8 amino acids which the body requires but cannot manufacture and must therefore obtain from foods.

essential fatty acid: either of 2 fatty acids which the body requires, cannot make from other substances and which must therefore be supplied by the food. The names of these 2 are linoleic acid (18:2*w*6) and linolenic acid (18:3*w*3).

essential fatty acid deficiency: shortage of one or both of the essential fatty acids and the attendant effects on health of this shortage.

essential nutrient: any one of about 45 different substances that are known to be necessary for body structure and physical health. About 20 minerals, 15 vitamins, 8 amino acids and 2 essential fatty acids must come from the foods we eat, since the body cannot manufacture them out of other substances.

esterify: to chemically link an alcohol or acid with another substance in a particular way called an ester linkage.

evening primrose: a weed whose seeds contain within them the essential linoleic acid (18:2*w*6) and also a product made from it, known as gammalinolenic acid.

fat: three fatty acids hooked to a glycerol molecule in an ester linkage. In common usage, it refers to those substances that fit the above description and are hard at room temperature because they contain mostly saturated fatty acids.

fatty acid: a carbon chain with an organic acid group at one end, and hydrogens attached to the rest of the carbon atoms in the chain. The chain length can vary from 4 to 26 or more.

fatty degeneration: fatty deposits which interfere with normal biological functions, commonly found in arteries, around tumours, in liver and other internal organs.

fiber: any one of several undigestible complex carbohydrates which make up the 'roughage' of plant material. They aid in bowel regularity, help to stabilize blood sugar and aid in the elimination of bile acids and cholesterol from the body.

flax: a plant whose seed oil contains both essential fatty acids in large quantities, especially the more rare linolenic acid (18:3*w*3). It also contains many other essential nutrients, as well as mucilage and fiber, which aid the body in the elimination of excess cholesterol, and help to prevent the reabsorption of toxic wastes from the large intestine.

free radical: a molecule or molecular fragment with a single or unpaired electron which, wanting to be paired, steals electrons from other pairs. Free radical reactions occur normally in biological processes.

free radical chain reaction: uncontrolled free radical reaction which is damaging to biological processes.

gammalinolenic acid: a substance made from the essential linoleic acid (18:2*w*6) by healthy cells, also found in mother's milk and evening primrose oil. It is used therapeutically in several conditions in which the body's ability to make it from linoleic acid is impaired.

GLA (18:3w6): see gammalinolenic acid.

glycerol: a molecule which consists of 3 carbon atoms, hydrogen and oxygen. It is the backbone of the fat or oil molecule and of the membrane's fatty component. Two glycerol molecules can be hooked together to make a sugar molecule.

glycogen: glucose molecules hooked together in long chains and stored in the liver and muscle of animals as energy reserves. It is also called 'animal starch'.

HDL: see high density lipoprotein.

high density lipoprotein: one of the vehicles found in the blood stream, which carries fats and cholesterol. It is the 'good' type of cholesterol, which returns excess cholesterol from the cells to the liver, where it is changed into bile acids and poured into the intestine to aid in fat digestion on its way out of the body.

hydrogenation: a commercial process by which oils are turned into fats, by destroying the double bonds in the fatty acids and saturating the carbon atoms with hydrogen.

isomer: a chemical substance which is identical to another in composition, but differs in its 3-dimensional spatial arrangement, and which therefore has different properties.

ketone: a type of toxic chemical substance, which is involved in acidosis, a condition of the blood and fluids of poorly managed cases of diabetes.

Krebs cycle: the body's main way of releasing the energy stored in the chemical bonds available for the body's requirements. Carbohydrates are its main fuel, but fats and proteins may also be used. It is also called the tricarboxylic acid cycle and the citric acid cycle.

LA (18:2w6): see linoleic acid.

LDL: see low density lipoprotein.

lecithin: a nutritional substance containing fatty acids, glycerol, phosphate groups and choline. Its health value resides in its content of essential fatty acids and choline. Soybeans are a good source of lecithin which contains both essential fatty acids. Lecithin is part of the structure of the membranes of cells and organelles.

life energy (or life force): sunlight energy stored in the chemical bonds between atoms in molecules, released in the process of metabolism, stored in special molecules called ATP which make this energy easily available to 'drive' the chemical reactions that build, maintain and repair the body and make activity possible.

linoleic acid: an 18 carbon fatty acid with 2 double bonds, positioned between *w* carbon atoms 6 and 7, and 9 and 10. It is one of the 2 essential fatty acids. The body cannot make it, requires it for life, and must therefore obtain if from food. It is sensitive to destruction by light, oxygen and high temperatures, and extremely important to the body's health. Its absence is fatal. Deficiency causes severe problems in every cell, tissue, and organ. The body makes several other important substances from it.

linolenic acid: an 18 carbon fatty acid with 3 double bonds, positioned between *w* carbons 3 and 4, 6 and 7, and 9 and 10. It is the second of the 2 essential fatty acids. The body cannot make it, requires it for life, and must therefore obtain it from food. It is extremely sensitive to destruction by light, oxygen and high temperature. Its absence is fatal. Deficiency is linked to degenerative disease. Modern diets contain only 1/5 as much of this essential substance as traditional diets.

lipid: the chemist's collective name for fats, oils and other fatty substances.

lipoprotein: fatty substances (fats, oils, phosphatides and cholesterol) associated with protein materials. Specifically, it refers to transport vehicles for fats and cholesterol in the blood and lymph.

LNA (18:3w3): see linolenic acid.

long chain fatty acid: a fatty acid containing more than 14 carbon atoms in its chain.

low density lipoprotein: vehicles which transport fats and cholesterol via the blood stream to the cells. An *excess* of these vehicles is associated with cardiovascular disease; hence it is also called the 'bad' cholesterol.

MDR: see minimum daily requirement.

metabolism: all of the chemical changes that take place in the body that make physical life possible.

methylene interrupted: in fatty acid chemistry, the situation where double bonds start 3 carbons apart. This is the usual case in fatty acids in their natural state.

mineral: any one of several of the basic elements, including the metals. In the body, about 20 minerals are required for biochemical life functions.

minimum daily requirement: also called the 'recommended daily allowance', it is the minimum amount of each of the 45 or so essential nutrients required daily to prevent the symptoms of deficiency in a normal, healthy person.

molecule: 2 or more atoms held together by means of electron pairs shared between them.

monounsaturated fatty acid; a fatty acid which contains one double bond between carbon atoms somewhere in the fatty chain. **MUFA:** see monounsaturated fatty acid.

oil: a liquid fat. The shorter the fatty acid chains or the more double bonds present in them, the more liquid the oil.

optimum: best. In nutrition, the term applies to that daily dose of a nutrient or nutrient combination which results in the most effective functioning of the organism. Optimum nutrition thus results in the best possible physical health.

organelle: literally, a little organ. In the cell, the various kinds of biochemical 'machinery' that carry out the different specialized cell functions. Mitochondria, lysosomes, vesicles, Golgi, nucleus and nucleolus are examples of organelles.

orthomolecular: literally, of the right molecules. In nutrition, it is the maintenance of health and the treatment of disease by varying the concentrations of substances normally present in the body (vitamins, minerals, fatty acids, amino acids, enzymes, hormones).

oxidize: the addition of oxygen, subtraction of hydrogen, or addition of electrons to a substance, usually accompanied by a release of energy.

omega: symbolized by *w*, it refers to the methyl end of a fatty acid.

partially hydrogenated: an oil in which some but not all of the double bonds have been destroyed by the addition, under pressure and high temperature, of hydrogen to the fatty acid molecules. A semi-solid fat results, and many chemical changes take place in the fatty acid molecules during this process.

phosphatide: also called phospholipid; a class of fatty compounds found in membranes, consisting of 2 fatty acid molecules, a glycerol molecule, a phosphate group, and some other groups hooked to the phosphate. Lecithin is the most famous example.

phospholipid: see phosphatide.

platelet: small, colourless discs in circulating blood, which aid in blood clotting. Depending on the type of fats and oils consumed, platelets become more or less sticky, and this changes the ease with which they form clots.

polymerize: the process of forming complex or giant molecules by linking together many smaller units. Fatty acids containing many double bonds may polymerize under certain conditions of processing. The body lacks the ability to metabolize such molecules.

polyunsaturated: a fatty acid which contains more than one double bond between carbon atoms in its chain. The term includes both natural, health-enhancing as well as unnatural health-destroying kinds.

precursor: parent substance; a substance out of which another substance is made by chemical modification.

preservative: any one of a very large number of possible compounds that slows down the chemical deterioration of substances.

prostaglandin: a fatty acid partially oxidized in a very specific and controlled way by enzymes made in the body for just this purpose. Prostaglandins have hormone-like functions in the regulation of cell activity. There are about 30 different prostaglandins known so far.

protein: a group of complex molecules with specific and precise structural and chemical functions. They are made by linking together amino acids (over 20 different kinds of amino acids are known) in a specific linear sequence and then folding these chains in particular 3-dimensional ways. Enzymes, muscle and egg white are examples of protein.

PUFA: see polyunsaturated.

RDA: see recommended daily allowance.

recommended daily allowance: the daily dosage of essential nutrients required by a healthy average person in order to prevent the occurrence of deficiency symptoms. It is the government-set minimum requirement, rather than an optimum for good health. It does not take into account the increased requirement during disease, stress, nor individual differences in the needs of biochemically different people.

refined: refers to processed sugars, starches and fats and oils. Essential substances are removed from foods, and thus refined substances rob the body of its stores of these essential nutrients, leading to deficiency diseases and degeneration. Refined is synonymous with deficient.

saturated fatty acid: a fatty acid with no double bonds in the carbon chain, and with every possible position on the carbon atoms taken up by hydrogen atoms.

short chain fatty acid: a fatty acid with 10 or less carbon atoms in its chain.

simple carbohydrate: a simple sugar. Glucose, fructose and lactose are examples. Simple carbohydrates are absorbed into the blood stream rapidly; excess consumption may lead to hypoglycemia, diabetes and cardiovascular problems, as well as obesity.

starch: glucose molecules hooked together into branching chains by plant cells. Starches are digested and absorbed slowly, and supply energy at about the rate at which the body uses it.

t- fatty acid: see *trans-* fatty acid.

toximolecular: literally, of toxic molecules. The use of substances foreign to the body in the maintenance of health and the treatment of disease. This commonly accepted approach of medical practice at this time does not make biological sense for the long-term health care of people.

trans- configuration: the spatial arrangement in which hydrogen atoms on the carbons involved in a double bond are found on opposite sides of the molecule.

trans- fatty acid: a fatty acid in which the hydrogen atoms on the carbon atoms involved in a double bond are situated on opposite sides of the fatty chain.

triglyceride: a molecule of fat or oil. It consists of 3 fatty acid molecules hooked to glycerol backbone. This is the form in which fatty acids are stored in the body's fat tissues and in the seeds of plants.

UFA: see unsaturated fatty acid.

unrefined: in its natural state; not altered.

unsaturated fatty acid: a fatty acid with one or more double bonds between carbons in its chain.

vegan: a person who eats no animal products whatsoever. No meat, no fish, no eggs, no dairy products.

very low density lipoprotein: vehicles made in the liver for carrying fats and cholesterol.

vitamin E: a natural antioxidant and essential vitamin which is found in seeds containing oils, required by the body to prevent the destruction of membrane fatty acids by oxidation.

vitamin: one of about 15 essential nutrients that the body cannot make from other substances, requires for health and life and must therefore obtain from external sources. Refining of foods removes much of the natural content of these nutrients and therefore aids in the cause of deficiency disease and degeneration.

VLDL: see very low density lipoprotein.

w: see omega.

Annotated Bibliography

Introduction

There are two different approaches used in published material on fats and oils. One approach serves the industry. It emphasizes the technical, complex nature of fats and oils, and stresses the processes by which raw materials can be changed into marketable products. This approach also concerns itself with customer appeal of products through taste, smell, colour, texture, convenience, shelf-life, etc. This material is generally written for other experts in the field, and is often quite boring to read. It downplays the health, nutrition, and safety aspects of fats and oils products.

The other approach serves the 'lay' public, and emphasizes the effects on health of fats and oils products. It also concerns itself with the nature of the chemical changes to which industry subjects natural raw food stuffs and the effect of these changes on nutritional qualities and health. Both kinds of published material contain valuable information, and both can contribute to our understanding. Therefore, references to both are given.

References marked with an * are, in the author's opinion, outstanding works.

Dr. Budwig's Work

The most thorough work that has been done in the area of fats, oils, nutrition, and health comes from Dr. J. Budwig in Germany. Dr. Budwig has published 11 books on fats, nutrition and health. She studied physics, chemistry, pharmacy, botany, biology, and medicine. Since 1979, she has been nominated every year for the Nobel Prize in Medicine.

Fats and Oils

Dr. Budwig did her basic research into the nature of fats at the University of Muenster, Germany; she worked in collaboration with several hospitals; she held a high government post in which she was responsible for monitoring the effects of drugs and processed foods on health. She left this post in 1953 to open a clinic in which she successfully treats terminal cancer by nutritional means.

Using her expertise in chemistry and biology, Dr. Budwig creates new food products with extended shelf life and superb taste, without compromising their natural nutritional qualities. She has several such products on the market, as well as a line of cosmetic products of extremely high quality.

All of her books are in German. They are listed in chronological order.

*Budwig, J. *Die elementare Funktion der Atmung in ihrer Beziehung zu autoxydablen Nahrungstoffen.* Freiburg, W. Germany. Hyperion Verlag. 1953. (The basic function of cell respiration in its relationship to auto-oxidizable nutrients [essential fatty acids and sulphur-rich proteins]). This book summarizes her ground-breaking research in lipid chemistry, oil-protein combination, human blood lipids, and cancer. She calls it "a contribution to the solution of the cancer problem."

Budwig, J. *Oel-Eiweiss Kost.* Freiburg, W. Germany. Hyperion Verlag. 1955. (Oil-protein combination). This is her cook-book. She says: "This cook book helps those who are ill."

Budwig, J. *Krebs ein Fett-Problem.* Freiburg, W. Germany. Hyperion Verlag. 1956. (Cancer is a fat problem). In this book, Dr. Budwig explains cancer briefly, and gives more recipes. The subtitle reads: "Correct choice and use of fats."

*Budwig, J. *Das Fettsyndrom,* Freiburg, W. Germany. Hyperion Verlag. 1959. (The Fat Syndrome). In this book Dr. Budwig describes the functions of the essential fatty acids in the various organ systems; she covers physical, chemical, and bio-chemical behaviour of fats; deficiency of essential fatty acids; she considers cancer as a "fat syndrome"; she suggests that cancer is not uncontrolled, but retarded growth of cells and explains why this is so; she looks at fats in nutrition and fats in clinical theory.

*Budwig, J. *Kosmische Kraefte gegen Krebs.* Freiburg, W. Germany. Hyperion Verlag. 1966. (Cosmic forces against cancer). In this book with fanciful title, Dr. Budwig describes the interactions of sunlight energy (cosmic power!) with the electrons of the double bonds in essential fatty acids (electron biology), and the relationship of these life processes with the cause and cure of cancer.

*Budwig, J. *Laserstrahlen gegen Krebs.* Freiburg, W. Germany. Hyperion Verlag. 1968. (Laser rays against cancer). This book deals with the relationship of light, electrons, oil-protein interaction, and health. The subtitle: "resonance phenomena as anti-entropy (anti-death) factors of life."

*Budwig, J. *Fette als wahre Hilfe.* Freiburg, W. Germany. Hyperion Verlag. 1972. (Fats as real help) against arteriosclerosis, heart attack, cancer. This is a collection of 3 lectures from a tour of Switzerland and France, on fats, sunlight, electrons, and cancer.

Budwig, J. *Der Tod des Tumors.* Freudenstadt, W. Germany. Budwig. 1977. (Death of the tumour). This book describes Dr. Budwig's research and inventions in legal language, as regards her biochemical insights, therapeutic innovations and applications for patents for improved food products for human consumption.

Budwig, J. *Der Tod des Tumors.* Band 2. Die Dokumentation. Freudenstadt, W. Germany. Budwig. 1977. (Death of the tumour. Vol. 2. Documentation). This book contains letters from cancer patients given up by doctors as 'terminal', who were cured by Dr. Budwig's oil-protein combination. It contains reprints of over 20 lectures and essays. It also contains a section on the tug-of-war between health considerations and the profit motive in the fats and oils business. Interesting reading for those inclined in this direction.

*Budwig, J. *Fotoelemente des Lebens.* Innsbruck, Austria. Resch Verlag. 1979. (Light energy in life processes). This is a concise and brilliant treatise which describes life processes and cancer in terms of the physics of light, the chemisdtry of electrons in bonds, and the biology of living systems in chemical and physical terms. She leans, in her explanations, on the work of Nobel prize winners in physics (Planck, Einstein, de Broglie, Ford, Bohr, Schroedinger, Feynman, Dessauer), chemistry (Meier, Pauling), and physiology-medicine (Rein, Schutz, Bauer, Warburg, Meyerhof, Szent-Gyorgyi). She manages to include health, cancer and human evolution.) All this in just 18 pages. Finally, the bibliography includes references to all her published work.

Budwig, J. *Fettfibel.* Freiburg, W. Germany. Hyperion Verlag. 1979. (Fat notebook). This book describes, in simple language, the oils which enhance health, the essential fatty acids, the problems with margarine, refined oils, and heating of oils.

For anyone who has terminal, medically untreatable cancer or who wants to avail themselves of alternate therapy, Dr. Budwig's address and phone number are given:

Dr. Johanna Budwig
Hegelstrasse 3
7290 Freudenstadt-Dietersweiler
West Germany
Tel: 011-49-7441-7667

To order her books, write to:

Hyperion Verlag
7800 Freiburg im Breisgau
W. Germany

Essential Fatty Acids

In English, probably the most comprehensive and readable review of essential fatty acids in health and disease is:

*Horrobin, D.F. *Essential Fatty Acids: A Review.* In: Horrobin, D.F. (ed) *Clinical Uses of Essential Fatty Acids.* London, England. Eden Press. 1982.

Fats, Oils, and Nutrition

Comprehensive works on fats and oils in nutrition include:

*Brisson, G.J. *Lipids in Human Nutrition.* Inglewood, NJ. Burgess. 1981. Contains an excellent section on hydrogenation and *trans-* fatty acids.

*Mead, J.F. and Fulco, A.J. *The Unsaturated and Polyunsaturated Fatty Acids in Health and Disease.* Springfield IL. Charles C. Thomas. 1976. Excellent background and overview of fatty acids.

*_Perkins, E.G. and Visek, W.J. (eds) Dietary Fats and Health._ Champaign, IL. American Oil Chemists' Society. 1983. Contains most recent research as well as statistics.

Sinclair, H.M. *Essential Fatty Acids.* London, England. Butterworths. 1958.

Somogyi, J.C. and Francis, A. *Nutritional Aspects of Fats.* New York, NY. Karger. 1977.

WHO/FAO. *Dietary Fats and Oils in Human Nutrition.* Report of an expert consultation. UN Food and Agricultural Organization. Rome, Italy. 1977.

Chemistry and Biochemistry of Fats and Oils

The chemistry and biochemistry of fats and oils is amply treated in:

Campbell, P.N. and Smith, A.D. *Biochemistry Illustrated.* New York, NY. Churchill-Livingstone. 1982.

*Gurr, M.I. and James, A.T. *Lipid Biochemistry.* 3rd Ed. London, England, Chapman and Hall. 1980.

Masoro, E.J. (ed) *Physiological Chemistry of Lipids in Mammals.* Philadelphia, PA. Saunders. 1968.

Pryde, E.H. (ed) *Fatty Acids.* Champaign, IL. American Oil Chemists' Society. 1979.

*Zubay, G. (ed) *Biochemistry.* Reading, MA. Addison-Wesley. 1983.

Industrial uses of fats and oils

Anderson, A.J.C. *Refining of Oils and Fats.* Williams (ed). Elmsford, NY. Pergamon Press. 1962.

Function and Biosynthesis of Lipids. *Advances in Experimental Medicine and Biology*, Vol. 83. New York, NY. Plenum Publishing Co. 1976.

Kirschenbauer, H.G. *Fats and Oils. An outline of their chemistry and technology.* 2nd Ed. New York, NY. Van Nostrand Reinhold. 1960.

*Swern, D. (ed) *Bailey's Industrial Oil and Fat Products.* 3rd Ed. New York, NY. Wiley and Sons. 1964.

*Swern, D. (ed) *Bailey's Industrial Oil and Fat Products.* 4th Ed. Volumes I and II. New York. Wiley and Sons. 1979. This is the oil chemist's bible.

*Weiss, T.J. *Food Oils and their Uses.* 2nd Ed. Westport, CT. Avi Publishing Co. 1983.

Experimental results

Journals

Foremost among reports of results from individual scientific studies are the technical journals, of which the main ones are:

American Oil Chemists' Society. *The Journal.* Champaign, IL. 1924-present.

Fette, Seifen, Anstrichmittel. (Fats, Soaps, Paints). In German. Leinenfelden-Echterdingen, W. Germany. Industrieverlag von Herrnhaussen. 1894 to present, with 5 changes in title during that time.

Journal of Lipid Research. Bethesda, MD. 1959 to present.

Lipids. Champaign, IL. American Oil Chemists' Society. 1966 to present.

*_Progress in Lipid Research._ Holman, T. (ed) Elmsford, NY. Pergamon Press. 1978 to present. This is a continuation of:

Progress in the Chemistry of Fats and other Lipids. Holman, T. (ed) Elmsford, NY. Pergamon Press. 1951 — 1977.

Symposia

Blix, G. (ed) *Polyunsaturated Fatty Acids as Nutrients.* Symposium of the Swedish Nutrition Foundation. Vol. IV. Stockholm, Sweden. Almquist & Wiksells. 1966

*Holman, T.(ed) Essential Fatty Acids and Prostaglandins. In: *Progress in Lipid Research.* Vol. 20, 1981. Elmsford, NY. Pergamon Press.

Body Composition

Behuke, A.R. and Williams, J.H. *Evaluation of Body Build and Composition.* Englewood Cliffs, NJ. Prentice-Hall. 1974.

Brozek, J.M. (ed) *Human Body Composition: approaches and applications.* New York, NY. Symposium Publications Division, Pergamon Press. 1965.

National Research Council. *Body Composition in Animals and Man.* Washington, D.C. National Academy of Science. 1968.

Parizkova, J. *Body Fat and Physical Fitness.* The Hague, Netherlands. Martinus Nijhoff BV/Medical Division. 1977.

Fat Tissue

Angel, A. (ed) *The Adipocyte and Obesity: Cellular and Molecular Mechanisms.* New York, NY. Raven Press. 1983.

Lundberg, O. *Brown Adipose Tissue.* New York, NY. Elsevier Books. 1970.

Membranes

Beck, J.S. *Biomembranes. Fundamentals in relation to human biology.* New York, NY. McGraw-Hill. 1980.

Bloch, K., Bolis, L., and Tosteson, DC. (eds) *Membranes, Molecules, Toxins, and Cells.* Littleton, MA. PSG Publishers. 1981.

Peeters, H. (ed) *Phosphatidylcholine.* New York, NY. Springer Verlag. 1976.

*Robertson, R.N. *The Lively Membranes.* Cambridge, England. Cambridge U. Press. 1983.

*Simons, P. *Lecithin. The cholesterol controller.* London, England. Thorsons. 1983.

General Nutrition

*Ballentine, R. *Diet and Nutrition: a holistic approach.* Hones dale, PA. Himalayan International Institute. 1978. Chapter 5 contains a good overview of fats and oils.

*Bland, J. (ed) *Yearbook of Nutritional Medicine*, New Canaan, C.T. Keats Publishers. 1985.

*Bland, J. *Your Health Under Siege: Using nutrition to fight back*, Battleboro, VT. The Stephen Greene Press. 1981.

*Cleave, T.L. *The Saccharine Disease.* New Canaan, CT. Keats Publishers. 1975.

*Colgan, M. *Your Personal Vitamin Profile.* New York, NY. Quill Books. 1982.

Davis, A. *Let's Get Well.* New York, NY. Harcourt Brace Jovanovich. 1965.

Fredericks, C. *Carlton Fredericks' High Fiber Way to Total Health.* New York, NY. Pocket Books. 1976.

Guthrie, H.A. *Introductory Nutrition.* 5th Ed. St. Louis, MO. Mosby, 1983.

Hoffer, A. and Walker, M. *Orthomolecular Nutrition.* New Canaan, CT. Keats Publishers. 1978.

*Kollath, W. *Die Ordnung unserer Nahrung* (The organization of our nutrition). Heidelberg, W. Germany. Haug Verlag. 1977.

Fats and Oils

*Kunin, R.A. *Meganutrition*. New York, NY. McGraw-Hill. 1980.
Mindell, E. *Earl Mindell's Vitamin Bible*. New York, NY. Warner Books. 1979.
Mindell, E. *Earl Mindell's Vitamin Bible for Your Kids*. New York, NY. Bantam Books. 1982.
Nutrition Reviews. *Present Knowledge in Nutrition*. 5th Ed. Washington, DC. Nutrition Foundation. 1984.
Passwaser, K.A. *Supernutrition*. New York, NY. Pocket Books, 1976.
*Pauling, L. *Vitamin C, the Common Cold, and The Flu*. San Francisco, CA. Freeman Book Co. 1976.
*Pfeiffer, C.C. *Mental and Elemental Nutrients*. New Canaan, CT. Keats Publishers. 1975.
*Philpott, W.H. and Kalita, D.K. *Brain Allergies*. New Canaan, CT. Keats Publishers. 1980.
Scharffenberg, J.A. *Problems with Meat*. Santa Barbara, CA. Woodbridge Publishers. 1979.
Schroeder, H.A. *The Poisons around Us*. New Canaan, CT. Keats Publishers. 1978.
Smith, L. *Feed Your Kids Right*. New York, NY. Delta Books. 1979.
*Williams, R.J. *Nutrition against Disease*. New York, NY. Bantam Books. 1971.
Williams, R.J. and Kalita, D.K. *A Physician's Handbook of Orthomolecular Medicine*. New York, NY. Pergamon Press. 1977.

Diets
Atkins, R.C. *Dr. Atkins' Diet Revolution*. New York, NY. Bantam Books. 1972.
Kunin, R.C. *Meganutrition for Women*. New York, NY. McGraw-Hill. 1983.
Pritikin, N. *The Pritikin Program for Diet and Exercise*. New York, NY. Bantam Books, 1979.
Reingold, C.B. *The Lifelong Anti-Cancer Diet*. New York, NY. Signet Books. 1982.
Schwartz, R. *Diets Don't Work*. Houston, TX. Breakthru Publishing. 1982.
Darling, K. *Weight No More*. Mill Valley, CA. Whatever Publishing. 1984.

Politics of nutrition, medicine, and environment
Carson, R. *Silent Spring*. New York NY. Fawcett Crest Books. 1962.
*Epstein, S. *The Politics of Cancer*. San Francisco, CA. Sierra Club Books. 1978.
Griffin, G.E. *World Without Cancer*. Westlake Village, CA. American Media. 1974.
*Hall, R.H. *Food for Nought: the decline in nutrition*. New York, NY. Random House. 1974.
Mendelsohn, R.S. *Confessions of a Medical Heretic*. New York, NY. Warner Books. 1979.

Psychological aspects of nutrition and disease
Cheraskin, E. and Ringsdorf, W.M. *Psychodietetics*. New York, NY. Bantam Books. 1974
Cousins, N. *Anatomy of an Illness*. New York, NY. Bantam Books. 1979.
Fredericks, C. *Psychonutrition*. New York, NY. Grosset & Dunlap, 1976.
*Simonton, O.C., Matthews-Simonton, S. and Creighton, J.L. *Getting Well Again*. New York, NY. Bantam Books. 1978.

Disease

Selye, H. *The Stress of Life.* New York, NY. McGraw-Hill. 1956.

Smith, L.H. and Thir, S.O. *Pathophysiology: The Biological Principles of Disease.* Philadelphia, PA. Saunders, 1981.

Serum lipids and cardiovascular disease

American Health Foundation. *Plasma Lipids: optimum levels for health.* New York, NY. Academic Press. 1980.

Day, C.E. and Levy, R.S. (eds) *Low Density Lipoproteins.* New York, NY. Plenum Press. 1976.

Hietanen, E. *Regulation of Serum Lipids by Physical Exercise.* Boca Raton, FL. CRC Press. 1982.

Life Style Counterattack. Symposium on diet, exercise, and health. Simon Fraser University, Burnaby, BC, Canada. April 13-15, 1984.

*Passwater, B.A. *Supernutrition for Healthy Hearts.* New York, NY. Jove Books. 1977.

Smith, L.L. *Cholesterol Autoxidation.* New York, NY. Plenum Press. 1981.

Cancer

Bodanski, O. *Biochemistry of Cancer.* New York, NY. Academic Press. 1975.

Booth, G. *The Cancer Epidemic: shadow of the conquest of nature.* Lewiston, NY. Edwin Mellen. 1979.

Busch, H. (ed) *Molecular Biology of Cancer.* New York, NY. Academic Press. 1974.

*Cameron, E. and Pauling, L. *Cancer and Vitamin C.* New York, NY. Warner Books. 1979.

Deutsch, E. (ed) *Molecular Base of Malignancy.* Stuttgart, W. Germany. Georg Thieme Verlag. 1976.

Galeotti, T. et al. *Membranes in Tumor Growth.* New York, NY. Elsevier Books. 1982.

Moss, R.W. *The Cancer Syndrome.* New York, NY. Grove Press. 1980.

*National Research Council. *Diet, Nutrition, and Cancer.* Washington, DC, National Academy of Science. 1982.

*Newbold, H. L. *Vitamin C against Cancer.* New York, NY. Stein and Day. 1979.

Nixon, D.W. *Diagnosis and Management of Cancer.* Reading, MA. Addison-Wesley. 1982.

Oppenheimer, S.B. *Cancer: a biological and clinical introduction.* Boston, MA. Allyn and Bacon. 1982.

*Szent-Gyorgyi, A. *The Living State and Cancer.* New York, NY. Dekker. 1978.

Tache, J., Selye, H., and Day, S.B. *Cancer, Stress, and Death.* New York, NY. Plenum Press. 1979.

Wolstenholme, G.E.W., Fitzsimmons, D.W., and Whelan, J. (eds) *Submolecular Biology and Cancer.* New York NY. Ciba Foundation. Excertpa Medica. 1979.

Wood, R. *Tumor Lipids: biochemistry and metabolism.* Champaign, IL. American Oil Chemists' Society. 1973.

Occupational Cancer

Peto, R. (ed) *Banbury Report: quantification of occupational cancer.* Cold Spring Harbor, NY. Cold Spring Harbor. 1981.

Shaw, C.R. *Prevention of Occupational Cancer.* Boca Raton, FL. CRC Press. 1981.

Aging

Masoro, E.J. (ed) *Handbook of Physiology in Aging.* Boca Raton, FL. CRC Press. 1981.

Pearson, D. and Shaw, S. *Life Extension.* New York, NY. Warner Books. 1983.

Multiple Sclerosis

Graham, J. *Multiple Sclerosis: a self-help guide to its management.* Wellingborough, North Hamptonshire. Thorsons Publichers. 1981.

Crime

*Schauss, A. *Diet, Crime, and Delinquency.* Berkeley, CA. Parker House. 1980.

Miscellaneous

Eckert, R. and Randall, D. *Animal Physiology: mechanisms and adaptions.* San Francisco, CA. Freeman Book Co. 1983.

Composition of Foods: raw, processed, prepared, Washington, DC, *Agriculture Handbook No. 8., USA Dept. of Agriculture.* 1963.

Graedon, J. *The People's Pharmacy.* New York, NY. Avon Books. 1976. Vol. 2, 1980.

Memmler, R.L. and Wood, D.L. *Structure and Function of the Human Body,* 3rd Ed. Philadelphia, PA. Lippincott, 1983.

Report of the Ad Hoc Committee on the Composition of Special Margarines. Ottawa, Canada. Supply and Services Canada. 1980.

Schreiber, J. and Fillip, J. *Edible Oils: the cold facts on 'cold-pressed'.* Whole Foods Magazine. 1978.

Levy, P. *Vegetable Oil: the unsaturated facts.* Talking Food. Salem, Mass. 1977.

Aquaculture, Vol. 25, 1981. pp. 161-172. Fatty acid composition of salmon oils. Amsterdam, Holland. Elsevier Scientific.

Enig, M.G. *Trans-fatty acid isomers in selected food items.* Thesis, University of Maryland. 1981.

The Merck Index. 10th Ed. Merck & Co. Rahway, NJ. 1983.

Technical Information Bulletin. *Efamol Research Institute.* Kentville, Nova Scotia, Canada. 1981.

Magazines

Rodale, R. (ed) *Prevention.* Emmaus, PA.

Vaughn, L. Getting the Most of the F complex (dietary fiber). *Prevention,* pp.48-54. Sept. 1984.

Vaughn, L. The Fish Oil Factor: healthy-heart gift from the sea. *Prevention*, pp. 64-69. March 1984.

Scientific American. New York, NY.

*Brown, M.S. and Goldstein, J.L. How LDL receptors influence cholesterol and atherosclerosis. *Scientific American*, pp. 58-66. Nov. 1984.

Both of the above magazines occasionally carry good articles on fats and health. Both are reputable. Articles found in magazines such as *Time* and *Vogue*, as well as the many articles recently being published in daily newspapers, indicate an increasing general interest in fats and oils nutrition, but are more journalistically interesting than scientifically accurate.

Index

Udo Erasmus

B.Sc. (Zoology, Psychology); plus 2 years post-graduate studies (Genetics, Biochemistry)
M.A. (Counseling Psychology)
M.S. (Nutrition)
Ph.D. (Nutrition)

Educator, Counselor, Author and Consultant specializing in **Fats, Oils, Cholesterol Control, Essential Fatty Acids, Omega 3's, Human Health** and **Natural Therapies.**

Available for **Individual Counseling, Group Education** and **Consultation** by **Telephone** on a Fee For Time basis.

Call **(604) 731-4255** for an appointment

You can use Udo's **expertise** to:
- **Educate** yourself
- Get information about **products**
- Explore the nature of **health**
- Discuss **natural therapies**
- Find out where to go for **help**
- Get **answers** to your questions

You can use the telephone to:
- **Instantly access information** vital to health
- **Avoid** the **costs** of travel, time and accommodations

Call to set a time: **(604) 731-4255**